"And Then The End Will Come"

"What will be the sign of Your coming,
and of the end of the age?"
(Matthew 24:3)

AND *THEN* THE END WILL COME
By D. E. Isom
First Edition, August 2017

Walk with the Word
P.O. Box 9265
Redlands, CA 92375
Website: WalkWithTheWord.org
Email: Servant@WalkWithTheWord.org

Other books by the author:
The Walk with the Word Psalm 119 Study Guide
Elijah to Come

ISBN

Any questions or comments should be directed to:
Servant@WalkWithTheWord.org.

Table of Contents

Introduction

I*t seems that one of the staples of nearly every work addressing even the edge of eschatology, regardless of the particular position defended, is a parallel attempt to revisit the history of the Church as early as possible.* This is most often efforted in order to make the case that the author's offered interpretation of Scripture was the primary one originally held "from the very beginning" of Church history. The assumption is this therefore sanctifies the particular position or viewpoint being espoused in the present as the "purest" or "truest" to what the first Christians believed. There is a common consensus of agreement that the closer an early source lived to the founding Apostles and to that original 1st century Church who can be favorably quoted, the more likely this was the most accurate and originally held interpretation of Christ's teachings. Especially when it comes to the treatment of eschatology, it is common to seek this sort of "historical provenance" to provide a kind of confirmation of one's position in order to make the case that a contemporary author's stance is what was originally held and therefore should be maintained today, or one to which we should return. But most often it is because the terms and concepts which have come into common use in recent Church history (mainly within the past 200 or so years) were never used in earlier writings.

There is no argument or rebuttal to the basic premise to be presented here, but rather it is the way this is applied which is in contention. There should be a natural hesitation to fully embrace the manner in which this assertion is often presented simply because a large body of writings by the hand of the very first generation of believers has not survived. Statistically speaking, there are very few extra-biblical documents for which we can be sufficiently confident their origin comes from the 1st century, so the de facto "earliest" writings which authors and scholars cite are most often found to actually date to the 2nd and 3rd centuries. Frequently the source being cited was not an actual member of the original Early Church, many of whom might have actually experienced Christ's ministry but certainly lived under the direct teachings of the Apostles. And, frankly, a principle of God's Word is the requirement for the presence of at least two witnesses, so it can be problematic to place all of our exegetical eggs into a single source's basket, so to speak.

To be sure, modern writers could be right in the conclusions they are drawing from early sources which are often anywhere from at least fifty to two hundred years removed from the very first and earliest generation of Christians. However, it is difficult to shake the feeling that it might be like someone today who writes a book about the American Civil War a hundred years after its conclusion. They can read what others wrote, examine items now saved in museums and collections, and even visit some of the sites where famous events took place, but by no stretch of the imagination are they firsthand "witnesses" of the conflict. Even if they restrict themselves to quoting the earliest sources possible, they are still filtering their findings based on personal opinion and their own worldview more than a century later. No matter how well-written a biography might be, it will always fall short of the same provenance and authority provided by an autobiography.

A famous instance is Polycarp, who lived from 69-155 AD and is believed to have been a disciple of the Apostle John because Irenaeus, Tertullian and Jerome mention him as such in their writings. Since he was not even born until some 35 years after Christ's Resurrection, Polycarp is not an original member of the very first generation comprising the Early Church. Even before his birth most of the founding Apostles had been martyred, and as an infant the destruction of the Temple and Jerusalem had already taken place. By his teens the Church was well into a transition from the second to third generations as a mostly Gentile entity no longer operating with any efficacy in Israel proper but growing exponentially in the rest of the mainly Gentile world. As someone who was head of the church in Smyrna, he obviously did not grow up in Israel where the original eyewitnesses of the First Coming lived. It is difficult to fully validate his late 1st century experience as being typical of the Church at large when he was a disciple of the last Apostle alive and long gone from Israel proper, much less comparable to that of the very first generation who experienced both Christ and all of the Apostles. He was "closer", but his experience under the latter ministry of the Apostle John is not a firsthand experience belonging to the very first original generation of believers. He is not even a first generation disciple of John. Polycarp's lone extant writing is *The Letter to the Philippians*.

But it gets more than a little complicated when we start placing things on an historical timeline. The authentication of Polycarp's ministry and standing come from Irenaeus (152-202 AD), a figure who was approximately 3 years old when Polycarp died, Tertullian just a few years later still but living longer overall from 155-240 AD but born the year Polycarp died, and Jerome who is even further down the line who arrives in the 4th and 5th centuries. (347-420 AD). Aside from Polycarp's lone writing, the authorities we quote concerning him actually come progressively later and later after Polycarp has largely come and gone, and in reality are not even his contemporaries. They are not actually firsthand witnesses of Polycarp, much less even belonging to his generation of the Church. This is not a chain of evidence which is beyond reasonable scrutiny.

Again, by no means is an argument being proffered to wholly disqualify these individuals or their associated works. This is being raised to highlight the greater issue of why quoting someone who heard or knew about someone who was a later disciple of the Apostle John should not be presented as a ringing endorsement of what the very first generation of the Early Church believed, even though he was "closer". Polycarp was probably no more than 26 years old when John was exiled to Patmos and when the first generation of the Church, then operating mainly outside of Israel, was already becoming a distant memory. At most he may be able to convey something of what the 2nd and 3rd generations of the mainly ethnic Gentile Church believed, but certainly not the first and earliest. We need to take into consideration the much shorter life expectancies to understand how few who were alive during Christ's ministry circa 30-34 AD were actually still around at the end of the 1st century when the book of Revelation became available.

Frankly, when it comes to handling Scripture, natural curiosity alone should make us wonder why an author or speaker is attempting to make their case based on writings from non-canonical sources. Often the implication is that something is being presented which for some reason was "lost" or, even more disturbingly, "unknown" to the centuries of Christians between the founding Church and us today. Even when well-intentioned, it is intrinsically problematic when the best and most powerful case cannot be made from Scripture alone, especially in tandem with an omission of the historical timeline which brings doubt, if not an outright refutation, of the assertion. The Scriptures are the best and only truly authoritative record of what the Early Church believed. But especially when it comes to eschatology, this is a familiar pursuit because the terms which in modern Church history have become common were never used for all but the latest generations of the Church. Many modern authors are therefore looking for parallels to their chosen "ism" going back as early as possible.

[For a more detailed discussion concerning what is probably one of the very few Christian writings originating from the actual time of the 1st century Church, see *Appendix B: The Didache*.]

The Importance of Chronology

In parallel to this skepticism concerning Early Church provenance, there appears to frequently arise an inherent confusion even among the most academically qualified when it comes to the chronology of eschatology as given in God's Word, especially where it concerns the Early Church and the attempt to use the earliest sources possible to justify a particular point or overall position. It seems to be regularly overlooked that the book of Revelation was not only given last after all the rest of God's Word, but provided quite late in the history of what is called the Early Church; so much so, that most of that very first generation had already passed away without ever knowing anything about it.

Many overlook the gap of time which the Early Church experienced of nearly sixty years between the Olivet Discourse and John's vision on Patmos; their eschatology could not even possibly include Revelation. Strictly speaking, the very first generation was all but gone and the publication of Revelation actually came when the Church was firmly in the grip of its third generation of believers. (Even the term "Early Church" is employed questionably; just because someone lived in the 1st century does not mean they all lived together at the same time, especially considering the shorter lifespans endemic in the ancient world.) Because of war, famine, disease and all the other life-shortening factors of living in the ancient world, there was a much quicker turnover of generations, not to mention that the Gospel spread exponentially outside of Israel creating a much newer, mainly ethnically Gentile Church by the time of John's vision. None of the letters to the seven churches given to John are even located in Israel, an indication of how far the ethnic identity of the Church had progressed in the nearly six decades before Revelation was written.

Consider carefully for a moment that eleven of the original Twelve Apostles and all the major foundational leaders of that generation who were eyewitnesses of Christ and belonged to its inaugural membership, even those such as Paul and Barnabas and their contemporaries, all died before the advent of Revelation, and yet lived in the expectancy of His Return. In fact, when any New Testament writer taught something touching on the Lord's Return, they could not possibly have been thinking about what was presented in Revelation, a work which would not be published in their lifetime. Although there may have been a handful of eyewitnesses to Christ's earthly ministry like the Apostle John still occasionally but decreasingly found, the fact is that Revelation was not available to the very first and earliest generation of believers.

At most, what that founding generation had in their possession were the Old Testament scriptures which had to be reinterpreted in light of Christ's main teaching on the subject, the Olivet Discourse, and the Apostolic commentary on Jesus' teachings in the New Testament writings, mainly through Peter, Paul, James and John. Like Revelation, the Apostle John's Gospel and Epistles would not be published until beyond the tail end of the life of that first generation of believers and after the other Apostles were gone, and yet even without Revelation, this did not prevent anyone from prolifically teaching about, and believing in, Christ's Second Coming for the first 60 years of the Church. For most of the lifespan of the Early Church, the Apostle John may have been actively teaching and ministering, but his writings preserved in the New Testament were non-existent for most of them, and even he could not teach the content of Revelation until experiencing the vision after all the other Apostles and most of that original generation had already gone to be with the Lord.

No mainstream author or scholar, even those belonging to competing eschatologies, disputes that the earliest Christians all expected Christ to return in their lifetime, and within that same group is usually found a common acceptance of the later date when John published Christ's vision in comparison with the rest of the New Testament canon. But it then follows that this means the Early Church's expectations for the Second Coming were first and foremost shaped by their understanding of the Olivet Discourse, the New Testament writings providing a commentary on it, and the Old Testament, and would have no parallel knowledge of how such things might be compared and contrasted to Revelation, a body of Scripture which was not revealed in the course of most of their lifetimes. The question of what the Early Church believed concerning the eschaton is answered in that it was completely founded upon the Olivet Discourse. This clarified for them the meaning of the Old Testament prior, and was what the New Testament writers were referring to which came immediately after.

By God's design, it was sufficient for that very first generation of believers to live in the expectation of Christ's Return based on what was taught in the New Testament writings given to that point, with John's contribution of Revelation still a distant prospect. And yet so many writers and scholars to this day superimpose upon the earliest Christians elements of eschatology which are uniquely ascribed to Revelation, something not merely yet to be revealed, but actually completely unknown to them. Modern commentators often represent 1st century eschatology as being fully cognizant of everything in Revelation long before it was ever written, and sometimes radically reverse the roles as if the New Testament references were written because of what is stated in Revelation, a timeline impossibility. Seldom do we find someone addressing the sixty year "silence" between the Olivet Discourse and the giving of Revelation, interrupted only by the New Testament writers commenting exclusively on the Olivet Discourse and the Old Testament texts. Nor are we often presented with an explanation of why God worked this way.

This is why we should automatically reject eschatology-themed books, articles and websites which attempt to stipulate that the Olivet Discourse is not for the Church, but only for Israel when it finds itself inside the final seven year period most generally labeled "*The* Tribulation" after the Church's removal. (And, yes, this is more commonly asserted today than we would like to believe.) For the approximately 60 years between the Resurrection and the Apostle John's vision on the Isle of Patmos, the Olivet Discourse was sufficient for the foundational members of the Church, not to mention all the Apostles and authors of the New Testament; it was enough scriptural light to allow the earliest Christians to live in compliance with God's Word where Christ's Second Coming was concerned. And in the same manner experienced by all Scripture when additional, newer Scripture came along, nothing was ever repealed, amended or replaced—in fact, the earlier texts always serve to prove the authenticity and authority of the newer, not the other way around.

A Reversal of the Order

This is also the major reason why it can be observed that one of the basic, most repeated problems when it comes to eschatology is that the order of study is often reversed. In other words, the presupposition is to begin with Revelation and establish it as an unalterable baseline, and then work backwards to integrate into it the perceived proper place of each prophetic piece of the puzzle from all of the remaining portions of God's Word. (Or worse, to then make a case to exclude previous portions of Scripture.) Everything is placed in subjugation to Revelation as not just being the foundation on which everything else is built, but as having to be the starting point, albeit with an occasional nod to other sections of God's prophetic Word. And, as pointed out, this is sometimes so rigidly applied that a reinterpretation of other Scriptures takes place, such as the extreme assertion that the Olivet Discourse has no meaning for the Church but for future Israel alone, or by those who reverse the order of the sequence provided by Paul in 2 Thessalonians 2. (Another twisting of Scripture which is all too commonly placed on prominent display in the present climate.)

Overwhelming visual evidence of this is provided by performing a Google search: elect to search by "image", type in "tribulation chart", and hundreds if not thousands of charts will fill the screen. Like snowflakes, no two are exactly alike. Google has not yet attained the ability to differentiate which charts belong to each particular eschatology, so they are all presented en masse, but even those asserting to be a member of the same "ism" are never identical. The Lord will surely return before anyone has the time to give each diagram even a cursory examination.

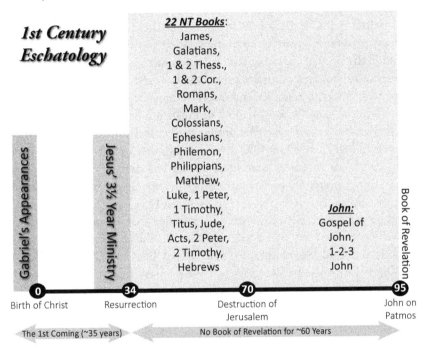

One of the shared assumptions behind the vast majority of these different timelines, which even a minimal examination will almost immediately make apparent, is how they seem to nearly always begin with Revelation as the baseline starting point. In fact, most of them will not even bother making an attempt to integrate the Olivet Discourse. They are most often centered around the three sets of Seals, Trumpets and Bowls of Revelation, a fixture not overtly specified in the Olivet Discourse nor previously documented in any portion of God's prophetic Word, or at least not given in that particularly expressed manner.

If we want to see things as the first generation saw them, if we want to understand God's prophetic plan the way they interpreted it, we have to make an attempt to understand the sequence by which God's Word was revealed to them and ultimately culminates with Revelation. We need to ask the hard question as to why it was sufficient for that first generation to only need the Olivet Discourse as their guide for such a long time, most even passing away with no knowledge of Revelation, and how this could provide the context for understanding the additional details to later arrive when Revelation finally did become available.

If we want to prove an eschatology belongs to the way Jesus' Return was "always" believed from the very beginning, we have to place ourselves in their exegetical shoes, metaphorically speaking. None of the twenty-six New Testament books preceding Revelation—not even John's Gospel and Epistles, were written with Revelation in the minds of those human authors or their readership when referring to anything relating to the eschaton—the Second Coming; the primary teaching which guided them was the Olivet Discourse. That it would not later contradict that which would be subsequently revealed is a testament to the guidance and inspiration of the Holy Spirit and the very reason why we assign it as a member of the canon of Scripture.

Remember, at Christ's First Coming, the expectation was that the Messiah would fulfill 100% of all the Old Testament prophecies spoken of Him during a single visit. At that time there was no talk of Daniel's "70th Week" nor a host of things presented in Scripture which we now know with the passage of time to only apply to His Second Coming. And the Early Church, equipped with Christ's teaching, the Apostolic commentary on that teaching, and the indwelling of the Holy Spirit to guide them in the correct interpretation of all Scripture available, maintained as their baseline for the Second Coming the Olivet Discourse because that was the primary teaching passed on from Christ Himself to them personally; everything for the earliest Christians was predicated on this, with absolutely no corroborating knowledge of Revelation at the time.

This is a very important exercise for us, if for no other reason than it helps us separate the plain meaning of Scripture from the outside teachings and concepts which have been superimposed. Returning to the primary authority of God's Word exposes those man-made assumptions we find the need to jettison, and to confrim the scriptural basis, if any, for the more recent terms the modern Church has adopted. Instead of trying to rely on making some kind of parallel connection to an ancient Christian author or writing, we engage the very best interpreter of God's Word to settle the issue--God's Word itself. Our primary Bible study rule should always be that God's Word is always the best interpreter of God's Word, and understand that an improper emphasis on human writers is sometimes used to take its place.

The Source of Verification

Furthermore, we need to consider seriously that when Revelation was initially distributed to the Church at large, its authenticity and authority would have therefore been tested against the Olivet Discourse (and the rest of Scripture, of course) and not the other way around. If those Christians could have created their own PowerPoint charts and websites depicting a consolidated End Times scenario to express their eschatology, the starting point would have been the Olivet Discourse. Only in this context would Revelation be first and foremost understood and even "integrated" with what they knew from that teaching, not the other way around as is presently so often the chosen approach regardless of the eschatology proffered.

Because the Olivet Discourse was the definitive teaching of Christ on the End Times—of which John was an original witness, they would have seen Revelation—His subsequent discourse revealed through John, as building on what He initially gave rather than replacing the original. They most certainly would not have entertained the notion that the Olivet Discourse, their chief guide for more than six decades, all of the sudden did not apply to the Church or had been superseded. It was the exclusive prism through which the Early Church viewed eschatology and tested all comers. This means that before one can understand Revelation, one must fully know and adhere to all the teachings of God's prophetic Word which came first, especially the Olivet Discourse.

Just to set the record straight so that the reader realizes this author is not presenting himself as yet another self-deceived know-it-all asserting to be the only one to get something right and can therefore wag a finger at all the authors, academics and experts who might be wrong, I arrived at this conclusion largely based on my own pathetic attempts to construct a highly customized master End Times chart. (It was not only incredibly detailed and formidable in its depth, but pretty, too!) Of course, my pride initially convinced me that I would finally get it right where everyone else had failed, because after viewing hundreds of those charts from the aforementioned Google search, I devised a "foolproof strategy" to make my end-all/be-all chart include integrated lines from every part of God's prophetic Word possible and not just limit it mainly to Revelation and Daniel. I thought I knew the path which would lead me to being able to correct everyone else's mistake, or at the least, their omissions. Instead, I would inevitably arrive at a place where something on my one-of-a-kind, integrated chart was irreconcilable with itself and would make yet another futile attempt from a slightly different approach, only to find myself at yet another irresolvable point of contradiction. It took some time to realize that I, too, was doing the very same thing, always starting with Revelation and making everything else subordinate and secondary to it.

Ever since I have recognized this in myself, many aspects of eschatology have become much more clear and uncluttered, not to mention some previously clouded points of misunderstanding have come into much better view, or at least are no longer inherently in conflict with each other. But even this effort, admittedly, is not without controversy and rightly subject to every reader's justified scrutiny, since it is primarily an attempt to shrug off a lifetime of man's influence in order to allow Scripture to speak for itself. This baggage is not easily jettisoned.

But this raises an important issue when it comes to God's Word which will be revisited in more detail, and that is the commonly accepted concept expressed as "the progressive revelation of God". God did not reveal everything about Himself or His plans from the outset to Adam and Eve, but we can point to milestones when new information was delivered such as in the times of Noah, Abraham, Moses, etc. God deemed it sufficient for many generations to live with a limited understanding which was appropriate for them, but greatly expanded upon for future generations going forward at God's appointed times of revelation.

Although new and additional information comes with each of these revelatory milestones, it never makes the previous obsolete, but rather sheds even greater light to affirm the foundation already laid for what is to come. In fact, that which was always given subsequently has always depending on what existed previously.

The "new" consistently reveals that it was always lurking in the "old" all along and makes the "old" even more relevant and valuable. (For instance, until Revelation 11 explained the existence and working of the Two Witnesses, we could not see the significance of the many types and activities of a pair of witnesses already present in many places in Scripture which all work in the character of the final pair, but they were nonetheless there all along.) Yet even though Revelation was provided last in the chronological sequence of God's canon of Scripture, far too many make it the first layer of the foundation and therefore essentially build everything backwards, when it is actually an extension of all that came before it and simply exposes what has been there all along, ultimately revealed according to God's will and timing.

To determine how the eschatology of the 1st century actually received and interpreted Revelation is to grasp that it was initially understood in the context of the Olivet Discourse. In our present time, much of the confusion within every eschatological camp can be traced to the propensity to reverse this order. They would not disagree with the concept of "the progressive revelation of God" in every other doctrinal area, but often do not apply it when it comes to their study of eschatology. The goal here is not to provide a comprehensive chart showing the placement of each and every detail, but to set the proper foundation so that at the God-given appointed time such events can be properly recognized in their appropriate scriptural context.

An Important Additional Issue

It is anticipated that the present-day believer will probably be most challenged by the raising of a repeated, additional issue throughout the body of this book which has resulted because of this approach. There are terms in common usage even across competing eschatologies which are rarely questioned and seem to be universally accepted which have become the building blocks of nearly every discussion, sermon or writing even skirting the fringes of eschatology regardless of their doctrinal affiliation or background. These terms are, indeed, found in Scripture, so they may provide the appearance of being supported by God's Word, but their actual usages and definitions in most cases are not precisely mirroring their given context in the exacting way Holy Spirit-inspired Scripture offers. They are often found to have been lifted from Scripture out of their originally-given textual usage and assigned definitions which do not precisely conform to their in situ context. Because such misusages have been adopted by the mainstream of Christian academia for so long, they have simply been accepted as is to the point it is assumed that this is what Scripture means whenever we come across them.

The over-ruling axiom of exegesis pursued in these pages is that Scripture is the best interpreter of Scripture, which means we have to investigate whether the teachings, concepts, or even individual terms someone employs, no matter how pure their intentions, conforms to Scripture's definition, or along the way have been reassigned to something else, even if it turns out to be a close or subtle variation. This is an exercise commonly accepted in all other cases of biblical doctrine, such as when it must be proven from Scripture what "elect" or "born again" mean, but seems to experience a glaring absence when it comes to the most common terms assigned to eschatology. This is a major reason why, unlike the academic format of so many books, very little space will be devoted to quoting other human authors and what they think so we can strive as much as possible to allow God's Word to be the deciding factor. When the paucity of such parallel human sources are identified, it is usually a reinforcement of Scripture interpreting Scripture, not citing them as an authority unto themselves.

Specifically to the point, there are probably no more important defining terms in this regard than "*tribulation*", "*great tribulation*", and "*the day of the Lord*". Most readers are probably going to find the ensuing discussion involving these terms the most imposing, because the issue is going to be repeatedly raised as to how they are handled by Scripture and the parameters it places on them, as opposed to the way many have lifted them out of God's Word for alternate meanings leading to other purposes.

If the reader is patient, it will be seen that these staples of biblical eschatology are not being discarded, nor actually moving the metaphorical goal post as far as one might initially think, but reestablishing the authority of God's Word over the most basic building blocks of the prophetic sequence of Scripture. This does not fall into the range of a technical argument which is really only interesting to academic wonks, but crucial to the rank-and-file constituents who earnestly seek and rely on the authority of God's Word first. 1st century eyes and ears were unencumbered by the predisposition of so many centuries of opinion upon opinion, and in the character of the Bereans, (Acts 17:10-12) confirmed Scripture with Scripture. Living in a post-printing press world, although we are blessed to each own many Bibles, there may be something to be said for those previous generations when commentaries could not deluge their personal libraries to overshadow the originally-given text. (Nor could they run to the Internet for a zillion offered answers.)

Many are the efforts to show how these terms were used and interpreted by previous generations going all the way back to the first one because, in actuality, the emphasis on the Second Coming has experienced different emphases at various points along the Church's historical timeline employing nuanced redefinition of terms along the way. Even good-faith efforts to string together a homogenous explanation for these variations in order to sanctify one's present assertions are difficult at best, and in the end require that the final decision is, as always, the authority of Scripture itself. A classic example is how the terms "Pre-Trib", "Post-Trib" or "Pre-Wrath" are actually relatively new in the Church's overall history, so there is the common pursuit to "prove" that although previous generations did not literally employ these labels in their writings or sermons, they were nonetheless somehow making a case with the terminology of their day to espouse those exact, same positions or concepts.

This has been a very long-winded attempt to suggest that we engage in an exercise, as much as possible, to first study the Olivet Discourse without any reference to Revelation, and then take that structure and overlay it on that very last Christ-given work. Just as nothing in the twenty-six books prior to Revelation revise in even the smallest detail what was presented in the thirty-nine books of the Old Testament, neither did Revelation replace even the smallest point of the eschatological landscape for anything which preceded it. As it turns out, both are essential to properly understand the other as long as the sequence of their publication is consciously retained and not reversed to suit us.

*[**One Technical Note**: It is this author's practice to study the Gospels synoptically— that is, to compare side-by-side accounts of the same event or teaching recorded in more than one Gospel and especially to note both the similarities and differences. Where the Olivet Discourse is concerned, the reader will note that a color-coded table format is provided to show where, exactly, each Gospel provides the same information as well as those items unique to each Gospel writer. Each account as a consolidated whole is worthy of study in its own right, but this approach facilitates our understanding of the overall Discourse and mitigates against taking just a portion of Scripture out of context to the exclusion of the rest of God's Word. This format is provided for the Olivet Discourse in its entirety in the included Appendix A: The Olivet Discourse in Parallel.]*

Part One:
Christ's First Revelation

1 ❖ The Second Coming in the Gospels

B<i>y far and away, that which Jesus teaches concerning His Second Coming is presented in its most concentrated and whole form in the Olivet Discourse.</i> That being said, however, there are additional relevant discourses and references made in the course of His earthly ministry which do not merely appear to supplement and compliment it, but actually provide a foundation building up to it. Although most of what Jesus refers to in an eschatological context has to do with His First Coming, and even though He most often addresses that particular issue during His 3-1/2 year ministry, there are still many instances prior to the formal giving of the Olivet Discourse which in some way directly refer to His Second Coming. In fact, it would appear that the Gospels record approximately sixty such references over those years of His ministry leading up to that definitive teaching which He provided during His final week on earth, and it must be kept in mind that in reality it was probably far more than that; a number of those teachings were most certainly repeated many more times than just the one or two recorded by the Gospel writers.

The point is that Jesus did not just begin talking about the Second Coming out of the blue a few days before His Crucifixion; it was a constant companion to His teachings during the whole course of His ministry because corrections to false assumptions about His First Coming required addressing misconceptions concerning His Second Coming still to come. But as we shall discover, the Olivet Discourse is the authoritative foundation for what will happen during the very last years when history transitions from the end of this age to the next. And if it had not been given, there would be five dozen or so specific references to things associated with the eschaton which would have to be collected, categorized and compared in order to be knit properly together.

In other words, the Olivet Discourse is not the beginning of New Testament eschatology, but the prism to view everything in the proper context, whether it comes before or after that sermon proper.

This is of particular importance for understanding why a select subset of four Apostles are recorded as inspired to ask on their own a very specific, multipart question regarding Jesus' Return which initiates the Olivet Discourse:

³As He was sitting on the Mount of Olives,	*³As He was sitting on the Mount of Olives opposite the temple,*
the disciples came to Him privately, saying,	*Peter and James and John and Andrew were questioning Him privately,* *⁷They questioned Him, saying,*
"Tell us, when will these things happen,	*⁴"Tell us, when will these things be,*
and what will be the sign when all these things are going to be fulfilled?" (Mk. 13:3-4)	*And what will be the sign when these things are about to take place?" (Lk. 21:7)*
and what will be the sign of Your coming, and of the end of the age?" (Mt. 24:3)	

Yes, at times the Apostles were confused as to some of the things Jesus said, and it is even documented in the Gospels that many events or references were not understood until Jesus' explanations after His Resurrection. But having heard years of sermons and teachings which contained specific mention of such things as *"the resurrection"* (Mt. 12:23; 22:30; Lk. 14:14, 35-36), *"the last day"* (Jn. 6:39-40, 44, 54; 7:37; 11:24; 12:48), *"the day of judgment"* (Mt. 10:15; 11:22, 24; 12:36), *"the harvest"* (Mt. 9:38; 13:39; 4:29), *"the time"* (Mt. 8:29; Lk. 13:35; 19:44), *"the end of the age"* (Mt. 13:39-40, 49), and even phrases such as *"until the Son of Man comes"* (Mt. 10:23; Lk. 18:8) or *"the Son of Man is coming at an hour that you do not expect"* (Lk. 12:40)—their tripartite question did not come completely unexpected as out of a vacuum, nor was it entirely uninformed. Many of the things Jesus wove together into a consolidated teaching to answer their questions in the Olivet Discourse had been touched upon previously at various points in Christ's ministry, steadily building up to that milestone discourse.

It is most telling that they did not limit their inquiry to, *"When will these things happen?"* or *"What will be the sign when all these things are going to be fulfilled?"*, which could be questions taken to be asking at which point in Christ's First Coming, simultaneous to the Apostles' lifetimes, such were going to be fulfilled, but they additionally specified, *"What will be the sign of Your coming?"* as well as *"…and the end of the age?"* They had clearly gained at least a minimal understanding from Christ's teachings those previous 3-1/2 years that there was some kind of future fulfillment yet to come apart from what was currently taking place, and they formed this question using the same terms they had repeatedly heard employed by Christ Himself. Jesus' answer will focus on what is going to take place at *"the end of the age"*.

But when making the case for what the Early Church believed where the Second Coming is concerned, as firsthand witnesses of Christ's teachings, and the continuation of being taught and discipled by Christ's inner circle of Apostles according to those teachings, that which is recorded in the New Testament writings would be axiomatic. And especially since the indisputable historical fact is that there was no such thing as the book of Revelation for the first 60 or so years of the Church, the Olivet Discourse in particular was unquestionably considered the most authoritative teaching in this regard. The source of the Early Church's eschatology centered on what would eventually be published in the Gospels, serving as the defining platform for everything which came both before them in the Old Testament Scriptures, and after in the emerging New Testament canon and John's vision on Patmos. This was the standard by which all things prophetic were measured and authenticated.

Although the premise of this writing is that the Olivet Discourse should be given precedence over what came more than 60 years later in the book of Revelation, we must first review the foundation which was being laid in Jesus' ministry prior to the Olivet Discourse to come during the last week of His earthly presence in those 60 or so prior teachings and references. In reality, the Olivet Discourse was not something entirely brand new which completely caught these Apostles by surprise, but was given at their request to consolidate together into the proper context the numerous and varied references to His Second Coming which they had heard Jesus use repeatedly throughout His teachings almost from the very beginning of the Apostles' relationship with Him.

Later we will additionally discuss in detail how their own curiosity may have been heightened by Jesus' response to the Pharisees' question in Luke 17 a few weeks or months prior to the Olivet Discourse, most of which is subsequently incorporated, but at that time was actually addressing a different inquiry. This "mini" Olivet Discourse in Luke 17 would be shown to be but a partial answer to the critical whole.

Prior to the giving of the Olivet Discourse, the statements *"the Son of Man comes"* and *"the Son of Man is coming"* are recorded six times, and as just mentioned, a mini-version of the Olivet Discourse itself was separately given just weeks or at most months prior as recorded in Luke 17 in response to the Pharisees' direct inquiry of Jesus *"as to when the kingdom of God was coming"*. (Lk. 17:20) The issue of the Second Coming was often woven in with His teachings to distinguish what was going to take place in His First Coming from that which was actually assigned for fulfillment in His Second Coming. This was a repeated topic Jesus visited many times prior to the Olivet Discourse, and it is present right up to His responses during His trial.

However, it is interesting to note that for a quartet of Apostles, that which took place on the Mt. of Olives may have been a sort of bookend to what was initiated on the earlier Mt. of Transfiguration. For these same Apostles, sans Andrew, that was one of the earliest documented instances establishing that a second visitation was not just possible, but an integral part of God's plan. This is the place where they witnessed Moses and Elijah discussing with Jesus His impending crucifixion in Jerusalem (Lk. 9:30-31) and Jesus' follow-on revelation specifying how Elijah had not only already appeared in the character of John the Baptist, but was going to return yet again, establishing the expectation of His Second Coming. (Mt. 17:10-13) It has been a long exegetical journey between these two mountains, during which repeated references to Christ's Second Coming were finally drawn together into consolidated detail. But for this select group of Apostles, their desire was for all of these references and teachings to be brought together categorically as a whole. We need to examine what they had previously heard to cause them to finally make this request of Jesus.

A Basic Outline

In surveying these 60 or so references recorded in all the Gospels, it would appear that they can be grouped together into three basic categories:

> ➤ ***This Present Age.*** These are clear indications that there is not just a large amount of work still to come before the Second Coming, but a divinely appointed plan by God which embraces it. Jesus keeps referring to things which will take place "*in this age*" as an historical period in which He was not only currently living, but would extend well beyond His Ascension and not going to end with the formal completion of just the 3-1/2 year ministry of His First Coming. That which came before His First Coming and which was to come future to His departure was referenced by Christ as variations of "*this present age*".

➤ *The End of This Age.* These are events and works directly associated with a period when believers, recognizing the signs of the times in relation to the impending fulfillment of God's prophetic Word, experience an unprecedented period of transition both spiritually and physically in a relatively compressed timespan compared to the whole of what comes in history prior. The unsaved in the world will not experience this kind of recognition and instead live in the character of the days of Noah, carrying on business as usual, and the days of Lot in an environment of increasing wickedness. Unspecified as to its exact length, it is nonetheless deemed not just detectable, but comes with accompanying warnings so as not to allow it to transpire unrecognized. This entire transitional period is what we presently call "the eschaton" or "The Second Coming". This is the concluding phase of *"this present age"* and not something separate from it.

➤ *The Age To Come.* We most often refer to this as "The Millennial Reign" or "Millennial Kingdom", but it was significant that Jesus began to reshape their understanding of Scripture not just for His day, but for all generations, as the common belief was that the Messiah would come and usher in this age within a single visitation. They did not fully understand at the time the concept of "one Messiah, two comings" and believed whenever He came, He would fulfill every prophecy concerning the Messiah the first time and within a single "age", which would then morph into the Messianic kingdom on earth. This age is definitely separate and distinct from *"the present age"*.

It is best at this point to avoid an apologetics level discussion of the various forms of "Dispensationalism", which many scholars embrace in order to assign specific names and designations to perceived historical periods past, present and future, except to say that there are those who are much more dogmatic about the details of this doctrine who would provide a chart of many more dispensations (periods or ages of history when it is believed that God worked in distinctly different ways) than will be designated in this book. For the sake of keeping it simple, a minimalist approach is going to be presented which accepts Jesus' teachings on this at the most cursory, plain text level. The specifics which are overtly and categorically recorded in Scripture by Jesus basically refers to five things from the perspective of His First Coming, three of which can be thought of more along the lines as "phases" of the same age:

1. The Old Testament Law and Prophets culminating with John the Baptist (Lk. 16:16), but making it more akin to the beginning of *"this present age"* rather than a distinct, previous era;

2. This present age, which continues unbroken through His First Coming until it ends with the completion of what we know to be Daniel's 70th Week and the end of all the kingdoms of the earth;

3. The end of the age, which is the final transition from this present age to the next age and accompanied by what we would call the specific events of the Last Days (these first three are all aspects or phases of *"this present age"*);

4. The age to come, which we often commonly refer to as His thousand year Millennial Reign; and,

5. Eternity, where there is no one left to still be resurrected, whether destined for heaven or hell.

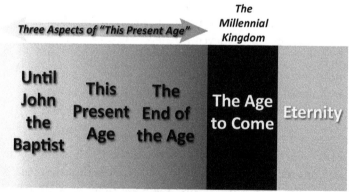

We will find that the Olivet Discourse concentrates on *"the end of the age"*, and that Revelation actually follows this same outline but instead employs a parallel set of terms to reflect the greater detail provided. We will also briefly examine some of the eschatological references to eternity Jesus provided in the contrast of *"a resurrection of life"* versus *"a resurrection of judgment"*, and various renderings of "hell" and "outer darkness".

Because of the great many times when Jesus specifically identified a wide variety of things to come for something future to His First Coming, we can understand that the Apostles' question initiating the Olivet Discourse did not materialize out of thin air for no reason or even with no prompting whatsoever. It was actually an intelligently, well-worded inquiry based on many references and teachings given over a long period of time by Christ Himself. And considering that the week in which it is all brought together in the Olivet Discourse began with the Triumphal Entry and all that was taking place in the Temple and in Jerusalem when some were acknowledging Jesus as Messiah and others opposing and rejecting Him, the Apostles did not believe that the whole of Scripture where the Messiah was concerned would go unfulfilled. Instead, they exhibited the faith to ask how to adjust their expectations appropriately. The very way they worded their multi-part question reveals their understanding, on a general level at least, to expect this present earthly age to give way to another before ultimately transitioning to eternity. This was based on their having paid attention to all Christ had taught about these things prior to His giving the Olivet Discourse, and of course their knowledge of the Old Testament Scriptures.

This Present Age

*¹¹While they were listening to these things, Jesus went on to tell a parable, because He was near Jerusalem, and **they supposed that the kingdom of God was going to appear immediately**. ¹²So He said, "A nobleman went to a distant country to receive a kingdom for himself, and then return. ¹³And he called ten of his slaves, and gave them ten minas and said to them, 'Do business with this until I come back.'*

¹⁴"But his citizens hated him and sent a delegation after him, saying, 'We do not want this man to reign over us.'

¹⁵"When he returned, after receiving the kingdom, he ordered that these slaves, to whom he had given the money, be called to him so that he might know what business they had done.

¹⁶"The first appeared, saying, 'Master, your mina has made ten minas more.'

¹⁷"And he said to him, 'Well done, good slave, because you have been faithful in a very little thing, you are to be in authority over ten cities.'

¹⁸"The second came, saying, 'Your mina, master, has made five minas.'

¹⁹"And he said to him also, 'And you are to be over five cities.'

> ²⁰*"Another came, saying, 'Master, here is your mina, which I kept put away in a handkerchief; ²¹for I was afraid of you, because you are an exacting man; you take up what you did not lay down and reap what you did not sow.'*
>
> ²²*"He said to him, 'By your own words I will judge you, you worthless slave. Did you know that I am an exacting man, taking up what I did not lay down and reaping what I did not sow? ²³Then why did you not put my money in the bank, and having come, I would have collected it with interest?'*
>
> ²⁴*"Then he said to the bystanders, 'Take the mina away from him and give it to the one who has the ten minas.'*
>
> ²⁵*"And they said to him, 'Master, he has ten minas already.'*
>
> ²⁶*"I tell you that to everyone who has, more shall be given, but from the one who does not have, even what he does have shall be taken away. ²⁷But these enemies of mine, who did not want me to reign over them, bring them here and slay them in my presence." (Luke 19:11–27)*

One of the reasons there are so many references to Christ's Second Coming prior to the formal giving of the Olivet Discourse is that He was constantly dealing with this issue, that *"they supposed that the kingdom of God was going to appear immediately"* in the course of His First Coming. His identity as Messiah was challenged by those who assumed everything Scripture spoke concerning Him would be fulfilled in a single visit. (This remains a staple of belief within Judaism to this day.) Over and over and over again Jesus supplies parables, illustrations and discourses involving different ways of teaching about *"the kingdom of God"*, nearly always in contrast to their preconceived notions.

As we shall see when examining the Olivet Discourse proper, Jesus provides parables and illustrations on this topic just like this one which regularly feature an authority figure who goes away for a long time, returns at a time the subordinates do not expect, and concurrent with his return delves out rewards and punishments which simultaneously take place in tandem with incorporating the righteous faithful and removing the wicked unfaithful. All of these elements are present in *The Parable of the Minas* which is given quite some time before the Olivet Discourse, regularly establishing the expectation for His Second Coming during the whole of His earthly ministry.

An additional common denominator of all these teachings which must not be overlooked is the manner in which they portray the right behavior by the servants in the interim while the Master is away. They are to faithfully carry out the work entrusted so as to be found "ready" when He returns because of the quality and consistency of their commitment to God's Word and ways. But the fact that a very long time of absence is featured in these teachings speaks to the very existence of *"this age"* extending much further out, even to future history, if you will, from Christ's First Coming. Regardless of which eschatology or timing of the Rapture we personally embrace, Jesus is simply specifying that *"this present age"* is in progress until He comes back and did not conclude with the cross so another could begin or a previous one come to an end; until the conclusion of the eschaton, He consistently speaks of it all as *"this age"*.

In the Meantime, Until the Day, the Time, the Judgment

> ¹⁴*"Whoever does not receive you, nor heed your words, as you go out of that house or that city, shake the dust off your feet.* ¹⁵*Truly I say to you, it will be more tolerable for the land of Sodom and Gomorrah **in the day of judgment** than for that city. (Matthew 10:14–15)*

Within the instructions Jesus gave in Matthew 10 when sending out the Twelve are found many similar references to things which will be repeated in the Olivet Discourse proper, such as difficulties which will be encountered when preaching the Gospel, opportunities to testify at the Spirit's leading, the divisions which will arise not just with governments and religious institutions but even one's family, and other aspects of persecution, apostasy and deception. But the work of *"this age"* is implied to be long and arduous just by the fact that the results will not be completely realized until *"the day of judgment"*.

> ¹⁰*"But whatever city you enter and they do not receive you, go out into its streets and say,* ¹¹*'Even the dust of your city which clings to our feet we wipe off in protest against you; yet be sure of this, that the kingdom of God has come near.'* ¹²*I say to you, it will be more tolerable **in that day** for Sodom than for that city.*
> ¹³*"Woe to you, Chorazin! Woe to you, Bethsaida! For if the miracles had been performed in Tyre and Sidon which occurred in you, they would have repented long ago, sitting in sackcloth and ashes.* ¹⁴*But it will be more tolerable for Tyre and Sidon **in the judgment** than for you.* ¹⁵*And you, Capernaum, will not be exalted to heaven, will you? You will be brought down to Hades!*
> ¹⁶*"The one who listens to you listens to Me, and the one who rejects you rejects Me; and he who rejects Me rejects the One who sent Me." (Luke 10:10–16)*

In the course of His instructions when sending out the Seventy in Luke 10, a similar set of conditions are again specified in parallel to what was provided previously to the Twelve, and this time with even more detail about the expected issues to be encountered and the spiritual consequences of rejecting the Gospel. Yet again, however, all the results will not be known until "*that day*" which is specifically defined as "*the judgment*".

> *²⁰Then He began to denounce the cities in which most of His miracles were done, because they did not repent. ²¹"Woe to you, Chorazin! Woe to you, Bethsaida! For if the miracles had occurred in Tyre and Sidon which occurred in you, they would have repented long ago in sackcloth and ashes. ²²Nevertheless I say to you, it will be more tolerable for Tyre and Sidon **in the day of judgment** than for you. ²³And you, Capernaum, will not be exalted to heaven, will you? You will descend to Hades; for if the miracles had occurred in Sodom which occurred in you, it would have remained to this day. ²⁴Nevertheless I say to you that it will be more tolerable for the land of Sodom **in the day of judgment**, than for you." (Matthew 11:20–24)*

In Matthew 11:20-24, Jesus provides this teaching for a third time in regard to Himself personally. In other words, what happened to Jesus is replayed again not just through the Twelve, and not just the Seventy, but shows how we should expect this to continuously and cyclically take place as an ongoing feature of "*this age*" until His Return. The perpetual persecution, apostasy and deception anticipated for every generation of believer serves to teach about its heightened, unprecedented form in the shadow of His Return when all things are dramatically drawing to a final conclusion and these activities are multiplied to levels never previously experienced. They may escalate in the Last Days as never before, but to one degree or another they are present for every generation during every historical period in the meantime.

But there is a clear indication of a significant length of time extending beyond the First Coming just by the fact that Jesus is mandating a life or work whose results will not be realized until "*the day of judgment*". In the meantime, it is the work of the Gospel which is to most preoccupy His servants.

> *²⁸When He came to the other side into the country of the Gadarenes, two men who were demon-possessed met Him as they were coming out of the tombs. They were so extremely violent that no one could pass by that way. ²⁹And they cried out, saying, "What business do we have with each other, Son of God? Have You come here to torment us **before the time**?" (Matthew 8:28–29)*

The underlying Greek word *"kairos"* is here rendered in the English as *"time"*. Whereas sometimes the word *"chronos"* (Strong's #5550) is used alternatively for *"time"* to describe a sequence of events or chronology, *"kairos"* (Strong's #2540) is usually employed for a timed event occurring with specific start and end points for a designated overall length. Jesus does not correct the demons' assumption that there is a specified schedule before they experience the inevitable consequences of their rebellion. For our purposes, it is a supporting footnote for the concept of *"this present age"* that this supernatural recognition of something to come is provided in this encounter, as well as a divine timing that is generally known in advance to exist as well, even in the spiritual realm.

> [15] *"Beware of the false prophets, who come to you in sheep's clothing, but inwardly are ravenous wolves. (Matthew 7:15)*

> [43] *"I have come in My Father's name, and you do not receive Me; if another comes in his own name, you will receive him. (John 5:43)*

Two of the most prominent and prolific features of the eschaton as specified by the Olivet Discourse are the *"many false prophets"* and the *"many false christs"*. (Mt. 24:23-26; Mk. 13:21-23) If Jesus was going to fulfill everything in His first visit, what would be the point of warning about the *"ravenous wolves"* disguising themselves *"in sheep's clothing"* and the counterfeits who will be accepted in the Messiah's place future to His present ministry? There is clearly something more to come, something in the future for which warnings can be issued.

> [16] *"**I have other sheep, which are not of this fold**; I must bring them also, and they will hear My voice; and they will become one flock with one shepherd. (John 10:16)*

The way this is worded was particularly powerful for the generation of that day. Whereas the popular interpretation of Scripture and the traditions erroneously built on it dictated that the Gentiles were rejected, or at most could only come to God through an arduous process, this is a very specific personal message about the work of the Messiah and especially the Church which would soon be fully realized. But also consider this in the context of Jesus' instructions first to the Twelve and then to the Seventy as to their preaching of the Gospel, and we can see that there is not only something which extends further than the Apostles and disciples, further beyond the first generation of Jews who come to faith in Christ, and even further to something much more comprehensive not just in depth of meaning, but the time necessary to accomplish such. Particularly powerful is the caveat, "*they will become one flock with one shepherd*".

In other words, if we take a step back and consider all of these things together, we are being told that the work of Christ must continue, the work of His servants must continue, Israel and the Gentiles will become "*one flock with one shepherd*", and there will be parallel spiritual impediments in the form of deception, apostasy and persecution not just through false prophets and false christs, and not solely at the hand of governments and courts, but by friends, family and church-based relationships. Such have cyclically returned during every historical period of the Church and characterize "*this present age*" as spiritually normative. That "*this present age*" will last for a considerable time is expressed in Jesus' parables repeatedly featuring a master who is away for a very long time, and even Jesus' own caveat to His disciples. This is not merely a metaphor, but plainly stated by Christ:

> *22And He said to the disciples, "The days will come when you will long to see one of the days of the Son of Man, and you will not see it. (Luke 17:22)*

But the more important takeaway is that these are the essential aspects of the Olivet Discourse as a whole, each element having been already established in Christ's ministry long before the Apostle's query on the Mt. of Olives.

The End of The Age

> *4"We must work the works of Him who sent Me as long as it is day; **night is coming** when no one can work. (John 9:4)*

The most common biblical metaphor for the End Times is darkness and night. It must be duly noted, however, how this provides a contrast to the previous instructions to persistently preach the Gospel from one place to the next as opposed to this warning that a time is going to come when such is no longer possible, or at the least, ceases to be effective. What is telling about the way this is worded is that when this spiritual night takes place, we will be here to experience it.

> *35"Be dressed in readiness, and keep your lamps lit. 36Be like men who are waiting for their master **when he returns** from the wedding feast, so that they may **immediately open the door** to him when he comes and knocks. 37**Blessed are those***

> **slaves whom the master will find on the alert when he comes;** *truly I say to you, that he will gird himself to serve, and have them recline at the table, and will come up and wait on them.* **[38]Whether he comes in the second watch, or even in the third,** *and finds them so, blessed are those slaves. (Luke 12:35–38)*

The teachings in Luke 12 come at least weeks, if not more likely months, before either what can be called the "mini" Olivet Discourse in Luke 17 or the proper one in Luke 21. This is evidence of what was stated before that these teachings in all likelihood were repeated many more times in the course of Christ's ministry than the one or two times they are recorded for space's sake in the Gospels. These parables and illustrations will be featured again in complimentary variations when we study the Olivet Discourse proper, but this instance proves how they were present in Jesus' teachings all along.

Again, notice that no one knows when the Master is coming and that His return is characterized as something which will probably take place at night in stating, "*Whether he comes in the second watch, or even in the third*".

> [39]*"But be sure of this, that if the head of the house had known at what hour the thief was coming, he would not have allowed his house to be broken into.* [40]*You too, be ready; for the Son of Man is coming at an hour that you do not expect." (Luke 12:39–40)*

This is especially one of those items which most likely rattled around in the Apostles' minds and led to their asking the opening questions to the Olivet Discourse as to the nature and timing of His coming. They already have the "*Son of Man*" with them, so the only way He can come at an hour they do not expect is for Him to go away and return! They likewise probably wondered why they could not anticipate when that return would take place much less the details of His going away and coming back.

> [41]*Peter said, "Lord, are You addressing this parable to us, or to everyone else as well?"*
> [42]*And the Lord said, "Who then is the faithful and sensible steward, whom his master will put in charge of his servants, to give them their rations at the proper time?* [43]**Blessed is that slave whom his master finds so doing when he comes.** [44]*Truly I say to you that he will put him in charge of all his possessions.* [45]*But if that slave says in his heart, 'My master will be a long time in coming,' and begins to beat the slaves, both men and women, and to eat and drink and get drunk;* [46]**The master of that slave will come on a day when he does not expect him**

> **and at an hour he does not know**, *and will cut him in pieces, and assign him a place with the unbelievers.* ⁴⁷*And that slave who knew his master's will and did not get ready or act in accord with his will, will receive many lashes,* ⁴⁸*but the one who did not know it, and committed deeds worthy of a flogging, will receive but few. From everyone who has been given much, much will be required; and to whom they entrusted much, of him they will ask all the more. (Luke 12:41–48)*

It would appear in the first illustration of waiting for the Master's return found in the wedding feast (Lk. 12:35-38) that the emphasis is to be ready by serving Him; in the second illustration of protecting one's household against an anticipated thief (Lk. 12:39-40) it is being prepared for the event of His return itself; this third follow-on teaching emphasizes being found prepared and ready by our treatment of others. These are three distinct aspects of the very same thing which ultimately mandates we are not only to practice God's Word and ways where our personal relationship with Christ is concerned and our individual understanding of God's prophetic Word, but in our relationships with and service to others as well. It is a trifold, overlapping sequence describing the entire fruits of a sanctified life which is the proper preparation for His return.

However, quite a while before the giving of the Olivet Discourse, Jesus will already have covered many of the fundamental teachings of that sermon in the need to be dressed and ready, prepared and alert, and most importantly, fulfilling the role of a biblical "servant". The end of this present age is characterized as placing great emphasis on who will be found ready and who will not, and simultaneously rewarding and welcoming the faithful versus punishing and banishing the unfaithful. This same standard as applied to Israel in the First Coming is equally in force for the Church in the course of His Second Coming.

End of the Age Parables

³⁶*Then He left the crowds and went into the house. And His disciples came to Him and said, "Explain to us the parable of the tares of the field."*

³⁷*And He said, "The one who sows the good seed is the Son of Man,* ³⁸*and the field is the world; and as for the good seed, these are the sons of the kingdom; and the tares are the sons of the evil one;* ³⁹*and the enemy who sowed them is the devil, and* **the harvest is the end of the age**; *and the reapers are angels.* ⁴⁰*So just as the tares are gathered up and burned with fire, so shall it be* **at the end of the age**. ⁴¹*The Son of Man will send forth His angels, and they will gather out of His kingdom all*

stumbling blocks, and those who commit lawlessness, ⁴²and will throw them into the furnace of fire; in that place there will be weeping and gnashing of teeth. ⁴³Then THE RIGHTEOUS WILL SHINE FORTH AS THE SUN in the kingdom of their Father. He who has ears, let him hear. (Matthew 13:36–43)

After the second or so full year of His ministry, which many characterize as transitioning to "The Year of Opposition" because of the noticeable change in attitudes on nearly all fronts, Jesus begins to speak in parables which were only fully understood by those who actually believed in Him. So in a teaching which may have been given as much as a year and half or more before the Olivet Discourse, Jesus is not just specifying the concept of *"this age"*, but that there is still a harvest to come of *"the sons of the kingdom"* versus *"the sons of the evil one"*.

Whereas it could be reasonably argued that the three previous examples from Luke 12 all deal with relationships within the Body of Christ as they use the metaphor of a wedding and a household which normally represent God's house, here we clearly see what is coming at the end of this age for believers versus non-believers. Whereas that which took place previously transpired by the unaided hand of the Master in dealing with His servants, here it is accomplished by supernatural agency of the angels by a permanent sorting and separation which is specified to eventually take place. And notice in Matthew 13:41 that this action is specified, *"they will gather out of His kingdom"*.

⁴⁷*"Again, the kingdom of heaven is like a dragnet cast into the sea, and gathering fish of every kind; ⁴⁸and when it was filled, they drew it up on the beach; and they sat down and gathered the good fish into containers, but the bad they threw away. ⁴⁹So it will be **at the end of the age**; the angels will come forth and take out the wicked from among the righteous, ⁵⁰and will throw them into the furnace of fire; in that place there will be weeping and gnashing of teeth. (Matthew 13:47–50)*

Similarly so, immediately following in *The Parable of the Dragnet*, the separation which takes place is between believer and non-believer, it is transacted by angelic agency, and it takes place *"at the end of the age"*.

It is of critical importance to mention that what is rendered here in English as *"take out"* (*"aphorizo"*, Strong's #873 in verse 49) is a different Greek word from that used in the Olivet Discourse to describe someone *"taken"*. (*"paralambano"*, Strong's #3880) In this case, it would be more accurate to translate this as *"separated"*. It is the same word used in Matthew

25 to describe how Jesus separates the sheep from the goats. One Greek lexicon even goes so far as to state that in everyday Greek it has the specific meaning "to separate locally". A harvest involving angelic agency is one of the main closing features of the Olivet Discourse, but something Christ's followers heard Him already teach throughout His ministry.

> ²⁶*And He was saying, "The kingdom of God is like a man who casts seed upon the soil; ²⁷and he goes to bed at night and gets up by day, and the seed sprouts and grows—how, he himself does not know. ²⁸The soil produces crops by itself; first the blade, then the head, then the mature grain in the head. ²⁹But **when the crop permits**, he immediately puts in the sickle, because **the harvest has come**." (Mark 4:26–29)*

This is something very important which should be considered in parallel with the parables of the *Tares* and *Dragnet* in particular. Jesus repeatedly uses the illustration of seasons to impress upon us that although we may not be able to know the precise day and hour of His Return, we will most certainly be assured of its nearness by signs in the character of a season, the same way in which we know that Spring or Winter is inevitably upon us. In this case, it is interesting to note that no farmer can simply go out and harvest a crop anytime he chooses or when it is convenient, but must wait until it is ready to be brought in—"*when the crop permits*". A farmer will tell you that although they can estimate the general time when a crop will be ready, they can never know or predict the exact day. They have to wait for it to properly ripen, and must be prepared to begin the harvest a little earlier or later if necessary. (This is actually the primary illustration used concerning the End Times which James employs in chapter 5 of his Epistle.)

A significant contributing reason for the Master being away for such a long time before returning may have to do with this present age not so much having a specific schedule to keep where a clock and calendar are concerned from our perspective, but rather that it is a chronology or sequence of events which must be accomplished in due course. In other words, we cannot proceed to "B" until "A" is completed, nor on to "C" until we are properly finished with "B" and so forth. Rather than each being constricted to a specific timespan and schedule, they are consecutive goals, which when achieved, then allows the procession to move on to the next. In this case, Winter must come before Spring, which must come before Summer. We cannot know the day or the hour each will be accomplished, but God certainly does from His eternal perspective. To us it's a sequence, but God already knows the day and the hour and the very minute when each will be fulfilled. That is why there is no contradiction between the fact that God has a schedule and knows the set day and hour, but we can only be aware of it generally as an overall sequence, just as we can be cognizant that one season inevitably leads into the next.

While terms such as *"the harvest"* and the *"end of the age"* speak more toward the general environment of what is anticipated to come, the repeated uses of variations of *"that day"*, *"day of judgment"*, and *"the judgment"* do not lend themselves to describing a general period of time, but the arrival of the absolute end. A feature of this final sequence of events which closes this age is in its likeness to Noah's environment. This is that point where everything is declared to be finalized by the Lord and He personally shuts the door on the ark. Permanently shutting the door is a feature of Jesus' parallel teachings on the eschaton.

Opposing Results

22And He was passing through from one city and village to another, teaching, and proceeding on His way to Jerusalem. 23And someone said to Him, "Lord, are there just a few who are being saved?"

And He said to them, 24"Strive to enter through the narrow door; for many, I tell you, will seek to enter and will not be able. 25Once the head of the house gets up and shuts the door, and you begin to stand outside and knock on the door, saying, 'Lord, open up to us!' then He will answer and say to you, 'I do not know where you are from.'

26"Then you will begin to say, 'We ate and drank in Your presence, and You taught in our streets'; 27and He will say, 'I tell you, I do not know where you are from; DEPART FROM ME, ALL YOU EVILDOERS.'

28"In that place there will be weeping and gnashing of teeth when you see Abraham and Isaac and Jacob and all the prophets in the kingdom of God, but yourselves being thrown out. 29And they will come from east and west and from north and south, and will recline at the table in the kingdom of God. 30And behold, some are last who will be first and some are first who will be last." (Luke 13:22–30)

This cannot have as its sole aim a lesson strictly applicable to the general rejection of Jesus by Israel in His First Coming as there is no place in Scripture which even suggests that God has permanently closed the door on Israel; during every historic period of the Church there have been Jewish converts to Christianity, and in the West, for instance, it is acknowledged that more Jews have presently come to faith in Yeshua since Israel's reoccupation of Jerusalem in 1969 than the total number combined from the previous 1,800 years. One has to go all the way back to the 1st century Church to find these kinds of large numbers of ethnic Jews embracing Jesus as Messiah which are being experienced at present.

The more important point is that a time comes when the door is shut, as it was on the ark, and there is nothing left but the wrath of God's judgment. This is a stark contradiction to a popular teaching within the Church which has largely arisen in the past thirty or so years from the arena of Christian fiction, but has achieved a very broad level of acceptance, that after the Church's removal by way of the Rapture, there is not just going to be a revival, but a "super-revival" by some estimates. This notion erroneously purports that the Rapture event in and of itself will be so powerful that it will initiate unprecedented worldwide numbers coming to faith in Christ.

This teaching has almost become so accepted and mainstream that it is compelling to keep revisiting the fact that, contrary to Christ's teaching as to the consequences of waiting until the door is shut, there is no such provision overtly stated in Scripture, but actually quite the opposite. (What kind of revival in Noah's day broke out as the ark floated away, or in Lot's day as he ran from the firestorm raining down from heaven?) It is apparent that this questionable teaching is actually an attempt to dilute the Church's primary mission of preaching the Gospel before that door is closed while there is still time to respond, and thus render ineffective the daylight still remaining to do His work.

Whereas references to *"the last day"* often refer in a broadly negative way to consequences for waiting too long, there is an interesting teaching recorded by the Apostle John which speaks of *"the last day"* in a positive light for believers:

> *⁵³So Jesus said to them, "Truly, truly, I say to you, unless you eat the flesh of the Son of Man and drink His blood, you have no life in yourselves. ⁵⁴He who eats My flesh and drinks My blood has eternal life, and **I will raise him up on the last day**. ⁵⁵For My flesh is true food, and My blood is true drink. ⁵⁶He who eats My flesh and drinks My blood abides in Me, and I in him. ⁵⁷As the living Father sent Me, and I live because of the Father, so he who eats Me, he also will live because of Me. ⁵⁸This is the bread which came down out of heaven; not as the fathers ate and died; he who eats this bread will live forever." (John 6:53–58)*

The keyword which provides the plain meaning of the metaphors of eating Christ's flesh and drinking His blood is *"abides"*. In fact, it is a reciprocal arrangement wherein obedience to Christ's Word and ways results in someone who *"abides in Me, and I in him"*.

This fits very well with the general New Testament teachings concerning the End Times in that the most important thing for believers is to be living a consistent life in accordance with His Word and faithfully serving Him in proportion to what He has entrusted into each one's care. For those found alert, ready and prepared in this manner, *"the last day"* has no negative connotation whatsoever.

> [8]*"I tell you that He will bring about justice for them quickly. However, **when the Son of Man comes**, will He find faith on the earth?" (Luke 18:8)*

Whether in the Old or New Testaments, translators have a choice when they encounter either the Greek or Hebrew words for *"faith"* as both have the dual meaning of *"faithfulness"*. In fact, if every time we come across the word *"faith"* in Scripture and read it again instead substituting *"faithfulness"* in its place, we will develop a much deeper understanding of God's definition and meaning. It has much to do concerning behavior, attitudes and actions and very little in common with blowing out the candles on a birthday cake and wishing really hard for a pony. But again, this passage comes earlier in Christ's ministry before His final week in Jerusalem and the giving of the Olivet Discourse, and yet He is making the bold statement, *"when the Son of Man comes"*.

Jesus specifically speaks of a future time when *"this present age"* is coming to an end. It is characterized as *"night is coming"* (Jn. 9:4), when all should *"expect Him at an hour he does not know"* (Lk. 12:46) and when the Master will simultaneously arrive to reward and welcome the faithful but punish and banish the unfaithful. This *"harvest"* separating the righteous from the wicked and carried out by angelic agency will be initiated *"when the crop permits"* (Mk. 4:26-29) and will mark a time when the door is shut to the joy of the rescued faithful and the ruin of those who are not. It is a time when everyone is measured against Christ's standard, *"When the Son of Man comes, will He find faith on the earth?"* (Lk.18:8) because ultimately this is not a test of knowledge, but faithfulness by biblical standards. This is a time of transition which culminates in a final period of judgment when the faithful are rewarded and all others are punished and cast out. At this time everyone will reap what they have sown in *"this present age"*. Jesus laid this foundation in the years leading up to His giving of the Olivet Discourse during His last week in Jerusalem, and as even a cursory reading of that Discourse will show, these are all prominently featured yet again.

The Age to Come

> *²⁷Then Peter said to Him, "Behold, we have left everything and followed You; what then will there be for us?"*
> *²⁸And Jesus said to them, "Truly I say to you, that you who have followed Me, **in the regeneration** when the Son of Man will sit on His glorious throne, you also shall sit upon twelve thrones, judging the twelve tribes of Israel. ²⁹And everyone who has left houses or brothers or sisters or father or mother or children or farms for My name's sake, will receive many times as much, and will inherit eternal life. ³⁰But many who are first will be last; and the last, first. (Matthew 19:27–30)*

Something which is fascinating about "*paliggenesia*", (Strong's #3824) the Greek word here translated "*regeneration*", is that it is being used to describe a literal, physical resurrection, whereas Paul uses it to describe our current spiritual "*regeneration*" which has already taken place in the meantime:

> *⁵He saved us, not on the basis of deeds which we have done in righteousness, but according to His mercy, **by the washing of regeneration and renewing by the Holy Spirit**, ⁶whom He poured out upon us richly through Jesus Christ our Savior, ⁷so that being justified by His grace we would be made heirs according to the hope of eternal life. (Titus 3:5-7)*

Something which the Holy Spirit has worked in us spiritually in this life is a literal mirror, and therefore very special assurance, of what is going to be completed physically and literally in the age to come. They are two sides of the same proverbial coin where believers are concerned, the one a promise of fulfillment in the other.

One of the most obvious aspects of this promise of Christ is the "re" in "**re**generation", because this is clearly describing something which cannot currently take place in this present age as things presently stand. This is referring to the Messianic or Millennial Kingdom as this is when "*the Son of Man will sit on His glorious throne*", and we know by Christ's own admission regarding this present age that, "*My kingdom is not of this world*". (Jn. 18:36) The "*regeneration*" is describing the age to come for all believers as not just a new kingdom but with an accompanying personal physical transformation, and with a change in assignment for the Twelve in particular.

This change in responsibilities is featured in *The Parable of the Minas* in Luke 19:11-27 when the servant who multiplied his one mina into ten was rewarded by His returning Master, "*you are to be in authority over ten cities*"

(Lk. 19:17) and the one yielding five, "*And you are to be over five cities*". (Lk. 19:19) The emphasis within those references to "*the age to come*" do not point to a need for separating the saved from the unsaved but rather to just those entrusted with the Master's work.

So prior to the Olivet Discourse, Jesus clearly established through His teachings that which was popularly expected in that day, that the Messiah would come and fulfill every prophecy in a single visitation, was not going to be transacted in that manner. His First Coming was to be part of "*this present age*", a very long time provided so that the work of the cross would be given the maximum opportunity to complete the primary mission of the First Coming; His return at His Second Coming would be the focus of "*the end of the age*" when during a comparatively shorter period of time all things would be brought to a close in anticipation of the establishment of His kingdom in "*the age to come*". (Mt. 12:32; Mk. 10:30; Lk. 18:30) It is the establishment of His earthly throne which closes out the Olivet Discourse.

Eternity To Follow

> [24]"*Truly, truly, I say to you, he who hears My word, and believes Him who sent Me, has eternal life, and does not come into judgment, but has passed out of death into life.* [25]*Truly, truly, I say to you, **an hour is coming and now is**, when the dead will hear the voice of the Son of God, and those who hear will live.* [26]*For just as the Father has life in Himself, even so He gave to the Son also to have life in Himself;* [27]*and He gave Him authority to execute judgment, because He is the Son of Man.* [28]*Do not marvel at this; for **an hour is coming**, in which all who are in the tombs will hear His voice,* [29]*and will come forth; those who did the good deeds to **a resurrection of life**, those who committed the evil deeds to **a resurrection of judgment**. (John 5:24–29)*

It is worth noting that this may have already experienced a literal, partial fulfillment in the course of Christ's First Coming when Matthew records the visible resurrection of Old Testament saints which took place upon the work of the cross being completed:

> [52]*The tombs were opened, and many bodies of the saints who had fallen asleep were raised;* [53]*and coming out of the tombs after His resurrection they entered the holy city and appeared to many. (Matthew 27:52–53)*

But the thing with which Jesus is concerned the most, that which is the most important goal where His Return is concerned, is that we become someone who "*hears My word, and believes Him who sent Me*", and by putting His Word and ways into practice "*does not come into judgment*". Those who do so will find that they have "*passed out of death into life*". Jesus repeatedly places His Return in the context of being the final junction with eternity, knowing that when everything achieves fulfillment, everyone will either "*come forth… to a resurrection of life*" or "*a resurrection of judgment*".

It is interesting how movies and books, particularly secular works but not exclusively limited to them, embrace the phrase, "The end of life on earth" as the end-all/be-all tragedy of their history-ending scenarios. Jesus understands how short-sighted this is because it completely ignores eternity. All life comes to an end on this planet, whether each generation physically dies or the last generation experiences rapture in the Second Coming, but no life ceases to exist because our immortal souls subsequently transition to eternity. The only real question for every individual, which is the most important question, is will it "*come forth…to a resurrection of life*" or to "*a resurrection of judgment*"?

Jesus keeps bringing His teachings back around to the fact that the way every single one of us is choosing to live now is going to conclude in one of these two end states. It has come, and still comes, for every person who experiences physical death as the inevitable end to each individual's life, but a time is coming when upon the completion of this age and the age to come, this planet's history comes to an end, bringing about an ultimate finality for each of us individually.

> ³⁴*Jesus said to them, "The sons of* **this age** *marry and are given in marriage,* ³⁵*but those who are considered worthy to attain to* **that age and the resurrection from the dead**, *neither marry nor are given in marriage;* ³⁶*for they cannot even die anymore, because they are like angels, and are sons of God, being* **sons of the resurrection**. ³⁷*But that the dead are raised, even Moses showed, in the passage about the burning bush, where he calls the Lord* THE GOD OF ABRAHAM, AND THE GOD OF ISAAC, AND THE GOD OF JACOB. ³⁸*Now He is not the God of the dead but of the living; for all live to Him." (Luke 20:34–38)*

The Sadducees, to whom Jesus is responding, simply did not believe in a resurrection, and so their attempt to manipulate the issue was restricted to what takes place in this temporal and limited life, and then making the erroneous effort to apply it to something eternal. This is the deception which Satan wishes to accomplish where everyone of every historical age is concerned, that they will not see that this life is but a temporary crossroad depositing us at one of these two final destinations.

> ²³*And someone said to Him, "Lord, are there just a few who are being saved?" And He said to them,* ²⁴*"Strive to enter through the narrow door; for **many, I tell you, will seek to enter and will not be able**. (Luke 13:23–24)*

> ¹³*"Enter through the narrow gate; for the gate is wide and the way is broad that leads to destruction, and there are many who enter through it.* ¹⁴*For the gate is small and the way is narrow that leads to life, and **there are few who find it**. (Matthew 7:13–14)*

This is why the Gospels record Jesus dedicating far more teaching to hell than to heaven; He warns the most for what appeals to the most. Jesus carefully draws this contrast not just for Jews alone when He came the first time, and not just for the last generation when He returns, but for everyone at every time in between.

When we say we are "saved" or "Jesus saves", consider seriously for a moment what it is, exactly, that He saves from—He effects a rescue from hell. That is where everyone is headed until they come into a saving relationship with Him. He saved Noah and his family from the Flood, Lot and his family from the fire, and Rahab and her family from Jericho's destruction. This is not just an illustration of the Rapture where earthly circumstances are avoided, but the greater work of salvation for the eternal benefit of our soul. They are events in this life which represent the greater spiritual result of being saved from hell.

In fact, Christ provided a series of teachings throughout the course of His earthly ministry which warned believers of every age, whether under the Old or New Covenants, of the eternal consequences for unfaithfulness. Beginning with ethnic Israel, the seven-fold example provided by Christ encompasses the entire spectrum of believers not only found within the scope of *"this present age"*, but those who will experience *"the end of the age"* as well. Each example of disqualification is met with not just being cast out, but cast out into hell characterized by the Hebrew idiom as a place of *"weeping and gnashing of teeth"* and will be examined in detail in the next chapter.

The Issue of the Final Seven Years

It would be extremely rare, and perhaps even suspicious, to find a mainstream Christian belonging to any "ism" where the Second Coming is concerned who does not believe that the very end of history will unfold in a final seven year period which the modern Church commonly calls "*The* Tribulation". It is something so universally agreed upon at present, that the main eschatologies have all acquired their names so as to delineate from the outset each one's relationship to this final seven year period regarding their proposed timing of the Rapture. Pre-Tribulationism, Mid-Tribulationism, Post-Tribulationism, and even Pre-Wrath in their very titles each express the fundamental difference of opinion as to the timing of the Rapture in relation to "*The* Tribulation", but none of them dispute either the number of years nor its name. And neither is there any disagreement even among these competing positions that the source of our collective knowledge establishing the existence of this final seven years comes from the Prophet Daniel.

> [24]"**Seconded weeks have been decreed** for your people and your holy city, to finish the transgression, to make an end of sin, to make atonement for iniquity, to bring in everlasting righteousness, to seal up vision and prophecy and to anoint the most holy place. [25]So you are to know and discern that from the issuing of a decree to restore and rebuild Jerusalem until Messiah the Prince **there will be seven weeks and sixty-two weeks**; it will be built again, with plaza and moat, even in times of distress. [26]Then **after the sixty-two weeks** the Messiah will be cut off and have nothing, and the people of the prince who is to come will destroy the city or and the sanctuary. And its end will come with a flood; even to the end there will be war; desolations are determined. [27]And **he will make a firm covenant with the many for one week, but in the middle of the week he will put a stop to sacrifice and grain offering; and on the wing of abominations will come one who makes desolate, even until a complete destruction, one that is decreed, is poured out on the one who makes desolate.**" (Daniel 9:24–27)

We will not repeat that which many very good studies have already explained in much greater detail, nor the intricate studies affirming these calculations, but summarize this basic End Times timeline for which there is little dispute.

Seventy weeks total are provided, but only sixty-nine have been accounted for to date. Those sixty-nine were divided into "*seven weeks and sixty-two weeks*" of years because it took "*seven weeks*"—or 49 years, to rebuild the Temple under Ezra's direction when Israel first returned from the Babylonian Captivity, followed by "*sixty-two weeks*" of years—434 years, until it was destroyed. That leaves a final week of years—7 years, which is commonly labeled "*The* Tribulation". Although history is presently frozen between the 69th and 70th Week of Daniel, that last week of years will officially begin when the Antichrist makes a seven year treaty ("*he will make a firm covenant with the many for one week*") which he will break at the midpoint ("*but in the middle of the week*") by committing the Abomination of Desolation. This will initiate a final sequence not just of unprecedented destruction brought about by the Antichrist, but his own inevitable demise as well.

Although a bit on the complicated side, this 70th Week is not in dispute even when other aspects of the eschaton are so passionately debated. But to be quite picky about it, there is no actual verse or statement here, nor anywhere else in Scripture, which calls Daniel's 70th Week "*The* Tribulation". This has been assigned primarily because of what was told Daniel, "*And there will be a time of distress such as never occurred since there was a nation until that time, and at that time your people, everyone who is found written in the book, will be rescued*", (Dan. 12:1) closely followed by Jesus' statement in the Olivet Discourse, "*Then they will deliver you to tribulation…*" (Mt. 24:9a)

However, nowhere in Jesus' teachings, much less within the Olivet Discourse, is there a hint, much less a plain reference, to a seven year period. In fact, neither can such a thing be found in the whole of Revelation. All one has to do is consult their concordance to discover that in the entire New Testament there is only one single, solitary instance of a mention of "*seven years*", and that is to the number of years Anna was married before becoming a widow. (Lk. 2:36) In the whole of the Old Testament, no such connection is likewise present.

This is not to say there is no such thing as Daniel's 70th Week, only that its assignment as "*The* Tribulation" is a relatively new association where the whole of Church history is concerned. It is something articulated mainly by Christians over the course of the past 150-200 years or so, and certainly not a mainstream teaching of the 1st century. At the time of Christ's First Coming and on through the end of the 1st century when Revelation was finally given, the concept of the 70th Week was neither a staple within either Judaism or early Christianity, especially while the Temple was still standing. The term "*tribulation*" is certainly present in Christ's teachings, but it has been lifted out of context and assigned to something similar sounding, but actually different enough from its scriptural meaning to be tangibly misleading.

This is important to our current discussion because we are trying to place ourselves in that first generation's shoes, who would accept Christ's teachings as being axiomatic where His Return is concerned. Whereas today nearly every Christian—scholar and student of Scripture alike—initiates their model of the End Times with an assertion of a seven year "Tribulation" in relation to the timing of the Rapture, the Early Church did not. That was not the teaching Christ provided in the Olivet Discourse proper, nor in the years of His ministry leading up to it, or by any of the New Testament writers in parallel to it. This is critical to understanding why it was not present when they first read and accepted Revelation as not only part of the canon of Scripture, but as a logical extension of the Olivet Discourse and all the New Testament End Times teachings which were published before it.

A more detailed examination of this will come, but the salient takeaway is that the earliest generations of believers did not superimpose a seven year period on either the Olivet Discourse nor Revelation in the same way as it has become normative to do so in the modern Church. Essentially when present-day academics moved the goal posts, instead of insisting they be returned to their original position, we fell into the trap of discussing how far they should be moved. This is one of Satan's cleverest ploys, to change the discussion just enough that we begin using the redefined jargon to make our own rebuttal, not realizing the terms themselves have been intrinsically compromised.

The important point in all of this is to understand that once we begin to use similar sounding terms to those found in Scripture, but assign them non-scriptural definitions, it begins to alter what God's Word is teaching. There is much confusion in the Church at present when it comes to Christ's Return which is not because of the purposeful nature of God's prophetic Word, but because we have accepted manmade alterations and accepted them as normative.

2 ❖ "Weeping & Gnashing of Teeth"

*¹⁶**All Scripture** is inspired by God and profitable for **teaching**, for **reproof**, for **correction**, for **training in righteousness**; ¹⁷so that the man of God may be adequate, equipped for every good work. (2 Timothy 3:16–17)*

Everyone *seems to want to simply jump straight to a chart which provides the proper place and timing for each and every End Times event.* So much so, that it is very easy to overlook the more important accompanying message. In our enthusiasm to "solve the puzzle", we often overlook the fact that all of God's Word is primarily intended to be personally applied, "*profitable for teaching, for reproof, for correction, for training in righteousness*". There is no exception, not even for those portions of God's prophetic Word, and it is especially so with the Olivet Discourse and Revelation, which are specifically given to and exclusively understood by Holy Spirit-filled believers. Its primary function is not to simply convey vital information, but properly equip us "*for every good work*"; it is intended to prepare us for His Return and not to merely provide information. We sometimes rush past the opening verse of Revelation and its provided context from the outset, "*The Revelation of Jesus Christ, which God gave Him **to show to His bond-servants**...*" (Rev. 1:1), and also tend to overlook the fact that Christ gave the Olivet Discourse to just a small, select group of believers for believers. It is crucial that we understand we are not simply waiting for Jesus to return, but are supposed to be actively preparing for it.

There is actually an additional series of foundational eschatological teachings which Jesus provided throughout the course of His 3-1/2 year earthly ministry which culminate within the Olivet Discourse, but began very early on and which He methodically revisits. To the casual observer, they appear on the surface to just repeat the same thing, but careful study of the details reveal something quite different which serves as the basis for what we are to personally do with Christ eschatologically. The word "eschatology" is derived from the Greek "*eschatos*" meaning "last". "Eschatology" is the study of the last things, and in this series of teachings Jesus designates what is coming last for everyone and everything whether it originated in heaven or on earth. For anyone who does not understand this teaching, the study of End Times events is completely useless.

While there are many who teach that one thing or another is the most important aspect of the Second Coming, most usually the Rapture but often other items such as the Antichrist, a new Temple or the like, the priority provided by Christ and the New Testament writers is actually squarely placed on spiritual faithfulness. What will be the state of readiness and spiritual preparedness the Master will find in every individual when He returns? This is, in point of fact, the more important message which consistently accompanies every instance of New Testament eschatological passages. And in the course of this seven-fold teaching He will close any perceived loopholes in order to apply the same standard to everyone, both Jew and Gentile, the saved and unsaved, both Israel and the Church, as well as those belonging to every historical period. That which is at stake is far more important than the End Times signs and associated chronology, and in fact, if this teaching is not given our undivided priority, any subsequent study of eschatology is pointless.

There are seven references recorded in the Gospels wherein Jesus refers to hell as a place where "*there will weeping and gnashing of teeth*", six within the Gospel of Matthew and one in Luke. These took place at various times during His 3-1/2 year ministry, the last two occurring during His final week within the Olivet Discourse. In some instances these characteristics are additionally supplemented with darkness or fire, but more important are the accompanying reasons why a particular person's or group's behavior is ultimately responsible for assigning them to this final destination. As we shall see, each of Jesus' warning as to who may find themselves at this most undesired terminus comprises different types who still share a common spiritual dilemma. None of these teachings are actually identical in terms of to whom they apply, except for the common result regardless.

"*The outer darkness*" depicts the worst spiritual condition of separation and loss contrasting sharply with one of the key features of heaven in that the light from the Godhead negates the ongoing need for a sun. (Is. 24:23; 66:19-20; Rev. 21:23) It is an idiomatic expression to describe the ultimate separation from God. "*Weeping*" refers to the emotional agony of loss, and "*gnashing of teeth*" to the physical agony of pain to express the ultimate separation from

God's love both emotionally and physically. All of these combine to describe hell as the absolute opposite of heaven.

It should be noted that these terms teach that being cast into hell is not a purely physical dilemma, but accompanied by being conscious not just of why one has been deposited there, but side-by-side with the stark knowledge of what one could have experienced instead! Each of these conditions unequivocally demands eternal consciousness on the part of the sufferer. While life on this planet may be mortal and come to an end, the soul is immortal, and whether it spends eternity in heaven or hell, it will consciously exist in either.

Eschatology has as its most basic, fundamental foundation the issue of what will happen when, one way or another in the end, we meet Jesus. Whether Jew or Gentile, saved or unsaved, or as belonging to Israel or the Church, we are all going to immediately "meet" Him whether through death and Resurrection or the one-time event most commonly called the Rapture or, for a decimated world population at the end of Daniel's 70th Week, when the eschaton comes to a close. It is an extremely binary state of affairs; either we are found ready by His standards and welcomed into eternity forever with Him, or determined to have fallen short to be forever separated and removed to the worst possible alternative. New Testament eschatology is not based on a chart or timeline of events, but the test of every individual's spiritual condition when they finally meet Jesus one way or the other.

The 1st Case: Ethnicity

5And when Jesus entered Capernaum, a centurion came to Him, imploring Him, 6and saying, "Lord, my servant is lying paralyzed at home, fearfully tormented."

7Jesus said to him, "I will come and heal him."

8But the centurion said, "Lord, I am not worthy for You to come under my roof, but just say the word, and my servant will be healed. 9For I also am a man under authority, with soldiers under me; and I say to this one, 'Go!' and he goes, and to another, 'Come!' and he comes, and to my slave, 'Do this!' and he does it."

*10Now when Jesus heard this, He marveled and said to those who were following, "Truly I say to you, I have not found such great faith with anyone in Israel. 11I say to you that **many will come from east and west, and recline at the table with Abraham, Isaac and Jacob in the kingdom of heaven; 12but the***

> **sons of the kingdom will be cast out into the outer darkness; in that place there will be weeping and gnashing of teeth."**
> [13]And Jesus said to the centurion, "Go; it shall be done for you as you have believed." And the servant was healed that very moment. (Matthew 8:5–13)

Matthew's first recorded instance of this reference comes in the context of a Gentile exercising faith in a manner not found to that point within Israel proper, and therefore is used as an example of those claiming to be God's people and belonging to the heritage of the Patriarchs—that is, Abraham, Isaac and Jacob. Jesus plainly warns they were in danger of not just losing their place in eternity—what is here expressed as *"recline at the table...in the kingdom of heaven"*, but being replaced by those whom the Jews of the day believed were automatically disqualified spiritually because of ethnicity. This is especially featured by His calling the Jewish listeners *"the sons of the kingdom"* who will be replaced by *"many...from east and west"*, an expression all Jews of the day would have understood to mean "Gentiles".

Just as it is to Israel Jesus first takes the Gospel and the opportunity to accept Him as their personal Savior and Messiah, they are the first to be warned of the consequences for rejection of same. In the context of presenting His first case, this is specifically applied to that generation of Jews who rejected Jesus in the course of His First Coming, but will be experienced by those acting in the same way during every historic age to the present. No one is automatically enrolled but must pass the minimum standards of God's Word where faith is concerned.

> [6]And **without faith it is impossible to please Him,** for he who comes to God must believe that He is and that He is a rewarder of those who seek Him. (Hebrews 11:6)

The 2nd Case: Proximity

> [22]And He was passing through from one city and village to another, teaching, and proceeding on His way to Jerusalem. [23]And someone said to Him, "Lord, are there just a few who are being saved?"
> And He said to them, [24]"Strive to enter through the narrow door; for many, I tell you, will seek to enter and will not be able. [25]Once the head of the house gets up and shuts the door, and you begin to stand outside and knock on the door, saying, 'Lord, open up to us!' then He will answer and say to you, 'I do not know where you are from.'

> ^{26}Then you will begin to say, 'We ate and drank in Your presence, and You taught in our streets'; ^{27}and He will say, 'I tell you, I do not know where you are from; DEPART FROM ME, ALL YOU EVILDOERS.'
>
> ^{28}**"In that place there will be weeping and gnashing of teeth when you see Abraham and Isaac and Jacob and all the prophets in the kingdom of God, but yourselves being thrown out. ^{29}And they will come from east and west and from north and south, and will recline at the table in the kingdom of God.** ^{30}And behold, some are last who will be first and some are first who will be last." (Luke 13:22–30)

The next instance recorded in Luke likewise applies to Israel, but with a broader scope of conditions and associated behaviors. Notice that the accusation is directed at those claiming to have a close proximity to Jesus without ever actually accepting Him personally. In this instance, they thought it was enough to have been near Him in some way: "*We ate and drank in Your presence, and You taught in our streets*". Compounding the problem highlighted in the previous instance of lacking faith is the false belief that one can be "close enough"; the results in both instances, however, are identical.

This very much mirrors the warnings from both Jesus and John the Baptist to that particular generation that although they claimed a special place and designation as ethnic descendants of Abraham and the Patriarchs, it did not overcome their not acting in faith and obedience to God's Word and ways. By not living in the character of those very same figures to which they ascribed their heritage, they were told that from God's point of view they were therefore not really children of Abraham. In fact, they were warned from the outset if they continued as such that God would replace them with real children of Abraham who were spiritually qualified. (Mt. 3:9; Lk. 3:8)

> ^{39}They answered and said to Him, "Abraham is our father." Jesus said to them, "If you are Abraham's children, do the deeds of Abraham. (John 8:39)

> ^{7}Therefore, be sure that it is those who are of faith who are sons of Abraham. (Galatians 3:7)

This passage captures Jesus' view that there are those who were treating Him in the exact, same way, claiming an association without following through from the heart.

Although still first and foremost applying to literal Israel, and especially to that generation rejecting Jesus at His First Coming, there is a general application which extends well beyond. To be sure, nearly every reader knows someone similar in character who openly admires Christ and speaks positively of Him, but who has never actually accepted Him as their personal Savior so as to live a changed life because of Him. (It always amazes me when I meet yet another person who testifies, "I went to church for thirty years, but I was never actually saved.") They feel as if they are "close enough" to be covered in some manner, having to some degree heard His Word but never having actually taken the plunge to become a doer of His Word. They substitute the necessary commitment to Him by "liking" Him and supporting what they think He stands for. They think they are "close enough". They may have had some kind of encounter where Christ approached them, but they never actually opened up the door of their heart and let Him in. They admit they came close enough to have heard His teachings, but their lack of appropriately following through in this regard assigns them to the category of *"evildoers"*.

But in either case, as when the Lord shut the door to Noah's ark and there was no further possibility of entry, those who thought their proximity and familiarity would qualify them for automatic inclusion and protection will find that from Jesus' point view they are as unfamiliar as total strangers with not even a passing attachment. They are dually rejected as they knock and plead from the outside trying to get in when it is too late: "*I do not know where you are from*". Their true identity and character will be exposed from Christ's viewpoint when He ends the discussion, "*I tell you, I do not know where you are from; depart from Me all you evildoers*".

It should be noted that the feature of a heavenly feast which is prominently given in these first two teachings primarily applying to Israel will also be featured as well in an iteration to come where the Church is concerned. It not only specifically addresses the shortfall of reaching the ultimate heavenly goal by those with more than a passing awareness of it, but a failure to achieve it because of problems in their earthly performance which cannot be dismissed. This will be an issue for those claiming proximity to Christ who are members of either Israel or the Church.

In the first instance provided in Matthew 8:10-12 we have an example of Hebrews 11:6, that "*without faith it is impossible to please God*", but this second case is a parallel to Romans 14:23, "*whatever is not from faith is sin*".

The 3rd Case: The Tares

²⁴*Jesus presented another parable to them, saying, "The kingdom of heaven may be compared to a man who sowed good seed in his field. ²⁵But while his men were sleeping, his enemy came and sowed tares among the wheat, and went*

away. ²⁶*But when the wheat sprouted and bore grain, then the tares became evident also.*

²⁷*"The slaves of the landowner came and said to him, 'Sir, did you not sow good seed in your field? How then does it have tares?'*

²⁸*"And he said to them, 'An enemy has done this!'*

The slaves said to him, 'Do you want us, then, to go and gather them up?'

²⁹*"But he said, 'No; for while you are gathering up the tares, you may uproot the wheat with them.* ³⁰*Allow both to grow together until the harvest; and in the time of the harvest I will say to the reapers, First gather up the tares and bind them in bundles to burn them up; but gather the wheat into my barn.'"*

³⁶*Then He left the crowds and went into the house. And His disciples came to Him and said, "Explain to us the parable of the tares of the field."*

³⁷*And He said, "The one who sows the good seed is the Son of Man,* ³⁸*and the field is the world; and as for the good seed, these are the sons of the kingdom; and the tares are the sons of the evil one;* ³⁹*and the enemy who sowed them is the devil, and the harvest is the end of the age; and the reapers are angels.* ⁴⁰*So just as the tares are gathered up and burned with fire, so shall it be at the end of the age.* ⁴¹*The Son of Man will send forth His angels, and* **they will gather out of His kingdom all stumbling blocks, and those who commit lawlessness,** ⁴²**and will throw them into the furnace of fire; in that place there will be weeping and gnashing of teeth**. ⁴³*Then THE RIGHTEOUS WILL SHINE FORTH AS THE SUN in the kingdom of their Father. He who has ears, let him hear. (Matthew 13:24-30, 36-43)*

In the third parallel teaching, the additional description of "*the furnace of fire*" is provided to round out this repeated reference to hell and its consequences. Those directed to this final destination in this case are identified as belonging to "*the tares*" whose identity is never left in doubt when called "*the sons of the evil one*" (Mt. 13:38) in an unmistakable association with outright unbelievers.

Because "*the field*" is defined as "*the world*", this parable is often interpreted as strictly referring to believers, who in the course of this life, must live side-by-side with the pretenders of all false religions. But in the accompanying explanation, the angels are instructed to gather and cast a group "*out of His kingdom*", a term which is most often used in the New Testament to refer to God's people, not an earthly institution or the Millennial Kingdom still to come or something which is entirely inclusive of the whole world. One of the primary works of God is to retake and remold Creation into that which He originally intended, an event we commonly call the Millennial Kingdom. All which will remain at that time is an earth which is reshaped into the character of His kingdom.

That many are extracted and separated out from those found within our walls as well is revealed by their designation as "*stumbling blocks*"—the New Testament metaphor describing someone who sets and trips traps comprised of sin, and "*those who commit lawlessness*"—someone who does not merely undermine God's Word but actively works against it. Their ill behavior has been directed at believers, those belonging to God's kingdom, as some worked their evil from inside the walls of the Church through cults and deception, while others from the outside in the guise of false religion, often making it difficult for non-believers to see the difference between the authentic and the counterfeit. Whereas the other six instances of this teaching address Israel, the Church, and unbelievers, the "*tares*" is addressing false believers of every type.

The removal of "*the sons of the evil one*" from both the world in general, and the simultaneous surgical extraction of the false spiritual influences within God's house results in the unprecedented result, "*Then the righteous will shine forth as the sun in the kingdom of their Father*". This separation and removal purifies both the venues of the earth proper and God's kingdom so as to feature those designated as "*righteous*" who, by definition, have proven their faith by obedience to God's Word and ways.

To the first two pictures of being cast out and replaced is provided the additional feature of "*the furnace of fire*" with an accompanying designation for avoiding this fate by being found biblically righteous. Note, however, that in none of Christ's teachings is a hint, much less stated provision, for some kind of "middle ground"; it is one or the other. But also pay attention to the sequence of these first three teachings, because Jesus is no longer applying them to Israel alone, but providing a bridge not only to the Church to come, but to the Gentiles in the world at large.

Some may wonder if the dual description of "*the darkness*" and "*the furnace of fire*" somehow cancel each other out or provide some kind of textual evidence that different locations are being specified for different conditions. Both will be equally experienced in the same place as one expresses the ultimate physical penalty of pain and suffering, while the other the ultimate emotional penalty of permanent spiritual separation. Any light from the fires of hell do nothing to illuminate the simultaneous and conscious experience of one's eternal separation from the Godhead. Again, this is illustrating hell as the complete opposite of heaven.

> ¹*Then I saw a new heaven and a new earth; for the first heaven and the first earth passed away, and there is no longer any sea. ²And I saw the holy city, new Jerusalem, coming down out of heaven from God, made ready as a bride adorned for her husband. ³And I heard a loud voice from the throne, saying, "Behold, the tabernacle of God is among men, and He will dwell among them, and they shall be His people, and **God Himself will be among them**, ⁴and **He will wipe away every tear from their eyes; and there will no longer be any death; there will no longer be any mourning, or crying, or pain; the first things have passed away**.*" (Revelation 21:1–4)

The 4th Case: The World's Wicked

> ⁴⁷*"Again, the kingdom of heaven is like a dragnet cast into the sea, and gathering fish of every kind; ⁴⁸and when it was filled, they drew it up on the beach; and they sat down and gathered the good fish into containers, but the bad they threw away. ⁴⁹So it will be **at the end of the age; the angels will come forth and take out the wicked from among the righteous, ⁵⁰and will throw them into the furnace of fire; in that place there will be weeping and gnashing of teeth**.* (Matthew 13:47-50)

This next iteration can probably be thought of as a subset of those identified in *The Parable of the Tares*, but are narrowed down to extracting and disposing of "*the wicked from among the righteous*" without assigning whether they originally resided on the earth in general or within God's house specifically.

For Jewish listeners at the time this was originally presented, however, "*the sea*" is a common biblical metaphor depicting the Gentile nations of the world, and "*fish*" as the individual people within those nations. (Remember the famous calling, "I will make you fishers of men"?) In other words, this same teaching has transitioned from being applied exclusively to Israel in the First Coming, to then referencing both Jew and Gentile, to now exclusively focused on just the Gentiles if these metaphors hold true so as to ultimately warn everyone. Just as the offer of salvation extends to all, likewise the consequences for rejecting it are universally applied.

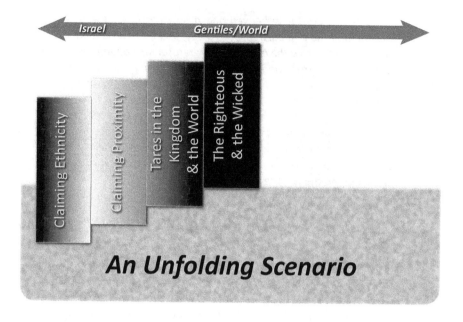

Israel   Gentiles/World

Claiming Ethnicity

Claiming Proximity

Tares in the Kingdom & the World

The Righteous & the Wicked

An Unfolding Scenario

The 5th Case: Those Not Ready

¹*Jesus spoke to them again in parables, saying,* ²*"The kingdom of heaven may be compared to a king who gave a wedding feast for his son.* ³*And he sent out his slaves to call those who had been invited to the wedding feast, and they were unwilling to come.*

⁴*"Again he sent out other slaves saying, 'Tell those who have been invited, "Behold, I have prepared my dinner; my oxen and my fattened livestock are all butchered and everything is ready; come to the wedding feast."'* ⁵*But they paid no attention and went their way, one to his own farm, another to his business,* ⁶*and the rest seized his slaves and mistreated them and killed them.*

⁷*"But the king was enraged, and he sent his armies and destroyed those murderers and set their city on fire.* ⁸*Then he said to his slaves, 'The wedding is ready, but those who were invited were not worthy.* ⁹*Go therefore to the main highways, and as many as you find there, invite to the wedding feast.'*

¹⁰*"Those slaves went out into the streets and gathered together all they found, both evil and good; and the wedding hall was filled with dinner guests.*

¹¹*"But when the king came in to look over the dinner guests, he saw a man there who was not dressed in wedding clothes,*

> *12and he said to him, 'Friend, how did you come in here without wedding clothes?' And the man was speechless.*
> *13"Then the king said to the servants, '__Bind him hand and foot, and throw him into the outer darkness; in that place there will be weeping and gnashing of teeth.__' 14For many are called, but few are chosen." (Matthew 22:1-14)*

The fifth instance within *The Parable of the Wedding Feast* should not be passed over quickly in the assumption it is just repeating all that came before, but recognized for having a very different focus even though it ends with the same, untoward final destination.

In Matthew 22:1-7 are descriptions of those who rejected the king's invitation—those "*invited*" but refusing to attend, and the reaction is, "*But the king was enraged, and he sent his armies and destroyed those murderers and set their city on fire*". (Mt. 22:7) It very much mirrors the literal historical fulfillment of Israel's destruction in the 1st century in the wake of their rejection of the Messiah, those originally "*invited*".

The king's servants are then instructed to go out and invite everyone possible to replace those who first received an invitation but refused to go, and it is specified, "*the wedding hall was filled with dinner guests*" in a prophetic parallel of the prolific success of the Gospel in the Church Age among the Gentiles. But the figure the king takes issue with in this instance is not one of the originally invited guests nor anyone else who refused to participate, but one of the invitees showing up to the feast!

In Scripture, soiled clothing is often associated with the works and deeds of unrighteousness, while clean clothing connects likewise to those of righteousness.

> *4He spoke and said to those who were standing before him, saying, "__Remove the filthy garments from him.__" Again he said to him, "__See, I have taken your iniquity away from you and will clothe you with festal robes.__" 5Then I said, "Let them put a clean turban on his head." __So they put a clean turban on his head and clothed him with garments__, while the angel of the LORD was standing by. (Zech. 3:4–5)*

> *7"Let us rejoice and be glad and give the glory to Him, for the marriage of the Lamb has come and His bride has made herself ready." 8__It was given to her to clothe herself in fine linen, bright and clean; for the fine linen is the righteous acts of the saints__. (Revelation 19:7–8)*

Here we have someone who was qualified to the degree that he gained entrance to the wedding feast, but was still found so personally lacking by the King that he is cast into hell. This is a powerful lesson that obedience to His Word and ways and faithful service in the interim leading up to His Return is the standard by which everyone is measured. This is but one of many scriptural examples of the Master returning to find someone unfit who is not simply rejected, but decidedly cast out, and there are examples of not just Israel under the Old Covenant and in the course of Christ's First Coming, but for the Church under the New Covenant all the way into His Second Coming.

For those of us in God's house to which this is directly aimed, it should also not be lightly glossed over that this person actually made it into the feast and experienced for a time what he was about to permanently lose forever before being removed, and therefore always living in hell with the memory of having tasted what he could have had. Likewise, we need to recognize that the emphasis for this particular instance of this teaching is focused exclusively on those invited by God, both Old Testament Israel and the New Testament Church, and not directed at outright non-believers. It is dealing with those who cannot make the case that they did not know any better.

Whereas the first two cases involving the feature of an anticipated heavenly banquet obviously first and foremost apply to Israel, the same is equally applied to the Church in this instance. The horizon presented in these first five teachings has spanned from Israel to the Gentiles to the Church. Why is it that so many fail to notice that Christ devotes far more time in these teachings to warning those who are supposed to comprise the ranks of the "saved" than the "unsaved"?

> [23]*And someone said to Him, "Lord, are there just a few who are being saved?"*
>
> *And He said to them, [24]"Strive to enter through the narrow door; for many, I tell you, will seek to enter and will not be able. (Luke 13:23–24)*

The 6th Case: The Hypocrites

> [45]*"Who then is the faithful and sensible slave whom his master put in charge of his household to give them their food at the proper time? [46]Blessed is that slave whom his master finds so doing when he comes. [47]Truly I say to you that he will put him in charge of all his possessions. [48]But if that evil slave says in his heart, 'My master is not coming for a long time,'*

> *⁴⁹and begins to beat his fellow slaves and eat and drink with drunkards; ⁵⁰the master of that slave will come on a day when he does not expect him and at an hour which he does not know, ⁵¹**and will cut him in pieces and assign him a place with the hypocrites; in that place there will be weeping and gnashing of teeth**. (Matthew 24:45–51)*

In the sixth case, the focus has now fully transitioned exclusively to the members of God's household who will experience "*the end of the age*" and Christ's Return. This is narrowly applied to those whom the "*master put in charge of his household*" and contrasted by a "*sensible slave*" versus an "*evil slave*". This cannot be applied in parallel to both Israel and the Church, or to believers and non-believers, but the Church alone.

Scripture repeatedly employs "*food*" and "*feeding*" as representative of the Word of God, and it is worth noting that the most valuable possession the Master entrusted, and for which they are judged, is the care and feeding of the fellow members of His household. Those failing to be found living up to His standard are identified as "*hypocrites*", and there is the additional designation of the severe punishment, "*will cut him in pieces*". In the previous example, those rejecting the invitation were destroyed, and it was the disqualified guest who was assigned to hell; in this case, both punishments are meted out, but now the emphasis has narrowed to the Church exclusively.

Note that where the Church is concerned, the behavioral litmus test is the treatment of others, unlike the previous examples which focused on whether someone had an authentic relationship with the Messiah. In the New Testament economy, the priority is placed on loving one another as Jesus loved, and here we find that such is precisely the yardstick by which believers are evaluated at the point of His Return. The focus in this series of teachings has shifted entirely from one end of the spectrum—exclusively applied to Israel, to the opposite end—exclusively applied to the Church, while incorporating everyone else along the way.

To understand how each of these teachings ultimately describe the same place, a close parallel to this teaching was previously provided by Christ:

> *⁴¹Peter said, "Lord, are You addressing this parable to us, or to everyone else as well?"*
> *⁴²And the Lord said, "Who then is the faithful and sensible steward, whom his master will put in charge of his servants, to give them their rations at the proper time? ⁴³Blessed is that slave whom his master finds so doing when he comes. ⁴⁴Truly I say to you that he will put him in charge of all his possessions.*

> 45"But if that slave says in his heart, 'My master will be a long time in coming,' and begins to beat the slaves, both men and women, and to eat and drink and get drunk; 46The master of that slave will come on a day when he does not expect him and at an hour he does not know, and **will cut him in pieces, and assign him a place with the unbelievers**. 47And that slave who knew his master's will and did not get ready or act in accord with his will, will receive many lashes, 48but the one who did not know it, and committed deeds worthy of a flogging, will receive but few. From everyone who has been given much, much will be required; and to whom they entrusted much, of him they will ask all the more. (Luke 12:41–48)

However, as mentioned previously, the fact is that Jesus can "come" for us at any time through our death so that the conditions specified here are not exclusively confined to His Return in the Second Coming. Death most often comes just as unexpectedly, but the conditions presented in all cases are still equally applied.

The Final Case: The Worthless & the Lazy

> 14"For it is just like a man about to go on a journey, who called his own slaves and entrusted his possessions to them. 15To one he gave five talents, to another, two, and to another, one, each according to his own ability; and he went on his journey.
>
> 16"Immediately the one who had received the five talents went and traded with them, and gained five more talents. 17In the same manner the one who had received the two talents gained two more. 18But he who received the one talent went away, and dug a hole in the ground and hid his master's money.
>
> 19"Now after a long time the master of those slaves came and settled accounts with them. 20The one who had received the five talents came up and brought five more talents, saying, 'Master, you entrusted five talents to me. See, I have gained five more talents.'
>
> 21"His master said to him, 'Well done, good and faithful slave. You were faithful with a few things, I will put you in charge of many things; enter into the joy of your master.'
>
> 22"Also the one who had received the two talents came up and said, 'Master, you entrusted two talents to me. See, I have gained two more talents.'

23"His master said to him, 'Well done, good and faithful slave. You were faithful with a few things, I will put you in charge of many things; enter into the joy of your master.'

24"And the one also who had received the one talent came up and said, 'Master, I knew you to be a hard man, reaping where you did not sow and gathering where you scattered no seed. 25And I was afraid, and went away and hid your talent in the ground. See, you have what is yours.'

26"But his master answered and said to him, 'You wicked, lazy slave, you knew that I reap where I did not sow and gather where I scattered no seed. 27Then you ought to have put my money in the bank, and on my arrival I would have received my money back with interest.

28"Therefore take away the talent from him, and give it to the one who has the ten talents.' 29For to everyone who has, more shall be given, and he will have an abundance; but from the one who does not have, even what he does have shall be taken away. **30Throw out the worthless slave into the outer darkness; in that place there will be weeping and gnashing of teeth**. *(Matthew 25:14-30)*

Likewise the last in the series found in *The Parable of the Talents* is exclusively focused on those in God's household proper who are ultimately characterized as, "*You wicked, lazy slave*", as opposed to the faithful slaves rewarded just prior. (Mt. 25:14-23) This is also applied to those living at "*the end of the age*" and that time leading up to Christ's Return, but in this case there is the added point that because of having failed to faithfully follow through with what was entrusted to them, this particular classification not only loses a potential reward, but experiences additional loss before permanent reassignment.

Whereas the previous case assesses our behavior and service within God's house to build up the Body of Christ, this last instance measures our behavior and service in the course of carrying out God's work in the world. Every Christian has dual responsibilities for ministry within the Church proper and in the course of their life out in the world. And there can be no mistaking that this is being exclusively applied to the Church by the fact that the Master "*called his **own** slaves*". The obvious failure in this example is not merely called "*lazy*", but further described as "*wicked*". This is because he did not act out of ignorance or some kind of lack of information, but by his own admission knew better.

In the first case the emphasis is on Israel's mistaken belief that ethnicity—the Old Testament standard of who belonged to God's house, was enough; in the sixth previous example is the mistaken belief of those in the Church—the

New Testament standard for God's house, to behave in any manner desired because they were household members. The second case involving those in Israel making a plea based on their proximity obviously is reflected in this last case for those in the Church. But as provided in the fifth case of *The Parable of the Wedding Feast*, members of both had expectations of attendance which fell short. There is no "loophole" for anyone; both Judaism and Christianity are held to the same standard, and even more so because they were both supposed to know better. Only one of the cases Jesus presented, the fourth, was purely devoted to simply separating the saved from the unsaved. Six of the seven scenarios presented by Christ personally are directed squarely at God's people not just of both Covenants, and not just for His First and Second Coming, but for every historical age.

In Conclusion

No two of these seven teachings are identical, and it is impossible not to notice that they follow a chronological order overlapping and transitioning from Israel to the Gentiles and then not just to the Church in "*this present age*", but extending into "*the end of the age*". They also follow an historical, chronological sequence beginning with Christ's initial approach of Israel in the First Coming, culminating in His Return for the Church in the course of the Second Coming. The consequences in each case is exclusion from "*the age to come*" and arriving at the worst possible destination for all eternity.

> 1. There are those with an ethnic connection but lacking spiritual obedience and faith who are warned where the path of their behavior and choices is ultimately leading. (Mt. 8:10-12)

> 2. There are those claiming the same kind of ethnic and cultural proximity to Christ which they attached to the Patriarchs who are warned where the path of their behavior and choices is ultimately leading. (Lk. 13:25-30)

> 3. There are "*tares*" of the world identified as "*sons of the evil one*" and additionally identified within the kingdom of God proper who are warned where the path of their behavior and choices is leading. (Mt. 13:40-43)

4.   Both the global generic "*wicked*" and the "*righteous*"
are warned where the path of their behavior and choices is
leading. (Mt. 13:47-50)

5.   Those who reject Christ's invitation, and those who
are invited but are not properly dressed and ready, are both
warned where the path of their behavior and choices is
leading. (Mt. 22:1-14)

6.   Those from within God's household proper who
are found to be "*evil slaves*" by their treatment of those
entrusted to them are warned where the path of their
behavior and choices is leading. (Mt. 24:45-51)

7.   A double caveat is provided to those within God's
household who fall short of faithful service to the world at
large and deemed a "*wicked, lazy slave*" who are likewise
warned where the path of their behavior and choices is
leading. (Mt. 25:26-30)

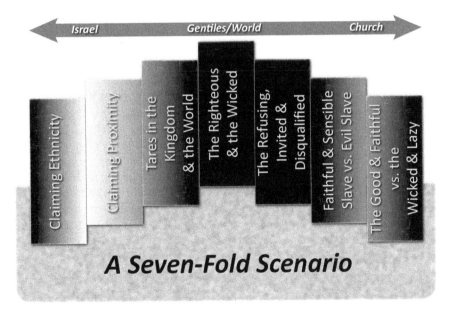

Jesus addresses the issue of the eternal consequences for falling spiritually
short in an overlapping fashion so as to nullify the possibility that there is
some kind of "loophole" or "exemption" when there is not. The same fate

awaits everyone across all ethnic groups, historical periods and responses to His calling, not just in *"this present age"*, but in the course of *"the end of the age"* as well. These do not simply apply to the Second Coming or the one-time event we call the Rapture, but reflect the spiritual state of anyone who "meets" Jesus by the more common occurrence of their life coming to an end. These all equally apply whether He comes for us today through our death, or tomorrow by the Rapture. It is respectfully suggested that since we neither know when either event will take place, there is an equally imperative motivation to put things right as soon as possible.

The bottom line is that there is no need to make any further inquiries into the meaning of God's prophetic Word if we are not striving *"to enter through the narrow door"*. (Lk. 13:24) But the wonderful alternative is that for those in compliance with this standard, any debatable deficiencies in their understanding of eschatology are not going to alter their final destination.

Jesus devotes much more time in the Gospels to the issue of hell than heaven because of the spiritual hurdle which first presents itself before attaining to all which will come after: *"…when the Son of Man comes, will He find faith on the earth?"* (Lk. 18:8) Not faith in proximity or heritage or other false hopes, but providing the evidence of a biblical faithfulness practicing obedience, service and steadfast commitment to His Word and ways alone. But the fact is that all aspects of eschatology can be distilled down to, depending on each reader's current path, as leading to one of two inescapable conclusions:

> [24]*"Truly, truly, I say to you, he who hears My word, and believes Him who sent Me, has eternal life, and does not come into judgment, but has passed out of death into life.* [25]*Truly, truly, I say to you, an hour is coming and now is, when the dead will hear the voice of the Son of God, and those who hear will live.* [26]*For just as the Father has life in Himself, even so He gave to the Son also to have life in Himself;* [27]*and He gave Him authority to execute judgment, because He is the Son of Man.* [28]*Do not marvel at this; for an hour is coming, in which all who are in the tombs will hear His voice,* [29]*and will come forth;* **those who did the good deeds to a resurrection of life, those who committed the evil deeds to a resurrection of judgment**. (John 5:24–29)*

The priority conveyed by this spectrum of spiritual conditions is to be properly reconciled and obedient to Christ in this life so as to be assured of avoiding the inevitable consequences for those who are not. What we will find accompanying every New Testament teaching on the End Times is the admonition to believers to remain faithful and obedient in spite of the circumstances so as to be found "dressed and ready" for His Return, to be found behaving and serving biblically as a Christian always should at any given time, and the warning to unbelievers to repent and accept Christ as their Savior while there is still time. Or as is stipulated by Christ through the angel to John in the closing verses of Revelation:

> [11] *"Let the one who does wrong, still do wrong; and the one who is filthy, still be filthy; and let the one who is righteous, still practice righteousness; and the one who is holy, still keep himself holy." (Revelation 22:11)*

In other words, the manner in which we are now currently living is exactly how we will live and behave then—there will not be time enough to change at that late date like those knocking to get in or taken by surprise at His Return. The repeated admonition is to be righteous and holy now so that we may be found righteous and holy then. This is specifically followed immediately by Christ Himself stating:

> [12] *"Behold, I am coming quickly, and My reward is with Me, to render to every man according to what he has done. (Revelation 22:12)*

In each of the seven instances of this teaching spanning the entire multi-layered range from Israel to the Church, from Jew to Gentile, and from believer to non-believer, the more important issue which will take place against the backdrop of all these End Times events will be the greater principle *"to render to every man according to what he has done"*. This is the focus of all End Times teaching in the New Testament in the repeated attempt to get us to understand that the more important issue is first and foremost our relationship with Christ as expressed by our visible witness to the world and treatment of others, not the ability to produce a proper diagram of the sequence of End Times events.

We will find that this spectrum of behaviors and outcomes are those which are most visited and emphasized by the New Testament writers, which boils down to warning the unsaved to accept and follow Christ, to Jews to accept and follow the Messiah, and to the Church that each member must be properly "dressed and ready" and not risk the ultimate consequences in the character of Lot's wife, or worse, as an outright hypocrite. The details of the Second Coming as provided in the Olivet Discourse, and Christ's groundswell of teachings leading up to it, emphasizes that which is the most important application to not just accept Christ, but to live and serve according to His

Word and ways in the interim so as to experience the full benefits of His Return. The New Testament writers reinforce how to avoid the "*broad*" way of destruction in favor of embracing the "*narrow*" way of obedience leading to salvation because, in the end, everyone is going to "meet" Jesus one way or the other.

This teaching is the real doctrinal heart and foundation for the greater area we call "eschatology", that which will befall everyone in the very end. No chart, graph, or debate-conquering knowledge of any of the aspects or events contained within the eschaton will do anyone any good if they are not spiritually prepared for His coming, whether through death and Resurrection or by way of supernatural extraction via the Rapture. Jesus spends more time warning believers than non-believers because they are supposed to know better and live accordingly, but so many will be found lacking because of the conditions specified in this spectrum of teachings. The true prerequisite for being ready to meet Jesus is living and serving as a Christian should according to His Word and ways. Christ has left no loopholes for those holding to biblically non-existent exemptions from actually practicing the faith.

3 ❖ Luke 17 & the Olivet Discourse

Whenstudying the Gospels in general, but especially when it comes to the Olivet Discourse, we are encouraged to study them "synoptically"—that is, to compare side-by-side the parallel accounts of the same teachings.* In this case, we are focusing on Matthew 24-25, Mark 13, and Luke 21 where each records the Olivet Discourse. [See *Appendix "A" • The Olivet Discourse in Parallel.*] This is the purpose of the multi-colored tables throughout this book which directly compare all three accounts.

However, there are instances when a teaching or event which seems identical in multiple Gospels is found to not actually be the exact, same thing, another good reason to scrutinize them synoptically. Just because the Gospels record a single instance of a teaching does not mean that Jesus did not give that lesson more than once at different times and places in the course of His ministry, and just because more than one account sounds like the same thing does not mean they are cloned copies of an identical discourse given for the same purpose or at the same time. There are instances where something sounding similar was taught at different points in His ministry but for a different overall context or audience. We just saw such an example in how seven different variations of *"weeping and gnashing of teeth"* are not identical and actually addressing seven distinct cases, even though there is a continuing, running theme throughout them all which connects them into an overall, broader message. When each is studied individually, we see the specific audience and context when each was given, but as a whole their sum is greater than their parts.

We have the same phenomenon where something with many similarities to the Olivet Discourse was given on a separate, earlier occasion, but with a different emphasis and audience in Luke 17, which has been referred to in these pages as the "mini" Olivet Discourse. We have to carefully consider whether this is something which should be harmonized with the Olivet Discourse proper, or emphasizing some of the same aspects for a different purpose when it comes to the Second Coming. As it turns out, we need to do both.

The Olivet Discourse is so named because the three parallel accounts all take place on the Mount of Olives in response to specific questions put to Jesus by his innermost circle of Apostles:

³As He was sitting on the Mount of Olives, the disciples came to Him privately, saying, "Tell us, when will these things happen, and what will be the sign of Your coming, and of the end of the age?" (Mt. 24:3)	*³As He was sitting on the Mount of Olives opposite the temple, Peter and James and John and Andrew were questioning Him privately, ⁴"Tell us, when will these things be, and what will be the sign when all these things are going to be fulfilled?" (Mk. 13:3–4)*	*⁷They questioned Him, saying, "Teacher, when therefore will these things happen? And what will be the sign when these things are about to take place?" (Lk. 21:7)*

However, the section of Scripture in Luke 17, although it closely parallels some of the points presented in the course of the Olivet Discourse in Matthew 24, actually takes place weeks or perhaps even months prior, "*While He was on the way to Jerusalem*". (Lk. 17:11) It not only does not take place in or near Jerusalem, but earlier while He is making His final journey there. And additionally in this case, Christ's response was not initiated by an inquiry from His disciples, but by a question posed by the Pharisees which is completely different from that which the Apostles would ask of Him later:

*²⁰Now **having been questioned by the Pharisees as to when the kingdom of God was coming**, He answered them and said, "The kingdom of God is not coming with signs to be observed; ²¹nor will they say, 'Look, here it is!' or, 'There it is!' For behold, the kingdom of God is in your midst." (Luke 17:20–21)*

Jesus immediately follows up, as recorded in verse 22, to provide an outline of His Second Coming using a skeletal structure of some of the same events and illustrations He will later build on in the much more expanded Olivet Discourse, but are here presented as a separate teaching which took place independently and earlier for a different audience and for a different purpose. It is critical that we not automatically treat this solely as a parallel part of the Olivet Discourse when it has a weight and purpose all its own in and of itself. Strictly speaking, Luke 17 is not 100% identical to its parallel in the Olivet Discourse, but a separate, earlier teaching with some significant differences for the audience and time it was originally presented:

> ➤ Whereas the Olivet Discourse is given on the Mt. of Olives during the last week of His ministry, the discourse in Luke 17 is given weeks or months before while still travelling to Jerusalem;

> ➤ Whereas the Olivet Discourse was given as a result of a tri-partite request initiated in private by four of Christ's Apostles, the discourse in Luke 17 was given publicly because of a completely different question raised by the Pharisees;

> ➤ Whereas the Olivet Discourse was only given to a quartet of Apostles, the discourse in Luke 17 was shared with all of His disciples who were present.

Again, this shows that Jesus often taught about different aspects of His Second Coming well before He formally provided the Olivet Discourse, and this instance in particular is an important foundational piece which began to reshape their thinking beforehand. It further shows that when they formed their subsequent question on the Mt. of Olives that it was derived from previous teachings and not simply a chance inquiry.

One Messiah, Two Comings

The repeated problem which everyone seemed to possess at Christ's First Coming, even the Apostles and John the Baptist himself, is that the common expectation was for the Messiah to come and fulfill every prophecy written about Him in one, single visit. In fact, their understanding of God's prophetic Word was even further afield than that because although there were Scriptures speaking of the Messiah as a "Suffering Servant" who would come and die for sin, by the time of Jesus' arrival this aspect was largely ignored. They instead over-realized those Scriptures describing the Messiah as the "Conquering King" who would establish His kingdom on earth from Jerusalem. The desire for someone to come and put the Romans in their place was so strong that it all but completely muted what Scripture had to say about the first and primary need for sin to be addressed. There is always a problem for those who only want the Messiah of the Second Coming without first accepting the Messiah of the First Coming.

> [44]Now He said to them, "These are My words which I spoke to you while I was still with you, that all things which are written about Me in the Law of Moses and the Prophets and the Psalms must be fulfilled."
> [45]**Then He opened their minds to understand the Scriptures,** [46]and He said to them, "Thus it is written, that the Christ would suffer and rise again from the dead the third day, [47]and that repentance for forgiveness of sins would be proclaimed in His name to all the nations, beginning from Jerusalem. [48]You are witnesses of these things. [49]And behold, I am sending forth the promise of My Father upon you; but you are to stay in the city until you are clothed with power from on high." (Luke 24:44–49)

It was not until immediately in the wake of Christ's Resurrection, after imparting to His disciples the Holy Spirit and then opening their minds to fully understand the whole of Scripture where the Messiah was concerned, when they were finally able to fully grasp the meaning of one Messiah, but two comings. With the benefit of their teachings, the guidance of the Holy Spirit, and hindsight, we personally now hold this to be axiomatic, that the Messiah had to first come to address the issue of sin once and for all in the work of the cross, but will return a second time to complete the work of what we most commonly refer to as the Millennial Kingdom.

This was not an unaddressed issue during the course of Jesus' 3-1/2 year ministry because it actually kept coming up time and time again. Just prior to that special vision to take place on the Mt. of Transfiguration, when on behalf of the disciples Peter acknowledged, "*You are the Christ, the Son of the living God*", (Mt. 16:16) Jesus began to distinguish between what had to take place in His First Coming from that which would come in His Second Coming.

> [21]From that time Jesus began to show His disciples that He must go to Jerusalem, and suffer many things from the elders and chief priests and scribes, and be killed, and be raised up on the third day.
> [22]Peter took Him aside and began to rebuke Him, saying, "God forbid it, Lord! This shall never happen to You."
> [23]But He turned and said to Peter, "Get behind Me, Satan! You are a stumbling block to Me; for you are not setting your mind on God's interests, but man's." (Matthew 16:21–23)

This was not an isolated incident, but a common, recurring issue which kept coming up over and over again. In fact, just eight days after this when Peter finds himself, together with James and John, on the Mt. of Transfiguration and shares a vision of Elijah and Moses talking with Jesus, Peter thinks that what we now associate with the Second Coming—the Millennial Kingdom, has arrived. This is the meaning of Peter's desire to make tabernacles, a practice strictly associated with the Feast of Tabernacles, still celebrated by Jews to this day as being representative of the Messiah's Millennial Kingdom to come.

> ³And behold, Moses and Elijah appeared to them, talking with Him. ⁴Peter said to Jesus, "Lord, it is good for us to be here; if You wish, I will make three tabernacles here, one for You, and one for Moses, and one for Elijah." (Matthew 17:3–4)

This teaching of the necessary preliminary work of the First Coming would come up over and over again and is recorded in the Gospels in Matthew 12:40, 17:9, 17:12, 17:22, 20:18, 27:63, Mark 9:12, 9:31, Luke 17:25, 18:32, 24:7, and John 2:19. And this is actually the greater teaching which underlies Luke 17:20-37, this "mini" Olivet Discourse, when the Gospels record Jesus presenting in greater detail than previously provided to that point the sequence and mechanics of how the Second Coming will transpire. Jesus is specifically addressing the false expectations for the Messiah's coming held by the Pharisees (and nearly everyone else at the time), which was such a pervasive teaching that it was even stubbornly held by Christ's own followers in spite of His repeated, unambiguous explanations to the contrary. It would not be until after His Death and Resurrection, and upon breathing into them the Holy Spirit, when their eyes would be fully opened not just to the whole of God's Word where the Messiah was concerned, but to the meaning of what Jesus had been teaching all along.

> ²⁰Now having been questioned by the Pharisees as to when the kingdom of God was coming, He answered them and said, "The kingdom of God is not coming with signs to be observed; ²¹nor will they say, 'Look, here it is!' or, 'There it is!' For behold, the kingdom of God is in your midst."
> ²²And He said to the disciples, "The days will come when you will long to see one of the days of the Son of Man, and you will not see it. ²³They will say to you, 'Look there! Look here!' Do not go away, and do not run after them. ²⁴For just like the lightning, when it flashes out of one part of the sky, shines to the other part of the sky, so will the Son of Man be in His day. ²⁵**But first He must suffer many things and be rejected by this generation**. (Luke 17:20–25)

Take note of the key qualifier in verse 25, "*But first He must suffer many things and be rejected by this generation*". This is one of the instances in the Gospels of a distinction being made for "one Messiah, two comings" which is accompanied by specific information as to how that second visitation will take place. Jesus is trying to not only adjust their expectations for His fulfillment of God's Word concerning His First Coming, but His Second Coming as well.

The Kingdom of God

It is important to distinguish the difference between "*the kingdom of God*" and that thousand year period of Messianic rule which we commonly refer to as the "Millennial Kingdom"—strictly and exegetically speaking, they are not the same thing. There is no contradiction in Jesus telling the Pharisees, "*The kingdom of God is not coming with signs to be observed*", (Lk. 17:20) and then immediately turning to His disciples and explaining the signs and conditions of His Second Coming. The "*kingdom of God*" is not the same thing as what we have come to know as the "Millennial Kingdom", and just as there was great confusion about this at Jesus' First Coming, it does not appear to be entirely settled in the minds of many to this day. The two related terms which are used repeatedly throughout the Gospels are "*the kingdom of God*" and "*the kingdom of heaven*". To avoid confusion, they will simply be referred to interchangeably as "*the kingdom*".

Essentially what it comes down to is that the term "*the kingdom*" describes something composed of people. Our earthly vision of a kingdom is to think in terms of the material aspects more than its human composition. We would define a kingdom as something which has physical boundaries around a body of land, a military and governmental structure subordinate to a ruler, and things like palaces, buildings, military strength and material possessions identified directly with the power and authority of the primary personality or entity serving as overall ruler. We might even think of it in terms of the ruler and the successive generations of their family members who reign from one succeeding period to the next. History has often defined this by describing various periods as belonging to the "Roman Empire", "Byzantine Empire", "British Empire" and so forth. Such are presented to us in the form of a map showing how much area they controlled and the capital from which they ruled.

The question posed by the Pharisees embodied the shared misconception prevailing at Christ's First Coming who saw the ultimate "kingdom" in earthly terms along the lines of the Roman Empire then ruling the known world, and perceiving that whatever was revealed in Scripture concerning the Messiah's Millennial Kingdom was merely God coming down to institute the ultimate version of that kind of earthly institution. However, when we look at teachings concerning *"the kingdom"*, they overwhelmingly reference people and their spiritual condition rather than the outward manifestations of a series of worldly fixtures.

Take, for instance, the parables recorded in Matthew 13 which all teach something about the character and nature of *"the kingdom"*:

> ➤ *The Parable of the Sower* (Mt. 13:3-23) is a kingdom parable which describes how each person either accepts or rejects the Word of God.

> ➤ *The Parable of the Tares* (Mt. 13:24-30, 36-43) is a kingdom parable describing how the saved and unsaved will be found living side-by-side until God's judgment separates them.

> ➤ *The Parable of the Mustard Seed* (Mt. 13:31-32) is a kingdom parable which uses the metaphor of "*the birds in the air*" to illustrate people.

> ➤ *The Parable of the Leaven* (Mt. 13:33) is a kingdom parable highlighting the issue of people's sin and false teaching (the meaning of the leaven).

> ➤ *The Parable of the Hidden Treasure* (Mt. 13:44) is a kingdom parable about a person's salvation.

> ➤ *The Parable of the Costly Pearl* (Mt. 13:45-46) is also a kingdom parable about a person's salvation.

> ➤ *The Parable of the Dragnet* (Mt. 13:47-50) is a kingdom parable about the eventual separation which final judgment will make between the wicked and the righteous—in other words, people.

In every instance, these teachings which Jesus qualifies with, "*the kingdom of heaven is like*", the object of the kingdom is people and their spiritual choices. There are no descriptions in these illustrations of a kingdom which fits with all the outward manifestations of an earthly domain defined by its palaces, boundaries, military might, great wealth or other earthly material associations or power structures.

Normally, from an earthly point of view, no one could become a citizen of a kingdom which has not yet come into being both literally and physically. A ruler would rise to power, conquer enemies and capture lands, and that kingdom would be physically established. Depending on your situation and position, you would become an active part of the kingdom seeking to support and expand it, or subjugated as part of that which was conquered, but either way it amounts to being a member of a visible earthly institution. But God's kingdom does not come about in this manner, because in reality it has already been established in eternity, even before the foundations of this world. (*"My kingdom is not of this world..."*—Jn. 18:36) And unlike earthly counterfeits which measure themselves by the amount of land they have conquered or occupy, in God's kingdom the first and foremost measurement of its occupation of the hearts of its citizens—people. It will not take earthly, physical shape until the Millennial Reign, and then over the entire planet.

> *19So then you are no longer strangers and aliens, but **you are fellow citizens with the saints, and are of God's household**, 20having been built on the foundation of the apostles and prophets, Christ Jesus Himself being the corner stone, 21in whom the whole building, being fitted together, is growing into a holy temple in the Lord, 22in whom you also are **being built together into a dwelling of God in the Spirit**. (Ephesians 2:19–22)*

In Luke 17, in response to the Pharisees' question, Jesus is saying that God's kingdom does not operate in the character of earthly kingdoms, and that by choosing salvation through Christ, one immediately becomes an active member of that kingdom, not someone expecting yet another earthly institution to come into existence and replace all the others. Not only does no one have to wait for the final version of God's physical kingdom to finally appear on earth and visibly show itself, but waiting until that happens before following Christ by faith would be a costly mistake taking place when it is too late. *"Behold, the kingdom of God is in your midst"* is Jesus' way of stating we must all make our choice here and now from the heart. Since His kingdom is already in existence, having been established in eternity past, we become members from the heart to join it in progress and on into eternity future.

He then follows this up with His disciples in the explanation that when God's kingdom does physically appear and replace all the kingdoms of the world, that it is still not going to happen in the way earthly kingdoms rise to power. The Second Coming—the total embodiment of the process by which

God's kingdom will come, will be just as unexpected and different according to human expectations as Christ's First Coming to initially perform the work of the cross was to everyone the first time. In both cases, whether for the First or Second Coming, it is about Jesus coming for His people.

Jesus' response to the Pharisees' question is they should become members of God's kingdom now by accepting Him as Messiah while there is still time because, as subsequently revealed, that "*kingdom*" (made up of people) is going to be extracted. It did not come the way they expected, so they needed to adjust their expectations. After the extraction described, there is nothing left except the wrath of God to come on the remaining "kingdoms" (made up of people) of the earth, and as we now know, in particular, on the kingdom of Antichrist when he consolidates and rules them for a time.

Luke 17:20-36 is an important, independent teaching in its own right to specifically address the misunderstood concept of "one Messiah, two comings", but is also a valuable milestone in Christ's teaching that neither the First nor Second Comings will meet human expectations, but God's Word and ways alone. It cannot be overly dogmatically asserted that this lesson may be one of the most important ones for Christians currently living in the shadow of Christ's Return, that we not repeat the mistake made at His First Coming supposing that God's prophetic Word will be fulfilled exclusively according to our presuppositions. The only defense against this is the prayerful pursuit of a sanctified, Spirit-led life immersed in His Word. But the warnings to us in anticipation of His Second Coming are to avoid the same behavior as commonly found in the course of His First Coming, that we not attempt to bypass our faith and relationship with the Messiah the Lamb of the cross and solely fixate on the Messiah returning on the white horse. (Rev. 19:11) Even among professing Christians, there is a danger in diminishing the Messiah of the First Coming in the process of over-realizing the Messiah of the Second Coming.

A Basic Foundation

> [20]*Now having been questioned by the Pharisees as to when the kingdom of God was coming, He answered them and said, "The kingdom of God is not coming with signs to be observed;* [21]**nor will they say, 'Look, here it is!' or, 'There it is!' For behold, the kingdom of God is in your midst.**" [22]*And He said to the disciples, "The days will come when you will long to see one of the days of the Son of Man, and you will not see it.* [23]**They will say to you, 'Look there! Look here!' Do not go away, and do not run after them.** [24]*For just like the*

> *lightning, when it flashes out of one part of the sky, shines to the other part of the sky, so will the Son of Man be in His day. 25But first He must suffer many things and be rejected by this generation. (Luke 17:20–25)*

The warning to the Pharisees, who represent non-believers and the apostate in this case, is to repent and become believers as soon as possible, the greater meaning of the statement, "*For behold, the kingdom of God is in your midst*". (The phrase "*in your midst*" can probably best be understood as "found within you if you would only accept Me as Messiah".) For the disciples as representative of all faithful believers, however, the priority is to avoid being deceived. But note how similar uses of the same kind of deception are employed in both cases, one to obfuscate the Messiah of the First Coming, and then to similarly inject the same kind of confusion at His Second Coming. "*Look, here it is…There it is!…Look there! Look here!*".

It is noteworthy that this is the overwhelming theme of the Olivet Discourse to come, as Jesus repeatedly warns against deception and admonishes us to remain alert and ready. The fact that both the primary teaching of the Olivet Discourse proper and this earlier related discourse recorded by Luke likewise warn that it will be too late for unbelievers, and a time of deception directed at believers, should not be taken lightly. We will later see that this is also the primary theme which the New Testament writers most frequently emphasize.

Something we understand in hindsight because we have been raised with the whole of God's Word, especially when it comes to our understanding of the events associated with the Last Days, is that a counterfeit christ is coming, preceded by many lesser counterfeit christs, and an ultimate, counterfeit kingdom. But from the outset, Jesus forewarns us that His kingdom is not going to come about according to earthly expectations. "*For just like the lightning, when it flashes out of one part of the sky, shines to the other part of the sky, so will the Son of Man be in His day*". (Lk. 17:24) This is actually the historical pattern by which earthly institutions give way to each other. Although the geo-political conditions may be observed for some time in advance, when the actual defining event takes place, its finality always takes us by surprise and seems to take place suddenly.

For the original listeners of this message at that time, Jesus specifically addresses their expectations by qualifying, "*But first He must suffer many things and be rejected by this generation*". But there is still a message relevant for us in that although we have the benefit of being able to look back and clearly see how the First Coming was actually carried out contrary to most expectations, we have to at least consider the possibility that neither will what is yet to come before us unfold precisely according to many modern, current assumptions if today we replay the stubbornness so prevalent then. (Is there any area within the Church today experiencing more confusion than eschatology—the many interpretations of how the Second Coming will take place? Even many, like the Sadducees, denying it completely?)

It is interesting to note that although the Apostles and the Early Church all expected to see Christ Return in their lifetime, Jesus specifically identifies a gap between His First and Second Comings which will be at least long enough so that, "*The days will come when you will long to see one of the days of the Son of Man, and you will not see it*". (Lk. 17:22) Christ Himself stipulated a sizable waiting period which, among other things, will shape the expectations of many concerning His Second Coming, and even lull the unbelieving into willful ignorance on the one hand, and some of the believing into deception on the other. These are all repeated features of the Olivet Discourse proper to come.

Examples of Judgment & Rescue

> [26]"*And just as it happened* **in the days of Noah, so it will be also in the days of the Son of Man**: [27]*They were eating, they were drinking, they were marrying, they were being given in marriage, until the day that Noah entered the ark, and the flood came and destroyed them all.* [28]*It was* **the same as happened in the days of Lot**: *they were eating, they were drinking, they were buying, they were selling, they were planting, they were building;* [29]*but on the day that Lot went out from Sodom it rained fire and brimstone from heaven and destroyed them all.* [30]**It will be just the same on the day that the Son of Man is revealed**. (Luke 17:26–30)

The initial illustrations which Christ employs to describe His "*apokalupto*" (Strong's #601)—"*the day that the Son of Man is **revealed***", are of events which each end in an example of final judgment, but which also exhibit a rescue of the faithful. In spite of Noah and Lot warning others, their contemporaries continued "business as usual". Noah's day is described in Scripture as "*filled with violence*" (Gen. 6:13) as a result of the fact that "*all flesh had corrupted their way on earth*". (Gen. 6:12) Sodom and Gomorrah was characterized as, "*their sin is exceedingly grave*" (Gen. 18:20) and "*were exceedingly sinners against the LORD*". (Gen. 13:13) Jude further elaborates that they "*indulged in gross immorality and went after strange flesh*". (Jude 7) The days of Noah and Lot, combining into a consolidated description of the character of the milieu out of which the Second Coming arises, lends itself greatly to the more expanded explanations of apostasy, deception and spiritual darkness which are staples of the eschaton in supporting Scriptures, but is clearly established here as a foundational part of the overall pattern.

But whereas earthly kingdoms come about as one power visibly conquering another, it is important to understand that what Christ is here emphasizing is not the physical destruction of the kingdom of Antichrist by the kingdom of Christ, but first and foremost warning of the greater portent of impending judgment which comes with it. Since in neither Noah's nor Lot's days there was found a sufficient level of spiritual preparedness, but rather willful ignorance in the pursuit of violence, sin and immorality characterized as "*sinners against the* LORD", the consequences of not belonging to the kingdom was final judgment resulting not just in physical death, but eternal. And to wait until that very point when "*the Son of Man is revealed*" (Lk. 17:30) is too late, just as it was too late for those who waited until the rain began to fall in Noah's day or the judgment of fire falling on Sodom and Gomorrah in Lot's case. The greater warning being conveyed here is to be prepared prior to the arrival of judgment so as to avoid the consequences.

An important aspect to both illustrations is that where the unsaved are concerned, everything changed for them at the point when the righteous in both cases were removed; all that was left for them was the wrath of God's judgment. This is an important reminder that the same thing is going to happen to those left behind after the Church's *Harpazo*.

For Christ's followers, these illustrations attempted to adjust their own expectations for the nature of the milieu out of which the Second Coming would arise. Just as Christ's First Coming did not establish a kingdom in the way that they expected, and they had to come to an understanding of the greater importance of what was taking place spiritually before they could grasp what was transacting literally, so it will be with the Second Coming; the kingdom will not fully disclose an alignment in accordance with earthly expectations. (The value of taking this into consideration in the course of every discussion cannot be overestimated as we undertake any aspect concerning the End Times in particular, or eschatology in general.)

As a side note, mention must be made that there are several variations of a serious false teaching most commonly coming under the umbrella of "Replacement Theology", also known in other iterations as Kingdom Now Theology, Dominionism, Triumphalism, Manifest Sons of Destiny, Supercessionism and other variants, all of which are debunked by Christ directly in this passage. The basic assertion of these false teachings is that Christ's Return will only come about when the Church has successfully evangelized the whole world, and therefore when the Church wins everyone to faith in Christ, Jesus will be visibly brought back to earth. Christ specifically stipulates here that not only will there obviously not be a worldwide acceptance of Him as Savior at His Return, but that the world at large will be gripped by the worst case of spiritual darkness and sin ever, and the remaining faithful but a small remnant among the greater unrepentant whole. Although in the End Times the Gospel may be "preached", that does not automatically mean it is universally, or even modestly, accepted.

A Time of Recognition

> *31 "On that day, the one who is on the housetop and whose goods are in the house must not go down to take them out; and likewise the one who is in the field must not turn back. 32 Remember Lot's wife. 33 Whoever seeks to keep his life will lose it, and whoever loses his life will preserve it. 34 I tell you, on that night there will be two in one bed; one will be taken and the other will be left. 35 There will be two women grinding at the same place; one will be taken and the other will be left. 36 Two men will be in the field; one will be taken and the other will be left." (Luke 17:31–36)*

First of all there is a warning for the faithful that there is going to come a time, however brief when, like Lot and his family, there is full recognition of what God is bringing about, and yet there is still a danger in looking back to the world instead of forward toward Christ. Every detail of the End Times, whether it be for a believer or non-believer, is not a test of knowledge, but a test of faith, even right up to the very end. Remember, it is Jesus Himself who warns against repeating the mistake of Lot's wife.

Second, there is a sharp scholarly divide as to the interpretation of the three examples of verses 34-36 where in each case one is taken and the other left behind. While there are nuanced variations, it basically breaks down to one side believing that what is being described is judgment of the unsaved, while the opposing view is that this is the *Harpazo*—the Rapture, or removal, of the Church. Some say the saved are "*taken*" as in rescued and the unsaved left behind, others that the unsaved are "*taken*" in judgment while the saved are left behind to continue on with their life.

Much of this confusion is immediately cleared up when we study the Gospels synoptically—that is, we examine the texts side-by-side. In this case, the similar passages found in Matthew 24 and here in Luke 17:

³⁷For the coming of the Son of Man will be just like the days of Noah. ³⁸For as in those days before the flood they were eating and drinking, marrying and giving in marriage, until the day that Noah entered the ark,	²⁶"And just as it happened in the days of Noah, so it will be also in the days of the Son of Man: ²⁷They were eating, they were drinking, they were marrying, they were being given in marriage, until the day that Noah entered the ark,

³⁹and they did not understand

until **the flood came and took them all away**;	and **the flood came and destroyed them all**. (Lk. 17:26-27)

so will the coming of the Son of Man be. (Mt. 24:37-39)

³⁴I tell you, on that night there will be two in one bed; one will be taken and the other will be left.

⁴⁰Then there will be two men in the field; one will be taken and one will be left.	³⁵There will be two women grinding at the same place; one will be taken and the other will be left.
⁴¹Two women will be grinding at the mill; one will be taken and one will be left. (Mt. 24:40-41)	³⁶Two men will be in the field; one will be taken and the other will be left." (Lk. 17:34-36)

Those focusing solely on Matthew's account see that where the sinners are concerned, the flood "*took them all away*", which is used by many to then assume when the English word "*taken*" is subsequently used in the examples of the pairs in bed, the field and at work grinding, that this is the same word. In other words, since the English in Matthew 24:39 says that the sinners were "*taken*", they interpret it to mean that the sinners in each of the three examples are also likewise sinners who are "*taken*". It is therefore assumed that the righteous, such as Noah, are the ones actually "left behind" to continue on in life. They end up reversing the traditional meaning of who is "*taken*" and who is "left behind" in an attempt to make the case that this is not actually referring to the Rapture of the Church.

In the first place, by a simple comparison of Matthew 24:39 and Luke 17:27, we can see that while Matthew states, "**the flood** came and **took** them all away", Luke records the meaning as, "**the flood** came and **destroyed** them all". So where the unsaved are concerned, they are not removed, but remain so as to experience the consequences of judgment.

In the second place, the Greek word for "*took*" ("*airo*", Strong's #142) in Matthew 24:39 is actually different from that used in Matthew 24:40-41 and Luke 17:34-36. ("*paralambano*", Strong's #3880) Our English translators are technically correct, but the "*took*" in Matthew 24:39 is the kind of "*took*" which is associated with being removed or taken out, or disposed of, or permanently cast out. In contrast, the "*taken*" applied to the three pairs of figures mentioned is used exclusively to refer to one person taking another person to himself. For instance, at the Mt. of Transfiguration, Jesus "*paralambano*"—that is, he took with Him, Peter James and John. (Mt. 17:1) Of the 49 times it is found within the New Testament, it refers to a person being taken by, to, or with another person 42 times, while the context of the other 7 are connected to instructions or teaching "received" between people. It is never used in the sense of a literal, physical "taking away". The three examples are Jesus taking beleivers to Himself.

Because this is incorporated into the Olivet Discourse proper, we will visit this again, but it is touched on here to give enough clarity as to what is taking place; sinners are left behind to experience judgment, the righteous are protected, rescued and exempted so as to be "*taken*" to another Person, in this obvious case to Christ Himself in the Rapture.

As mentioned previously, God's "*kingdom*" is actually comprised of people, and Jesus' warning to the Pharisees who envision an earthly institution akin to the Roman Empire is that they are misunderstanding the whole concept. Because of Christ, that kingdom is currently available and is obtained by accepting Yeshua as Lord and Savior—that is, by personally embracing the seminal work of the First Coming in the cross. However, as Jesus will categorically state, "*My kingdom is not of this world*". (Jn. 18:36) In other words, Jesus does not just come down and take over the world as it currently exists and operates, and therefore becomes its new, worldwide Ruler; the old must be judged and destroyed in order to be removed and replaced. He started all things anew at the Creation, again with the Flood, started over with Israel, rebooted Israel (so to speak) in their return from the Babylonian Captivity, effects it spiritually through the cross by making us a "new creation" in the new iteration of the Church, but yet again both for the Millennial Reign and finally following that in eternity with the New Heaven and New Earth.

This is what is significant about Jesus then turning to His disciples, and of all the End Times events to come, focusing on the *Harpazo*—the removal of His "*kingdom*", or the believers who actually comprise it. This event signals that there is no longer any opportunity to become members of His kingdom as it will return with Him to be established in a completely new and divine manner. Those left behind have nothing to look forward to except the final judgment of God's wrath poured out on the remaining "*kingdom*"—that is, the people of the earth who have effectively selected an alternate king.

This is yet another exegetical nail in the coffin for the false yet popular notion currently proposed that the Rapture in and of itself will be such a powerful sign that it will initiate a worldwide revival, or just the assertion of a post-Rapture revival by itself. Just as the removal of Noah and his family, or Lot and his family, ended the chances of all those "left behind" who then had nothing remaining to experience except the wrath of God's judgment, that is all that awaits those left behind in the wake of the Church's removal. The *"kingdom"* of God has temporarily left only to return again with Christ when all things anew are established in the Millennial Kingdom. Exegetically speaking, the Millennial "Kingdom" is also not strictly describing an institution either, but is also something comprised 100% of people.

Luke 17:20-37 is a valuable, standalone teaching in and of itself when it comes to the doctrine of "one Messiah, two comings", but is not a whole and complete teaching independent of the rest of what Jesus has to say about His Second Coming as we shall see when He greatly expands upon this partial skeletal structure to present a far more completed overall construct in the Olivet Discourse. As mentioned earlier, this is a teaching which requires both an independent study in its own right, but side-by-side with the later given Olivet Discourse as well.

The Final Condition

> [37]And answering they said to Him, "Where, Lord?"
> And He said to them, "Where the body is, there also the vultures will be gathered." (Luke 17:37)

There is much symbolism and deeper meaning to this concluding remark regarding His Second Coming. In the context of Jesus' description of what conditions will be like on the earth prior to his Return, what is rendered here in the English as *"body"* could be better translated as "corpse". It is describing something of incurable moral and spiritual corruption which is decaying and appealing to the vultures, a picture of unclean carrion eaters representing non-believers.

Jesus uses this illustration to answer the disciples' question as to what the conditions will be like immediately preceding His Return. As this is also recorded in Matthew's account of the Olivet Discourse, it will be discussed in more detail later, but in this context it is a powerful illustration of the ultimate conditions arising from a time which will embody both the spiritual nature of the days of Noah and its propensity for violence, and the intense moral decay of the days of Lot. They fuse together into the representation of a rotting corpse on which the world is feasting, and again, contradict the notion of Kingdom Now Theology proponents that the world in its entirety will be won to Christ by the Church in order to precipitate His Return.

However, the heart of this teaching touches on the same fundamental topic elaborated in the sevenfold teaching employing the common feature of *"weeping and gnashing of teeth"*, that every individual needs to attain to a good standing in Christ now before it is too late.

4 ❖ "The End of the Age"

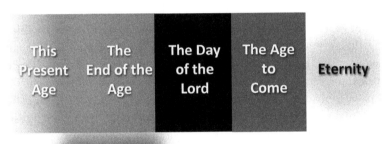

Having provided the overall foundation in His previous teachings leading up to it, Jesus in the Olivet Discourse narrows the discussion to the events exclusively associated with "the end of the age" with a closing reference to the transition to "the age to come". The Olivet Discourse's focus on "the end of the age" characterizes it as consisting of different phases, making no reference whatsoever to prophetic measurements of time found elsewhere in Scripture such as 3-1/2 years, 42 months, 1,260 days, or even seven years. The first phase which Jesus describes is presented in the character of "birth pangs".

⁸But all these things are merely the beginning of birth pangs. (Mt. 24:8)	*These things are merely the beginning of birth pangs. (Mk. 13:8b)*

As readers will be repeatedly reminded in the course of this discussion, the exercise here is to give priority to the Olivet Discourse by placing ourselves in the shoes of the earliest believers who were never aware of the book of

Revelation. As such, we must remember that nowhere in the Olivet Discourse (or Revelation, for that matter) is a seven year period ever mentioned. In fact, in the whole of the New Testament, there is only one, solitary reference to "*seven years*", and that is to specify the length of time Anna was married before she became a widow. (Lk. 2:36) This is something to take into very serious consideration, that although we can have no doubt that the Prophet Daniel's designation of a final week of years yet to come is absolutely true, there is no indication in the New Testament as to its exact beginning; we are only provided corroboration of its precise middle and ending milestones. And when we can muster up enough to imagine what it was like to hear or read the Olivet Discourse with no knowledge or influence from Revelation, we are left to interpret the terms as Jesus originally presented them rather than as they have come to be used in relatively recent Church history.

The events contained in the Olivet Discourse are not framed by this seven year period, often referred to as "Daniel's 70th Week" (Dan. 9:25-27), the way present day academia most often chooses. Instead we find that the beginning is cloaked in events which gradually increase in strength and frequency before we can possibly and dogmatically affix a place on a timeline. Ironically, this is the actual meaning of the Greek word "*apokalupsis*" which we translate as "*revelation*", that it is like a veil being raised the closer we come within its proximity so that what lies behind comes into gradually sharper focus and, eventually when completely pulled back, into plain view. What we shall see, however, is that it is not the entirety of Daniel's 70th Week which clearly presents itself as we draw closer, but some very specific and key aspects.

Instead of a timeline of milestones laid out according to a calendar, the Olivet Discourse is structured more in the form of a sequence of phases, beginning with what Jesus identifies as "*birth pangs*" in the initial stage. It is not specified how many obstetric waves there will be, nor how long of a period of time they can be expected to take place, but like an impending birth they allow us to know how close we are to the event itself. Although no one can know the day or the hour, we can certainly know the nearness of His Return by the increasing intensity of these events leading up to some very specific, unmistakable milestones.

That being said, the label used by Jesus to describe what the "*birth pangs*" transition to is "*tribulation*"—not a seven year period so many presently call "*The* Tribulation" and attribute to something the whole world will experience, but rather a specific time period of unprecedented (in their intensity) spiritual issues corresponding in their direct focus on the Church in the forms of deception, apostasy and especially persecution. Jesus does not use this term to describe either the 70th Week as a whole or even its first half. In fact, unlike its common usage today, He does not actually apply it to something the whole world experiences, but if we carefully examine the text, instead assigns it as a specific, intense period directed exclusively at believers. The persecution, deception and apostasy which has always been present in every historic age of the Church, even though at times extremely bad, have been precursors teaching something about the worst and final one yet to come.

If we were to attempt to depict this on our own End Times timeline, it would be something which begins gradually, gaining intensity as it approaches a series of specific, ultimate events. But overall, it is characterized by a sequence of phases:

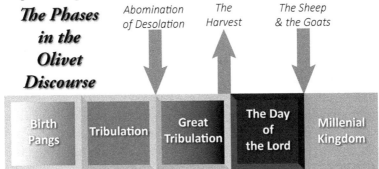

The Phases in the Olivet Discourse

Abomination of Desolation — The Harvest — The Sheep & the Goats

Birth Pangs | Tribulation | Great Tribulation | The Day of the Lord | Millenial Kingdom

It is worth noting that the time after the Church's removal is prolifically taught in Scripture as *"the day of the Lord"*. Because this time is the literal pouring out of God's wrath in judgment, and believers are exempt from His wrath (a doctrinal reason for their removal via the Rapture), there is more scriptural real estate devoted to this ultimate time of darkness than any other event featured in God's prophetic Word. This is why it is particularly noteworthy that although it will be greatly detailed in the book of Revelation to come, and already exhaustively established and described in the Old Testament, it was a feature of the Olivet Discourse only to the degree of identifying the timing of the Church's removal in the overall sequence; this is because Christ is providing what is most important for the Church, which is exempt from the wrath of God poured out on the world in *"the day of the Lord"*.

If we are faithful so as to navigate this time successfully by the standards of His Word leading up to *"the day of the Lord"*, believers are removed and exempted with its impending onset and know that the next stop for them is to leap over it and arrive at the Millennial Kingdom. Instead of defining our eschatology based on being exempted (or not) from the entirety of a mischaracterization of Daniel's 70th Week most call *"The Tribulation"*, the biblically textual standard is to avoid the final phase of the overall eschaton designated as *"the day of the Lord"*, which is its final, darkest period. Jesus shows how that is possible for the faithful Church in this critical teaching.

But this is one of the primary reasons a major reassignment of the Olivet Discourse so as not to apply to the Church has taken place in modern Church history. By erroneously designating the entirety of Daniel's 70th Week as being synonymous with *the day of the Lord*", a term which they correctly understand to be that time of God's wrath from which the Church is exempted, they think they can place the timing of the Rapture as taking place entirely before those final seven years. (Or just as erroneously, at their end.) But since the text of the Olivet Discourse plainly refutes this, they resort to a series of complex arguments to claim it has no meaning for the Church, but only for Israel to come when they are left to experience it alone. As we shall see, this results in something far more serious than just an academic argument where the timing of the Rapture is concerned, but is contributing to a complete lack of proper preparation of the Church for what Jesus says we will face in the shadow of that removal. Like the academic elite of the First Coming in the way of the Pharisees, Sadducees and Scribes, in the shadow of the Second Coming we likewise have those who are more concerned for protecting the doctrines and positions of man rather than first and foremost upholding the plain meaning of God's Word. What happened then is taking place again.

This "slice and dice" of New Testament Scripture leads to some other serious consequences, one being that there are those who even go so far to say that there are some books of the Bible which are only for the Church and others only for Israel. Just as one unaddressed sin always leads to more serious sin, unaddressed error always leads to deeper and more serious error. So it is no wonder that we often see parallel errors in the fundamental doctrines accompanying these teachings.

"Birth Pangs"

⁴And Jesus answered and said to them, "See to it that no one misleads you. ⁵For many will come in My name, saying, 'I am the Christ,'	*⁵And Jesus began to say to them, "See to it that no one misleads you. ⁶Many will come in My name, saying, 'I am He!'*	*⁸And He said, "See to it that you are not misled; for many will come in My name, saying, 'I am He,'*
and, 'The time is near.'		
and will mislead many.		*and will mislead many.*
Do not go after them.		

⁶You will be hearing of wars	⁷When you hear of wars	⁹When you hear of wars
and rumors of wars.	and rumors of wars,	
and disturbances,		
See that you are not frightened, for those things must take place, but that is not yet the end.	do not be frightened; those things must take place; but that is not yet the end.	do not be terrified; for these things must take place first, but the end does not follow immediately."
⁷For nation will rise against nation, and kingdom against kingdom,	⁸For nation will rise up against nation, and kingdom against kingdom;	¹⁰Then He continued by saying to them, "Nation will rise against nation and kingdom against kingdom,
...and earthquakes.	there will be earthquakes in various places;	¹¹and there will be great earthquakes,
and in various places plagues		
and in various places there will be famines...	there will also be famines.	and famines;
and there will be terrors and great signs from heaven. (Lk. 21:8-11)		
⁸But all these things are merely the beginning of birth pangs. (Mt. 24:4-8)	These things are merely the beginning of birth pangs. (Mk. 13:5-8)	

Jesus begins with a warning about deception, which is a point He will return to throughout the Olivet Discourse and repeat more than any of the other features which will characterize the environment just prior to His Return. Where believers are concerned, there are direct, repeated warnings about deception, apostasy and persecution more than any other particulars.

It is important to note, however, that while we all know and cite that there will be many false christs coming before the ultimate, final Antichrist, that it is only when comparing the Gospel accounts of the Olivet Discourse that we discover something which Luke alone captured, stipulating that danger will not only come from those claiming, "*I am the Christ*" (Mt. 24:5), but those over-asserting, "*The time is near*". (Lk. 21:8)

The Chicken Little Syndrome

It is obviously logical that Jesus would not provide such an extensive teaching to instruct us in how to know when His Return is imminently close and then, when recognizing the impending fulfillment, tell us it would be wrong to announce, "*The time is near*", so this must be understood in its proper context. Just as there will be those who falsely represent themselves to be Christ, there are going to be those who present false interpretations of events so as to declare, "*The time is near*" so often that, like the many false christs who disguise the ultimate one to come, there are many false declarations about the End Times so as to obfuscate the authentic and final true fulfillments. The many false prophets are in the business of making false and misleading prophecies, whereas the "*time is near*" pundits engage in misinterpreting what are actual fulfillments, or talk so much about anything and everything that it spiritually desensitizes their audience.

This is especially a current epidemic in our Western pop culture and media, facilitated by the recent advent of the Internet, where there are already too many movies, television series, books, articles and websites all devoted to the theme of the end of the world, so prolific in fact, that it has its own designated category as "apocalyptic" whether it is something biblically based or not. Satan is certainly hard at work generating a lot of "noise" from worldly sources in an attempt to drown out, or at least render ineffective, the truth about what is coming by employing a myriad of voices across the entire audio/video/textual media landscape to intone, "*The time is near!*" It is so pervasive that one of the most common jokes found nearly every week in the comics involves a figure wearing a sandwich board bearing this slogan and basically found on every street corner.

At the time of this writing, there are at least a dozen secular television series based on an apocalyptic premise regularly broadcast, not to mention the dozens of movies in the past few years which are likewise themed. (At the time of this writing, the A&E Network has aired a weekly series titled "Damien" based on "The Omen" movies, dedicated to following the life and rise to power of the Antichrist, and HBO is finishing up its third season of a series on the Rapture titled tongue in cheek, "The Leftovers". These are actually tame compared to the SyFy Channel's "Aftermath".) Who knows how many film and television productions on just the theme of a "zombie apocalypse" alone have been made and are planned for future release. Or the many plots revolving around the end coming due to climate change. And this does not even begin to graze the number of books, articles and websites similarly devoted in the whole of human literature and media outlets.

However, and quite disturbingly, this false declaration is actually and presently on display every day on so-called Christian television and an untold number of websites, podcasts and newsletters where false or deceived teachers either run from one manufactured set of signs to another, or give "prophecy updates" declaring practically anything and everything as some kind of fulfillment of God's prophetic Word. It has gone way beyond claiming something in Scripture is currently being literally fulfilled when it is not, but heaping attention on a myriad of "signs" which are not even hinted at in God's prophetic Word.

The history of such is far too long to document here, but just in the past few years alone we have witnessed a New York Times best seller called *The Harbinger* falsely misrepresent End Times events using the attacks of 9/11 as the centerpiece, a host of false personalities espousing variations of "the blood moons" false teaching connecting cosmological eclipses to the Hebrew festal calendar and End Times events—none of which came true, an attempt to link all American financial calamities to the Torah's requirement to give the land rest and forgive all debt every seven years, and various assertions espoused in the guise of "Christian Fiction". There is no end of reporting on Islam and political events which cannot be found in Scripture. The "apocalyptic" genre is a thriving profit center in the secular world, but neither can it be measured in its opportunities for money making and attention grabbing forms within the current walls of the Church. Many of these things have successfully crossed back and forth to capture both a secular and Christian audience.

These are but a very few examples of false or compromised teachers using something to whip up a frenzy around the theme, "*The time is near*", but many of these personalities, and certainly their spiritual counterparts, have been running from one unfulfilled thing to another for decades now. Not surprisingly, when each of these teasers fizzles out, these false teachers merely move on to the next "Chicken Little" apocalyptic fad because there always seems to be an appetite for it and a good paycheck to boot. (I know of one prominent false teacher of the blood moons error who, when confronted as to why he does not write books or speak about the more orthodox features of God's prophetic Word actually replied, "It wouldn't sell". Well, he should get some points for a moment of honesty, I suppose.) And largely due to the more recent inventions of the Internet and social media, although many of these false cries have been around, they are increasing with each new round exactly in the character of "*birth pangs*". Yes, we can find approximate parallels in history past, but such were never propelled by an Internet-driven mass media which can propagate a lie or deception to every person on the planet in well under 24 hours. No previous generation experienced the intensity of birth pangs which is currently taking place.

But there has arisen yet another extreme in this area from within Christian academia based on an aggressive application of what is referred to in academic circles as the "Doctrine of Imminency". In its simplest form, it is an acknowledgment that we should expect that Jesus can return at any time, which is certainly something stated in Scripture. But what some prominent personalities have done is to take this to such an extreme that they claim there is no "trigger" for the Rapture. This is their way of attempting to make a case, contrary to Christ's plain teaching to the contrary, that there will be no warning signs whatsoever so that a "secret" Rapture takes everyone completely and totally by surprise. The problem is that many of them have now gone so far as to dogmatically declare that nothing we have witnessed nor is taking place now is a "sign" of the nearness of Jesus' return. On one extreme there are the false declarations seeing practically everything as a prophetic fulfillment, but at the same time is the opposite notion that nothing is currently being fulfilled and equally loud calls to ignore it all.

In the previous example we have those who are making up and presenting false signs, here we have those suppressing and dismissing the authentic signs. Their own false cries, "*The time is near!*" undermines everything Jesus teaches for believers to not be deceived by properly responding to the signs of His imminent Return. On the one end are "Chicken Little" fanatics declaring anything and everything as a sign that "*the end is near*", and on the other equally impassioned pleas to ignore everything, even the actual signs which Jesus Himself presented. In all cases, heed Christ's direct admonition, "*Do not go after them*".

The bottom line here is that Jesus' warning is to maintain a watch list based on the signs and events He gives, not the ones which false teachers will attempt to substitute or dismiss. In the past few years there seems to be an industry rising out of publishing regular "prophecy updates" which loves to assign some vague prophetic End Times fulfillment to any and every evil thing happening in the world; such clouds what is actually important by weekly announcing, "*The time is near!*" Satan does not want us reading and applying Scripture in the first place, but when he cannot accomplish that, his next preference is to offer a counterfeit in the name of misapplying and misinterpreting God's given Word. We are specifically and directly warned, "*Do not go after them*". (Lk. 21:8)

Wars & Disturbances

The second caveat is to not be frightened, but to have faith that God is in control, knowing that things are unfolding precisely according to His plan. Here, too, it is revealing when we compare the Gospel accounts, because while we most often quote from memory that there will be "*wars and rumors of wars*" (Mt. 24:6; Mk. 13:7), we rarely include the additional mention in Luke 21:9 of "*and disturbances*".

⁶You will be hearing of wars	⁷When you hear of wars	⁹When you hear of wars
and rumors of wars.		and rumors of wars,
and disturbances,		
See that you are not frightened, for those things must take place, but that is not yet the end. (Mt. 24:6)	do not be frightened; those things must take place; but that is not yet the end. (Mk. 13:7)	do not be terrified; for these things must take place first, but the end does not follow immediately." (Lk. 21:9)

Whereas we are told to anticipate *"wars"*—*"polemous"* (Strong's #4171), and *"rumors of wars"*—*"akoas polemon"* (Strong's #189), *"disturbances"*—*"akatastasias"* (Strong's #181) is an additional, distinct category describing commotion, tumult, disorder and confusion. This sign might be even more revealing to us at present because not just within the traditional walls of Christianity, but even among secular social and political observers there is a near universal acknowledgment that there seems to be a worldwide lack of leadership and general societal breakdown creating a tumult, disorder and confusion on an historic scale as never before experienced.

In America alone, the office of the President seems to be gripped with irrationality, the Congress is paralyzed within itself, the judicial system has taken to legislating from the bench, stances on moral issues no longer sharply divide people who go to church and those who do not, and that is just the tip of the proverbial iceberg as this pattern replays itself across the globe. This issue of anticipating there will not just be wars and rumors of wars, but disturbances, reminds us of the admonition by the writer of Hebrew that everything will be shaken.

> ²⁵See to it that you do not refuse Him who is speaking. For if those did not escape when they refused him who warned them on earth, much less will we escape who turn away from Him who warns from heaven. ²⁶And His voice shook the earth then, but now He has promised, saying, "YET ONCE MORE I WILL SHAKE NOT ONLY THE EARTH, BUT ALSO THE HEAVEN." ²⁷This expression, "Yet once more," denotes **the removing of those things which can be shaken, as of created things, so that those things which cannot be shaken may remain.** ²⁸Therefore, since we receive a kingdom which cannot be shaken, let us show gratitude, by which we may offer to God an acceptable service with reverence and awe; ²⁹for our God is a consuming fire. (Hebrews 12:25–29)

It would appear that while the primary purpose of the *"birth pangs"* is to alert the biblically faithful, a supplemental important function where the entire world is concerned is to begin to shake things up so as to loosen what is not going to survive the unprecedented events to come.

The Nature of the "Birth Pangs"

But then in warning us specifically that these things are not the end, but merely presage the greater things still to come, we are provided with a list which details the exact character and nature of the *"birth pangs"* in this preliminary, opening period:

➤ *"...nation will rise against nation..."*

➤ *"...kingdom against kingdom..."*

➤ *"...earthquakes in various places..."*

➤ *"...in various places plagues..."*

➤ *"...in various places there will be famines..."*

➤ *"...terrors and great signs from heaven."*

All these *"birth pangs"* can be summarized "wars, rumors of war and disturbances". The *"disturbances"* are not just limited to earthquakes, plagues and famines, which are occurrences commonly taking place to disrupt and disturb what is taking place on the earth and in nature, but *"terrors and great signs from heaven"* representing disturbances coming from above.

We live at a time when not only are UFO sightings increasing in relationship to all manner of extra-terrestrial claims, but government funding of detection and destruction of inbound meteors and comets is no longer a movie plot line. Additional research is being expended on the scenario of solar flares anticipated to eventually come which have the potential to globally destroy the ability to produce electricity, literally sending the planet back to the dark ages. The *"birth pangs"* seem to not just be coming in increasingly powerful and more concentric waves where the earth below is concerned, but the heavens above as well. And at present, we seem to be more aware of many more potential occurrences within these categories than any past generation.

One of the things to note about this list is that these are the same kinds of things recorded in the Old Testament as being used by God to render judgment on earth in order to first and foremost provoke repentance and a spiritual return to Him, but to also warn that failing to do so would inevitably lead to experiencing the wrath of final judgment. For instance, these are the same things God used to warn both Israel and Judah while they still had a chance to repent, before proceeding with the wrath of His final judgment by even greater events destroying the land, the Temple and Jerusalem as they were given into the Babylonian Captivity. God used the same things to shake up His people which were in turn used to shake up and ultimately judge the Gentile nations opposing them for their respective spiritual failures. According to Jesus, we are to expect that these *"birth pangs"* of judgment, in tandem with a time of increasing deception, will prefigure and point to the end to come. And we are to anticipate they will unfold with ever-increasing frequency and strength. As physical calamities increase, so will their parallel spiritual counterparts.

However, Jesus specifies a caveat to put all of this into the proper context: *"These things are merely **the beginning**"*. It can be argued that we are already in that period, where events since the early 20th century have been fulfilling these obstetric waves whether it be WWI, WWII, the re-establishment of the state of Israel, the recapturing of Jerusalem, or a number of other such things in the character of *"birth pangs"* coming ever more frequently with greater and greater intensity. (The steady increase in earthquakes alone as charted by secular agencies over the past one hundred years is interesting in its own right.) However, the Olivet Discourse does not constrain these things as having to take place within a final seven year period, but rather characterizes a much broader span with no single, clearly recognizable starting point. But in the character of *"birth pangs"*, each round is more intense than the last and coming with ever-increasing frequency, even though there may be periods of respite between, and actually taking place over a period much longer than seven years. Again, *"These things are **merely** the beginning"*.

It fades in like "birth pangs"...

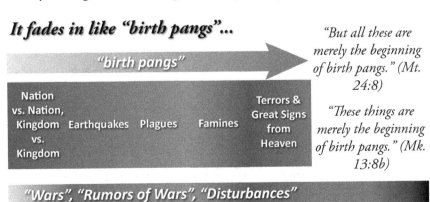

"But all these are merely the beginning of birth pangs." (Mt. 24:8)

"These things are merely the beginning of birth pangs." (Mk. 13:8b)

It may be an important point to keep in mind that for the more than thirty years in the First Coming prior to Jesus' public ministry of three-and-a-half years initiated by His baptism, that ~14% of the more than 325 Old Testament prophecies concerning His earthly ministry were fulfilled. In other words, there was a period of prophetic fulfillment much longer than seven years leading up to that final three-and-a-half year period when everything finally became plainly and overtly public for everyone to see.

"Tribulation"

⁹"Then they will deliver you to tribulation, and will kill you, and you will be hated by all nations because of My name.

⁹"But be on your guard; for they will deliver you to the courts, and you will be flogged in the synagogues, and you will stand before governors and kings for My sake, as a testimony to them.	¹²"But before all these things, they will lay their hands on you and will persecute you, delivering you to the synagogues and prisons, bringing you before kings and governors for My name's sake.
¹¹When they arrest you and hand you over, do not worry beforehand about what you are to say,	¹³It will lead to an opportunity for your testimony. ¹⁴So make up your minds not to prepare beforehand to defend yourselves;

but say whatever is given you in that hour; for it is not you who speak, but it is the Holy Spirit.

¹⁵for I will give you utterance and wisdom which none of your opponents will be able to resist or refute.

¹⁰At that time many will fall away and will betray one another and hate one another.

¹²Brother will betray brother to death, and a father his child; and children will rise up against parents and have them put to death. ¹³You will be hated by all	¹⁶But you will be betrayed even by parents and brothers and relatives and friends, and they will put some of you to death, ¹⁷and you will be hated by all
because of My name,	because of My name.

¹⁸Yet not a hair of your head will perish.

¹¹Many false prophets will arise and will mislead many.

¹²Because lawlessness is increased, most people's love will grow cold.

¹³But the one who endures to the end, he will be saved.	but the one who endures to the end, he will be saved.	¹⁹By your endurance you will gain your lives. (Lk. 21:12-19)
¹⁴This gospel of the kingdom shall be preached in the whole world as a testimony to all the nations, and then the end will come. (Mt. 24:10-14)	¹⁰The gospel must first be preached to all the nations. (Mk. 13:9-10)	

While the *"birth pangs"* describe earthly judgments which will affect everyone alike, both believer and non-believer, there are additional events which are specific to just believers: persecution and apostasy. And what is particularly revealing is that while the *"birth pangs"* describe severe elements putting the whole world through ever-increasing and more intense anguish, affliction and distress, it would appear that the world will deal with it by in turn heaping it on the Church directly when "**they** will deliver **you** to tribulation". (Mt. 24:9)

It is important to note that the events mentioned as belonging to *"tribulation"* no longer involve signs in the natural realm such as wars, famines or earthquakes, but are all focused attacks with a spiritual agenda beginning with the persecution of believers. And although deception will equally effect everyone regardless of their spiritual state, the overwhelming emphasis of this time of *"tribulation"* is the pressure it brings to bear on believers and the call for them to not just endure deception, apostasy and persecution, but to continue to preach the Gospel. This will in turn induce unparalleled turmoil within the Church when, *"At that time many will fall away and betray one another and hate one another"*. Historically unrivaled deception, apostasy and persecution are the chief characteristics of this period of *"tribulation"*.

It may seem overly nitpicky to strictly espouse Scripture's narrow definition of *"tribulation"* as being contrary to its manmade misapplication such as when the final seven years of the eschaton is universally called *"The* Tribulation", but we must recognize what has actually taken place. A term which Christ used to exclusively apply to a specific phase for something which is experienced by the Church alone has been reassigned a meaning as applying to the whole world and the unsaved alike. In reality, nothing Jesus specifies as taking place during *"tribulation"* is experienced by the world at large, but it is rather a period when the world's actions are exclusively directed toward the goal of permanently eliminating and silencing the Church. (Just as at the end of Christ's 3-1/2 year ministry they tried to permanently eliminate and therefore silence Christ, so it will be visited upon His Bride in her final hours.) The list of the associated features of what Christ calls *"tribulation"* is exclusive to what the Church will experience. Well-meaning or not, we have taken something out of its original context and applied it to something never intended, and it ends up producing tangible errors downstream, so to speak, and inserts a new meaning in place of Christ's. Instead of being prepared to deal with the coming "*tribulation*", Christians are being falsely told they will be exempt from it.

A brief review of a concordance's list of the uses of "*tribulation*" will show that it is a term which is rarely used to describe something experienced by non-believers, but is exclusively applied to believer's alone, such as in Christ's statement, "*In the world you have tribulation*". (Jn. 16:33) The five uses of the term by Paul all describe something exclusively experienced by believers alone. (Rom.2:9; 5:3; 8:3; 12:12; 1 Th. 1:6) In the New Testament it is found 45 times in 43 verses, and that which the whole world will experience is qualified as "**great** *tribulation*", a term we will get to shortly.

[Note: It is ironic that Pre-Tribulationism, probably still the most popular eschatology held by the Western Church at this time, is dogmatic that the Church will not enter what they call "*The* Tribulation"—that is, the whole of the final seven years, and yet Christ in the Olivet Discourse plainly states that the very nature of the "*tribulation*" is a time of testing of the Church before it is raptured. This is an example of the effect of using a biblical term out of its original context. This additionally provides an explanation as to why so many of its adherents in recent years have come to teach that the Olivet Discourse has no application for the Church but for Israel alone after the Church is removed. Without this subtle redefinition of a single term so as to produce such a dramatic reinterpretation of Scripture, they cannot present their proposed exemption. However, we cannot move past the fact that the term "Pre-Tribulationism" is an oxymoron; the Church cannot leave before and escape from something which only the Church itself can experience.]

Jesus warned in general, and for every believer of every age or generation, that "...*in the world you have tribulation*..." (Jn. 16:33), the underlying Greek word being "*thlipsis*" (Strong's #2347). To gather a greater understanding of the meaning of the word, in Matthew 13:21 it is rendered "*affliction*", in John 16:21 as "*anguish*", in 1 Corinthians 7:28 as "*trouble*", and in Philippians 1:17 as "*distress*". The root word it comes from means to crush, press, compress, or squeeze. The point of this grammatical exercise is to remind us that none of the uses of the word "*tribulation*" in Scripture is directly referring to that final seven year period we most often hear referred to as "The Tribulation" with capital "T's"; Christ does not use it to refer to either the whole of the final seven years or to even one of its halves, but designates it as the chief characteristic of a specific phase coming with the onset of the "*birth pangs*" which is solely directed for a time at believers. While the "*birth pangs*" will most likely continue in parallel in the background, an even greater problem will be exclusively added and experienced by the Church.

The concept to grasp here is that while there is a period of intense anguish, affliction and distress which will come about as the expression of God's wrath poured out exclusively on the world and the kingdom of the Antichrist, prior to that is a specific period of *"tribulation"* for believers coming with the onset of the *"birth pangs"*. Rather than being in the character of "wrath", *"birth pangs"* are best understood as "judgment" which is experienced by believer and non-believer alike. But when Jesus refers to the *"birth pangs"* giving way to *"tribulation"*, note that this period is characterized by a different set of signs. *"Birth pangs"* involve the earthly signs of wars, disturbances, plagues, famines, earthquakes and visible heavenly signs, while *"tribulation"* consists of the spiritual agenda of deception and apostasy and the physical effect of persecution, but borne exclusively by the believer. Nothing Jesus mentions pertaining to *"tribulation"* is aimed at the world, but rather it is the unsaved taking out its own wrath exclusively on the saved.

It is unfortunate that what Jesus is referring to in the Olivet Discourse has been so dogmatically attached as exclusively applying to the entirety of Daniel's 70th Week alone; this is not specifically stated and not the pattern of Scripture. (But because we do at present know the contents of Revelation, it probably has not eluded readers that the *"birth pangs"* and the sequence spoken of so far in the Olivet Discourse mirror each of the Seal judgments in Revelation 6, something we will specifically visit.)

"It Begins With Us First"

¹⁷For it is time for judgment to begin with the household of God; and if it begins with us first, what will be the outcome for those who do not obey the gospel of God? (1 Peter 4:17)

This might be the best way to understand why there is a period of intensifying tribulation experienced by the Church followed by a separate, far more intense "wrath of God" to come upon the world. Peter expresses a concept which is found repeatedly throughout Scripture that judgment begins with the house of God first before it is applied to the world at large. (Think of the example of Jesus first cleaning out the Temple.) But in addition to the obstetric character of wars, rumors of wars, disturbances, earthquakes, plagues, famines and cosmological signs, for members of the Body of Christ there is going to be an escalation to tribulation accompanied by the additional sign of our very public persecution:

➤ *"...**they** will deliver **you** to the **courts**..."*

➤ *"...**you** will be flogged in the **synagogues**..."*

➤ *"...delivering **you** to...the **prisons**..."*

➤ *"...bringing **you** before **kings** and **governors**..."*

Notice that it is not just persecution by governments, but the judicial system; and it is not solely experienced at the hands of earthly institutions alone, but the inclusion of *"synagogues"* describes those claiming some kind of heritage to God and those who may have at one time been devoted to Christ turning against His true followers. For quite some time, the Early Church continued to use synagogues as their primary meeting spot, and it was not just the Romans or Gentile governments who persecuted early Christians, but very often non-believing Jews from those shared facilities of worship. For a number of years now, in the United States, the number of believers leaving traditional denominations to form their own churches and fellowships has numbered in the millions, and their persecution by the very ones they have separated from has increased exponentially.

But just as we were previously admonished not to fear when we see the activities of the *"birth pangs"* ever-increasingly unfold, knowing that these things were divinely foreordained and ultimately in God's control, likewise for this period of *"tribulation"* of the true followers of Christ; even this comes about by His appointment and for His purpose. We are again told, *"...do not worry beforehand what you are to say"* (Mt. 24:11) and assured that *"it will lead to an opportunity for your testimony"*. (Lk. 21:13)

If we truly understand that the judgments being replayed by the *"birth pangs"* are the same ones God historically used to motivate repentance and a spiritual return to Him before that opportunity is lost forever, then this parallel *"tribulation"* for the Body of Christ can be seen as the chief agent of that greater purpose. While on the one hand the physical calamities of the *"birth pangs"* are testifying to the world's need for acceptance of Christ as Lord and Savior, on the other is the coinciding supporting testimony and visible witness of the Church in its tribulation as they are publicly persecuted and brought to the foreground of all that is taking place. This worldwide testimony of the Gospel will have a supernatural impact because we are promised, *"I will give you utterance and wisdom which none of your opponents will be able to resist or refute,"* (Lk. 21:15) and the end result will be, *"This gospel of the kingdom shall be preached in the whole world as a testimony to all the nations"*. (Mt. 24:14) However, what is here promised is that the Gospel will finally reach *"the whole world"*, not a guarantee that it will be accepted by the whole world.

Many seem to believe that the Church will not finish all that Jesus instructed in Acts 1:8 to *"be My witnesses...even to the remotest part of the earth"* and therefore introduce scenarios where someone else accomplishes this mission. The most popularly proposed candidates to resolve this alleged "failure" are the Two Witnesses or the 144,000 sealed Jews, neither of which is mentioned in Scripture for the first time until provided in Revelation, and even then without a syllable of text supporting such a role. This is often put forth because they see the end goal as reaching everyone on earth and Jesus' command for the Church to deliver the message to everyone as falling short and needing to be finished by someone else after the Church is removed, or sometimes that one of the reasons for the Rapture **IS** this perceived failure of the Church where the Gospel is concerned.

The plain text of Christ's instructions, however, provides that the Gospel will be *"preached in the whole world as a testimony"*, realizing it is every individual's choice as to what to do with it. This time of *"tribulation"* is going to allow the Church to fulfill Christ's command where preaching the Gospel is concerned, albeit as it gets progressively darker and darker spiritually. And exegetically speaking, this is what the Early Church would have embraced as axiomatic, incapable of even making the modern-day connection to something yet to come in Revelation in the way of either the Two Witnesses or the 144,000 sealed. (Again, in modern times, the order gets reversed so that the latter is allowed to override the former.)

Just as the persecutions of the first generation of the Early Church by the Roman Empire actually provided the opportunity for the Gospel to be preached and received by a far greater audience than ordinarily possible, so this will be replayed yet again, but with an even greater efficacy to the entire planet. But when it is falsely taught that a revival yet to come does not take place until after the Church's removal, such directly contradicts Christ's explicit teaching that this is actually a key indicator that the Rapture is about to take place. Such a false notion reverses the order so as to render Christians ineffective while there is still time and before it becomes too dark to work.

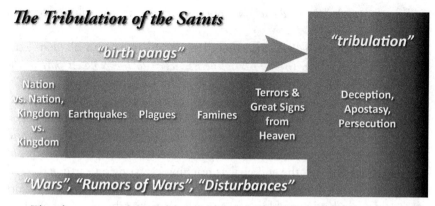

The Tribulation of the Saints

"birth pangs" → "tribulation"

Nation vs. Nation, Kingdom vs. Kingdom — Earthquakes — Plagues — Famines — Terrors & Great Signs from Heaven — Deception, Apostasy, Persecution

"Wars", "Rumors of Wars", "Disturbances"

The obstetric model of increasing signs of judgment in the earthly realm experienced by everyone gives way to a period of "*tribulation*" exclusively brought upon the Church, or at most continues in the background in parallel. It does not encompass the entire final seven years of the eschaton, nor even fully span its first half as popularly taught. It is a period of unprecedented deception, apostasy and especially persecution heaped on the saints by the unsaved. This will not merely refine the Church spiritually, but will also result in the unprecedented accomplishment of the Gospel reaching the ears of the entire planet.

It is worth noting that this is not entirely without precedent. Before the final plagues of the Exodus Narrative, which are obviously replayed again in the Last Days, there was a preceding period of intense persecution of God's people which actually served to prepare them for what was to come. (Ex. 5-6)

5 ❖ "The Great Tribulation"

> ²⁰"But when you see Jerusalem surrounded by armies, then recognize that her desolation is near.

¹⁵"Therefore when you see the ABOMINATION OF DESOLATION which was spoken of through Daniel the prophet, standing in the holy place (let the reader understand),	¹⁴"But when you see the ABOMINATION OF DESOLATION standing where it should not be (let the reader understand),

¹⁶Then those who are in Judea must flee to the mountains.	then those who are in Judea must flee to the mountains.	²¹"Then those who are in Judea must flee to the mountains,

¹⁷Whoever is on the housetop must not go down to get the things out that are in his house.	¹⁵The one who is on the housetop must not go down, or go in to get anything out of his house;
¹⁸Whoever is in the field must not turn back to get his cloak. (Mt. 24:15-18)	¹⁶and the one who is in the field must not turn back to get his coat. (Mk. 13:14-16

> and those who are in the midst of the city must leave, and those who are in the country must not enter the city;

> ²²because these are days of vengeance, so that all things which are written will be fulfilled. (Lk. 24:20-22)

Now we have moved from the Church's "thlipsis" (Strong's #2347)—or "tribulation", to Jerusalem's "eremosis" (Strong's #205)— "desolation", along with an "eremosis" to likewise take place in the Temple, which are critical elements of what is now identified as the next phase labelled "megale thlipsis", (Strong's #3173) or "great tribulation". (Mt. 24:21)

It is no doubt significant that just prior to giving the Olivet Discourse, Jesus specifically predicts the *"eremosis"*—the *"desolation"* of Jerusalem in an exchange with the Pharisees:

> ³⁷*"Jerusalem, Jerusalem, who kills the prophets and stones those who are sent to her! How often I wanted to gather your children together, the way a hen gathers her chicks under her wings, and you were unwilling.* ³⁸**Behold, your house is being left to you desolate!** ³⁹*For I say to you, from now on you will not see Me until you say, 'BLESSED IS HE WHO COMES IN THE NAME OF THE LORD!'" (Matthew 23:37–39)*

There are those who argue that at least this part of the Olivet Discourse has already been fulfilled by the destruction of both Jerusalem and the Temple by the Romans in 70 AD and that there is no further, outstanding or unrealized fulfillment. There are others who assert that because some of the details associated with this event were not witnessed in the course of what took place in 70 AD that this proves it was not a fulfillment on any level and speaks only of events yet to come. However, this is yet another example of prophecy working as pattern and fulfillment, and what took place in 70 AD is a partial fulfillment which teaches something about the final, ultimate one to come, which is confirmed by Jesus' prediction quoted in Matthew 23. The events which Jerusalem and the First Temple experienced at the hands of the Babylonians in 586 BC were again experienced at the hands of the Romans in 70 AD, and will ultimately occur a final time in the course of the eschaton. Rather than cancel each other out, they complement our understanding of the final one to come.

> ⁴¹*When He approached Jerusalem, He saw the city and wept over it,* ⁴²*saying, "If you had known in this day, even you, the things which make for peace! But now they have been hidden from your eyes.* ⁴³*For the days will come upon you when your enemies will throw up a barricade against you, and surround you and hem you in on every side,* ⁴⁴*and they will level you to the ground and your children within you, and they will not leave in you one stone upon another, **because you did not recognize the time of your visitation**." (Luke 19:41–44)*

Jesus is obviously and unambiguously speaking to the generation of His time who repudiated Him and specifically addressing the consequences of that rejection. We cannot deny that much of what is spoken of in both Matthew 23 and Luke 19 literally took place, but must equally recognize those elements which did not experience historical fulfillment. History records that when

Simeon, then leader of the Church in Jerusalem, recognized the temporary withdrawal of the Roman armies attacking Jerusalem and led the Christians out of Jerusalem and into the Jordanian wilderness before the final onslaught, there is no doubt that he was responding to this prediction by Christ of what was specifically going to happen to Jerusalem. By following Jesus' admonition to flee Jerusalem when it was surrounded by Gentile armies, Simeon saved the lives of the Jerusalem Christians at that time, yet it foreshadows a final similar event with these same characteristics yet to come.

In tandem with a military encirclement of Jerusalem, however, what is also stipulated here is the parallel occurrence of the Abomination of Desolation. Every Jew at this time, whether or not they were a Christian, understood exactly what the Abomination of Desolation was because of its previous fulfillments both by Antiochus Epiphanes IV in the Hasmonean Period per Daniel 11, and the actions of the Roman General Pompey about a hundred years after that. In particular, the Maccabean Revolt which defeated Epiphanes IV and retook the Temple is at the center of what is celebrated within Judaism as Hanukkah even to this day. Jesus Himself would have had to have been aware of this as He likewise celebrated the anniversary of this event in John 10, what at that time was called "*the feast of dedication*".

It is worth mentioning that in the course of events in 70 AD, one of the ways we know this was not the literal, final fulfillment of these things is that the order was reversed. The armies circled Jerusalem, the Christians fled during a temporary Roman cease fire, but it was only after the destruction took place and much later that a temple to Jupiter was erected on that site and another Abomination of Desolation in a series of same took place. In other words, the instructions in the Olivet Discourse are to flee upon witnessing the Abomination take place, but it did not occur in that order in 70 AD.

What is also worth mentioning at this point is that the admonition, "*let the reader understand*" specifically directs attention to the overall writings of the Prophet Daniel, who provided more details concerning the Antichrist and his associated activities than were restated by Jesus. It is a challenge by Jesus to investigate the Word of God further where more details and information about them can be found.

> [26] "*Then after the sixty-two weeks the Messiah will be cut off and have nothing, and the people of the prince who is to come will destroy the city and the sanctuary. And its end will come with a flood; even to the end there will be war; desolations are determined.* [27] *And* **he will make a firm covenant with the many for one week, but in the middle of the week he will put a stop to sacrifice and grain offering; and on the wing of abominations will come one who makes desolate,** *even until a*

complete destruction, one that is decreed, is poured out on the
one who makes desolate." (Daniel 9:26–27)

Daniel specifically speaks of a window of a final week of years in which these things are going to take place, and that the seven year clock starts ticking when the Antichrist makes a seven year treaty—*"a firm covenant"* with Israel. *"But in the middle of the week"*—at the half-way point in this final seven year period which coincides with the length of the treaty, the Abomination of Desolation takes place. God's wrath then follows to bring about the same kind of destruction and desolation upon the Antichrist which he himself inflicts. Neither Jesus nor any of the New Testament writers mention the covenant as the starting point, but rather begin with what will unambiguously take place *"in the middle of the week"* when Scripture states the agreement will be broken by the Abomination of Desolation.

This also conforms to that which Daniel emphasizes concerning the 70th Week. Although he provides the milestone of the treaty as the starting point, the overwhelming emphasis he expounds is on the second half initiated by the Abomination of Desolation. In other words, Jesus, Paul and Daniel (and as will be seen later with John in Revelation) purposely place the most importance on the second half of the 70th Week. There is a manmade overemphasis on the "seven" which distracts away from Christ's focus on the "three-and-a-half".

The Precedence of the New Over the Old

A principle of biblical exegesis which is fully endorsed here is that the New Testament takes precedence over the Old. For instance, the Gog and Magog scenario detailed in Ezekiel 38-39 is not the same one described in Revelation 20; therefore the priority is on the final one provided in Revelation 20, and the one offered in Ezekiel 38-39, while it may be a pattern or precursor teaching something about the final one to come, does not have the weight and importance of the New Testament occurrence. It is most likely a "shadow" which on a smaller scale prefigures and teaches about the ultimate, worldwide fulfillment.

It has been observed that just as there are many antichrists to disguise the final Antichrist, many false prophets to disguise the final False Prophet, and many Babylons and Abominations to disguise the final ones, so we have already seen many treaties which may be part of Satan's ploy to try and disguise the final fulfillment of this one as well. (Recently, at the time of this writing, it was revealed that the Pope entered into a treaty with the Palestinians which no one publicly knew about for the past two years. This is not the treaty, but an example of how it is possible to not really know the beginning of such a thing except in hindsight.) Nevertheless, the scriptural admonition which can be applied to all these things is that Holy Spirit-filled, Bible-immersed Christians are not to be deceived by the "many" counterfeits attempting to deceive us, but to recognize the final, authentic ones according to God's Word alone.

Of course, this may also be an obvious extension of the teaching that we cannot know the day or hour of His Return in that we will not automatically recognize this treaty's enactment. After all, there have already been many treaties—the Oslo Accords, the Camp David Accord, a little known proposal by the Clinton administration which actually contained a provision for the Temple Mount, and many different peace initiatives proposed by various parties up to this very hour—which all probably serve to disguise the final, authentic one to come, just as there are many antichrists and false prophets to camouflage the final Antichrist and False Prophet. But in spite of the fact that the only scriptural statement defining the start of this final 70th Week is the institution of this treaty, it is the repeated assertion of the majority of scholars and authors that the 1st Seal of Revelation (Rev. 6:1) is the metaphorical starter's pistol.

If we go back to the Google image search for "tribulation chart" spoken of earlier, it is not only difficult to find a graphical timeline which does not assign the 1st Seal as the starting point of the final seven years, but we will find that a large number of them do not even mention Daniel's treaty; they place all the emphasis on Revelation, and particularly the Seals. This in itself is proof of reversing the order of Scripture and using Revelation to cancel out, or at least mute or demote, what came before it.

All that being said, there is a much more important point of discussion being revealed here which many would rather obfuscate by either redirecting our attention to Revelation away from the Olivet Discourse, or by making the extreme assertion that the Olivet Discourse has no application at all for the Church but only for Israel after the Church's removal by the Rapture, and that is the fact that this clearly shows that the Church is present and goes into the final seven years, however one chooses to define it. There is no seven year period explicitly stated in the Olivet Discourse, and even if it was implied by the Early Church based on their reading of Daniel, it would be obvious to them that they would experience at least part of it because the Abomination of Desolation does not take place until the 70th Week's midway point.

A staple of Pre-Tribulationism is that the Rapture, by their account, must take place entirely before the whole of what they call the final seven year Tribulation, and therefore the Church will not be present to experience any of the events assigned to take place within the boundaries of those seven years. This is why there are extreme Pre-Tribulationists who insist that the Olivet Discourse does not apply to the Church, because it plainly and overtly conflicts with this assumption.

But we cannot ignore the historical fact that for more than sixty years, the Olivet Discourse was the all-sufficient eschatology for Christ's Return where the Early Church was concerned—both Jew and Gentile believers alike, and that they had no expectation of being exempted from the whole of Daniel's 70th Week. We can even go so far as to state that in order to prove that the very first believers held to a "Pre-Tribulational" eschatology, it would have to be proven from the Olivet Discourse alone, because that was the primary teaching given them. And yet many of that position's teachers take the contrarian view that the Olivet Discourse does not apply to the Church! Such antagonists are disproven by the historical timeline.

Because of Jesus' unambiguous statement that they would witness the Abomination of Desolation—the very event defining the precise middle of Daniel's 70th Week, the Early Church had every reason to believe they would enter into and experience it. In fact, they expected to experience the *"birth pangs"*, unprecedented persecution and apostasy in the *"tribulation"* phase, and witness the unveiling of the Antichrist before having to themselves flee from it all in anticipation of the onset of the fulfillment of God's whole prophetic Word, a sequence Paul would later affirm in 2 Thessalonians 2. This is because they understood the difference between *"thlipsis"*—*"tribulation"*, and *"orge"*—God's *"wrath"*, which at present seems to elude many.

Not Since the Beginning

19"But woe to those who are pregnant and to those who are nursing babies in those days!	17"But woe to those who are pregnant and to those who are nursing babies in those days!	23"Woe to those who are pregnant and to those who are nursing babies in those days;
20But pray that your flight will not be in the winter, or on a Sabbath.	18But pray that it may not happen in the winter.	
21For then there will be a great tribulation,	19For those days will be a time of tribulation	for there will be great distress
such as has not occurred since the beginning of the world until now, nor ever will.	such as has not occurred since the beginning of the creation which God created until now, and never will.	

upon the land	
and wrath to this people;	
²⁴and they will fall by the edge of the sword, and will be led captive into all the nations; and Jerusalem will be trampled under foot by the Gentiles until the times of the Gentiles are fulfilled. (Lk. 21:23-24)	
²²Unless those days had been cut short, no life would have been saved; but for the sake of the elect those days will be cut short. (Mt. 24:19-22)	²⁰Unless the Lord had shortened those days, no life would have been saved; but for the sake of the elect, whom He chose, He shortened the days. (Mk. 13:17-20)

The initial caveat is that this flight specifically applies to "*those who are in Judea*" (Mt. 24:16; Mk. 13:14; Lk. 21:21) so that this obviously and literally applies to whoever is physically present in the land at this time. However, this is not a blanket endorsement that the Olivet Discourse as a whole is only for Israel and not for the Church. There may be a geographical constraint expressed here, but it is not limited to just ethnic Jews who happen to be living in the land at the time. It may even be argued that the specific designation of "Judea" rather than "Israel" restricts this to the area immediately in the vicinity of Jerusalem and not the whole country entirely. (But if you are actually close to the area when this happens, who would have the nerve to risk it?) But when this happens, both Jew and Christian alike would have enough scriptural light to recognize what is taking place and act accordingly.

It is understandable that in such a time of flight, persecution and turmoil, no one would want to be doubly burdened by the hardship of pregnancy or the hazards of inclement weather, but many have pointed to the added designation of "*or on a Sabbath*" (Mt. 24:20) as at the least puzzling, and at the most an indication that this is not for the Church but for Israel alone because of observance of the Sabbath.

Recently it has been aptly pointed out that even in modern-day Israel, having to take flight on that day of the week would be extremely problematic whether one is an adherent of Judaism or not, as the country tends to shut down on the Sabbath, particularly in the area of mass transportation upon which many are dependent. This was a huge problem in the course of the Maccabean Revolt because the rebels were often killed when they would not fight on a Sabbath. In other words, there is such a huge cultural issue when it comes to the Sabbath for anyone physically located in Israel, that it becomes a significant hindrance in and of itself, whether or not one is a practicing Jew; it affects everyone living there. It would be like saying to tourists vacationing in America, "Pray you don't have to drive on New Year's Eve" or "Good luck getting a camping reservation for the 4th of July". Whether or not you celebrate these holidays, the associated cultural activities and congestion produced affects everyone in the land regardless. Jesus may not be speaking of the Sabbath in terms of some kind of violation of a biblical commandment, but including it in a list of times of added difficulty such as pregnancy or severe weather.

But here we find another significant description of the specific nature of the "*great tribulation*" which sets it apart from all other "*tribulation*", in that "*those days will be a time of tribulation as has not occurred since the beginning of creation which God created until now, and never will*". (Mk. 13:19) In spite of how bad things were in 70 AD, they were much worse in the Bar-Kochba Revolt of 132-135 AD, even worse in subsequent persecutions such as the Spanish Inquisition in the 15th century, and worse still in the Holocaust of the Second World War. The point is that what took place in 70 AD could not be the ultimate fulfillment of what was predicted because many times since, much worse things have taken place. (And in the character of an increasing "birth pang".) Again, each are examples teaching something about what the ultimate, final fulfillment will be like, the last one being worse than any previous instance.

In the course of World War II it is estimated that a third of worldwide Jewry were killed, but Zechariah 13:8 stipulates there is yet a holocaust to come which will fully take two-thirds. As horrible and incomprehensible were the events we recently witnessed in World War II, they do not rise to the level of a far worse finale still to come. World War II numbers its casualties in the millions; by the end of the Seals and Trumpets alone the numbers are in the billions.

While even non-believing Jews of the 1st century would almost universally acknowledge that the destruction of Jerusalem and the Temple came about per the Old Testament prophecies such as those of Daniel, Christian Jews would affirm an additional endorsement as coming directly from Christ through the Olivet Discourse and preliminarily in His response to the Pharisees in Matthew 23. Paul's teachings on the temporary condition of Israel in Romans 9-11 would have provided a parallel affirmation of the Church's view that what would come about in 70 AD was by the will of the Lord, particularly what Paul taught concerning "*the fullness of the Gentiles*", but that the final end had still not arrived.

> *25For I do not want you, brethren, to be uninformed of this mystery—so that you will not be wise in your own estimation— that **a partial hardening has happened to Israel until the fullness of the Gentiles has come in**; (Romans 11:25)*

In the wake of 70 AD, the Early Church would most certainly have seen what took place as at least a partial fulfillment of what Christ here spoke in the Olivet Discourse.

The Amputation

The intensity of this final period cannot be underestimated, especially in the reference to having to be "*cut short*", or in Greek "*koloboo*" (Strong's #2856)—that is, "amputated", but also due to the additional reference, "*wrath to this people*". (Lk. 21:23) Whereas previous events can be characterized as judgments which God historically used for both believers and non-believers alike, an escalation to "*wrath*"—"*orge*" (Strong's #3709) in the Greek, indicates a radical change to come in this sequence of events, noting that Scripture specifies that although Christians may experience God's judgment, we do not experience God's wrath.

> 9*Much more then, having now been justified by His blood,* **we shall be saved from the wrath** *of God through Him. (Romans 5:9)*

> 9*For* **God has not destined us for wrath**, *but for obtaining salvation through our Lord Jesus Christ, (1 Thessalonians 5:9)*

However, once again we need to take note that nowhere are these events specified as having to span an entire 3-1/2 year period or "half" of a "seven". What is described takes place over a much shorter, more intense period of time and fulfills all the requirements of the "*great tribulation*" without having to be anchored to either a 7 or 3-1/2 year timespan. In fact, the "*birth pangs*" giving way to "*tribulation*" disqualifies this from being limited to a 3-1/2 year period, as well as the fact that the Church enters that period of "*great tribulation*" and for their sake divine intervention cuts it short. These terms are used in the Olivet Discourse to describe phases within the eschaton which are not assigned to either a seven year whole or as corresponding to the whole of either of its 3-1/2 year halves. They are the final and most powerful "*birth pangs*", so to speak, to come just before the "birth" event itself. However, because the milestone event of the exact middle of Daniel's 70th Week is also the defining event highlighted by Christ, we can see that like Daniel, Christ is placing the emphasis on the second half of that final seven years. (And when Revelation arrives, this is the same emphasis John provides with added details for the "*birth pangs*" leading up to it.)

In other words, for that first generation of believers expecting Jesus' Return to take place in accordance with the Olivet Discourse alone, and having no reference to Revelation and the seven year structure the modern-day Church places upon it, they would have taken the Olivet Discourse on face value as beginning with a longer period of "*birth pangs*" giving way to a specific phase of "*tribulation*" directed exclusively at the Church, which then sharply transitions to a much more intense period identified as "*great tribulation*" for the whole world initiated by the milestones of the Abomination of Desolation and the surrounding of Jerusalem. They would not have assigned these things either to an overall seven year period or the whole of one of its halves, and would have expected to personally experience them.

But again, because modern scholarship has removed "*great tribulation*" from its original context referring to a very short but specific phase initiating the second half of Daniel's 70th Week which actually has a defined beginning (the Abomination of Desolation) and ending (the Rapture), additional and even greater errors result. It is not uncommon to find it stated, "The first half is called 'Tribulation', but the more intense second half is called "Great Tribulation" when referring to Daniel's 70th Week. This is not at all the context or meaning of these terms, and as it turns out, this actually matters.

If Possible, Even the Elect

²³Then if anyone says to you, 'Behold, here is the Christ,' or 'There He is,' do not believe him. ²⁴For false Christs and false prophets will arise and will show great signs and wonders, so as to mislead, if possible, even the elect. ²⁵Behold, I have told you in advance.	²¹And then if anyone says to you, 'Behold, here is the Christ'; or, 'Behold He is there'; do not believe him; ²²for false Christs and false prophets will arise, and will show signs and wonders, in order to lead astray, if possible, the elect. ²³But take heed; behold, I have told you everything in advance. (Mk. 13:21-23)

²⁶So if they say to you, 'Behold, He is in the wilderness,' do not go out, or, 'Behold, He is in the inner rooms,' do not believe them. ²⁷For just as the lightning comes from the east and flashes even to the west, so will the coming of the Son of Man be. ²⁸Wherever the corpse is, there the vultures will gather. (Mt. 24:23-29)

Think of this section as a sort of overall recap to this point of the more important issues for believers in spite of all the events specifically identified so far. Jesus begins to incorporate what had been previously taught a few weeks earlier in Luke 17, and emphasizes that for Christians the more pressing danger does not come from the judgments of the *"birth pangs"*, the persecution, or even the onset of the final fulfillment of all things beginning with the Abomination of Desolation, but the greater issue of deception.

There are many who hold that the interpretation of *"if possible, even the elect"* means it is not possible, but the context and qualifier, *"Behold, I have told you in advance"* specifically reveals that this is a dire warning that it is possible. In fact, the ever-increasing apostasy and deception we are witnessing at present proves it is not just possible, not just likely, but already taking place.

In 1987, at my final Army posting at Ft. Hood, Texas with just a couple of weeks to go before being discharged, I was reading the personal ads in *The Dallas Morning News* and came across an entry announcing that Jesus was not only already here, but actually stated outright, "He is waiting for you in the inner room". Perhaps this was someone's idea of a joke, but it was nonetheless startling to see a very real and literal fulfillment of this warning. (And no, I did not call the number or go to see if it was true, as Jesus warned explicitly not to do that. I have yet to find a Scripture suggesting Jesus will first secretly return to a motel in Texas and I still wonder what He's been doing there in that room for nearly three decades aside from watching TV and having pizza delivered.)

While Jesus has been mainly answering the first part of the tripartite question put to Him, *"When will these things happen"*, (Mt. 24:3) this reminder of the greater danger of deception also seems to be serving as a transition for answering, *"and what will be the sign of Your coming"*? (Mt. 24:3)

It is sobering to ponder how at a time when God's judgments are at work through the ever-increasing frequency and intensity of the *"birth pangs"*, culminating in the visible rise and working of the Antichrist, the environment can be obscured by such spiritual deception that there will not only be a host of claims from false christs and false prophets alike, but an extensive working of false signs and wonders. But even at present one does not have to look any further than YouTube to see these very things already on display in order to begin to grasp the breadth of what is coming. If someone cannot discern the difference between the authentic and the counterfeit in the present climate when so much is outright faked or manufactured in Photoshop, what are the odds they will be able to turn it around when the ultimate Antichrist and False Prophet appear and begin to work real signs and wonders?

> [1]*"If a prophet or a dreamer of dreams arises among you and gives you a sign or a wonder, [2]**and the sign or the wonder comes true**, concerning which he spoke to you, saying, 'Let us go after other gods (whom you have not known) and let us*

> serve them,' ³you shall not listen to the words of that prophet
> or that dreamer of dreams; for the LORD your God is testing you
> to find out if you love the LORD your God with all your heart and
> with all your soul. ⁴You shall follow the LORD your God and fear
> Him; and you shall keep His commandments, listen to His voice,
> serve Him, and cling to Him. (Deuteronomy 13:1–4)

> ²²"When a prophet speaks in the name of the LORD, **if the
> thing does not come about or come true**, that is the thing
> which the LORD has not spoken. The prophet has spoken it
> presumptuously; you shall not be afraid of him. (Deuteronomy
> 18:22)

The spiritual depravity and moral decay of the times is portrayed as a dead and rotting corpse to which those of the earth, represented by the vultures, are attracted, and it seems that this already appears to be taking place, at least in its formative stages. But in the midst of this ever-growing spiritual darkness and among the intensifying *"birth pangs"* giving way to *"great tribulation"*, when Christ's coming for the Church itself takes place, it will occur *"just as the lightning comes from the east and flashes even to the west"*. This is what it means when Jesus says, *"Behold, I am coming quickly"*. (Rev. 22:7, 12) When it finally comes, it will take place quicker than we can grasp the flashing of lightning.

One way to explain that there is no conflict in knowing the "season" but not the "day", and likewise how Jesus is actually coming *"quickly"* in spite of witnessing a long, preceding period of the fulfillment of prophecy, is in how America was drawn into World War II. Although the specific attack on Pearl Harbor itself came as a surprise in 1941, the overall declaration of hostilities was seen to be coming for decades. The Japanese navy defeated Russia in a series of conflicts in 1904-1905, the conclusion of which was facilitated by the President of the United States' mediation, and military expansion ensued from that point on in ever greater ways for the next thirty-five years. Many pointed out the inevitable conflict which was coming between Japan and America, the most notable documented at the court martial of Colonel Billy Mitchell, who in 1924 not only predicted war with Japan, but specifically the attack on Pearl Harbor—some 17 years before it happened. In other words, there was a prolonged, visible environment in which hostilities escalated, so that although the day and the hour of the sneak attack on Pearl Harbor was not known, it nonetheless took place as expected against a backdrop of intensifying events, or "signs", leading up to it. When it finally happened, it was quick and devastating, but it was certainly not unanticipated. Although expected to come for decades, it still took everyone by surprise on a Sunday morning and was over in just a few hours, changing everything forever.

There are many historical examples like this which mimic the eschaton where the defining event came suddenly and could not have been precisely predicted, but was inevitably anticipated due to the prolonged and intensifying climate out of which it arose. A biblical example is Babylon falling in one night to the Medo-Persian Empire, or the sudden fall of Jericho after six previous days of warning, or Noah and his family entering the ark seven days before the rain and the 120 years before when God's declared that particular end. (Gen. 6:3) There was a period of inevitability leading up to them, but when it finally transpired it still took everyone by surprise.

It is worth mentioning again that while we will absolutely know the day and the hour of the end of Daniel's 70th Week, and that we will absolutely know the day and the hour of the half-way point, the beginning seems to be purposely cloaked. And we must understand that it is intentionally planned this way because ultimately this is not a test of knowledge, but faith. That being said, it would appear that the next phase identified by Jesus in the Olivet Discourse is probably the one End Times period which seems to be spoken of by more passages of Scripture than any other single item, when time runs out and all that is left is "*the day of the Lord*", but for which He spends the least amount of time because it the phase from which the Church is truly exempt.

But before this ultimate time of spiritual darkness comes upon the earth dwellers who are left behind, there is an intense but shortened parallel which everyone, the Church included, experiences which the Lord supernaturally cuts short. Again, this "*great tribulation*" is not the whole second half of Daniel's 70th Week, but the final phase shortly characterizing the very beginning of the final 3-1/2 years just prior to the Church's removal.

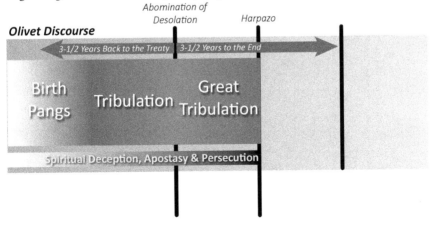

6 ❖ "The Day of the Lord"

There are seven main terms around which all eschatologies revolve: *Daniel's 70th Week, "tribulation", "great tribulation", "the times of the Gentiles", "the fullness of the Gentiles", and "the time of Jacob's trouble".* It is interesting to note that while they are all important, Daniel's 70th Week is only mentioned a handful of times, *"tribulation"* just a few, *"great tribulation"* even fewer, *"times of the Gentiles"* and *"fullness of the Gentiles"* but once each, *"the time of Jacob's Trouble"* also in a single instance, and yet no one would have enough time in the whole of their life to read all that has been written on those subjects. However, *"the day of the Lord"* is spoken of more than a couple dozen times within the context of more than a hundred verses accompanied by an enormous amount of supporting text. There is far more information given throughout Scripture about this particular feature than all the others combined, and yet this is the term on that list which most divides scholars, commentators and authors.

By just taking the Olivet Discourse on its face, this is the provided sequence:

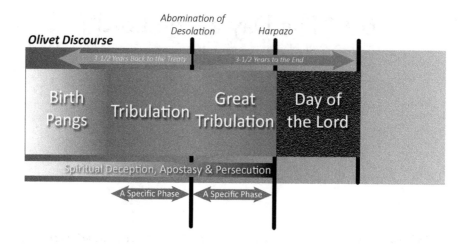

Immediately After

[29]"But immediately after the tribulation of those days	[24]"But in those days, after that tribulation,	
THE SUN WILL BE DARKENED, AND THE MOON WILL NOT GIVE ITS LIGHT, AND THE STARS WILL FALL from the sky,	THE SUN WILL BE DARKENED AND THE MOON WILL NOT GIVE ITS LIGHT, [25]AND THE STARS WILL BE FALLING from heaven,	[25]"There will be signs in sun and moon and stars,
and on the earth dismay among nations, in perplexity at the roaring of the sea and the waves, [26]men fainting from fear and the expectation of the things which are coming upon the world;		
and the powers of the heavens will be shaken. (Mt. 24:29)	and the powers that are in the heavens will be shaken. (Mk. 13:24-25)	for the powers of the heavens will be shaken. (Lk. 21:25-26)

This next milestone signals the end of that time particularly focused on the Church called "*tribulation*" giving way to the world's "*great tribulation*", and specifies that which will foretell of its imminent conclusion, at least where the Church is concerned. In the opening round of the "*birth pangs*" the signs were earthly events experienced by everyone on earth, and during the "*tribulation*" deception, apostasy and persecution comes upon the Church like never before accompanied by the opportunity to preach the Gospel and be a witness to the whole world. But after comes signs everyone will again experience coming from the heavenlies. This produces "*dismay*", "*perplexity*" and "*fear*" among non-believers because of their "*expectation of the things which are coming upon the world*". Everyone—both the saved and unsaved alike, albeit from different perspectives, see and respond in their own way to the signs of the times and know God is working, although from different viewpoints and opposing interpretations leading to opposite results. For the Christian it is an affirmation of the nearness of Christ's Return to remove and rescue them; for the non-believer it is the fear of the impending release of the wrath of God in a sequence of final judgment. Matthew and Mark quote just one of many Old Testament references which associates these signs with a time when all that is left is the outpouring of God's wrath known as "*the day of the Lord*", such being an announcement which is visible and experienced by everyone.

As stated, the most prolifically used and documented term concerning the End Times found throughout Scripture is "*the day of the Lord*". What is most interesting about the Old Testament quote recorded here is that these are signs which are repeated over and over again throughout God's Word and used most often in association with "*the day of the Lord*". Examples can be found in Isaiah 13:10, 24:23, Ezekiel 32:7, Joel 2:10, 31 and 3:15, Amos 5:20, 8:9, and Zephaniah 1:15, for instance, and we will see them affirmed yet again in Revelation. These cosmological signs in combination with a great shaking are commonly stipulated in Scripture as the events identifying the onset of "*the day of the Lord*", which is not a single twenty-four hour period, but a span or period of time when God's wrath is poured out. Think of it more as an announcement in the earthly realm of something impending to be released from the heavenly. These signs, repeatedly documented in Scripture, signal what is about to happen. This is that tipping point when the only thing which remains is to experience the wrath of His final judgment. Think of it in the character of the last sign of the Exodus when the angel of death came, and if the blood of the Passover lamb had not already been applied, it was too late to avoid the finality of the consequences.

This is a very important concept to grasp because the Early Church would have understood from the Olivet Discourse that there was a period of judgment which the Church would co-equally experience with the rest of the world in the "*birth pangs*", with the additional burden of unparalleled apostasy, deception and persecution coming on believers in the "*tribulation*", that everyone would then witness the unveiling of the Antichrist by way of the Abomination of Desolation and together experience "*great tribulation*", and finally would come the wrath of God, described by so many Scriptures as "*the day of the Lord*", something familiar to all Jews whether they were believers or not.

Foundational from the Outset

Additionally, the Early Church would have understood from Peter's "*kerygma*"—his Gospel message explaining on the Day of Pentecost the events taking place when the Holy Spirit was outpoured upon the Church, and Peter's citation of Joel therein, that "*the day of the Lord*" would definitively mark the end of the Church's time on earth.

> ¹⁴*But Peter, taking his stand with the eleven, raised his voice and declared to them: "Men of Judea and all you who live in Jerusalem, let this be known to you and give heed to my words.* ¹⁵*For these men are not drunk, as you suppose, for it is only the third hour of the day;* ¹⁶*but this is what was spoken of through the prophet Joel:*
>
> ¹⁷'AND IT SHALL BE IN THE LAST DAYS,' GOD SAYS,
> 'THAT I WILL POUR FORTH OF MY SPIRIT ON ALL MANKIND;
> AND YOUR SONS AND YOUR DAUGHTERS SHALL PROPHESY,
> AND YOUR YOUNG MEN SHALL SEE VISIONS,
> AND YOUR OLD MEN SHALL DREAM DREAMS;
> ¹⁸EVEN ON MY BONDSLAVES, BOTH MEN AND WOMEN,
> I WILL IN THOSE DAYS POUR FORTH OF MY SPIRIT
> AND THEY SHALL PROPHESY.
> ¹⁹AND I WILL GRANT WONDERS IN THE SKY ABOVE
> AND SIGNS ON THE EARTH BELOW,
> BLOOD, AND FIRE, AND VAPOR OF SMOKE.
> ²⁰THE SUN WILL BE TURNED INTO DARKNESS
> AND THE MOON INTO BLOOD,
> BEFORE THE GREAT AND GLORIOUS DAY OF THE LORD SHALL
>   COME.
> ²¹*And it shall be that everyone who calls on the name* OF
>   THE LORD WILL BE SAVED.' (Acts 2:17–21)

Peter is describing the beginning and ending limits of the entire Church Age. Wherein there have already been recorded untold numbers of believers who have experienced visions, prophecies and dreams—the outpouring of Christ's Spirit, Peter then describes things which are yet to come—the signs also cited in the Olivet Discourse which he specifies will transpire, "*Before the great and glorious day of the Lord shall come*". Just as Jesus tells the Apostles in the Olivet Discourse that these things will take place in the shadow of His Return, so Peter affirms the very same on Pentecost which should be expected to signal the transition from the Church Age, or what many call "The Age of Grace", to "*the day of the Lord*", as the anticipated final outpouring of God's wrath prefacing final judgment. Peter affirms what Jesus taught, that the Church is present up to the edge of that time when judgment turns into wrath, and it should not be glossed over that it was stated on the very first day of the Church.

Affirming this sequence may have been one of the primary reasons for Jesus' discourse prior to the Olivet Discourse in Luke 17. As discussed in *Chapter 3, Luke 17 & the Olivet Discourse*, Jesus corrects the Pharisees' notion that God's Kingdom will take over all the existing kingdoms of the earth in an uninterrupted conclusion to the work of the Messiah, and qualifies to the disciples that the *"kingdom"*—which is actually comprised of people, will be supernaturally removed. In other words, the old must be judged and destroyed so that those returning with Jesus will experience something completely new and spiritually pure. It replays the command to destroy all the wicked out of Canaan so God's people can occupy the Promised Land being rid of all the false spiritual influences.

It is also worth mentioning that this is the exact sequence the Apostle Paul provides and is why the Apostolic writings are continually characterized as a commentary on the Olivet Discourse, not just because Revelation did not exist at the time any of the Epistles were authored, but because this teaching of Jesus concerning the End Times was considered to be their primary road map, so to speak.

> *¹Now we request you, brethren, with regard to the coming of our Lord Jesus Christ and our gathering together to Him, ²that you not be quickly shaken from your composure or be disturbed either by a spirit or a message or a letter as if from us, to the effect that **the day of the Lord** has come. ³Let no one in any way deceive you, **for it will not come unless the apostasy comes first, and the man of lawlessness is revealed**, the son of destruction, ⁴who opposes and exalts himself above every so-called god or object of worship, so that he takes his seat in the temple of God, displaying himself as being God. (2 Thessalonians 2:1–4)*

But in general, what would have been understood from the Olivet Discourse is that as bad as the periods characterized as *"birth pangs"*, *"tribulation"* and *"great tribulation"* will be for believers, this will ultimately be followed by an unprecedented period which will be even far worse for non-believers, which was already described prolifically in Scripture as *"the day of the Lord"*. This is why some scholars divide Daniel's 70th Week into two halves, designating the first half as the "Tribulation" and the second half as the "Great Tribulation" in order to identify an escalation of intensity. This is truly part of the pattern, but in reality it is not so tightly tied to specific halves of a final seven year period as popularly presented, but rather more in the character of phases within the overall eschaton. They are actually short phases on either side of the Abomination of Desolation at the halfway point.

For present-day readers' sake, this is important to keep in mind in order to understand the Early Church's interpretation of Revelation. When we visit this in more detail to come, we will realize that the Seal judgments in Revelation parallel the phases in the Olivet Discourse of "*birth pangs*", "*tribulation*" and "*great tribulation*", and that "*the day of the Lord*" commences with the Trumpet judgments when God's wrath is poured out on those remaining. We will see this same sequence involving events of the very same description and character, but accompanied by even more detail. Revelation does not replace the Olivet Discourse (after all, Jesus provided both) but builds upon it.

Something many do, which cannot be found stated in Scripture and must therefore be superimposed upon it, is to say that "*the day of the Lord*" and Daniel's 70th Week are the exact same thing. By designating the entire seven year period as "*the day of the Lord*", everything therefore within it becomes "God's wrath". This is how they justify placing the *Harpazo* of the Church as occurring before that entire timespan and subsequently assert that none of these things will be experienced by the Church, who will also be absent in that scenario before the advent of the Antichrist. Unfortunately, such is clearly not what Jesus nor the Apostles taught. This is usually arrived at by those who prioritize Revelation over all other portions of prophecy, and often omit reference to the Olivet Discourse altogether. And such proponents never have a satisfying answer as to why, if it is all God's "wrath", that believers are martyred as the sole activity of the 5th Seal (Rev. 6:9-11), something which completely contradicts the very character and working of God Himself.

It Is No Secret

[30]And then the sign of the Son of Man will appear in the sky, and then all the tribes of the earth will mourn,

and they will see THE SON OF MAN COMING ON THE CLOUDS OF THE SKY with power and great glory.	[26]Then they will see THE SON OF MAN COMING IN THE CLOUDS with great power and glory.	[27]Then they will see THE SON OF MAN COMING IN A CLOUD with power and great glory.

[28]But when these things begin to take place, straighten up and lift up your heads, because your redemption is drawing near." (Lk. 21:27-28)

³¹And He will send forth His angels	²⁷And then He will send forth the angels,
with A GREAT TRUMPET	
and THEY WILL GATHER TOGETHER His elect from the four winds, from one end of the sky to the other. (Mt. 24:30-31)	and will gather together His elect from the four winds, from the farthest end of the earth to the farthest end of heaven. (Mk. 13:26-27)

Notice that the signs in the heavenlies prepare the stage for an even narrower set of cosmological signs specifically signaling the nearness of the *Harpazo*. For the believer it is a time to *"straighten up and lift up your heads, because your redemption is drawing near"*, but for the rest of mankind, *"then all the tribes of the earth will mourn"*. This is further scriptural proof that everyone will be aware from their own particular spiritual state and viewpoint that God is working, and that although the day and the hour of Christ's coming cannot be predicted, it nonetheless is presaged by obvious signs of its nearness and does not take place in secret or without no warning whatsoever.

What is usually portrayed in movies and animations when the Rapture is depicted is most often in the nature of a "secret" Rapture, something which occurs without warning and as a complete surprise to everyone, especially Christians who are the only ones who believe in it in the first place. A representative example is a popular YouTube video a church made showing several hundred people in attendance at a typical Sunday morning service when a loud thunder clap sound effect coincides with all but a handful of congregants instantly disappearing and the remaining few falling to their knees instantly in repentance. This is what is meant by a "secret" Rapture; it comes unexpectedly and without any warning whatsoever. Its proponents are often fond of saying there is no event or sign which will "trigger" the Rapture. This is a teaching which is based on only a hand-picked selection of verses which conveniently omits the whole counsel of God's Word on the subject, such as in this passage where there are signs in the sky and a trumpet sounding.

Granted, we cannot know the day or the hour in advance so as to predict the date, but Scripture actually states that there are both visible and audible signs signaling it is about to happen, much in the character of what took place at Jericho. They are so powerful that they are universally recognized by everyone on earth, believer and non-believer alike, and cause each to react accordingly, even if there is but a sliver of a timespan between these signs and the event; believers will look up in expectation that their *"redemption is drawing near"*, the rest *"will mourn"*. The one group will hear the trump of God as sounding the victory of their salvation, the other will hear it as their consignment to judgment. Although this may take place in very quick succession, it nonetheless is not "secret" and therefore completely unforeseen. It is, however, a "surprise" to the degree it will be a very happy one for believers, and the worst possible kind for non-believers, each acting accordingly as they simultaneously experience this visible and audible announcement of what is about to take place.

Jesus said the precedent for what is to come parallels that which transpired in the days of Noah and Lot. It would be difficult to make a case that either event came without any warnings or out of environments which gave no clue as to what was about to happen. For Noah, God originally narrowed it down from 120 years to just 7 days. (Gen. 6:3; 7:4) The precise day of the actual Flood in Noah's time or the hour of the Fire in Lot's may not have been predictable, but the inevitable nearness was unquestionable. Who, actually recognizing the signs of the times, would have been taken by complete surprise as if with no clue whatsoever? As it turns out, only the willfully ignorant.

It is important to note that the Greek word "*episunago*" (Strong's #1996) underlies the English "*gather*" in Matthew 24:31, which is derived from "*episunagoge*" the word *used* in Scripture to describe both the Raptured and Resurrected gathering together in the air to meet with Jesus. This is the same description Paul uses in 2 Thessalonians 2:1 for "*our **gathering** to Him*", and it is this very thing about which Paul dogmatically insists to not be deceived, because that gathering cannot occur before the apostasy first takes place followed by the revealing of the Antichrist. Paul is merely affirming what readers of the Olivet Discourse already knew from Jesus' teaching.

It is important to note that at this juncture, when Christ "*will send forth His angels*", that the harvest is exclusively comprised of "*His elect*"—the Church. There is no mention made of harvesting non-believers at this time because that is what is actually going to happen to them by their being left behind, the metaphorical chaff to be destroyed after the harvested crop is separated and removed. The Church experiences a "*harvest*" of salvation, the rest a "*harvest*" of judgment. (This will be overtly revisited in Revelation 14:14-20 as well when the harvest of the righteous removes them first while the wicked are left behind to experience their own harvest of wrath in the winepress of God.) Or as John the Baptist phrased it:

> [17]"*His winnowing fork is in His hand to thoroughly clear His threshing floor, and to gather the wheat into His barn; but He will burn up the chaff with unquenchable fire." (Luke 3:17)*

"*The day of the Lord*" is the time when the "*chaff*"—those left behind, experience the consequences of their choices. This is further textual proof that the Olivet Discourse is for the Church because the *Harpazo* is provided a specific place in the overall sequence which takes place well into the thick of it all.

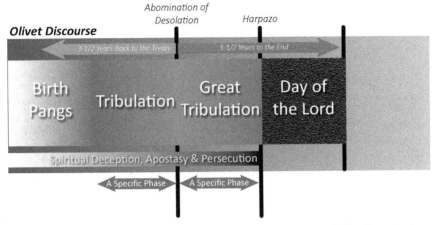

As a reminder, it can be acknowledged that it is very difficult to look at this in isolation from Revelation, because we have lived our whole Christian lives not only with the whole of God's Word, which is a very good thing, but also with the baggage of presuppositions which have been commonly drilled into us about how to interpret it, and such have not always been perfect. This is just a pause to remind us that the purpose of this exercise is to understand what that first generation of the Early Church believed when it came to Christ's Return, keeping to the knowledge that for at least the first 60 years or so the book of Revelation did not exist and their primary source was the Olivet Discourse, the Apostolic commentary in the way of their writings and teachings, and the Old Testament. God deemed it sufficient for those Christians, and even all the Apostles save John, to have lived their entire lives in expectation of Christ's Return with the Olivet Discourse as their crucial and primary guide. And, as a repeated reminder, when Revelation finally became available, it would have been interpreted in light of what was established by the Olivet Discourse and not the other way around as is so often the process in the present climate. Even without Revelation, Christ's prior teachings are actually sufficient.

In brief, the timeline or sequence of events the Early Church would have derived from the Olivet Discourse is a period of "*birth pangs*" of increasing wars, rumors of wars, disturbances, famines, plagues and cosmological signs against a backdrop of ever-intensifying apostasy, deception and persecution segueing to its most intense visitation upon the Church in what is termed *"tribulation"*. This is followed by the milestone of the Antichrist committing the Abomination of Desolation to inaugurate a much more intense and compact period of calamity termed *"great tribulation"* closely followed by the onset of "the day of the Lord", at which time the removal of the Church takes place as all that remains for the world is to experience God's wrath in *"the day of the Lord"*.

The Parable of the Fig Tree & All the Trees

³²"Now learn the parable from the fig tree: when its branch has already become tender and puts forth its leaves, you know that summer is near; ³³so, you too, when you see all these things, recognize that He is near, right at the door.	²⁸"Now learn the parable from the fig tree: when its branch has already become tender and puts forth its leaves, you know that summer is near. ²⁹Even so, you too, when you see these things happening, recognize that He is near, right at the door.	²⁹Then He told them a parable: "Behold the fig tree and all the trees; ³⁰as soon as they put forth leaves, you see it and know for yourselves that summer is now near. ³¹So you also, when you see these things happening, recognize that the kingdom of God is near.
³⁴Truly I say to you, this generation will not pass away until all these things take place.	³⁰Truly I say to you, this generation will not pass away until all these things take place	³²Truly I say to you, this generation will not pass away until all things take place.
³⁵Heaven and earth will pass away, but My words will not pass away. (Mt. 24:32-35)	³¹Heaven and earth will pass away, but My words will not pass away. (Mk. 13:28-31)	³³Heaven and earth will pass away, but My words will not pass away. (Lk. 21:29-33)

Although we are told we cannot know the day nor the hour, we are unambiguously instructed that we should know the season, meaning that all of the *"birth pangs"* and accompanying spiritual decay serves as proof of the nearness of His Return. This is not merely mentioned in passing, but what follows in Jesus' continued teaching on the subject in the Olivet Discourse is a series of reminders reinforcing the fact that we should understand the signs of the times and live accordingly. Again, there are those at present who are claiming that no event or series of events can serve as a "trigger" for the Rapture to take place, and insist it will be a "secret" Rapture which will catch everyone completely unaware. This not only contradicts what we just read, that immediately before the Rapture takes place there are special signs which the whole world recognizes signaling His Return, but Jesus uses many illustrations to teach us the importance of understanding what all these things mean when Christians do witness them.

It would seem that a major feature (and error) of the First Coming is being replayed yet again, when in the span of just thirty years, they went from taking God's Word literally ("He will be born in Bethlehem" in Mt. 2), to superimposing alternative interpretations which were entirely manmade ("no one will know where He is from" in Jn. 7). At one time it would have been extremely difficult to find an adherent of Pre-Tribulationism promoting such things as "no trigger" or signs of any kind preceding the Rapture, or that the Olivet Discourse has absolutely no meaning for the Church, but in the past thirty or so years these have become prominent assertions on display in growing parts of that fractured camp. What happened then is happening yet again. Yes, there have been changes to the discussion of eschatology in the whole of Church history, but just like the extreme swing which took place in the thirty years between Christ's birth and public ministry when many literal prophetic fulfillments took place, the same has already replayed itself in parallel again at present. It is a clear sign that we are already in the Last Days when Christian academics so radically alter their positions and associated terms.

There is an important detail captured by Luke which is not precisely mirrored by Matthew and Mark when it comes to this parable. Whereas Matthew and Mark call it *"the parable from the fig tree"*, Luke identifies it as *"the fig tree **and all the trees**"*. What Jesus may be referring to here is not just the immediate lesson of a fig tree's synchronicity with the seasons, but also to a parable in Judges 9:7-14 about many trees, the fig tree included. This is worth a separate study in its own right. (One suggested study is a sermon by Jacob Prasch of Moriel Ministries, *This Generation*.)

This "Generation"

Risking the danger we will become sidetracked too far afield from our present aims with this study, I feel compelled to share my belief that so much of the damage, deception and misinterpretations in various elements of eschatology at present can be traced in my lifetime to a massive mishandling of what is stated in Matthew 24:34, Mark 13:30 and Luke 21:31, *"this generation will not pass away until all these things take place"*.

In the early 80s, a large swath of teachers, scholars and authors across nearly every denominational divide, crossing nearly every eschatological aisle, and even normally opposed to each other based on contra-theological grounds, uniformly embraced the notion that the definition of "*generation*" was a set period of forty years. This gained a near universal appeal because the state of Israel was re-formed in 1948, and it was somehow deemed that "***this generation***" could only possibly mean that Jesus would return in 1988 by the 40th anniversary of Israel's statehood. It is not difficult to believe that all of the "usual suspects" in the form of false teachers marched so enthusiastically to this banner, but it is still painfully difficult to reverently explain why so many normally rational and even prominent men and women of God joined with them and embraced such a thing which has no scriptural foundation. This is one of those rare times when both the false and so many of the good teachers joined together in agreement and sometimes even collusion.

In those pre-Internet days, it was captured and embraced in one of the most popular books of that time, *88 Reasons Why the Rapture Will Be in 1988* by Edgar C. Whisenant. In fact, he even went so far as to predict the Rapture would take place that year sometime between September 11-13 during the Feast of Trumpets. On those dates, the Trinity Broadcasting Network (TBN) took the extraordinary step of interrupting their normal programming to broadcast special instructions on how to make preparations for the Rapture.

But make no mistake, this was not one of these crazy things gaining some whack-a-doodle kook their fifteen minutes of media fame, but was endorsed or at least given very serious consideration and positive public attention, by some of the biggest and most respected names in Evangelicism at that time. Even more miserably still, when this obviously did not happen, this did not stop Whisenant from publishing *The Final Shout: Rapture Report 1989* which basically asserted 89 reasons why the Rapture would take place the following year in 1989, a third book titled *23 Reasons* as a prediction the Rapture would take place on Rosh-Hashanah in 1993, and yet a fourth book, *And Now the Earth's Destruction by Fire, Nuclear Bomb Fire* predicting the end in 1994!

The simple, exegetical explanation from the text is that the generation who witnesses the specific things identified by Christ as heralding His Return will see the whole thing come about, but it is not the mathematical equivalent of the number forty, nor did Christ ever specify any milestone connected to Israel obtaining political statehood—nowhere can that be found in Scripture. Ethnic Jews returning to the physical land of Israel is prolifically stated, but not a political reconstitution. But the fallout from so many mainstream, across-the-board Christians embracing the date of Christ's Return as specifically being 1988 had, I believe, very serious repercussions with which we are having to still deal with today in the area of eschatology and related teachings concerning Christ's Return.

In the wake of their obvious error when this interpretation failed to come true, instead of those espousing or even simply endorsing this false teaching publicly repenting and leading a church-wide return to the Scriptures, there was mainly anger and outrage on one end of the spectrum, and denial in the form of a reinterpretation of God's prophetic Word on the other. In other words, in most cases, the right lesson was not humbly learned, but pride seemed to take most from either side of the aisle into new directions even further afield from the truth, even if it was in opposite directions from each other. They started out together in the wrong place and ended up in their own respective wrong places, albeit at opposite extremes. This is not a surprising reaction for false teachers, but there were many good teachers who had joined with them in this particular instance and acted in the same character. The one error gave birth to many errors. One of the most obvious ones is the notion that the Olivet Discourse does not apply to the Church, something rarely espoused prior to this debacle, and certainly not by orthodox, mainstream Evangelicals as is the case today.

In my opinion, one of the most regrettable items to come out of this was the rise of so-called "Christian fiction", which by its very name conveys the implied right of an author to stray from the strict confines of biblical truth. (After all, it's just "fiction", right?) Today we have vast numbers within the Church whose only knowledge of eschatology comes from the "Christian Fiction" section of their local bookstore, an aisle which never previously existed until the relatively recent burst of works in this genre. And more recently we have intial publications touted as Christian fiction, but once they become popular, are subsequently outed by their authors as actually being not just true, but actual doctrine. They hide behind the guise of Christian fiction until their sales are high enough that they can come out of the closet with their true intentions.

One of the few positive things which seemed to come out of this is that during this same timeframe a re-examination of Scripture took place in parallel to this craze which led to the publishing of a new eschatology termed "Pre-Wrath", the most notable seminal works being authored by Marv Rosenthal in 1990 and Robert Van Kampen in 1992. Whereas the Pre-Tribulational position holds that the Rapture takes place entirely prior to the whole seven year tribulational period, Pre-Wrath asserts the Church enters the the 70th Week and is not raptured until just before the onset of "*the day of the Lord*" between the 6th and 7th Seals.

While I would agree with them on this particular point, the problem with all the major, published eschatologies is that they have differing interpretations regarding many other aspects of the eschaton—it is not exclusively and solely limited to a differing assignment as to the timing of the Rapture. My personal burden is that there are some things with which I agree from each of the camps, and some things with which I strongly disagree. In the case of Pre-Wrath, because they so often insist that the Restrainer of 2 Thessalonians 2 is not the Holy Spirit but rather the Archangel Michael, I do not want to give a full endorsement to that position just because I agree with their timing of the Rapture, and prefer the recently coined term "Intra-Seal" put forth by Jacob Prasch of Moriel Ministries. [See *Appendix "C": Intra-Seal.*]

But this interpretation of *"generation"* is an example of the old time saying, which D. A. Carson ascribed to his father, that when it comes to interpreting Scripture, "A text without a context is a pretext for a proof text". Another popular variation goes, "A text out of context in isolation from its co-text becomes a pretext". Unfortunately, it did not end there, but seems to have served as a springboard into even greater error, which is another tried and true axiom, "Error leads to even more serious error".

At present we are dealing with eschatological and doctrinal error on an unprecedented scale because, among other things, a major contributing factor of what germinated in the 80s with the embrace of a wrong interpretation of *"this generation"*. This led many to directly violate Jesus' warning that no one could or should set the date of His Return, and then by not fully repenting of this error, resulted in even more egregious deviations. And it should be noted that all the present false teachings and predictions involving the Hebrew festal calendar are not new, but a regurgitation of what has been taking place for at least the past forty plus years. What germinated in 1988 with a prediction of Christ's Return on Rosh Hashanah yielded many subsequent false predictions connected to the Hebrew festal calendar, the most recent notable being the failed "Blood Moons" falsehood and an attempt to link America's financial tragedies to those holidays. Instead of repenting of the error to tying End Times milestones to the Hebrew festal calendar, they keep trying to "correctly assign" something to it, blind to the fact that it is an error and false assumption to begin with.

Summary

In brief, *"the day of the Lord"* was not at all a new concept to the Early Church, and when described by Jesus at this particular juncture in the Olivet Discourse, and by Peter on Pentecost in designating its relationship to the Church Age, would have been clearly understood both for its accompanying signs and how it pertained exclusively to the final outpouring of the wrath of God. Unfortunately, in more modern times, it has been the source of doctrinal division as eschatologies argue over its definition, and in particular attempt to equate it in ways Scripture does not stipulate.

It may be important to note that the very fact that Christ does not continue at this point to provide a detailed explanation of what will take place during "*the day of the Lord*" is itself a textual proof that the Olivet Discourse is, indeed, for the Church. Events basically end where the Church is concerned with the divine direction to the angels to remove the Church and Christ lets stand at this time all that is known about "*the day of the Lord*" from the Old Testament. He will provide much more detail about this final phase of the eschaton in Revelation, but the Olivet Discourse provides believers all they need to know to properly prepare for their part in His Return.

7 ❖ "Be On Guard"

Just as the Olivet Discourse begins with warnings to be alert and on guard, and are repeated in the body of the overall message, so they are found in concentrated form yet again as a reminder to believers of what should be most important to them. Jesus devotes more time to this point than anything else where events of the End Times are concerned, even more than the individual signs pointing to His Return which will be witnessed by everyone.

34"**Be on guard**, so that your hearts will not be weighted down with dissipation and drunkenness and the worries of life, and that day will not come on you suddenly like a trap; 35for it will come upon all those who dwell on the face of all the earth. 36But **keep on the alert** at all times, praying that you may have strength to escape all these things that are about to take place, and to stand before the Son of Man." (Lk. 21:34-36)

36"But of that day and hour no one knows, not even the angels of heaven, nor the Son, but the Father alone. (Mt. 24:36)

32But of that day or hour no one knows, not even the angels in heaven, nor the Son, but the Father alone.

33"**Take heed**, **keep on the alert**; for you do not know when the appointed time will come.

34It is like a man away on a journey, who upon leaving his house and putting his slaves in charge, assigning to each one his task, also commanded the doorkeeper to **stay on the alert**.

35Therefore, **be on the alert**—for you do not know when the master of the house is coming, whether in the evening, at midnight, or when the rooster crows, or in the morning— 36in case he should come suddenly and find you asleep.

37What I say to you I say to all, '**Be on the alert!**' " (Mk. 13:32-37)

In just this section recorded by the synoptic Gospels, we are told...

➤ *"Be on guard..."* (Lk. 21:34)

➤ *"...keep on the alert at all times..."* (Lk. 21: 36)

➤ *"...keep on the alert..."* (Mk. 13:33)

➤ *"...stay on the alert".* (Mk. 13:34)

➤ *"...be on the alert..."* (Mk. 13:35)

➤ *"...Be on the alert!"* (Mk. 13:37)

Previous to this we are told...

➤ *"... See to it that no one misleads you..."* (Mt. 24:4; Mk. 13:5; Lk. 21:8)

➤ *"...Do not go after them."* (Lk. 21:8)

➤ *"...be on your guard..."* (Mk. 13:9)

➤ *"...do not believe him...I have told you in advance..."* (Mt. 24:23-25; Mk. 13:21-23)

➤ *"...do not go out...do not believe them".* (Mt. 24:26)

➤ *"...Do not go away, and do not run after them".* (Lk. 17:23)

Again, as a supporting editorial comment, the fact that Jesus keeps revisiting throughout the whole of the Olivet Discourse admonitions to be on guard, to keep alert, and to not be misled argues against those maintaining that this message is not for the Church, but only for Israel in a designated seven year Tribulation proper after the Church has been removed. Just taking it on face value, why would a group which going into the Last Days and who already rejected Jesus be repeatedly warned to be alert and avoid deception? They are already, biblically speaking, "asleep" and deceived!

For Christians, the biggest problem is going to be apostasy and deception, and this is very strong textual proof mitigating against the notion of a "secret" Rapture or the Rapture taking place in a vacuum and occurring with absolutely no warning whatsoever. If that were the case, why would the Gospels record Jesus stating fourteen times some variation of a warning to be alert, to not be misled, to be on guard? Paul will dramatically and explicitly elaborate in this regard, "*But you, brethren, are **not** in darkness, that the day would overtake you like a thief*". (1 Th. 5:4)

Notice that it is not just the danger of metaphorically falling asleep because it has been such a long time waiting for an unknown appointed time when He will return, but Luke records there are certain factors which will greatly contribute to the problem, "*so that your hearts will not be weighted down with dissipation and drunkenness and the worries of life*". (Lk. 21:34)

"*Dissipation*" (Greek "*kraipale*", #2897) is basically descending into debauchery or a wild self-indulgence. When this is considered in connection with "*drunkenness and the worries of life*", we understand this to be a picture of someone who is living to please themselves in this life rather than exclusively according to God's Word and ways for the next. But this is particularly worth noting because at the heart of every false teaching currently attacking the Church is the common denominator of trying to make this present life temporarily better at the expense of achieving the eternal benefits of the one to come. In the Western Church today we actually see prominent false teachers encouraging this kind of behavior and twisting Scripture so as to make it appear such is permissible to Christians. We actually have publicly popular personalities within the Church who openly use vulgar and obscene language in concert with promoting the same kind of sensuality and lust as the world's, but calling it "Christian love".

The illustration of the man who goes on a journey, which represents Christ, and leaving his slaves in charge, a representation of us as believers, is yet again an example that there is a long period when Jesus will be away and shows that the Olivet Discourse is targeted at the Church. (After all, it is the Church who is charged with His work in the meantime and not Israel who rejected Him.) This first illustration contains the elements common to those to follow, that the Master will temporarily be away, we are to continue to be vigilant in both the work of the Kingdom and our anticipation of His Return, and we should therefore not be taken by surprise when it all finally takes place and He returns. Again, the overall eschaton, or Return of Christ, as well as the Rapture event contained within it, do not transpire in a vacuum with no warning or prefiguring events; the bigger issue for us is failing to look for and live according to those things and the nearness of His Return to which they are pointing. In particular, the Master returns to assess whether we are carrying out our assigned Christian duties and behaving like proper members of His household.

Think of this in terms of the literal birthing process. We already know that the period of pregnancy is approximately nine months, but we never immediately know when it began and only become aware of its beginning in hindsight after being into it a bit. Even then, however, the projected date of birth can only be at best approximated, and as it approaches it could take place days or weeks on either side of the end of that estimate. There is no absolute box we can circle on the calendar, but knowing the general time of arrival is unavoidable. When the birth pangs begin to take place, we know for sure the final event is impending and that it is now only a matter of a couple of days or even just hours away, but we are still unable to precisely declare the exact time. We have a general expectancy during the nine months, it heightens in the final days and hours of ever-increasing birth pangs so as to narrow the time down to an inevitably smaller window, but the birth itself is ultimately a "surprise" to us in the sense that we could not know in advance precisely when it would take place, even when the birth pangs started; it is sheer joy that the waiting is over and the expected child has arrived, even within that known nine month span, and yet we are surprised!

But just because we cannot circle a date and time on our calendar to plan in advance when the birth will actually occur, it would be the epitome of foolishness to ignore the nine month gestation period as if nothing was going on, and even more so to dismiss the birth pangs in denial that a baby is going to be born very, very soon. (Will it go away if you simply choose to ignore it?) Such is the tension we have to maintain in our understanding of the Scriptures telling us that although we cannot know the day or the hour, we will most certainly recognize the season (the nine month gestation period) and the events immediately preceding His Return (the "birth pangs").

It is interesting that in Mark's account, Jesus is recorded as stating that this warning is not just for His inner circle of Apostles, but "*for all*". It is applicable not just for the partial events fulfilled in 70 AD, but for their ultimate, final fulfillment.

Noah & Lot

³⁷For the coming of the Son of Man will be just like the days of Noah. ³⁸For as in those days before the flood they were eating and drinking, marrying and giving in marriage, until the day that Noah entered the ark,	²⁶"And just as it happened in the days of Noah, so it will be also in the days of the Son of Man: ²⁷They were eating, they were drinking, they were marrying, they were being given in marriage, until the day that Noah entered the ark,
³⁹and they did not understand	
until the flood came and took them all away;	and the flood came and destroyed them all.
so will the coming of the Son of Man be. (Mt. 24:37-39)	

²⁸It was the same as happened in the days of Lot: they were eating, they were drinking, they were buying, they were selling, they were planting, they were building; ²⁹but on the day that Lot went out from Sodom it rained fire and brimstone from heaven and destroyed them all. ³⁰It will be just the same on the day that the Son of Man is revealed.

³¹On that day, the one who is on the housetop and whose goods are in the house must not go down to take them out; and likewise the one who is in the field must not turn back.

³²Remember Lot's wife. ³³Whoever seeks to keep his life will lose it, and whoever loses his life will preserve it. (Lk. 17:28-33)

The illustration in both examples compares and contrasts the vigilance of the believer and the willful ignorance of the non-believer. It is particularly telling that Noah is described by Peter as a *"preacher of righteousness"* (2 Pe. 2:5) ignored by a wicked generation and Lot as a righteous man who was *"oppressed by the sensual conduct of unprincipled men"* and was *"tormented day after day by their lawless deeds"* (2 Pe. 2:7-8). In each case, the wicked simply chose to live "business as usual" until it was too late to avoid final judgment, but the righteous remnant lived faithfully in the presence of ever-growing spiritual darkness.

According to what was previously disclosed in the Olivet Discourse, the point at which *"the Son of Man is revealed"* is when there is a cosmological signal of the Rapture about to take place, (Mt. 24:29-30; Mk. 13:24-25; Lk. 21:25-26) and all those about to be left behind—those in the character of the people living in Noah's and Lot's days, recognize it too late and will universally mourn, as opposed to believers who will lift their heads in anticipation of being taken. (Lk. 24:28)

This definitely fits with the old time Larry Norman song about the Rapture once so popular in the 60s and 70s, "It's too late to change your mind, the Son has come and you've been left behind" and what was once universally believed concerning the working of the Rapture. That is what happened to those in Noah's day who finally understood what the rain meant, and those in Lot's day who finally understood why he had gone out of the house to warn them before the fire fell.

It is important to note that Noah was first given a 120 year countdown (Gen. 6:3) which was dramatically narrowed to a much smaller window when his family were instructed to enter the ark and remain there a full seven days before the Lord shut the door. (Gen. 7:1-10) This is an example of not knowing the day or the hour but properly recognizing and responding to the season, so to speak. Likewise, Lot continued to plead, first with the men pounding on his door and then with his future sons-in-law right up to the very end, but was met by those who continued to pursue their wicked desires in spite of being struck blind, or thought he was jesting and did not take him seriously. (Gen. 19:6-14)

But for believers there is a particularly important caveat in the example of Lot's wife. Apparently there will be those who believe and take the right actions up to a point, but who will still fail to be rescued because, as stated previously, they are "*weighted down with the…worries of life*". (Lk. 21:34) Both Noah and Lot are examples of those who were willing to completely forsake or "lose" their old life in favor of trusting God to provide a better "new" life. What transpired for them literally also occurred spiritually; clinging to this life had the opposite result for Lot's wife. For Christians, she is the most powerful caveat because the danger for us is that even though we can reject acting in the character of the unbelievers who were left behind in both the cases of Noah's and Lot's particular times, we may still act in her character, turning back in the midst of all that is taking place even at the latest moment possible.

One Taken, One Left

³⁴I tell you, on that night there will be two in one bed; one will be taken and the other will be left.	
⁴⁰Then there will be two men in the field; one will be taken and one will be left.	³⁵There will be two women grinding at the same place; one will be taken and the other will be left.
⁴¹Two women will be grinding at the mill; one will be taken and one will be left. (Mt. 24:40-41)	³⁶Two men will be in the field; one will be taken and the other will be left."
[See v.28]	³⁷And answering they said to Him, "Where, Lord?" And He said to them, "Where the body is, there also the vultures will be gathered." (Lk. 17:34-37)

Previously in the Olivet Discourse, when Jesus spoke of a group "*taken*" (or "*gathered*") from the earth, it was preceded by the sign of the Son of Man in the sky, the sighting of Jesus, the sounding of the trumpet, and angelic agency removing believers; there was no mention or inference that non-believers are "*taken*", but rather left behind to experience the wrath of God's judgment. (Mt. 24:29-31)

There is much disagreement on this point, most of which has to do with the Greek word "*paralambano*" (Strong's #3880) which underlies the English rendering of "*taken*". The argument is that the people of Noah's and Lot's times were the one's "*taken*" into judgment while Noah and Lot themselves "remained" on earth and their lives continued. However, this fails to recognize that Noah and Lot were respectively "*taken*" out of, or rescued from, the final judgment while everyone else was "left behind" and forced to experience the Flood on the one hand and the fire on the other. In the context of the Olivet Discourse it is the same in that judgment is coming upon the whole world, beginning with God's House first, but when it transitions to the finality of the wrath of God, believers are removed and exempted from that ultimate experience, but non-believers remain behind to suffer the consequences—exactly as was the case for both Noah and Lot.

But the main mistake most are making is to assume that because the English in Matthew 24:39 says of non-believers in Noah's day, "*the flood came and **took** them away*", that the same meaning can be applied in verses 40-41 to, "*one will be **taken** and one will be left*" to mean the unsaved are "*taken*" and the saved remain. This could be easily resolved if they simply looked at the parallel passage to Matthew 24:39 in Luke 17:27 where it is stated, "*the flood came and **destroyed** them all*". The "*taken*" in Matthew is confirmed as not possibly applying to unbelievers in Luke by the parallel description they are "*destroyed*".

While this might be confusing in English, the Greek word for "*took*" in verse 39 is "*airo*" (Strong's #142), but "*taken*" in verses 40-41 is "*paralambano*" (Strong's #3880). "*Airo*" was used by Jesus to describe the violent taking or cutting off of bad branches (Jn. 15:2), and also describes a person being taken away to be killed (Is. 53:8; 57:1-2; Acts 8:33) It is "*taken*" in the sense of removal with the idea of an accompanying act of violence and authority. "*Paralambano*", however, is used in the New Testament to describe one person taking another person into their possession, such as when Jesus "*took*" Peter, James and John with him to the Mt. of Transfiguration or to witness Him raise Jairus' daughter from the dead. It is only English speakers who are confused by this issue because while the translation is technically correct, it still requires more detail for the difference to be made clear to the strictly English reader. But the Early Church, fluent in Greek, would have never confused "*airo*" and "*paralambano*" in this manner. They would have understood that the unsaved were being left behind to be "*taken*" into judgment while the saved were being removed or "*taken*" into the personal possession of Christ.

I have personally always found this teaching to have a comforting aspect to it because it does not show Christians as preparing bunkers or taking extraordinary measures of self-protection, but rather continuing to live exactly like Christians should right up to the very end. As in the previous illustration of being faithful in their Master's absence, and the similar examples to come, one of the applications of these teachings is that when we recognize the nearness of His Return, we are not to act differently, but are called to live even more Christ-like, just as we are always supposed to do in the first place. In other words, what is normally required of us in the course of the mundane, is even more important in the shadow of the profound.

But to address the narrow but often asserted argument that regardless, "*paralambano*" as "*taken*" cannot possibly be the Rapture, since they say only the Greek word "*harpazo*"—that is "snatched away", describes that specific event, consider that the mechanics of speech work in Greek exactly the way it works in English.

Anyone could say, "My wife was **snatched** by kidnappers right off the street", and if asked, "When did this happen?", could in turn further state, "They **took** her today right after lunch." We would not start screaming at them, "Which is it, Mr. Pants-On-Fire! Was she 'snatched' or was she 'taken'? Can't you make up your mind?" As a native English speaker, you knew without need of any explanation that "snatched" was first used to emphasize the action, and the subsequent use of "taken" when the emphasis was on the timing of that exact, same event. It is no different in the Greek, where more than one term is used to describe the Rapture depending on the emphasis being made by the context of the particular passage. "*Harpazo*" emphasizes the action, "*paralambano*" the timing.

Be Ready

> ⁴²"Therefore **be on the alert**, for you do not know which day your Lord is coming.
>
> ⁴³But be sure of this, that if the head of the house had known at what time of the night the thief was coming, **he would have been on the alert** and would not have allowed his house to be broken into. ⁴⁴For this reason **you also must be ready**; for the Son of Man is coming at an hour when you do not think He will.
>
> ⁴⁵"Who then is the faithful and sensible slave whom his master put in charge of his household to give them their food at the proper time? ⁴⁶**Blessed is that slave whom his master finds so doing when he comes**. ⁴⁷Truly I say to you that he will put him in charge of all his possessions. ⁴⁸But if that evil slave says in his heart, 'My master is not coming for a long time,' ⁴⁹and begins to beat his fellow slaves and eat and drink with drunkards; ⁵⁰**the master of that slave will come on a day when he does not expect him and at an hour which he does not know**, ⁵¹and will cut him in pieces and assign him a place with the hypocrites; in that place there will be weeping and gnashing of teeth. (Mt. 24:42-51)

Theses illustrations highlight the dual aspect of being prepared and ready for ourselves and yet effective and responsible in our dealings with others on both a personal level and as a member of the Church at large.

The first parable stresses personal protection against a thief breaking into one's house. Satan and his false shepherds are characterized in Scripture as a "*thief*" (Jn. 10:1, 10), and Jesus as one who comes "*like a thief*". (1 Th. 5:2, 4; 2 Pe. 3:10; Rev. 3:3, 16:15). But in this first illustration, the emphasis is on protecting our own house, of being personally aware and faithful so as to not be "*broken into*"—that is, deceived, misled, unaware, not ready.

Whereas there was a previous parable in Mark 13:33-37 of the slaves being put in charge of their master's house to be ready for his return in general, this second parable in Matthew addresses the responsibility of the slave left in charge to rightly treat the rest of the household in the master's absence and not succumb to temporal sensuality. The emphasis here is on protecting everyone in the Body of Christ—the house of God—corporately in the course of our service and ministry within the Church. We are not just supposed to attain solely to personal readiness, but proving it outwardly in our care and feeding of the Body of Christ so as to equally prepare them as well. But it is also a clear warning from Christ Himself that the first ones He will hold responsible are the shepherds He left in charge of His flock.

Again, these two aspects of what it means to be found awake and ready at Jesus' Return can only have primary application to the Church leading up to and overlapping into Daniel's 70th Week. For the Church living during that sixty year period before Revelation when it was deemed sufficient by God that they live in expectation of His Son's Return according to the primary teaching of the Olivet Discourse, they understood that they should be alert and ready, watching for the "*birth pangs*" giving way to an intense period of "*tribulation*" when deception, apostasy and persecution would rise to unprecedented levels, and able to identify the Abomination of Desolation signaling the start of "*great tribulation*", the spiritually darkest period of all to be supernaturally cut short for the sake of the Elect by the *Harpazo*. They would equally recognize from the accompanying parables and illustrations that this was a time when it was more important than ever to live like a biblical Christian should.

8 ❖ "The Age to Come"

T*he Olivet Discourse does not go into but the briefest of references when it comes to the Millennial Kingdom, inferring its beginning with the opening description of what will take place with the judgment of the nations, "But when the Son of Man comes in His glory, and all the angels with Him, then He will sit on His glorious throne".* (Mt. 25:31) Since believers are exempt from the wrath of God, and the Olivet Discourse is directed at believers, a portion of the eschaton is left mostly blank; not to mention details about *"the day of the Lord"* which have already been provided prolifically throughout the Old Testament Scriptures with which the Early Church would have been very familiar (and so should we). So it should not be that surprising when it picks up again with the Millennial Kingdom, something commonly known through already given Scripture as a shared experience to come for all believers of every age.

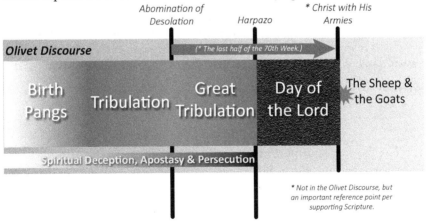

The Sheep & the Goats

....

³¹"But when the Son of Man comes in His glory, and all the angels with Him, then He will sit on His glorious throne. ³²All the nations will be gathered before Him; and He will separate them from one another, as the shepherd separates the sheep from the goats; ³³and He will put the sheep on His right, and the goats on the left.

³⁴"Then the King will say to those on His right, 'Come, you who are blessed of My Father, inherit the kingdom prepared for you from the foundation of the world. ³⁵For I was hungry, and you gave Me something to eat; I was thirsty, and you gave Me something to drink; I was a stranger, and you invited Me in; ³⁶naked, and you clothed Me; I was sick, and you visited Me; I was in prison, and you came to Me.'

³⁷"Then the righteous will answer Him, 'Lord, when did we see You hungry, and feed You, or thirsty, and give You something to drink? ³⁸And when did we see You a stranger, and invite You in, or naked, and clothe You? ³⁹When did we see You sick, or in prison, and come to You?'

⁴⁰"The King will answer and say to them, 'Truly I say to you, to the extent that you did it to one of these brothers of Mine, even the least of them, you did it to Me.'

⁴¹"Then He will also say to those on His left, 'Depart from Me, accursed ones, into the eternal fire which has been prepared for the devil and his angels; ⁴²for I was hungry, and you gave Me nothing to eat; I was thirsty, and you gave Me nothing to drink; ⁴³I was a stranger, and you did not invite Me in; naked, and you did not clothe Me; sick, and in prison, and you did not visit Me.'

⁴⁴"Then they themselves also will answer, 'Lord, when did we see You hungry, or thirsty, or a stranger, or naked, or sick, or in prison, and did not take care of You?'

⁴⁵"Then He will answer them, 'Truly I say to you, to the extent that you did not do it to one of the least of these, you did not do it to Me.' ⁴⁶These will go away into eternal punishment, but the righteous into eternal life." (Mt. 25:31-46)

....

A Logical Ending for Everyone

For the first generation of believers in the Church, this ending to the overall sequence would seem very natural since they would have had more than a cursory knowledge of all the Old Testament had to say both about the Millennial Kingdom and *"the day of the Lord"* preceding it, especially the Old Testament references to other nations taking part in the Millennial Kingdom. In fact, there is far more material on those subjects in the Old Testament than the New Testament, which does not see the need to revisit what has already been documented. God's Word is not divided into testaments or books, but is actually a single, combined whole. Something not mentioned in the New Testament is not "erased" or "nullified", but stands on its own equal merits and authority. If there is a change, which always comes by way of a fulfillment and not a replacement, God's Word clearly documents its.

The Early Church would see their removal as members of the Church before the onset of *"the day of the Lord"* proper as the fulfillment of their exemption from God's wrath in the same character of the Exodus account wherein everyone experienced the first third of the plagues, but escaped the last two-thirds culminating in a kind of final judgment in the working of the angel of death, and ultimately being saved by the blood of the Lamb. Their next stop was the Promised Land. But even after all the events associated specifically with God's wrath were concluded in the Exodus narrative, there were still Gentile survivors who came out alongside Israel, which means that what is here presented in the Olivet Discourse is not unprecedented. Such had to abide by the same standards as the ethnic Jews they accompanied.

And because of the expectations provided by Scripture that Israel would rule over the rest of the world at the behest of the Messiah, judgment of the Gentile nations as covered in passages dealing with *"the day of the Lord"* would be seen as finally being fulfilled in this New Testament account as the Messiah's first action after assuming His throne. Additionally, one of the prominent features of Scripture when it speaks about things pertaining to this thousand year kingdom is to persistently describe its citizens as still composed of nations. God's Word repeatedly describes the roles of nations, the behavior of nations, and even specifies nations which will be included in this time and those who will be left out, and the role of the Messiah as Judge and King over them is specified and therefore expected. But it would have also served as Christ once again differentiating His work in the First Coming from that in the Second Coming. This expected rule of the Messiah was going to take place, but not according to the presuppositions dominating His first visitation.

So for believers in the 1st century, particularly those raised with the Old Testament Scriptures, it would not seem out of place that after the removal of the Church and the fulfillment of all that Scripture predicts for *"the day of the Lord"* that a judgment of all remaining within the nations takes place at that transition point into the Millennial Reign. And in addition to this, there was an expectation that the Messiah would establish His throne in Jerusalem and rule all the nations of the earth not just among adherents of Judaism, but even more so among Christians. In other words, it would be a primary expectation of the Early Church that the eschaton ends, *"when the Son of Man comes in His glory, and all the angels with Him, then He will sit on His glorious throne*" (v.31) and serves as the answer to the opening question of the Olivet Discourse, "*Tell us…what will be the sign…of the end of the age?*" (Mt. 24:3) It is important to note that Jesus omits the Battle of Armageddon, which many assign as "*the end of the age*", but rather designates this event selecting who is included or excluded from entering the Millennial Kingdom as "*the sign…of the end of the age*". That event involving Armageddon is at the conclusion of "*the age to come*".

Because we are intrinsically aware of the content of Revelation, we know that more information is forthcoming to expand upon what is given here, but the underlying timeline and purposes will not be altered. In fact, from a purely Christian point of view for whom the Olivet Discourse was primarily designed in the first place, the basic sequence presented contains all that is most important for us. We will go through a time of "*tribulation*" giving way to a shorter, more intense period of "*great tribulation*" before being removed on the cusp of the initiation of "*the day of the Lord*", and rejoin everyone in the Millennial Reign. For the first sixty or so years of the Early Church, this was the complete teaching on the Second Coming, and it would not have been altered by the introduction of Revelation; instead, John's vision would have been affirmed by the fact that when taken on its face, it conforms to this sequence.

It may help to revisit the Apostles' original question to which Jesus is responding:

³*As He was sitting on the Mount of Olives,*	³*As He was sitting on the Mount of Olives opposite the temple,*	
the disciples came to Him privately, saying,	*Peter and James and John and Andrew were questioning Him privately,*	⁷*They questioned Him saying,*
"Tell us, when will these things happen,	⁴*"Tell us, when will these things be,*	
and what will be the sign when all these things are going to be fulfilled?" (Mk. 13:3-4)	*And what will be the sign when these things are about to take place?" (Lk. 21:7)*	
and what will be the sign of Your coming, and of the end of the age?" (Mt. 24:3)		

As noted previously, there are really three parts to their compound question:

➤ When will these things happen?

➤ What will be the sign that these things are going to be fulfilled by Your coming?

➤ What will be the signs of the end of the age?

Notice that the inquiry is limited to the eschaton, or the entire sequence of Christ's Second Coming which is specifically confined to "*the end of the age*". It does not extend into "*the age to come*" nor eternity beyond because it is assumed from all they knew from the Old Testament that when the Messiah comes He will establish the Millennial Kingdom to usher in a new age. What Christ introduces for the first time is that before He inaugurates the "*age to come*", there will first be a separation of believers from non-believers by way of the *Harpazo*, followed by a separation of those left behind who experienced the whole of Daniel's 70th Week represented here as the sheep and the goats. There will be those rejected who "*go away into eternal punishment, but the righteous into eternal life*".

For those who recognized that the Old Testament example of Israel and Judah leading up to their respective captivity was a pattern of "*the end of the age*", they may have seen that sequence as a pattern for the final one. Whereas there were actually four deportations in the form of the Northern Kingdom of Israel first taken by the Assyrian Empire, followed by three such increasingly stronger forced evacuations effected by the Babylonian Empire against the Southern Kingdom of Judah—all in the character of the four invasions of the locusts prophesied by Joel, (Joel 1:4) an argument could be made for this kind of pattern in the eschaton. There was already a resurrection of Old Testament believers in the course of the Crucifixion, then the anticipated *Episunagoge* kicking off "*the day of the Lord*" with the Rapture and Resurrection of the saints, this separation of the sheep and the goats at the beginning of the Millennial Reign, and the Final Judgment to come at its conclusion. Whether or not this turns out to be the case, or whether this is the correct one-for-one assignment, the greater point is that a judgment event like this would not be completely unprecedented scripturally.

But within the greater context of the Olivet Discourse, this teaching is not oriented toward the unsaved but the saved. This final event seems to be included to answer the repeated questions throughout Jesus' ministry as to when the establishment of the Millennial Reign could be expected. The establishment of His throne and the ensuing judgment of the nations perfectly complements the large body of Old Testament Scripture speaking directly to this point. It is just that it does not come about precisely according to their preconceived notions.

9 ❖ More For Us Than Them

The most important lesson Christians can derive from the Olivet Discourse is that it is mainly directed more for us than it is for non-believers. This is what is particularly troubling when we come across the assertion that the Olivet Discourse has no application for the Church and is only intended for literal Israel in the Tribulation after the Church is removed, or is omitted from End Times discussions in favor of limiting the discussion to just the contents of Revelation. The warnings and caveats are overwhelmingly directed at those who have long been awaiting His Return, not those who have not.

> ➤ It begins with a direct, personal warning, "*See to it that no one misleads you*" in an opening disclosure that we should expect many false personalities and signs of judgment which "*is __not yet__ the end*" and characterized as "*merely __the beginning__ of birth pangs*". (Mt. 24:4-8; Mk. 13:5-8; Lk. 21:8-11)

> ➤ This is followed up with extensive warnings about the inevitable world's heaping upon the Church unprecedented persecution, accompanied by apostasy and deception in a time called "*tribulation*". This will serve as a vehicle to provide an opportunity to witness for Christ and preach the Gospel to the whole world. This intense phase in the course of "*the end of the age*" applies exclusively to believers. (Mt. 24:9-14; Mk. 13:9-13; Lk. 21:12-19)

➤ The onset of an even greater time of *"great tribulation"*, whose beginning is identified by the surrounding of Jerusalem and the Abomination of Desolation, is directed at believers who are supposed to comprehend what is taking place and to flee Judea. Christ's instructions for what to do when these things are recognized are aimed solely at believers, and it is for their sake that this time is cut short. (Mt. 24:15-22; Mk. 13:14-20; Lk. 21:20-24)

➤ Jesus then warns again to not be deceived by false christs and false prophets whose purpose is *"to mislead, if possible, even the elect"*. (Mt. 24:23-27; Mk. 13:21-23; Lk. 17:22-25) The world is already deceived, so this is affirmation of the primary purpose of the Olivet Discourse as a guide directed exclusively at the Church.

➤ When the milestone signs associated with *"the day of the Lord"* signal the impending harvest of the Church, the specific admonition to believers is, *"Straighten up and lift up your heads, because your redemption is drawing near"*. (Mt. 24:28-31; Mk. 13:24-27; Lk. 21:25-28)

➤ *The Parable of the Fig Tree and All the Trees* is directed at those alone who can recognize the prophetic signs of the times. (Mt. 24:32-35; Mk. 13:28-31; Lk. 21:29-33) By definition, anyone living in sin without the aid of the Holy Spirit cannot understand Scripture, much less the signs it designates; their personal recognition of what is happening always comes too late.

➤ Jesus' warning to *"Be on guard...keep alert at all times, praying..."* and to not fall into worldly behaviors *"weighted down with dissipation and drunkenness and the worries of life"*, is hyper-directed at believers who will otherwise *"stand before the Son of Man"* if they remain spiritually alert and avoid those obstacles to a practicing faith. (Lk. 21:34-36)

> ➤ The illustrations of the master away on a journey who has left a slave in charge, the days of Noah, the days of Lot, the head of the household who should expect a thief, and the slave placed in charge of the household who is to take care of his fellow slaves and not abuse them are all directed at believers. The common caveat for each is, "*Therefore be on the alert, for you do not know which day your Lord is coming*". (Mt. 24:36-51; Mk. 13:32-37; Lk. 17:26-37)

> ➤ *The Parable of the Wise and Foolish Virgins* is a warning to those in the Church and the consequences if they are not ready through the Holy Spirit's anointing in the Word. Neither group of virgins represents non-believers. (Mt. 25:1-13)

> ➤ *The Parable of the Talents* is a warning to those in the Church and the consequences if they are not responsibly carrying out their assigned work of the kingdom. (Mt. 25:14-30)

> ➤ Even the closing teaching of the judgment of the nations in the separation of the sheep and the goats conveys a warning to anyone surviving all that has transpired to that point that it is Christ's standards which will still matter more than anything else. (Mt. 25:31-46)

That which Jesus establishes in the Olivet Discourse are the fundamentals which matter most to those who claim to have a relationship with Him and are supposed to be living in expectation of His Return. (This cannot be the present-day adherents of Judaism because they are expecting a Messiah, not Yeshua the Messiah.) This is why, of all the prophetic events spoken of in the whole of God's Word which have yet to find their final fulfillment, Jesus' main emphasis is on those which are leading up to the Rapture—those which matter most to believers and tell them what to anticipate and how to live in both the expectation and shadow of His Second Coming.

But to understand what to foresee from the worldly non-believing majority in the shadow of Jesus' Return, their anticipated behavior will revolve around a few aspects which are to be normative at any time, but will be particularly accelerated in their intensity and depth in the Last Days:

➤ Many will live as in the days of Noah when "*all flesh had corrupted their way on earth*" and these will completely ignore everything except that which pleases themselves.

➤ Many will live as in the days of Lot in the most extreme forms of sensuality and lawlessness, despising authority.

➤ Many will apostatize and some even turn back at the latest possible moment in the character of Lot's wife.

➤ Many will give in to the pressures of "*dissipation, drunkenness and the worries of life*" so as to be found not ready.

➤ Many will be deceived by the many false christs and false prophets, much less the ultimate Antichrist and False Prophet they foreshadow; many by those desensitizing others to what is taking place by incessantly intoning, "*The time is near*".

➤ Many will participate not just in the persecution of believers, but in seeking to put us to death, even though we might be family or at one time close friends.

➤ For those who survive the earthly judgments of the "*birth pangs*", "*tribulation*" and "*great tribulation*" to follow, they will experience an additional judgment.

Both believers and non-believers alike will witness and experience firsthand the cosmological and associated signs of the Son of Man and see Jesus as the Rapture takes place, but while it is a time of redemption to be embraced by the believer, it will be a turning point of open mourning for all those about to be left behind. The final "revival" will come just prior during an intense period of persecution of the Church at which time we will be witnesses and preach the Gospel to the whole world, whether they accept it or not—it will not come after we are removed when all that is left is the wrath of God in "*the day of the Lord*".

A 1st Century Chart

The End Times "chart" for the 1st century Church would begin with a longer introductory period of the "*birth pangs*" comprised of wars, rumors of wars, disturbances, famines, earthquakes, pestilence, giving away to a specific period of "*tribulation*" when the Church experiences unprecedented levels of apostasy culminating in unparalleled persecution. The hardships experienced by Christians at this time provide the opportunity to preach the Gospel to the whole world, but it would be a time marked with an increase in the rise of many false christs and false prophets working to counter the Gospel with previously unseen levels of deception.

This time of "*tribulation*" gives way to an even more intense period of "*great tribulation*" for the entire planet which is initiated by the surrounding of Jerusalem, the Abomination of Desolation, and the flight of those in Judea at that time into the wilderness. This phase will end with the "*harvest*" of the elect—the Rapture when the Church is "*taken*", and leaving behind the rest in the same way that those of both Noah's and Lot's days were "left behind" to suffer a type of final judgment. What then follows is "*the day of the Lord*", at the end of which Christ literally returns to earth and assumes His throne to establish what was commonly expected in the way of His Millennial Kingdom, at which time a judgment of the nations takes place.

But it is perhaps the way that the sequence provided in the Olivet Discourse ends in each of its three synoptic iterations which testifies to the Church being its main, target audience. It is only in Matthew's account that there is a brief mention of the Messiah returning to assume His throne and initiate what we have come to call the "Millennial Reign". In other words, the Olivet Discourse is singularly concerned for teaching about things pertaining to the period of the eschaton leading up to the Rapture, whereas Revelation and supporting Scripture extend beyond into expanded accounts not only of the Millennial Kingdom, but of eternity to come. Yet all three of the accounts basically end their timeline of the milestone events not just with the Rapture taking place, but the visible sign immediately preceding it:

> [30]"And then the sign of the Son of Man will appear in the sky, and then all the tribes of the earth will mourn, and they will see THE SON OF MAN COMING IN THE CLOUDS OF THE SKY with power and great glory. (Matthew 24:30)

> [26]"Then they will see THE SON OF MAN COMING IN CLOUDS with great power and glory. (Mark 13:26)

> [27]*"Then they will see* THE SON OF MAN COMING IN A CLOUD *with power and great glory. (Luke 21:27)*

In other words, the Olivet Discourse is focused on revealing that which will be experienced by the Church up until its removal. What is provided in this critical teaching, and why it must be viewed as the fundamental starting point, is because these are the things which are most vital to the faith of the Church as we live out these events, and that is why the focus of the overall teaching after the sign of the Son of Man is witnessed is a review of what is most important about Christian behavior awaiting the Master's Return:

> ➤ It begins with warnings to faithful Christians expecting the Second Coming not to be deceived in a time of growing apostasy, deception and persecution.

> ➤ For the faithful, what looks like the worst or most tragic of circumstances will be used by the Lord so that they can preach the Gospel and be a visible witness for Him to the whole world.

> ➤ All the parables and illustrations are directed at those who are supposed to be living and serving the Master faithfully until He returns—that is, putting His Word and ways into practice, living as a Christian should, carrying out His work both within the Church and to the world.

> ➤ And it ends just as it did in the days of Noah and Lot, when a remnant was "*taken*" in the ark and a remnant "*taken*" out of the city, and the wicked, unbelieving were left behind to experience the wrath of God.

If the earliest generation of Christians drew a chart to visually represent their eschatology, it would describe the events leading up to their removal as the final materialization of "*the day of the Lord*" descends upon those who have chosen to follow Satan and the kingdom of Antichrist. But their chart would overwhelmingly be focused on the details relating specifically to the Church, and could not possibly apply to an Israel who still rejects the Messiah, nor to a class of believers some claim will come into existence only after the Church has been removed. The Olivet Discourse is, again, hyper-directed at the Church.

Eschatology in the 1st century had little to do with what will happen to "them" and much more to do with what will happen to "us". And even though we have been blessed with extensive supplemental information in this regard in the giving of the book of Revelation, even today the Olivet Discourse is sufficient to prepare every Christian in advance for Christ's Second Coming.

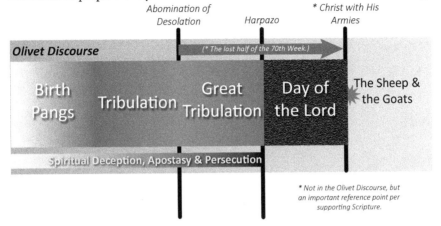

Part Two:
The Apostolic Affirmation

10 ❖ James' Commentary

While we will not be able to engage in an exhaustive study of each and every verse of the New Testament touching on some aspect of the eschaton, an overall survey of the New Testament writings other than the Gospels and Revelation shows that eschatological teachings and references overwhelmingly conform to Christ's establishment of "the present age", "the end of the age", and "the age to come". The details subsequently provided in this regard very much parallel those of the Olivet Discourse when it comes to dealing with *"the end of the age"*. This is why the Epistles have been repeatedly referred to as essentially functioning as a "commentary" on the Olivet Discourse.

All of these works, of course, and even including the later publication of John's Gospel and Epistles, all came prior to Revelation. James and Peter in particular provide very strong parallels to that which is already provided in the Olivet Discourse, and the amount of new, supplemental details overall is not only very narrow in scope, but never fundamentally alter anything Christ presented. These will be visited as well as the eschatological substance of John's Epistles, written as the "last Apostle standing" at the tail end of what can be broadly defined as the Early Church, and Paul's dealing with the church at Thessalonica, which is recorded as the one New Testament congregation experiencing outright difficulties with eschatology. It can be reasonably argued that what occurred in Thessalonica on the local level is at present being replayed again on a much greater churchwide stage. For the purposes of this discussion, we will focus on James, Peter, Paul at Thessalonica and John, acknowledging we will not comprehensively address every New Testament passage referencing the eschaton.

However, it is worth repeating the caveat that none of the New Testament writers, not even the Apostle John himself, could have possibly authored anything with conscious knowledge of what was never revealed to them in the way of Revelation at the time of their writings. Everything on their part was a commentary on the Olivet Discourse and the Old Testament Scriptures, and that it would later be found absent of any conflict with Revelation testifies not only to being Holy Spirit inspired, but reinforces how the Olivet Discourse is the bi-directional prism to view all things both before and after. By and large, however, the content of the New Testament writers mostly parallels the parables and illustrations Christ gave in the Olivet Discourse dedicated to how believers should conduct themselves while awaiting the Master's Return, and warn most about that which Christ emphasizes the most concerning deception, apostasy and persecution.

"The Coming of the Lord is Near"

> *¹James, a bond-servant of God and of the Lord Jesus Christ,*
> *To the twelve tribes who are dispersed abroad: Greetings.*
> *(James 1:1)*

The Epistle of James is most likely the earliest of all the New Testament books to have been written and circulated within the Early Church. The fact that it is addressed "*To the twelve tribes who are dispersed abroad*" indicates it was written so early in Church history that this was still a time when the Church's membership was mainly comprised of ethnic Jews, a time before Peter's experience at Cornelius' house when the Church began to formally expand and regularly incorporate Gentile believers. (Acts 10)

> *⁷Therefore be patient, brethren, until **the coming of the Lord**. The farmer waits for the precious produce of the soil, being patient about it, until it gets the early and late rains. ⁸You too be patient; strengthen your hearts, for **the coming of the Lord is near**. ⁹Do not complain, brethren, against one another, so that you yourselves may not be judged; behold, **the Judge is standing right at the door**. (James 5:7–9)*

The main theme of James' contribution to New Testament eschatology is patience and endurance. In just these few verses we are presented with a complement of similar attributes such as "*patient*" (v.7, 8), "*waits*" (v.7), and followed in verses 10-11 with "*patience*", "*endured*" and "*endurance*". But the opening example of patience and endurance in the illustration of the farmer is particularly relevant. Like the promise of Jesus in John 14:1-3 that He will return even though it is to our benefit that He be away for a time, and His statement in Luke 17:22 that He will be away for such a length of time that they will long for Him, and the many examples in the Olivet Discourse of a master or bridegroom being away for an extended period of time, all generally parallel the imagery of the patience and working of a farmer, especially in the context of seasons.

What is clearly implied, first of all, is that a farmer must experience the seasons, caring for the soil and the crops, only expecting it to ultimately be ready and available at harvest time. Crops blossom and mature not on a particular day, but only during a specific season, so no farmer would expect he could skip past the other seasons to go directly to the harvest—they are actually necessary and required precursors in order to achieve the desired end result. This closely parallels Jesus' admonition in the Olivet Discourse to pay attention to the signs of the times in the character of seasons.

In addition, there is reference to the specific seasonal conditions of the *"early and late rains"*, something unique to Israel because of its geographical location and climate. Many have pointed out that this reference to the two periods of expected rain for the meteorological conditions specific to Israel is a metaphor relating to God's working through the outpouring of the Spirit. Just as there is an expected separation of time on the Hebrew calendar between the early and late rains, this most likely has the dual meaning of what took place on the Day of Pentecost in Acts 2 as the first of these rains, and then a second similar outpouring yet to come in the Last Days in the character of the first. But in both this example and that of the farmer, there is the unavoidable parallel of a specific lapse of time which takes place as well between the expected rains so crucial to the harvest crop.

There is also something particularly interesting about this overall sequence, in that the farmer must pay attention to seasons, must be faithful to carry out the appropriate work at the appropriate times, but ultimately has no control over the weather or nature, which will inevitably take place in an anticipated sequence for varying lengths of time, and of course cannot be expected to arrive on a day or hour which can be precisely predicted. Each season always comes in the same sequence, but not only are the exact starting and ending dates of each impossible to pinpoint in advance, but often overlap in such a way that it is difficult to be sure when the transition from one season to the next has permanently taken hold. It is usually only from hindsight when the farmer can look back and pinpoint the exact day or week in which the current season actually began, even though it comes in the general timeframe expected.

It is further telling to juxtapose this against what is eschatologically revealed, in that the overall timing of the eschaton is also recorded in Scripture by Jesus' statement, *"When the crop permits"*. (Mk. 4:29) These things precisely mirror what has already been foundationally established concerning Christ's Return, that it was going to take place future to the Early Church, could not be precisely predicted by setting a specific date, but would arrive in an unmistakable environment of foreshadowing signs and events so that its nearness is so obvious it cannot reasonably be ignored. For Christians in particular, there is a repeated admonition to not just be ready and waiting, but to be consistently faithful in carrying out the work and responsibilities of the Body of Christ in the example of the farmer.

"The Endurance of Job"

> *10As an example, brethren, of suffering and patience, take the prophets who spoke in the name of the Lord. 11We count those blessed who endured. You have heard of* **the endurance of Job** *and have seen the outcome of the Lord's dealings, that the Lord is full of compassion and is merciful. (James 5:10–11)*

Of particular note, however, is the example of Job who is offered to explain just how deep the expectations of patience and endurance for the End Times penetrates. We could probably write an entire, separate book comparing and contrasting in minute detail all the parallels between what took place in the book of Job and that which the End Times Christian is to expect in the season of Jesus' Return, but here are a few highlights:

➤ The earthly events which take place, although permitted by God, are actually carried out by Satan.

➤ What happens to Job is not the result of sin or as a deserved consequence of his own actions, but is actually a test of faith.

➤ Everyone turns against Job, not just worldly enemies who take his physical possessions, but his closest friends and even his wife, just as in the Olivet Discourse Jesus warns that family and those previously close to us will turn against us in addition to the usual earthly suspects.

➤ Job was not exempted from earthly trials, but required to participate in and endure them, although still preserved by God through them. By faith he ultimately overcame them.

> ➤ At the time all these things took place, Job did not fully understand them, and it was only in hindsight that everything was explained and completely understood.

> ➤ When these things began to take place, they occurred very quickly and in rapid succession in an attempt to overwhelm him.

However, what may be most important about the example of Job where Christians are concerned is his spiritual condition before going into his time of tribulation:

> ¹*There was a man in the land of Uz whose name was Job; and that man was **blameless, upright, fearing God and turning away from evil**. (Job 1:1)*

Where the example of Job is concerned, and in light of the most important aspects of the Olivet Discourse previously discussed, what may be most relevant for us is that prior to all that would come upon Job, he was a practicing, righteous believer who entered into a time of distress "*blameless, upright, fearing God and turning away from evil*". We could probably write yet a whole additional book on the quality of one's walk based on these four crucial attributes of someone who is spiritually ready for that time of unprecedented testing in their Christian life because they are spiritually prepared to this degree. The "*endurance of Job*" carries with it the prerequisite of the faithfulness of Job in the first place. He did not obtain these qualities in his time of tribulation, but in the course of his whole life leading up to it.

As a side note to the overall discussion of eschatology, the example of Job and the prominent role of Satan in what took place in his life is one of the primary reasons we should reject the oft-proposed notion that the Church will be raptured before the appearance of the Antichrist (who is literally possessed by Satan) and will therefore be exempt from meeting and experiencing him. What would be the point if Satan only comes against someone who is unfaithful or unbelieving in the first place? Even Jesus Himself was subject to testing by Satan. (Mt. 4:1-11)

Many of the same commentators who insist the Church will be raptured before the rise to power of the Antichrist also tell us that just as Christ had some years of ministry in His First Coming, so Satan will demand his own equivalent period in the course of the Second Coming to explain the references to 3/1-2 year time periods in both Daniel and Revelation. What would be the point of only testing the unfaithful, unbelieving, and/or apostate, which would be the case if the Church does not face him? No, just as in the case of

Job, Satan will demand and be given the opportunity to send the Antichrist, whom he personally possesses, against everyone. Just as God once presented to Satan, "*Have you considered My servant Job?*" (Job. 1:8), so a time comes when it is replayed as, "Have you considered My Bride, the Church?"

In combination with this, it must also be pointed out that even for those who will be born in the Millennial Reign after Satan is temporarily imprisoned for a thousand years, (Rev. 20:1-10) that he is still provided the opportunity to deceive those who grew up without him, resulting in the final war climaxing the transition to eternity. There is no biblical instance where someone is exempted from having to face Satan, not even for those growing up in the Millennial Reign while he is imprisoned and not actively working.

It can be further argued that this is the pattern replayed over and over in Scripture, that whenever a rescue takes place (a figure of the Rapture), the faithful have been present to be tested before their extraction is transacted. Noah and his family had to endure the sin and wickedness of their time, Lot and his family lived among such corruption that God could not allow it to continue, Israel followed God in Egypt in spite of an antichrist figure in Pharaoh and their many false gods, Rahab and her family were a minority of believers in the God of Israel amongst the majority who were not, and so on. All ultimately escaped the wrath of God which came upon their contemporaries for yielding to Satan's ways, but in every case, God's faithful were not exempt from Satan making every effort to entice them as well. Everyone was equally tested even though the faithful were ultimately exempted from the consequences of God's wrath reserved for those failing the test. Even the raptured Enoch lived in the shadow, so to speak, of Satan.

> [10]*As an example, brethren, of suffering and patience, take the prophets who spoke in the name of the Lord. (James 5:10)*

We could work up the same kind of profile as Job for the "*suffering and patience*" of "*the prophets...of the Lord*", showing that in every case they entered into their own times of tribulation as spiritually prepared servants. They did not become faithful in times of testing, persecution and trial, but achieved it well before in the course of everyday life. Like Job, they were hopelessly outnumbered, often betrayed by those closest to them, and assigned the role of preaching God's Word in spite of the circumstances—all attributes which will be shared by the End Times Christian according to the caveats of the Olivet Discourse.

These two examples of Job and the Prophets actually fit in with the opening example of the farmer, in that just as their pursuit of always living according to God's Word and ways prepared them spiritually for the season of testing and necessary endurance to come, the farmer likewise must faithfully accomplish all the required work in the seasons leading up to the harvest in order to reap its benefits when the crop matures and finally becomes ripe for the impending harvest.

The Example of Elijah

It can be no coincidence that at the beginning of chapter 5, James refers to the farmer patiently awaiting the rains, and then we find at the end of the same chapter the reference to Elijah and his relationship to the rain:

> *[17]Elijah was a man with a nature like ours, and he prayed earnestly that it would not rain, and it did not rain on the earth for three years and six months. [18]Then he prayed again, and the sky poured rain and the earth produced its fruit.(James 5:17–18)*

It is first and foremost notable that both Jesus and James refer to the literal, historical Elijah, but whereas Jesus casts him in the context of His First Coming, (Lk. 4:24-26) James' usage is for the Second Coming.

Jesus specifically stated that John the Baptist was the fulfillment of the prophetic expectation of someone coming in the spirit and power of Elijah immediately preceding the Messiah's First Coming, and further stipulated that Elijah should be expected to come yet again. (Mt. 17:10-13) However, there is no specific nor overt mention of Elijah in either the book of Revelation or the Olivet Discourse. One of the reasons for this may be the fact that just as John the Baptist came in the character of Elijah at the First Coming exclusively to literal and ethnic Israel, that the "Elijah to come" in the Second Coming will replay that role once again, explaining something about the process of Israel finally coming to accept Jesus as Messiah in the End Times. If so, his omission from the Olivet Discourse would be another confirmation that Jesus' teaching is primarily for the Church and not limited, as some assert, to only Israel.

But just as the illustrations of the farmer and Job have much to teach concerning expectations for End Times Christians, so the life of Elijah can contribute to the same, most notably in the fact that he does battle with an antichrist figure in Ahab, a system of spiritual seduction in the character of Mystery Babylon in the parallel of Jezebel and the prophets of Baal, and lives at a time when the remaining faithful have become just a small remnant. (1 Ki. 17-19) Most importantly, of course, he is someone who was not only literally raptured, but lived for a short period when his imminent rapture was not merely anticipated, but conspicuously expected. (2 Ki. 2:1-11) They recognized that Elijah's rapture was going to take place soon even though they did not know the day or the hour.

But whereas Jesus uses Elijah to illustrate what was taking place in the course of His First Coming, drawing a parallel to being rejected by Israel and then going to the Gentiles in a replay of events similar to Elijah's life, James instead highlights the withholding and restoring of rain as the seminal event mirroring the Second Coming.

One of the primary lessons specifically applicable to us in this example is that it was not Elijah's natural talents or abilities which made him an effective, great man of prayer, but rather his dedication and faith, things achievable by every believer—"*a man with a nature like ours*". It was the quality of his faithfulness in everyday life which was the best preparation for the extraordinary power and faithfulness which would come when times were hardest and darkest.

This is the repeated lesson concerning the condition of the End Times Christian which New Testament eschatology from beginning to end attempts to establish as pivotal. Elijah's participation in a spiritual battle of epic proportions in his encounters with Ahab, Jezebel and the prophets of Baal so as to withhold rain and then restore it to bring an end to a drought was accomplished by someone whose faithfulness in times of relative peace prepared him for those times of extraordinary testing. Remember, James preceded this example of Elijah by first asserting, "*The effective prayer of a righteous man can accomplish much*" (Ja. 5:16b), something which exists as well in a parallel to the righteousness of Job.

Summary

The founding generations of the 1st century Church would have understood this earliest of the rest of the Epistles yet to come as perfectly compatible with what was established in the Olivet Discourse. At this early point in Church history, James does not provide new and additional information to what was given in the Olivet Discourse, but rather an exhortation for patience and faithfulness in the examples of Job, Elijah and the Prophets, and as it applies in the illustration of the farmer working toward a future, inevitable harvest. That which James offers supplements and parallels that which Christ originally provided.

Whereas Jesus mentions Elijah's ministry as a parallel to what takes place in the course of His First Coming, James' usage highlights the Second Coming. Although Jesus specifically stated that all should expect Elijah to come again in the course of His Second Coming, because of there being no mention of Elijah in the Olivet Discourse (or the rest of the New Testament except for a brief mention by Paul in Romans 11), it is most likely they would have understood this in the context of the Old Testament Scriptures directly speaking of Elijah's arrival and ministry to come. Or perhaps, as so many of us do at present, seeing that John the Baptist came the first time "*in the spirit and power of Elijah*", (Lk. 1:17) that this would be replayed again in the course of Christ's Return when someone would come yet again to Israel in the character of Elijah to prepare for the coming of the Messiah. (A separate book on the subject of Elijah in the Second Coming, *Elijah to Come*, can be read or downloaded for free from the Walk with the Word website, or as an inexpensive Kindle eBook from Amazon.)

11 ❖ Peter's Commentary

Peter & the Gospel of Mark

A very common assertion across even otherwise contrasting theological and eschatological divides is that the Gospel of Mark was authored by way of Peter's dictation, or at the very least transcribed by Mark as he heard Peter's teachings firsthand. This would mean that Peter's mainstay instruction where the Second Coming is concerned would be one of the three renderings of the Olivet Discourse itself, in this case the one found in Mark 13. It would therefore be unavoidable to conclude that Peter's writings were anything but a commentary on the Olivet Discourse.

The First Epistle of Peter is thought to have been written shortly before 62 AD prior to the beginning of the severe persecution at the behest of Nero. The Second Epistle of Peter is believed to have been written not much longer after and shortly before Peter's death as in it he specifically mentions his belief that the end of his life is imminent, (2 Pe. 1:14-15) which would date it to approximately 64 AD. Most arguments for the date of the publication of the Gospel of Mark fall within this same general timeframe, plus or minus a few years.

Tradition holds that the signatory on the Gospel of Mark is the John Mark mentioned as the son of a certain Mary in Jerusalem (Acts 12:17) and a cousin of Barnabas (Col. 4:10) who accompanied Paul and Barnabas on their first missionary journey, (Acts 12:25; 13:5) but returned to Jerusalem upon reaching Perga. (Acts 13:13) This same John Mark is thought to have accompanied Barnabas on a subsequent missionary journey to Cyprus (Acts 15:37-39) and was later found in Paul's company in Rome. (Col. 4:10; Philemon 23-24) Tradition further holds that at some point while in Rome, he served as Peter's interpreter and would ultimately found and lead a church in Alexandria.

This is a necessary exercise so as to understand that if the source of the work bearing Mark's name holds true, this would mean that Peter authored the Gospel of Mark by close proximity with Mark and in the same general timeframe as when he authored his Epistles, certainly not more than a few years before his death and no more than ten or so before the destruction of Jerusalem and the Temple in 70 AD. This would also mean that Peter would have been relaying the Olivet Discourse in his own ministry for some thirty or so years from the Resurrection of Christ to his own death, and it would most certainly be foremost in his memory as he authored his Epistles as well. In other words, although the Gospel of Mark is located at the front of the New Testament, and it takes a while to read through the other works to get to 1 & 2 Peter located in the latter half, it appears they were authored within a few years of each other.

But in any case, the fact is that regardless of whether or not Peter is the primary source for the entire Gospel of Mark, Peter is only one of four sources from which Mark could have possibly learned about the Olivet Discourse:

> [3]*As He was sitting on the Mount of Olives opposite the temple,* **Peter and James and John and Andrew were questioning Him privately,** [4]*"Tell us, when will these things be, and what will be the sign when all these things are going to be fulfilled?" (Mark 13:3–4)*

If Mark did not get it from Peter, it had to come from one or more of these Apostles, and even if Mark's account is not a verbatim transcript of Peter's firsthand witness of this teaching, Peter unquestionably knew every detail of the Olivet Discourse without the aid of any other writings.

Because of the order and grouping of the New Testament books, we tend to think of the Gospels as the earliest and "first" books everyone in the Early Church was familiar with because that is what we read first in the way our modern Bibles are organized, and the Epistles as coming much later. This is true in terms of their historical content, but not necessarily pertaining to the sequence as to when they were literally authored and subsequently distributed as many of the Epistles actually arrived prior to the Gospels. In fact, most Bible dictionaries and commentaries will offer that the Gospel of Mark was the first Gospel published of the four.

In Peter's case, the contents of the Olivet Discourse would have been very "fresh" and relevant to him, not just because he may have relayed it to John Mark in the penning of his Gospel in the same timeframe when Peter would author his Epistles, but as stated, was one of the elite quartet of original witnesses. It was obviously a mainstay of his ministry's teaching, as would be all that was published in the Gospel of Mark if this scenario holds true, but he would nonetheless not be dependent on this or any of the Gospels, seeing how he is actually one of the sources they depended on for their content.

This historical background of Peter's writings is important to keep in mind because they are being produced when he believes that his death is imminent. He is therefore writing with the same reaction and motivation we would all have when presented with concrete knowledge that we only have a short time to live—that is, to relay to our loved ones the things we think are of the most importance.

Where the Second Coming of Christ is concerned, whether or not Peter has just provided the foundation of the Olivet Discourse through Mark, what "supplements" it in his Epistles released in that same general timeframe is naturally supportive as one of the only original witnesses of it. The substance of his Epistles, therefore, relates far more to specific Christian behavior rather than events of an eschatological nature. In other words, what was deemed as important to Peter in his Epistles was not setting down yet again the general sequence or individual milestones of the Second Coming, but the greater message originally conveyed by Christ in the Olivet Discourse and related teachings as to how believers should be found living when such events finally unfold.

This Salvation

*³Blessed be the God and Father of our Lord Jesus Christ, who according to His great mercy has caused us to be born again to a living hope through the resurrection of Jesus Christ from the dead, ⁴to obtain **an inheritance** which is imperishable and undefiled and will not fade away, **reserved in heaven** for you, ⁵who are protected by the power of God through faith for **a salvation ready to be revealed in the last time**. ⁶In this you greatly rejoice, even though now for a little while, if necessary, you have been distressed by various trials, ⁷so that the proof of your faith, being more precious than gold which is perishable, even though tested by fire, may be found to result in praise and glory and honor at **the revelation of Jesus Christ**; ⁸and though you have not seen Him, you love Him, and though you do not see Him now, but believe in Him, you greatly rejoice with joy inexpressible and full of glory, ⁹obtaining as the outcome of your faith **the salvation** of your souls. (1 Peter 1:3–9)*

Peter opens with multiple references to Christ's Second Coming with an emphasis on the fact that what is taking place in this life will be transcended by what is to come in the next, the milestone of crossing over here identified as "*the revelation of Jesus Christ*". (v.7) This is supported by references to "*an inheritance...reserved in heaven for you*" (v.4) and "*obtaining as the outcome of your faith the salvation of your souls*". (v.9) The eschatological focus, where Peter is concerned, is the greater spiritual end result of the completed work of salvation more than anything else, which he describes eschatologically, "*a salvation ready to be revealed in the last time*". (At present, there seem to be many who think the "end" is the Rapture, rather than realizing they must be equally qualified spiritually whether the end comes by Rapture or Resurrection.)

He further specifies that leading up to the completion of the work of salvation that there are "*...for a little while...various trials..*" which refine our faith so that we are being "*tested with fire*". (v.6-7) The events of the eschaton which are anticipated to come are not going to produce faithfulness in and of themselves, but rather that which is experienced in the course of this life leading up to it. Whereas Peter states here that believers will be "*tested with fire*", he will later contrast this to unbelievers being "*reserved for fire*". (2 Pe. 3:7)

> ^{10}As to **this salvation**, the prophets who prophesied of the grace that would come to you made careful searches and inquiries, ^{11}seeking to know what person or time the Spirit of Christ within them was indicating as He predicted the sufferings of Christ and the glories to follow. ^{12}It was revealed to them that they were not serving themselves, but you, in these things which now have been announced to you through those who preached the gospel to you by the Holy Spirit sent from heaven—things into which angels long to look. (1 Peter 1:10–12)

This is an interesting extension of the Olivet Discourse's teaching, "*But of that day and hour no one knows*" (Mt. 24:36; Mk. 13:32) and how Jesus said that at the time even He and the angels of heaven did not know, but the Father alone. Here we can add to that list of those who cannot supply a specific date the Prophets of Scripture as well. (Remember this the next time someone invents a "Bible code" or reinterprets a prophecy to calculate a date—even the Prophets do not know.) In the opening verses is found an important caveat that in the shadow of the Last Days, new eschatological revelations have been provided to a special group, "*announced to you through those who preached the gospel to you by the Holy Spirit*". (v.12) The entirety of the work for both the First and Second Comings is again labeled, "*this salvation*", (v.10) something cast in a positive light for believers rather than the doom of God's wrath for non-believers, but the overall understanding of which is not possible for any except Holy Spirit-filled believers.

"Revelation" and "Visitation"

> *¹³Therefore, prepare your minds for action, keep sober in spirit, fix your hope completely on the grace to be brought to you at **the revelation of Jesus Christ**. ¹⁴As obedient children, do not be conformed to the former lusts which were yours in your ignorance, ¹⁵but like the Holy One who called you, be holy yourselves also in all your behavior; ¹⁶because it is written, "YOU SHALL BE HOLY, FOR I AM HOLY." (1 Peter 1:13–16)*

The keyword "*therefore*" indicates that Peter is summing up the meaning of the teaching to this point, and the admonition to maintain faithfulness and live in accordance with God's Word and ways very much parallels what is characterized as the most important behavior of Christians in the Last Days as conveyed by the Olivet Discourse. The direct connection to the Second Coming is here expressed, "*fix your hope completely on the grace to be brought to you at the revelation of Jesus Christ*". (v.13); it is not to fix our hope on an event such as the Rapture, which will take care of itself if we are consistently faithful to Christ, but rather the contrast of forsaking "*the former lusts*" in the pursuit of being "*holy yourselves also in all your behavior*".

One of the things which many commentators point out in the course of understanding New Testament Scripture in general is that there is actually a reason when the text provides His name in the order "*Jesus Christ*" as opposed to "*Christ Jesus*". We are told that "*Jesus Christ*" places the emphasis on His earthly ministry or working in the earthly realm, whereas the opposite order "*Christ Jesus*" stresses the context of His heavenly ministry and working in the eternal. This hermeneutic would indicate that Peter's reference to the "*revelation of Jesus Christ*" is a literal appearance in this earthly arena and not some kind of heavenly spiritualization.

> *¹⁷If you address as Father the One who impartially judges according to each one's work, conduct yourselves in fear **during the time of your stay on earth**; ¹⁸knowing that you were not redeemed with perishable things like silver or gold from your futile way of life inherited from your forefathers, ¹⁹but with precious blood, as of a lamb unblemished and spotless, the blood of Christ. ²⁰For He was foreknown before the foundation of the world, but has appeared **in these last times** for the sake*

of you *21who through Him are believers in God, who raised Him from the dead and gave Him glory, so that your faith and hope are in God. (1 Peter 1:17–21)*

In making reference to the ultimate judgment of our work we are admonished, *"conduct yourselves in fear during the time of your stay on earth"* (v.17), something which very much parallels the many examples in Christ's teachings of believers ultimately being held accountable for their deeds while awaiting the Master's return. But Peter provides an additional, wonderful affirmation that His *"appearance in these last times for your sakes"* (v.20) is actually something *"foreknown before the foundation of the world"*, (v.20) a reassurance that this is all going according to God's specific, prearranged plan.

It may be of further importance that the underlying Greek word *"chronos"* (Strong's #5550) is used for *"times"* as in *"these last times"*. The English renderings of *"time"* or *"times"* throughout the New Testament are actually two different Greek words, *"kairos"* (Strong's #2540)—which is mostly used in the character of a clock to denote something with a specific start and end, or a timed event, and *"chronos"*—which is most often used in the sense of a chronology, which is a sequence of events taking place without necessarily being timed by a clock or calendar. In other words, Peter is not setting a specific date because no one can know the day or the hour, but rather affirming that the definition of the *"last days"* is a sequence, which when achieved in its foreordained order, brings about ultimate fulfillment.

*22Since you have in obedience to the truth purified your souls for a sincere love of the brethren, **fervently love one another from the heart**, 23for you have been born again not of seed which is perishable but imperishable, that is, through the living and enduring word of God. 24For,*

"ALL FLESH IS LIKE GRASS,
AND ALL ITS GLORY LIKE THE FLOWER OF GRASS.
THE GRASS WITHERS,
AND THE FLOWER FALLS OFF,
25BUT THE WORD OF THE LORD ENDURES FOREVER."

And this is the word which was preached to you. (1 Peter 1:22–25)

This summation elegantly supports the Olivet Discourse's concerns that in spite of the End Times' environment, Christian love is in danger of growing cold (Mt. 24:12) and that vigilance needs to be maintained where God's Word is concerned. (Mt. 25:1-13) Again, the priority is placed on our behavior during the End Times more than precisely plotting the individual milestones defining it.

> *¹¹Beloved, I urge you as aliens and strangers to abstain from fleshly lusts which wage war against the soul. ¹²Keep your behavior excellent among the Gentiles, so that in the thing in which they slander you as evildoers, they may because of your good deeds, as they observe them, **glorify God in the day of visitation**. (1 Peter 2:11–12)*

The specific use of the phrase *"the day of visitation"* carries with it the meaning of God "visiting" men to reward for righteousness or alternatively to "visit" in order to render punishment for evil. Jesus used this phrase in the closing days of His earthly ministry to describe the literal consequences of destruction which was going to come on Jerusalem and the Temple for that generation's rejection of Him at His First Coming.

> *⁴³"For **the days will come** upon you when your enemies will throw up a barricade against you, and surround you and hem you in on every side, ⁴⁴and they will level you to the ground and your children within you, and they will not leave in you one stone upon another, because you did not recognize **the time of your visitation.**" (Luke 19:43–44)*

But in either case, this parallels Peter's use of *"the revelation of Jesus Christ"* to describe the literal return of Christ. Accompanying this are warnings about believers' personal behavior and witness to the world at large, another staple of the Olivet Discourse.

The underlying Greek word for *"visitation"*—*"episkope"* (Strong's #1984), is the same word from which we get the office of *"overseer"* or *"bishop"*. What is being conveyed in its usage as *"the day of visitation"* is the idea of intently observing or inspecting so as to pass and protect the faithful, but at the same time to judge and condemn the faithless. The appearance to all of the One Judge has a simultaneous, but opposite effect for both the righteous and the wicked when they are "visited" by Him.

A Few Brought Safely Through

> *[18]For Christ also died for sins once for all, the just for the unjust, so that He might bring us to God, having been put to death in the flesh, but made alive in the spirit; [19]in which also He went and made proclamation to the spirits now in prison, [20]who once were disobedient, when the patience of God kept waiting **in the days of Noah**, during the construction of the ark, in which a few, that is, eight persons, were **brought safely through** the water. (1 Peter 3:18–20)*

Practically whole books, much less countless papers, articles and commentaries have been dedicated to these verses, and the purpose of this author is not to visit this to that degree of detail, but only to highlight the greater message which is being illustrated. These verses emphasize that there is a greater power of the working of Christ, whose end did not come in the course of physical death, but instead overcame it by the Resurrection—"*made alive in the spirit*". The point is that just as believers were brought safely through what was sure death for non-believers in the events of Noah's days, so in similar fashion believers in Christ will be saved in spite of the same kind of cataclysmic world judgment in the Last Days.

A point not to be quickly passed over is the reference, "*when God kept waiting in the days of Noah, during the construction of the ark*". (v.30) While Scripture does not seem to overtly state how long the construction of the ark took, we do know that God's announcement of His intentions specified judgment would come upon the earth at that time within 120 years of His announcement to Noah:

> *[3]Then the LORD said, "My Spirit shall not strive with man forever, because he also is flesh; nevertheless his days shall be one hundred and twenty years." (Genesis 6:3)*

So there was an extended time period when Noah would have made known God's intentions not only by what he had been told, but subsequently by the length of time it took for the construction for the ark as well. As the nearness of the Flood approached, there was the gathering of animals to be taken on board additionally testifying to the increasing nearness of what was to come, but then just seven days before the rains came, God commanded Noah and his family to enter the ark. (Gen. 7:1-5)

> *[10]It came about after the seven days, that the water of the flood came upon the earth. (Genesis 7:10)*

In other words, there was a progression of events which were plainly visible to everyone which testified to what God was about to do which became more intense and closer together before the final closing of the door of the ark by the Lord (Gen. 7:16) and the onset of the Flood, (Gen. 7:17-24) but the remnant was nonetheless saved. However, it was not a "secret" flood which came without any warning whatsoever, but rose out of a general visible environment which escalated into a much more intense, compact period briefly before the end; there were plenty of signs leading up to it with God Himself narrowing the timeframe for Noah and his family.

This very much parallels the timeline of the Olivet Discourse which denotes that we should first recognize the season and the harvest which is about to take place, and like those in Noah's days who were warned and subsequently saw the signs in the sky of the gathering of clouds for the unprecedented rain about to come, so will everyone ultimately see "*the sign of the Son of Man*" which "*will appear in the sky*" (Mt. 24:30)

Christian Living

> [7]**The end of all things is near**; *therefore, be of sound judgment and sober spirit for the purpose of prayer. [8]Above all, keep fervent in your love for one another, because love covers a multitude of sins. [9]Be hospitable to one another without complaint. [10]As each one has received a special gift, employ it in serving one another as good stewards of the manifold grace of God. [11]Whoever speaks, is to do so as one who is speaking the utterances of God; whoever serves is to do so as one who is serving by the strength which God supplies; so that in all things God may be glorified through Jesus Christ, to whom belongs the glory and dominion forever and ever. Amen. (1 Peter 4:7–11)*

This is an affirmation of what is most important for Christians living in the shadow of the Second Coming, that the priority is on our behavior and faithfulness:

➤ "*…sound judgment…*" (v.7)

➤ "*…sober spirit…*" (v.7)

➤ "*…for the purpose of prayer*". (v.7)

➤ "*…fervent in your love…*" (v.8)

➤ *"…hospitable…without complaint"*. (v.9)

➤ Using our gifts *"serving one another…"* (v.10)

➤ *"…good stewards…"* (v.10)

➤ *"…speaking the utterances of God…"* (v.11)

➤ *"…serving by the strength God supplies…"* (v.11)

This list of behaviors closely reflects those qualities expounded in the illustrations and parables within the Olivet Discourse such as the *Wise Virgins*, the *Faithful Steward* and so forth, but paying particular attention that the common denominator of these behaviors is our love and treatment of others, not designing an End Times chart or merely waiting for God to judge the wicked.

Once again, when the time is near, the admonition is not for Christians to act or prepare for these events differently, but that it is even more important than ever for us to live and behave according to God's Word and ways, especially toward one another just as we always have ostensibly lived. The repeated New Testament theme consistent with the examples provided in the Olivet Discourse is a call to always walk faithfully so as to be found at the moment of His coming to be living and working for Him, not changing things up or acting differently at the last possible moment so as to save ourselves. Being ready "then" is actually an exercise in being ready "now" by our example of the full work of salvation on display.

It Begins with the Household of God

[12]*Beloved, do not be surprised at the fiery ordeal among you, which comes upon you for your testing, as though some strange thing were happening to you;* [13]*but to the degree that you share the sufferings of Christ, keep on rejoicing,* **so that also at the revelation of His glory you may rejoice with exultation.** [14]*If you are reviled for the name of Christ, you are blessed, because the Spirit of glory and of God rests on you.* [15]*Make sure that none of you suffers as a murderer, or thief, or evildoer, or a troublesome meddler;* [16]*but if anyone suffers as a Christian, he is not to be ashamed, but is to glorify God in this name.* [17]**For it is time for judgment to begin with the household of God; and if it begins with us first, what will be the outcome for those who do not obey the gospel of God?** [18]*AND IF IT IS WITH DIFFICULTY THAT THE RIGHTEOUS IS SAVED, WHAT WILL BECOME OF*

THE GODLESS MAN AND THE SINNER? ¹⁹*Therefore, those also who suffer according to the will of God shall entrust their souls to a faithful Creator in doing what is right. (1 Peter 4:12–19)*

Peter's admonition greatly parallels what to do when the greater issues of apostasy, deception and persecution arise in the End Times, as well as James' parallel teaching of the endurance of Job. Just as the illustrations and parables of the Olivet Discourse demand endurance until the return of the Master and Bridegroom, likewise the task presented here occupies us until "*the revelation of His glory*".

It is important to note in verse 17 the very specific reason which is given as to why the Church will have to endure these things in the earthly arena, "*For it is time for judgment to begin with the household of God*". As stated previously, it is important to differentiate between "*judgment*", which is something which everyone must undergo, and "*wrath*", which is only experienced by those rejecting Christ. Judgment begins with God's people and escalates to everyone, but only ends badly for those ultimately rejecting Him. (This is literally seen in both the Olivet Discourse, where the "*tribulation*" of the Church is experienced before the "*great tribulation*" of the whole world, and in Revelation when the 5th Seal of the Church's persecution first comes before the wrath poured out on those remaining in the 5th Trumpet.)

A biblical illustration of this is the distinction which took place between Israel and Egypt in the Exodus account. In that series of events, which seems to be replayed again in the course of the Second Coming, the first three plagues rendered through Moses and Aaron were experienced by everyone, both Israelite and Egyptian alike. (Ex. 7-8) Between the third and fourth plagues, however, God declared that a distinction would be made going forward where only the Egyptians would experience the rest of the plagues and His people would be exempt. (Ex. 8:22-23) One way of looking at this is that basically no one was exempt from the first third of the plagues as a common judgment upon everyone, but after that it was only non-believers who experienced the final plagues of God's wrath poured out on Pharaoh's kingdom, a biblical representation of the kingdom of Antichrist. But prior to the plagues taking place, when Moses and Aaron first appeared on the scene, Israel experienced the persecution of Pharaoh, which turned out to be a time God used to prepare His people both spiritually and physically for what was about to come and their ultimate removal. In fact, things got much harder for God's people before they got better.

This is an important lesson in order to fully understand Peter's statement, "*Therefore, those also who suffer according to the will of God shall entrust their souls to a faithful Creator in doing what is right*". (v.19) Just as there was a purpose in what turned out to be the necessary preparation of God's people as they entered into and experienced at least the beginning of these things along with everyone else, so it again takes place for the Church as it enters into what the Olivet Discourse calls "*tribulation*", escalating into the briefer more intense period of "*great tribulation*" before being exempted from the full onset of "*the day of the Lord*", which answers the rhetorical question, "*What will become of the godless man and the sinner?*"

Conduct within the Household of God

*¹Therefore, I exhort the elders among you, as your fellow elder and witness of the sufferings of Christ, and a partaker also of **the glory that is to be revealed**, ²shepherd the flock of God among you, exercising oversight not under compulsion, but voluntarily, according to the will of God; and not for sordid gain, but with eagerness; ³nor yet as lording it over those allotted to your charge, but proving to be examples to the flock. ⁴And **when the Chief Shepherd appears**, you will receive the unfading crown of glory. ⁵You younger men, likewise, be subject to your elders; and all of you, clothe yourselves with humility toward one another, for GOD IS OPPOSED TO THE PROUD, BUT GIVES GRACE TO THE HUMBLE. (1 Peter 5:1–5)*

Just as the Olivet Discourse addresses not only how servants of the Master should conduct their selves while He is away, but directly targets those left in charge of the others in the Master's household as well, so Peter specifies the behavior expected of Christian leadership in the whole of the time leading up to His Return. Whereas the Olivet Discourse emphasized the danger of those in charge thinking they can misuse their position and details those abuses and misbehavior, Peter emphasizes the positive characteristics of a true and faithful shepherd living and acting consistently until the appearing of Christ the Chief Shepherd. Peter then adds caveats for those who should be subject to that leadership until the appearing of Christ, again emphasizing personal behavior, especially humility, one of the best biblical antidotes for addressing the common destructive root cause of pride, humility's exact opposite.

The Importance of the Word

*¹⁹So we have the prophetic word made more sure, to which you do well to pay attention as to a lamp shining in a dark place, **until the day dawns and the morning star arises in your hearts**. ²⁰But know this first of all, that no prophecy of Scripture is a matter of one's own interpretation, ²¹for no prophecy was ever made by an act of human will, but men moved by the Holy Spirit spoke from God. (2 Peter 1:19–21)*

This is an excellent commentary in support of *The Parable of the Wise and Foolish Virgins,* (Mt. 25:1-13) elaborating on the importance of God's Word as a lamp and the admonition to remain not just vigilant in His Word but in the anointing of the Holy Spirit, and particularly singling out *"the prophetic word"*. There are those who propose that biblical prophecy is not a hard and fast requirement of the faith, that is all up for debate, which then renders those who accept that proposition dead and blind to all the warning signs and indications of His coming.

We could probably also write a book concerning just this statement alone that *"no prophecy of Scripture is a matter of one's own interpretation"*. (v20) This flies directly in the face of the many times we have heard it said or seen it written that since more than one party cannot agree on what a particular passage or aspect of prophetic Scripture is conveying, that all concerned should "agree to disagree". We would not do such a thing if it concerned a fundamental doctrine such as something pertaining to salvation, justification or sanctification, and yet this seems to apply the same kind of rigidity which is most often exempted from prophetic portions of God's Word. But it cannot be overstated that it cannot come about by *"one's own interpretation"* as *"an act of human will"*, but has to be pursued through the Holy Spirit. It was only the *Wise Virgins,* having the Word through the anointing of the Holy Spirit, who were ultimately found ready and allowed to enter with the arrival of the Bridegroom, and the accompanying text even specifies the inclusion of *"the prophetic word"*.

However, there is a condition which must be met here in the caveat, *"until the day dawns and the morning star arises in your hearts"*. (v.19) This appears to fit well with the definition of the word *"revelation"* (Greek *"apokalupsis"*— Strong's #602), something being unveiled and coming into clearer and clearer focus the closer we approach and enter into its proximity. This is a call to continually study prophecy, vigilant to do so even in a growing climate of spiritual darkness, so that we will be able to fully understand what is taking place when it matters the most. In tandem with Peter's reminder that in the shadow of Jesus' Return it is more important than ever to behave and act accordingly so as to be spiritually prepared by the quality of our faithfulness, likewise we are to remain equally faithful and committed to God's prophetic Word so that at every stage along the way it will be *"made more sure"* to us personally. (v.19) It is not something open-ended which allows for mutually exclusive interpretations.

This can be characterized as a call to continually seek the true meaning of scriptural passages of prophecy rather than merely assigning to it many varied and possible scenarios. We might consider the Prophet Daniel as the model for this, someone who not only specified that as the Last Days draw closer our understanding would become clearer, (Dan. 12:10) but became aware of the fulfillment of prophecy in his own time while studying God's Word (Dan. 9:1-2) and reacted accordingly:

> ³So I gave my attention to the Lord God to seek Him by prayer and supplications, with fasting, sackcloth and ashes. (Daniel 9:3)

It would seem that these are the kinds of activities which should be pursued by those who truly recognize the signs of the nearness of His Return.

What It Will Really Be Like

> ⁴For if God **did not spare** angels when they sinned, but cast them into hell and committed them to pits of darkness, reserved for judgment; ⁵and **did not spare** the ancient world, but **preserved** Noah, a preacher of righteousness, with seven others, when He brought a flood upon the world of the ungodly; ⁶and if He **condemned** the cities of Sodom and Gomorrah to destruction by reducing them to ashes, having made them an example to those who would live ungodly lives thereafter; ⁷and if He **rescued** righteous Lot, oppressed by the sensual conduct of unprincipled men ⁸(for by what he saw and heard that righteous man, while living among them, felt his righteous soul tormented day after day by their lawless deeds), ⁹Then the Lord knows how to **rescue** the godly from temptation, and to **keep** the unrighteous under punishment for the day of judgment, ¹⁰and especially those who indulge the flesh in its corrupt desires and despise authority. (2 Peter 2:4–10a)

As to the continual question of who exactly is "*taken*", note that in the case of the rebellious angels God "*cast them into hell*" (v.4), in Noah's day God "*preserved Noah*" but "*He brought a flood upon the world of the ungodly*" (v.5), and that He "*rescued righteous Lot*" (v.5) but "*condemned the cities of Sodom and Gomorrah to destruction by reducing them to ashes*". (v.6) The overall summary used by Peter to describe what God does regarding both groups is, "...*the Lord knows how to **rescue** the godly...and to **keep** the unrighteous under punishment...*" (v.9) God's people are "*taken*" so as to be exempted, the wicked are not and therefore "left behind" to experience the worst to come.

Those who are identified as parties who will experience God's judgment exhibit the spiritual conditions of having "*sinned*" (the angels in v.4), are "*ungodly*" (in Noah's day and Lot's in v.5-6), and engaged in "*sensual conduct of unprincipled men"* (v.7), *"lawless deeds"* (v.8), *"indulge in the flesh in its corrupt desires"* (v.10), and finally who *"despise authority"*.

In the growing spiritual darkness which the Olivet Discourse describes as unprecedented apostasy, deception and persecution, Peter does not merely offer that God eventually rescued the righteous from what the rest of the world would experience in the days of Noah and Lot, but shows how they were preserved through it in terms of something even more important than being rescued from the physical judgments: they were able to be *"an example to those who live ungodly lives"* (v.6) and rescued *"from temptation"* (v.9).

This can be seen as a commentary delving deeper into the Olivet Discourse's assertion that one of the primary activities of Christians in the Last Days is to be afforded the opportunity to preach the Gospel to the whole world and to personally testify at every level concerning Christ and their faith. The primary examples of Noah and Lot are not simply models of an ultimate escape, but in the consistency of their faith and work right up to the very end. It was God's intention that they be around to serve as visible testimonies of faithfulness to those who were going to suffer the consequences of what was coming for their faithlessness.

> *³Know this first of all, that **in the last days** mockers will come with their mocking, following after their own lusts, ⁴and saying, "Where is the promise of His coming? For ever since the fathers fell asleep, all continues just as it was from the beginning of creation." ⁵For when they maintain this, it escapes their notice that by the word of God the heavens existed long ago and the earth was formed out of water and by water, ⁶Through which the world at that time was destroyed, being flooded with water. ⁷But by His word the present heavens and earth are being reserved for fire, kept for **the day of judgment** and destruction of ungodly men. (2 Peter 3:3–7)*

This hits home personally for me because in the first half of my life, everyone I knew or heard or read were in unanimous agreement that Jesus is about to Return, but in the second half of my life I have witnessed so many of them actually turn completely around to ask, *"Where is the promise of His coming?"* There are very public figures who can be documented as having become such mockers, and it is frankly quite disturbing because it often comes from those claiming some kind of membership within the Church rather than from the usual host of detractors attacking from a distance. This is an aspect of the deception which can be expected to be encountered in the Last Days, and like many other things discussed so far, has already begun to manifest itself. Unfortunately, what is transpiring today in this regard is a sign in itself of being closer than ever to His Return.

But a core reason for this behavior is attributed to those who are no longer following Jesus according to His Word, but *"following after their own lusts"*. Those whom I've witnessed becoming such antagonists have shared this common behavior in some way, engaging in what makes them feel good in some worldly sense in contradiction to the standard of God's Word, some even becoming devoted to a lifestyle of sin. We need to recognize that there are those who cannot be rescued just by telling them the truth, but only by repenting and genuinely turning away from the underlying issue of sin at the source of it all.

> *8But do not let this one fact escape your notice, beloved, that with the Lord one day is like a thousand years, and a thousand years like one day. 9The Lord is not slow about His promise, as some count slowness, but is patient toward you, not wishing for any to perish but for all to come to repentance. 10But **the day of the Lord** will come like a thief, in which the heavens will pass away with a roar and the elements will be destroyed with intense heat, and the earth and its works will be burned up. 11Since all these things are to be destroyed in this way, what sort of people ought you to be in holy conduct and godliness, 12looking for and hastening the coming of **the day of God**, because of which the heavens will be destroyed by burning, and the elements will melt with intense heat! 13But according to His promise we are looking for new heavens and a new earth, in which righteousness dwells. (2 Peter 3:8–13)*

When it comes to abuses of God's prophetic Word, there are few snippets of Scripture which have been taken advantage of more than a particular phrase contained in these verses. For some reason this *"one day is like a thousand years, and a thousand years like one day"* is persistently twisted into a license for so-called "Bible codes" and the application of wild and fanciful mathematical manipulation of almost any passage mentioning a number so that date after date after date of Christ's Return has been set, even though Scripture explicitly commands against it.

We can agree that there have been six 1,000 year periods recorded in biblical history from Adam to the present, and when combined with the 1,000 year Millennial Reign yet to come, it certainly seems like a case can be made for a "week" of days, each being roughly 1,000 years in length. But even if that is something being suggested here, this is not a coded message which can be used to predict the day or the hour, much less even the year, of His Return, but an unambiguous and direct warning against that very thing! This is a message about the incomprehensible depth of God's grace, specifying He is *"not wishing for any to perish but for all to come to repentance"*. (v.9) And once more the very definition of *"the day of the Lord"* is affirmed as that time when repentance is no longer possible and the only thing left is the destruction of final judgment. For us to have to endure in the character of Noah or Lot is to do so for the sake of the unsaved, seeking the maximum time possible for their repentance before that chance comes to an ultimate, conclusive end.

It is very interesting to note that in verses 12-13, Peter admonishes believers that they are not supposed to be looking forward to *"the day of God"*—another way of describing *"the day of the Lord"*, which is automatically associated with the destruction of the earth because of sin and wickedness, *"But according to His promise we are looking for new heavens and a new earth, in which righteousness dwells"*. (v.13) Godly believers are burdened by the knowledge of what happens to non-believers when *"the day of the Lord"* finally arrives and their time runs out, not rooting for some kind of comeuppance for the wicked. Instead, those striving for *"holy conduct and godliness"* (v.11) set their sights on that place *"in which righteousness dwells"*. (v.13) This is because it is a future extension of how we are supposed to be living in the present, that just as our focus is supposed to be on living righteously in this present life, our future vision is fixed on living in righteousness in the next. Just as the message of the Olivet Discourse and the Apostolic commentaries on it are that Christians are supposed to be living faithfully all the time, not just in the Last Days, so our hope is fixed on achieving the right behavior and spiritual condition not just for this life, but the one to come.

> *14Therefore, beloved, **since you look for these things**, be diligent to be found by Him in peace, spotless and blameless, 15and regard the patience of our Lord as salvation; just as also our beloved brother Paul, according to the wisdom given him, wrote to you, 16as also in all his letters, speaking in them of these things, in which are some things hard to understand, which the untaught and unstable distort, as they do also the rest of the Scriptures, to their own destruction. 17You therefore, beloved, knowing this beforehand, **be on your guard** so that you are not carried away by the error of unprincipled men and fall from your own steadfastness, 18but grow in the grace and knowledge of our Lord and Savior Jesus Christ. To Him be the glory, both now and to **the day of eternity**. Amen. (2 Peter 3:14–18)*

Are those who "*look for these things*" directed to make charts, predict dates, or become obsessed with all things pertaining to the events of the eschaton?

> "*...be diligent...*" (v.14)

> "*...found by Him in peace...*" (v.14)

> "*...spotless and blameless...*" (v.14)

> "*...regard the patience of our Lord as salvation...*" (v.15)

Not only does Peter re-emphasize the importance of personal faithfulness where the End Times are concerned, but affirms the same through the teachings of the Apostle Paul. Notice that Peter specifically warns to "*be on your guard*" against a greater danger which challenges our personal faithfulness in the form of a "*fall from your own steadfastness*". (v.17) Again, it is the steadfastness of a consistent faith and walk in Christ each and every day as we patiently await His Return which renders us ready, alert, and prepared at His appearance, no matter when it happens.

But there is also something particularly relevant for our present time, and that is Peter's warning that when it comes to Paul's writings to be aware that there are those who "*distort, as they do the rest of the Scripture*". (v.16) As will be seen in the upcoming discussion in chapter *12 • Paul & the Thessalonians*, there seems to be an endless supply of those who distort what Paul states, particularly in 2 Thessalonians 2:1-12. Some of the most prominent speakers, authors and professors claiming membership in the Evangelical community are not just exchanging at will the translation of the English from the underlying Greek, but have actually taken the unprecedented step of reaching down into the original Greek text itself and making changes to their liking! (For those who are interested in a detailed examination of what has specifically taken place, please read a Walk with the Word commentary published on the website titled, *When Change is Expressly Forbidden.*)

Summary

There is nothing new which Peter adds in his Epistles which was not originally covered in his account of the Olivet Discourse captured by Mark in his Gospel or from Christ's related teachings. And there are certainly no references to Revelation, something to come decades distant from his life and writings. At a time when Peter believes it has been divinely revealed to him that his own time on earth is quickly drawing to a close, the emphasis is on that which he deems is most important, those aspects of the Olivet Discourse which are focused on how a Christian should be found living in the shadow of Jesus' Return.

Rather than focusing on the return of Christ in the event of what is elsewhere referred to as the *"Episunagoge"*—that is, the gathering of the resurrected and raptured to Jesus preceded by the whole world's sighting of Him, Peter emphasizes what is the more important successor to that event, that our ultimate focus is, *"But according to His promise we are looking for new heavens and a new earth, in which righteousness dwells."* (2 Pe. 3:13) Peter keeps using terms such as *"this salvation"*, *"the revelation"*, *"visitation"* and *"the day of eternity"* in various forms to emphasize that it is the very end of the entire process which is most important for us and for which we are actually striving, rather than any intermediary goal or event along the way. (Imagine how different a prophecy conference would be if all the emphasis was placed on being spiritually qualified for the end result rather than whipping everyone into a frenzy over one of the milestone events or an End Times personality.)

Even when he provides parallel material to the illustrations and parables presented in the Olivet Discourse, they overwhelmingly emphasize these aspects of faithful Christian living. Yes, Noah and his family were rescued, and likewise Lot, but the greater takeaway from their examples, according to Peter, is how they faithfully endured and bore witness to God through their steadfast faith right up to the very last moment possible. Such are those found ready in the illustrations of the Olivet Discourse in the returning Bridegroom and Master; such are those found "dressed and ready" for the Master's wedding feast.

It is at the least interesting to note that it is not just that Peter had spent some thirty plus years of ministry teaching about Christ's Return with no knowledge of the book of Revelation (still thirty or so additional years distant) and exclusively with the Olivet Discourse as his chief guide, but he did not see the need to supplement or expand upon it. Not only is the timeline of the Olivet Discourse enough for Peter, his message, and his ministry, but it is those aspects of Christian living emphasized within it which he affirms as the most important qualities which he reinforces in what amounts to his own commentary on it.

12 ❖ Paul & the Thessalonians

*I*t must be kept in mind that although not an eye witness of Christ's earthly ministry, Paul possessed at least two things which placed him in the same standing as the other founding Apostles. The first was the fact that he had a direct encounter with Christ, not just on the road to Damascus in the course of his conversion experience, but was soon after sent into the wilderness for a number of years where he received instruction from Christ. (Gal. 1:15-18) This is seen in his teaching on Communion and the Last Supper where he relates, as a direct witness, not what he heard from others, but had personally "*received from the Lord*". (1 Co. 11:23) Much of what Paul teaches came to him as the result of direct instruction from Christ and is the main reason that he is certainly on equal footing with the original Apostles where the authority of his teaching is concerned.

> *11For I would have you know, brethren, that the gospel which was preached by me is not according to man. 12For I neither received it from man, nor was I taught it, but **I received it through a revelation of Jesus Christ**. (Galatians 1:11–12)*

But secondly, it is important to remember that one of his traveling companions at various times was Luke, the physician by trade who researched and authored the Gospel of the same name as well as the book of Acts. We see this in Acts where the pronouns often change to say "*we*" went here or there and "*we*" did this or that to indicate he was actually present with Paul at those times. It is thought that it was during the years of Paul's having to endure the bureaucratic process of hearings at the various levels leading up to his ultimate appearance before the emperor of Rome when Luke interviewed the witnesses of Jesus' life and ministry which ultimately resulted in the Gospel of Luke. It is therefore quite likely that Paul would have had more than just a passing familiarity with Luke's material and, for the purposes of this discussion, the Olivet Discourse included in his Gospel. It would be hard to imagine that they spent so many years together as traveling companions and ministry partners without ever discussing Luke's research, interviews and writings.

There is the additional fact that Paul not only crossed paths with Peter to the degree that they obviously spent significant time together, but according to tradition, ended up in Rome around the same time to suffer their fates at the hand of Nero. Paul would have been familiar with Peter's teachings and writings as well, especially the Gospel of Mark which often parallels the Gospel of Luke, and likewise, Peter made specific reference to Paul's writings, personally endorsing his authority. (2 Pe. 3:15-16) In other words, Paul was in a unique position which may have allowed him to be more than just acquainted with most of the New Testament writers and their writings, perhaps almost more than anyone during his lifetime and that of the first generation of believers; or at the least he possessed a working knowledge of their sources which was far above average because of his contact with Luke and those who witnessed Christ's ministry including Peter and the other Apostles and New Testament authors with which he had such a close association.

Of all the New Testament texts directly relating to the eschatology of Christ's Second Coming, it is one assigned to Paul which is the metaphorical tempest in a tea pot and seems at times to be debated more than the Olivet Discourse, the book of Revelation, and the whole of Old Testament prophecy combined. Apparently the confusion concerning *"the day of the Lord"* and related events experienced by the church at Thessalonica has cyclically resurfaced at various times in Church history, but especially so at this present hour. For some reason, the same errors keep turning up, and even more so today. The main issue which has given rise to the main eschatologies embraced today are united in their disagreement over *"the day of the Lord"*; their opposition on the timing of the Rapture stems from a dramatic conflict of their respective definitions of *"the day of the Lord"*.

That being said, we have preserved Paul's writings to many of the earliest churches more than those from any other Apostle, and the common theme of each letter shows that Paul by nature was a problem solver. Each Epistle is largely aimed at addressing specific issues unique to that particular person or church, and there is often found in each one a distinct area of doctrine addressed in far more detail than within any of the other Epistles because of what is at issue in that particular church or person. In the case of eschatology, Thessalonica was the place experiencing the most difficulty and requiring a much deeper treatment of the subject than any of the others.

To be sure, there is much material in the rest of Paul's writings, but for the purposes of our discussion we will focus on the church at Thessalonica.

The Background of Thessalonica

It is highly recommended that readers acquire the book *Harpazo* authored by Jacob Prasch of Moriel Ministries, (print edition available from Moriel Ministries and the eBook from Amazon), especially for its detailed treatment of what was taking place in Thessalonica in *"Chapter 22: Imminency & the Harpazo"*. This is a more thorough explanation of the issues involved not just at the time of Paul's original writing, but in how they are presently being replayed yet again where a misconceived concept of imminency escalates to produce a wrong notion of the precise order and sequence of End Times events.

Nonetheless, the fact is that the reader needs to pay particular attention to how any author or speaker handles 2 Thessalonians 2:1-12, as in recent years there has been a gross mishandling of these verses (especially 2 Thessalonians 2:3) by figures holding prominence in the Church proper which is historically unprecedented in what is so heinously taking place. So-called Evangelicals are cutting and pasting not only parts of 1 Thessalonians 5 with 2 Thessalonians 2 so as to make Scripture appear to say something it absolutely does not, but they have now reached down into the Greek text itself to cut-and-paste the original language to suit themselves. By replacing the Greek *"apostasia"* (Strong's #646, meaning a spiritual "falling away") in 2 Thessalonians 2:3 with their preference of *"aphistemi"* (Strong's #868, a literal "departing"), they actually attempt to make the case that the definition of *"apostasy"* in this instance does not refer to a spiritual departing or "falling away", but to the actual departure of the Church in the Rapture itself! They do this to rearrange the sequence so that the Church will "depart" before the arrival of the Antichrist, by editing the original, inerrant manuscripts of God's Word and making their own changes to it! As Peter warned, we are once again experiencing those who distort Paul's teachings. (2 Pe. 3:15-16) (For those who are interested in a detailed examination of what has specifically taken place, please read a Walk with the Word commentary published on the website titled, *When Change is Expressly Forbidden.*)

While 2 Thessalonians 2 has long been the center of far more eschatological disputes than most of the rest of God's prophetic Word combined, it has not been until the last ten years or so that this heresy has not just become public, but is growing more and more mainstream within the walls of the Church. A Jehovah's Witness or Muslim or outside critic of orthodox Christianity would not risk their academic or intellectual credibility by engaging in this obviously deceitful "cut-and-paste hermeneutic", but so-called Evangelicals within the Church proper are not just embracing it, but teaching it with the accompanying outrageous claims that this has "always" been the correct interpretation. It is at best ironic that the oldest lie of them all is to never present something as "new" but misrepresented as having "always" been around.

Just as it originally transpired where Thessalonica was concerned, today we have those coming along behind the Apostle Paul who are attempting to twist the plain teaching of God's Word not just into something which he did not state in the first place, but nearly into the complete opposite of what he actually and unambiguously documents, just as Peter warned. In a very real sense, we are re-living at present an even more serious variation of what false teachers introduced in the church at Thessalonica within the Western church at large today.

1 & 2 Thessalonians

*⁹For they themselves report about us what kind of a reception we had with you, and how you turned to God from idols to serve a living and true God, ¹⁰and **to wait for His Son from heaven**, whom He raised from the dead, that is Jesus, **who rescues us from the wrath to come**. (1 Thessalonians 1:9–10)*

These are the most basic elements of the Second Coming established by the Olivet Discourse where believers are concerned, that we no longer trust in this life but look forward, waiting *"for His Son from heaven"*, knowing that we will be rescued from what is inevitably to result for the rest of the world in the ultimate consequences, *"the wrath to come"*. The warnings for Christians as to the things which will prevent them from living in accordance with God's Word and ways in the Last Days mainly have to do with becoming comfortable with this life to the point of no longer living in expectancy of His Return, in combination with losing sight of the lessons from the days of Noah and Lot when headlong pursuit of this life gave way to the wrath of His judgment.

It is an interesting point of rare harmony that while there are a host of things, particularly when it comes to eschatology, for which there is no consensus of agreement whatsoever, there is something approaching universal agreement across nearly all theological divides that the wrath of God is eventually coming upon the unsaved, but will not be experienced by the saved. Regardless of when someone declares the Rapture will take place in the course of End Times events, each position nearly always (but not always) points to a period when God finally pours out His wrath as coming just after the removal of His people, often in the character of Noah or Lot. One of the key reasons we have competing eschatologies is a fundamental disagreement as to when, exactly, God's wrath begins in the scheme of things, in spite of widespread agreement that we will not experience it; all parties simply cannot agree as to when God's wrath begins in the sequence.

> *¹⁹For who is our hope or joy or crown of exultation? Is it not even you, **in the presence of our Lord Jesus at His coming**? (1 Thessalonians 2:19)*

The parables of the Olivet Discourse largely feature the difference between those who are establishing their good deeds in Christ by their treatment of others versus those who will suffer loss for the mistreatment of same. The message is that personal faithfulness is not something limited to just what we believe, but additionally visible in our dealings with others. It was not just Noah who was rescued by himself, but his family as well; it was not Lot alone, but his family, too; it was not just Rahab, but along with her family. In Peter's inaugural message at Pentecost he declared:

> *³⁹"For the promise is **for you and your children** and for all who are far off, as many as the Lord our God will call to Himself." (Acts 2:39)*

There is much more at stake than just ourselves not just in terms of judgment, but in what it means to have accomplished a good job according to God's point of view, which is bringing along others into the kingdom, discipling them, and thus delivering complete Christians and whole families.

> *¹¹Now may our God and Father Himself and Jesus our Lord direct our way to you; ¹²and may the Lord cause you to increase and abound in love for one another, and for all people, just as we also do for you; ¹³so **that He may establish your hearts without blame in holiness before our God and Father at the coming of our Lord Jesus with all His saints**. (1 Thessalonians 3:11–13)*

The pursuit of not only right relationships with others, but building them up in love in the Body of Christ, is offered as a key behavior which actually prepares us for *"the coming of our Lord Jesus"*. Paul draws a direct connection between achieving the necessary spiritual state of possessing *"hearts without blame in holiness before our God and Father"* and *"love for one another"*. In other words, even during ordinary and normal times, the primary commandment of Christ is to love others as He has loved us, (Jn.

13:34; 15:12) but in the End Times this is even more critical than ever before. And this is the responsibility of every Christian during every historic age of the Church, because whether by *Harpazo* or by Resurrection, we will still be evaluated at that time for whom and what we delivered.

The personal question we need to ask ourselves is if we believe that either in the case of our selves personally, or Christian friends and family close to us, what might be the nature of the consequences if we (or they) are not living in this manner now? Can we expect to be on the inside or the outside of the ark, so to speak, if our love continues to fall short of this standard? Will we really achieve the necessary qualifications of *"holy and blameless"* when the Master returns, imparted then for how we are acting now, or will we, like Lot's wife, the *Foolish Virgins*, or the *Lazy Slave* suffer deserved loss? The more difficult question is whether we think we are really doing family members and friends a favor by not addressing their present contra-biblical behavior because we do not think anyone is in danger of being left behind, not just when it comes to the Rapture, but even more pressingly, the Resurrection.

No Room for Misinformation

> ¹³But **we do not want you to be uninformed**, brethren, *about those who are asleep, so that you will not grieve as do the rest who have no hope.* ¹⁴*For if we believe that Jesus died and rose again, even so* **God will bring with Him those who have fallen asleep in Jesus**. ¹⁵*For this we say to you by the word of the Lord, that* **we who are alive and remain until the coming of the Lord, will not precede those who have fallen asleep**. ¹⁶*For the Lord Himself will descend from heaven with a shout, with the voice of the archangel and with the trumpet of God, and the dead in Christ will rise first.* ¹⁷*Then we who are alive and remain will be caught up together with them in the clouds to meet the Lord in the air, and* **so we shall always be with the Lord**. ¹⁸*Therefore comfort one another with these words.* (1 Thessalonians 4:13–18)

The word translated as *"uninformed"* comes from the Greek word *"agnoeo"* (Strong's #50), and this is the third time it has arisen in Paul's writings. Some translations render it as "ignorant", as the meaning is a misapplication of knowledge in the sense of someone who acts upon their wrong notions, convinced they are anything but ignorant and misinformed. They are not operating in the absence of the truth or without information, but plunging headlong operating according to their error in place of the truth.

Although this is the word from which modern English derives the term "agnostic", the way we use it in English today is significantly different from its original Greek meaning. Whereas we characterize someone who is "agnostic" as merely not knowing one way or another whether God exists as if they simply do not yet have enough information to make a decision, "*agnoeo*" in the original Greek means the person is acting on the wrong information in spite of the availability of the truth. They are either applying the misinformation in a mishandling of the truth so as to arrive at an erroneous result or destination rather than simply operating in the absence of the necessary data; they have already made a decision which turns out to be wrong and will continue to apply it to make things even worse.

A recent modern-day example would be a probe sent to Mars which crashed in spectacular fashion because it acted on the information it had, which was absolutely wrong. According to the information it was going by, it thought it was just beginning to enter into the atmosphere when it was actually just a couple of miles off the ground. The exploration device was not operating without any information as it was making its landing, and it actually was not given the wrong information technically speaking if it had been in the place it was supposed to be, but out of stunning ignorance to its position, applied what it was given to produce such a stellar failure as it never slowed for the landing. Like a Looney Tunes cartoon, the parachute did not deploy until after the crash. This is closer to the original meaning of the term. We are not being warned to fill in our data "gaps", but to wake up and stop operating on the wrong information inevitably leading to a catastrophic end.

It is interesting that there are three things for which Paul clearly specifies no Christian should be uninformed or ignorant, or "*agnoeo*": spiritual gifts (1 Co. 12:1), God's plan for literal Israel (Rom. 11:25), and the "*episunagoge*"— "*caught up together with them in the clouds to meet the Lord in the air*". (v.17) It probably has not escaped your noticed that these three things are at the center of nearly every doctrinal controversy within the Church, and yet they are the three things about which Paul specifically says there should be no misunderstanding.

On one end of the spectrum we have Cessationists who insist that the spiritual gifts—at least the so-called "charismatic" ones anyway, ceased to exist with the death of the foundational Apostles and the first generation of the Church as the New Testament became available; on the opposite extreme we have the Charismaniacs displaying false gifts or insisting that someone who does not speak in tongues is not saved.

On one extreme are the many forms of Replacementism, be it Dominionism, Triumphalism, or Kingdom Now Theology, which all commonly assert that God is through with Israel, the Church should therefore replace every instance of "*Israel*" in the Bible as transferring all those promises so that they now only apply to the Church, and in many cases that

Jesus will not actually return until the Church wins every soul on earth to Christ. At the opposite end we have Messianic factions which insist that to become a Christian, one must first fulfill the Old Testament requirements as interpreted by Orthodox Judaism, a way of stating that one must become a Jew, at least culturally, before they can become a Christian spiritually. There is much *"agnoeo"* when it comes to both the gifts of the Spirit and God's plan for Israel, and this is but a minimal presentation of many existing examples in just those two arenas.

This final caveat is no less polarizing within the Church with eschatologies straddling the spectrum when it comes to when this gathering is to take place, or whether it really is a literal event at all. Placement of the *Episunagoge* ranges from before the entire seven year **T**ribulation, around the mid-point or shortly thereafter, to not until the very end of the seven years. For the church at Thessalonica, false teachers wreaked great confusion by claiming *"the day of the Lord"* had already come, or with variations which falsely asserted that those who had already died would miss out on what is yet to take place; today we have the same kind of confusion rendered by dogmatic assertions of the timing of its rendering which conflict with each other. And of course there are those who are sowing "pre-confusion" (to coin a new term) by misrepresenting the timing of *"the day of the Lord"* in the overall eschaton.

As previously noted, no term associated with eschatology in Scripture is more disputed than *"the day of the Lord"*. This is quite ironic because while the other critical terms combine to occupy only a handful of total verses throughout the entire Bible, it is *"the day of the Lord"* which is discussed more than all of them combined many dozens of times over. Almost no one disagrees that there is a final seven year period, which is only known from a couple of verses, and yet the one term which is spoken of the most in God's Word is the one upon which there is dogmatic disagreement.

> *¹⁵For this we say to you by the word of the Lord, that we who are alive and remain until **the coming of the Lord**, will not precede those who have fallen asleep. (1 Thessalonians 4:15)*

In reality, the Rapture and the Resurrection are two sides of the same coin, two aspects of the same thing. In 1 Corinthians 15:20, Paul explains that Jesus' Resurrection was *"the first fruits of those who sleep"*, meaning He is just the first of many more to be resurrected. As it has been famously articulated so often by so many, we are not actually waiting for the Resurrection and Rapture to take place, but rather waiting for our place in it. It already began with Christ Himself, shortly followed by a resurrection of Old Testament saints (Mt. 27:52-53), and is subsequently completed by all who have "*fallen asleep*" in Christ to this point with the *Harpazo* bringing it all together.

> *⁵⁰Now I say this, brethren, that flesh and blood cannot inherit the kingdom of God; nor does the perishable inherit the imperishable. ⁵¹Behold, I tell you a mystery; we will not all sleep, but we will all be changed, ⁵²in a moment, in the twinkling of an eye, at the last trumpet; for the trumpet will sound, and the dead will be raised imperishable, and we will be changed. ⁵³For this perishable must put on the imperishable, and this mortal must put on immortality. (1 Corinthians 15:50–53)*

That first generation of Christians raised exclusively with the foundation of the Olivet Discourse would have clearly seen this as fitting with exactly what Jesus taught:

> *³¹"And He will send forth His angels with A GREAT TRUMPET and THEY WILL GATHER TOGETHER His elect from the four winds, from one end of the sky to the other. (Matthew 24:31)*

They would have sensed no conflict in Paul's teachings with Jesus' sequence of this taking place after the Abomination of Desolation at the end of a short but extremely intense "*great tribulation*". As this signals the onset of "*the day of the Lord*", 1st century Christians would have deemed it quite appropriate that Paul moves on to a discussion of that particular anticipated event.

The Day of the Lord

> *¹Now as to the times and the epochs, brethren, you have no need of anything to be written to you. ²For you yourselves know full well that **the day of the Lord** will come just like a thief in the night. ³While they are saying, "Peace and safety!" then **destruction will come** upon them suddenly like labor pains upon a woman with child, and they will not escape. ⁴But you, brethren, are not in darkness, that the day would overtake you like a thief; ⁵for you are all sons of light and sons of day. We are not of night nor of darkness; ⁶so then let us not sleep as others do, but let us be alert and sober. ⁷For those who sleep do their sleeping at night, and those who get drunk get drunk at night. ⁸But since we are of the day, let us be sober, having put on the breastplate of faith and love, and as a helmet, the hope of salvation. ⁹For **God has not destined us for wrath**, but for obtaining salvation through our Lord Jesus Christ,*

> *10who died for us, so that **whether we are awake or asleep, we will live together with Him**. 11Therefore encourage one another and build up one another, just as you also are doing. (1 Thessalonians 5:1–11)*

All of the salient elements pertaining to *"the day of the Lord"* are all present and succinctly summarized for us here. But it is important to note that within the original historical context of Paul's letter, he is not communicating anything to the Thessalonians which they are not already aware of. In other words, this is actually elementary material which is not in dispute.

Although it will overtake those who are in spiritual darkness and metaphorically *"of night"* and therefore *"they will not escape"*, believers are *"sons of light and sons of day"* who will not be overtaken by this event. Whereas our counterparts *"sleep"* and *"get drunk at night"* so that *"destruction will come upon them suddenly"*, we are starkly differentiated as *"sober"* and *"not destined…for wrath"*. The teaching of Christ's coming *"like a thief in the night"* is not so much about the literal event of the *Episunagoge*, but places a greater emphasis on who is and who is not spiritually prepared regardless of when Jesus comes for them. This is not limited to being ready just for the one-time event we call the Rapture, but *"whether we are awake or asleep, we will live together with Him"*—it is about spiritual preparedness regardless of whether we participate in the *Episunagoge* through death and Resurrection or supernatural rescue through the Rapture.

All the examples and parables of the Olivet Discourse reflect this in each one's example of those who are welcomed by the Bridegroom and Master as opposed to those who are rejected and removed. The right examples of Christian behavior in the interim are spiritually prepared by continuing to live and serve faithfully so as to be found ready, none of whom are actually taken by surprise when He finally arrives. They may not have been able to predict in advance the precise day or hour of His Return, but because they have been living in faithful obedience to His Word and ways, they are not spiritually found wanting with no oil in their lamps, having mishandled the talent entrusted to them, failing to take care of God's household or, worse, taking advantage of them.

> *23Now may the God of peace Himself sanctify you entirely; and **may your spirit and soul and body be preserved complete, without blame at the coming of our Lord Jesus Christ**. 24Faithful is He who calls you, and He also will bring it to pass. (1 Thessalonians 5:23–24)*

This is why the previous statement was made that when it comes to living in the shadow of the End Times, for the unbeliever it is all about the last chance for salvation, but for the believer the issue is sanctification. This summarizes what Paul has been previously highlighting in terms of the End Times behavior of believers, which is the faithful pursuit of sanctification so as to be found putting into practice God's Word and ways. In all the examples of the Olivet Discourse, the right attitude in each case is held up to be the one consistently putting faith into practice. Paul identifies the ultimate work of sanctification as attaining an eschatological trifecta so that "*may your spirit and soul and body be presented **complete***", the definition of "*sanctify You **entirely***". It is a mistake to think that preparation for either the Resurrection or *Harpazo* is limited to recognizing the nearness of the event; we must be spiritually qualified, or "*presented complete*" to this greater degree.

> *⁶For after all it is only just for God to repay with affliction those who afflict you, ⁷and to give relief to you who are afflicted and to us as well **when the Lord Jesus will be revealed from heaven** with His mighty angels in flaming fire, ⁸dealing out retribution to those who do not know God and to those who do not obey the gospel of our Lord Jesus. ⁹These will pay the penalty of eternal destruction, away from the presence of the Lord and from the glory of His power, ¹⁰**when He comes to be glorified in His saints on that day**, and to be marveled at among all who have believed—for our testimony to you was believed. (2 Thessalonians 1:6–10)*

Because 1st century adherents of the Olivet Discourse were more than familiar with its emphasis on the apostasy, deception and persecution facing believers, this would powerfully supplement their understanding of that teaching, especially in its assurance that while Christians will have to endure such things, "*it is only just for God to repay with affliction those who afflict you*". It is a call for endurance to the very end as this promise will only be realized "*when the Lord Jesus will be revealed from heaven with His mighty angels*".

But notice who it is who will "*pay the penalty of eternal destruction*", that it is not just "*those who do not know God*", but additionally includes "*those who **do not obey the gospel** of our Lord Jesus*". This again parallels the Olivet Discourse in that Jesus offers that persecution is not just going to come from secular institutions such as governments and court systems, but from "*synagogues*"—those with some kind of knowledge of and claim to spiritual things. They know about the Gospel but do not actually obey it.

And again, in alignment with what was originally offered in the Olivet Discourse, as the onset of "*the day of the Lord*" takes effect, the dual reactions

Paul offers that at this time "*He comes…to be marveled at among all who believed*" as opposed to unbelievers who "*will pay the penalty of destruction, away from the presence of the Lord and the glory of His power*" echoes the side-by-side reactions of the redeemed looking up in expectancy of their salvation versus the mourning of those realizing the consequences of their choice.

The earliest Christians would not have seen anything in Paul's writings as contrary to what they had come to expect from the Olivet Discourse, and even more so, found it to be very supportive not just of the individual milestones in the timeline leading up to "*the day of the Lord*", but reinforcing the very same things held to be most important for the Christians who will be required to endure and experience them.

The Apostasy Comes First

As stated previously, the twelve verses below appear to reside at the center of more exegetical controversy than all the rest of God's prophetic Word combined—Revelation included. Every time we think we have heard or read every possible variation or outright heresy that can be possibly constructed from a misinterpretation of any part or the entirety of this passage, yet another seems to rear its ugly head. As of two minutes ago, as this author began to work on this very section, that infernal contraption known as email spit out yet another "new" one which I could have never imagined someone calling themselves a saved, born again Evangelical could even make up as a joke, much less use as the basis to publish an entire book and then charge a fee to make public appearances to "teach" it to the sheep. Sadly, that is not the case.

It would be very easy to give in to the flesh at this point and dedicate this section as a response to all of these false teachings, so this is mentioned as a personal motivation to instead concentrate more on the straightforward comparison of this with the Olivet Discourse with as few sidebar diversions as possible to these present-day dysfunctions. Let us first perform an overall read-through of the entire passage before examining in more detail some of the particulars.

> *¹Now we request you, brethren, with regard to **the coming of our Lord Jesus Christ and our gathering together to Him**, ²that you not be quickly shaken from your composure or be disturbed either by a spirit or a message or a letter as if from us, to the effect that **the day of the Lord** has come. ³Let no one in any way deceive you, for **it will not come unless the apostasy comes first, and the man of lawlessness is revealed**, the son of destruction, ⁴who opposes and exalts himself above*

> *every so-called god or object of worship, so that he takes his seat in the temple of God, displaying himself as being God. ⁵Do you not remember that while I was still with you, I was telling you these things?*
>
> *⁶And you know what restrains him now, so that in his time he will be revealed. ⁷For the mystery of lawlessness is already at work; only he who now restrains will do so until he is taken out of the way ⁸Then that lawless one will be revealed whom the Lord will slay with the breath of His mouth and bring to an end by __the appearance of His coming__; ⁹That is, the one whose coming is in accord with the activity of Satan, with all power and signs and false wonders, ¹⁰and with all the deception of wickedness for those who perish, because they did not receive the love of the truth so as to be saved. ¹¹For this reason God will send upon them a deluding influence so that they will believe what is false ¹²in order that they all may be judged who did not believe the truth, but took pleasure in wickedness. (2 Thessalonians 2:1–12)*

Verses 1-3 present a basic sequence for which the overall passage provides more information, which is *"the apostasy comes first"*, then *"the man of lawlessness is revealed"*, after which will come *"the day of the Lord"*. False teachers were able to upset the Thessalonians by telling them *"the day of the Lord"* had already come because the Thessalonians whom the false teachers were trying to deceive knew without a doubt the timing of the *Episunagoge*— *"our __gathering__ together to Him"*—because of Paul's previous teaching, and that it takes place just prior to *"the day of the Lord"*. In other words, the deceivers attempted to alter the timeline. Notice that the false teachers at that time did not attempt to redefine or reinterpret what Paul originally taught for these individual items or to change the specific sequence, but instead declared that something was already fulfilled so as to deceive them overall. (Even those original false teachers did not have the gall to attempt to change the sequence or Paul's words, which shows how much further today's false teachers, who actually do, have fallen.)

This is a good example of what Jesus warned about in the Olivet Discourse, to not go after those who *"...will come in My name, saying...'The time is near'"*. (Lk. 21:8) As can be seen here, such are just as destructive as the many false christs and false prophets we are expected to deal with, but we need to consider how this is a particularly powerful deception; instead of having to evaluate a claim of being Christ or being a prophet, we have to know God's prophetic Word well enough in concert with understanding the signs of the times so we can biblically discern someone who is making the false claim, *"The time is near"*. They embellish a particular aspect of God's Word which in its proper context is not controversial, but their misrepresentation corrupts the meaning so as to redefine someone's overall understanding of the eschaton.

This is very much in the character of those today who replay the same error by over-realizing things like the Hebrew festal calendar, the blood moons, or passages of Scripture such as Psalm 83 or Ezekiel's Gog and Magog scenario. (It is hard to stop with this short list which, if properly expanded, could be a whole series of books as to the number of false teachings presently espoused.) Especially when combined with those who assign a specific biblical fulfillment which is never overtly stated in Scripture to current events such as the attacks of 9/11, or attempt to make America or the Church subject to the same covenant as Old Testament Israel, the false teachers of our times are not only corrupting an understanding of God's prophetic Word, but at the same time obscuring how to discern the existing signs of the times. This all works together for a very complete work of deception. Their running from one "The end is near!" false proclamation to the next is specifically identified by Jesus as something we should both recognize and purposely avoid.

Let No One Deceive You

> ³*Let no one in any way deceive you, for **it will not come unless** the apostasy comes first, and the man of lawlessness is revealed, the son of destruction, ⁴who opposes and exalts himself above every so-called god or object of worship, so that he takes his seat in the temple of God, displaying himself as being God. (2 Thessalonians 2:3–4)*

It is unrealistic to expect that we can rationally explain how it is possible that a passage of Scripture which begins with the unambiguous mandate, "*Let no one in any way deceive you*" and is followed by the simplest of sequences is at the center of more deception, error and questionable interpretation than any other portion of contested Scripture of which we are aware. But to avoid going into such length and detail of these "alternatives" so as to take us too far astray from our present purpose, a brief personal observation will be offered for your prayerful, yet future consideration for which the reader is encouraged to pursue further and separate study as led by the Holy Spirit. But in an attempt to trace these things back to their root cause, there appears to be a two-part, common denominator which crosses not just opposing eschatologies, but even doctrinal divides which often occurs for something related exclusively to eschatology, but is especially prolific here: a change in hermeneutics in parallel with the wrong prioritization of Revelation.

What is meant by a "change" in hermeneutics is that when it comes to the handling of the prophetic portions of God's Word, the particular teacher or author in question abandons or significantly modifies the rules they normally use to handle Scripture, treating prophecy as an "exception" to how the rest of God's Word is exegeted or, at the least, as needing to be treated with a completely different toolset. In the case of outright false teachers, they will purposely manipulate even their own rules to manufacture an unsanctioned meaning.

But even in instances of the well-intentioned, time and again it can be witnessed that there are those who handle the underlying Greek and Hebrew completely differently for eschatology than any other area of doctrine. Or the many who group and handle similar words and passages in an almost contrary manner from normal when it comes to terms associated with prophecy, or define them completely differently from other uses in Scripture and give them "one time" exceptions. Or many times it is departing from the way one normally accounts for the different types of biblical literature and/or historical context. Whether they are doing these kinds of things consciously or not, there is an almost uncountable number of examples which can be cited where they essentially exegete prophetic passages with a completely different approach than what they normally use for the rest of Scripture. These are not out-and-out false teachers, but brothers and sisters in the Lord with whom we would normally agree concerning the fundamental teachings, but find ourselves suddenly very far apart when it comes to eschatology.

But on the heels of this practice it is also usually closely followed by the very premise of this writing, that the book of Revelation is assigned the wrong level of authority in relation to the rest of God's prophetic Word, especially in regards to the Olivet Discourse. They not only feel compelled to make all things conform first and foremost to Revelation and frequently omit related passages from the rest of Scripture, but often diminish the importance of the Olivet Discourse if not completely dismiss it outright. The combination of simultaneously changing one's rules of interpretation in parallel with placing all their exegetical eggs in the Revelation basket is the most common explanation which has been observed for the concentrated controversy surrounding 2 Thessalonians 2:1-12, not counting the antics of out-and-out false teachers or extreme cult beliefs.

The point is that far too many come to this passage demanding a tailored fit with what they have already predetermined from a combination of prioritizing Revelation in the above manner, which was not even written when the Holy Spirit supplied this teaching through Paul, and the "alternate" rules of exegesis they employ just for issues relating to eschatology and nothing else. Because they have made "adjustments" to Revelation and the Olivet

Discourse, it is necessary for them to do something with Paul's teachings in Thessalonians to bring a semblance of order to their overall proposition.

So if because of such things one has predetermined that the Church will be removed before the Antichrist makes his appearance, they cannot accept the simple sequence here and instead jump through impossible hoops to undo it. Nor can those who assert that "no trigger" initiates the Rapture, or others who have an unorthodox interpretation of what *"the day of the Lord"* might mean if they allow the plain text to stand. Such are but a few examples of why there are incredibly audacious, mind-numbing and outlandish twists and manipulations for these verses which at times defy even simple, common sense; it is the hermeneutical equivalent of not just trying to fit the round peg in the square hole, but getting out one's knife to whittle away the corners to make the cylindrical peg fit into something so mutilated, in the end it is not the exact, same perfectly square hole it started out as. They whittle a bit at Revelation, even more at the Olivet Discourse, and by the time they get around to 2 Thessalonians 2 they've carved it into something completely different from its plain, original form.

1st century Christians would be very comfortable with how this perfectly mirrors Christ's Olivet Discourse sequence, that the Church is present against the backdrop of ever-increasing apostasy, the Abomination of Desolation takes place as the Antichrist *"takes his seat in the temple of God, displaying himself as being God"*, followed by the onset of *"the day of the Lord"*. Paul's is a rudimentary, bare bones timeline mirroring the essential elements of the more completed one originally established by Christ.

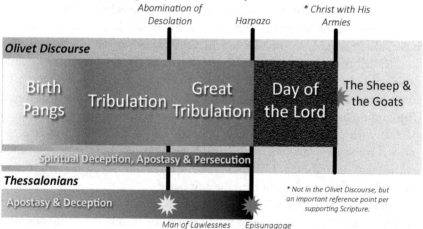

The Man of Lawlessness

As previously mentioned, this basic sequence precisely mirrors that which was established in the Olivet Discourse, that a longer, very general period of spiritual activity eventually gives way to a very specific public event categorically revealing the Antichrist. This milestone, originally identified by the Prophet Daniel as marking the exact halfway point of the final seven years of the eschaton, is affirmed by both Jesus and Paul, and tells us that although the beginning of the final sequence to come will by design be difficult to know, and perhaps only by way of hindsight, that this mid-milestone unmistakably kicks off the final, most intense period of time remaining for the Church culminating in the *Episunagoge*.

> ³*Let no one in any way deceive you, for it will not come unless **the apostasy comes first, and the man of lawlessness is revealed**, the son of destruction, ⁴who opposes and exalts himself above every so-called god or object of worship, so that **he takes his seat in the temple of God, displaying himself as being God**. (2 Thessalonians 2:3–4)*

It is no coincidence that in Scripture there are only two figures who are specifically called *"the son of destruction"*, or alternatively rendered, *"the son of perdition"*, which is the Antichrist and Judas. (Jn. 17:12) In both cases the underlying Greek is exactly the same, *"tes apoleias"* (Strong's #684), although translators may choose different English renderings. Many may have been demon-possessed, but it is only these two individuals who are satanically-possessed—that is, into whom Satan personally enters. (Jn. 13:27) Judas is the primary example in Scripture whose character and actions tell us what most to expect from the Antichrist to come.

From our current historical perspective, we might read these verses and say, "Aha! If he '*takes his seat in the temple of God*', then that must mean a temple has to be rebuilt!" But for those to whom Paul is originally writing, the Temple is still intact and operating, and having experienced in recent history past the Abomination of Desolation having taken place twice before in the Inter-Testamental Period in that very Temple, first with Antiochus Epiphanes IV and then the Roman General Pompey, they knew exactly what to expect. But in the present situation, we are keenly aware of current efforts such as those of The Temple Institute in Israel to not just rebuild the Temple, but revive the priesthood operating it, and it would be unwise to ignore what many popularly refer to as the "Tribulational Temple" being built.

187

It is worth noting again that this is the pattern of the First Coming, that there was a longer period of approximately 31-1/2 years when many things took place and prophecies concerning the Messiah's coming were already being fulfilled, but it was the dramatic milestone of Jesus' baptism by John, and the signs of the Spirit as a dove accompanied by God's vocal confirmation which initiated the much more intense and final 3-1/2 year public ministry. It is not 7 years which is the focus of the Second Coming in the New Testament because that was not the primary object of the First Coming; it is actually 3-1/2 years. But just as Christ's time was initiated by an authentic testimony of His deity, the Antichrist's will be inaugurated by an outrageous yet equally public counterfeit.

It was not the case that no one was aware of any milestone prior to the baptism, but they were few and not universally shared with everyone until much later. Zacharias and Elizabeth knew something, the people at the Temple when Zacharias emerged unable to speak knew something, friends and family at John the Baptist's birth knew something when Zacharias was no longer mute and prophesied, the Magi, the shepherds, as well as Simeon and Anna in the Nativity Narrative all knew something, and even those experiencing, advocating and carrying out Herod's persecution of the babies all knew something. Twelve years after His birth, those who encountered the child Jesus in the Temple all knew something, but even his parents, who were the only ones probably even aware of the totality of these events, did not comprehend it all. (Lk. 2:19; 33) And those in this list outside of his parents would be witnesses to just the one thing they participated in and not everything which took place during these three decades. That 31-1/2 year or so period containing these initial activities was shrouded from total view until the final 3-1/2 year period was publicly kicked off by Jesus being identified with the very attributes of God in the visible work of the Holy Spirit and the audible confirmation supplied by the Father.

Likewise, in a Satanic counterfeit, the Antichrist is publicly inaugurated in an act of self-deification *"above every so-called god or object of worship... displaying himself as being God"*. Satan is not content with simply getting equal time to do his work, but jealously imitates nearly every detail in an attempt to be like God. Remember, the "anti" in "Antichrist" does not mean "against" as in opposed to, but rather "in place of" as in an attempt to displace as a replacement or substitute.

It would appear that because Jesus had 3-1/2 years that Satan demands and is granted his own 3-1/2 year equivalent which, for the world, becomes plainly visible with the Abomination of Desolation. This does not mean there is no seven year period, but rather that the first half is not clearly identifiable to everyone universally; it is the last half of that seven years which is unmistakable. But one of the sources of confusion seems rooted in the assertion that many state so matter of factly that Satan will demand and be given seven years in order to justify their notions of a seven year **Tribulation**, when in fact that cannot be found anywhere in Scripture, and the only New Testament references are to periods closely aligned with a quantity expressing some form of 3-1/2 years. Even Daniel places all the emphasis on the second half.

But just as Christ was supernaturally "announced" at the beginning of His public 3-1/2 year ministry at the baptism by John, so Satan through the Antichrist desires some kind of replay of that announcement when he commits his public act of self-deification through the Abomination of Desolation, "*displaying himself as being God*". (See also Is. 14:14 & Eze. 28:2)

The Activity of Satan

> [9]That is, **the one whose coming is in accord with the activity of Satan**, with all power and signs and false wonders, [10]and with all the deception of wickedness for those who perish, because they did not receive the love of the truth so as to be saved. (2 Thessalonians 2:9–10)

First of all, this should tell us that to understand the Antichrist, we need to study that which Scripture reveals about Satan. There is a wealth of information in God's Word which speaks about him directly and subsequently by way of example through those who act in his character.

Second, notice that he employs deception not just "*with all power and signs and false wonders*"—something in the character of Pharaoh's magicians Jannes and Jambres (2 Ti. 3:8) who not only deceived with false works, but "*with all the deception of wickedness*"—spiritual deception resulting in spiritual death. The result is falling short of being saved.

It does not take a long and detailed search of YouTube to witness in our present environment a nearly endless series of examples of false spiritual activity already on public display. But what is most baffling is when false personalities claim to have performed miracles or signs which no one can verify (or can easily debunk), and yet ever-increasing crowds still blindly accept them as real and they are performed by these con artists over and over again. If someone is deceived by such easily provable fraud now, what will happen when the "real deal" comes along and performs actual "*signs and false wonders*"? If someone is fooled by the fake and counterfeit or even a complete lie, how will they possibly see through something that is not?

> [1]*"If a prophet or a dreamer of dreams arises among you and **gives you a sign or a wonder,** [2]**and the sign or the wonder comes true**, concerning which he spoke to you, saying, 'Let us go after other gods (whom you have not known) and let us serve them,' [3]you shall not listen to the words of that prophet or that dreamer of dreams; for the LORD your God is testing you to find out if you love the LORD your God with all your heart and with all your soul. (Deuteronomy 13:1–3)*

Likewise, what is plainly on display with these false figures is an accompanying teaching which achieves "*the deception of wickedness*" so as to corrupt the quality of their followers' spiritual walk and faith as well as general behavior. If such amateurs can so effectively and successfully accomplish this today in times of relative peace and prosperity, what do you suppose will result when the master of deception goes to work as day gives way to night? Will those who cannot resist the acolytes manage even a modest protestation against the ultimate connoisseur of manipulation to come? At present it is the spirit of antichrist at work foreshadowing what the final figure will with much more efficacy perpetrate upon the world.

We also have here an explanation as to why, after the removal of the Church, the repeated documentation of God's prophetic Word is that the rejection of Christ which led to their being left behind actually intensifies to overt rebellion and, ultimately, public blasphemy of God personally rather than melting into repentance: "*they did not receive the love of the truth so as to be saved*".

As discussed earlier, there is a well-known YouTube video created by a well-meaning church which shows several hundred people gathered at a typical Sunday morning service when a loud thunderclap sound effect coincides with all but a very small handful being unexpectedly taken by the Rapture and, by video magic, all disappearing instantly. The few left behind, recognizing what just happened, all fall to their knees in repentance, an example of those who teach that the Rapture itself will initiate a worldwide revival, and offering that even when it takes place, it is still not too late to repent and be saved.

Assuming for argument's sake that the mechanics of the Rapture works like this to begin with, what is the spiritual condition of those who are left behind? "*They did not receive the love of the truth so as to be saved*". Having rejected the truth and instead immersed in deception before the Church is removed, these same individuals, under the full sway of the now-revealed Antichrist and absence of the Church, are not going to finally repent and change their ways, but rather they are going to be fully given over to what they have been pursuing all along, and become even more militantly so.

> ¹¹*For this reason **God will send upon them a deluding influence so that they will believe what is false,** ¹²**in order that they all may be judged*** who did not believe the truth, but took pleasure in wickedness. (2 Thessalonians 2:11–12)

A primary name of the Antichrist provided to describe one of his most important and recognizable spiritual traits is *"man of lawlessness"*, which is closely followed with *"son of destruction"*. (2 Th. 2:3) It should be noted how closely this fits one of the primary characteristics of the deceived who follow him, that they *"took pleasure in wickedness"*. The word translated *"wickedness"—"adikia"* (Strong's #93), is not just strictly referencing sin, but applying it in the context of injustice and unrighteousness—something falling well short of God's standard and a sort of bookend to the Antichrist's character of *"lawlessness"* and *"destruction"*. It is not just tolerating evil or acting out of complete ignorance of God's standard, it is doing evil and ultimately being given over to evil so as to become its partner, accessory and active enabler.

It is important to note that there is some period of time which transpires between when the Antichrist is plainly and publicly revealed for who he is, and when the *Harpazo* takes place. Those not taken will have lived in willful ignorance not just of everything which took place in the years of the *"birth pangs"*, but they will dismiss all the unmistakable milestones such as the rebuilding of the Temple, the surrounding of Jerusalem, and the Abomination of Desolation which will kick off the even more intense *"great tribulation"* which is so unprecedented in its ferocity that Jesus says if those days were not supernaturally *"cut short"*, (Mt 24:22) that *"no life would have been saved"*. Those left behind have steadfastly ignored all of these things for themselves, dismissed every warning from Christians at every turn concerning each of these events, and perhaps even participated in some of them against believers as predicted by Jesus, and yet there are those who insist that the singular act of the Rapture will instantly change them? No, Daniel provides the hard truth about what will really happen at this time: *"Many will be purged, purified and refined, but the wicked will act wickedly; and none of the wicked will understand…"* (Dan. 12:10)

The practitioners of evil in Noah's day did not repent or understand even when the rain came and God shut the door; the practitioners of evil in Lot's day, even though blinded, still tried to force their way into the house and did not repent or understand even as the fire fell; Pharaoh's army acknowledged that God was working on behalf of Israel in the Red Sea and all the previous plagues but did not repent and understand as the passage collapsed around them; neither was there either repentance or understanding at Jericho even though it was acknowledged they had witnessed God working in Israel for the previous forty years and watched the daily parade each day for a week before the walls fell, nor by any of the soon-to-be conquered Canaanite nations witnessing that which took place there and even after the previous multiple encounters with Egypt and other nations in the wilderness.

People who practice wickedness continue to do so regardless because they are given over to that lifestyle by their own choice, and in the course of abiding by that course of behavior lose the ability to understand what is taking place even as it unfolds before their very eyes. Ultimately, because they so consistently pursue that lifestyle and steadfastly refuse to repent, which is why they were left behind in the first place, God turns them over to it: "*For this reason God will send upon them a deluding influence so that they will believe what is false*". They cannot recover even when they witness a sign or miracle—they never have, and they never will. Just look at all the examples of those who witnessed Christ's miracles in the course of His earthly ministry who, because of the hardness of their heart, steadfastly refused to believe. This is why Scripture never speaks of a worldwide revival after the removal of the Church and only documents nothing but unrepentance, rebellion and continued rejection of Christ, ultimately culminating in open blasphemy.

The Restrainer

As stated many times already, the most pressing features of the eschaton for believers is the growing spiritual darkness defined by ever-increasing apostasy, deception and persecution. While these things have existed historically many times before, and an argument can be made that to one degree or another they all exist at various times during every generation of the Church, the reason that this final darkness is unprecedented is due to a coming change in the working of the Holy Spirit.

> [6]*And you know what restrains him now, so that in his time he will be revealed.* [7]*For the mystery of lawlessness is already at work;* **only he who now restrains will do so until he is taken out of the way**. *(2 Thessalonians 2:6–7)*

There are repeated warnings provided by Jesus, Daniel, Paul and John concerning antichrist figures which prefigure the ultimate and final Antichrist to come. In the meantime, the Apostle John informs us that the spirit of antichrist is presently active, which Paul describes as "*the mystery of lawlessness…already at work*". But Paul adds the detail that this final, ultimate figure cannot make his final appearance until "*he who now restrains…is taken out of the way*". And although at the time of Paul's writing to the Thessalonians they did not possess the information about the Antichrist which would later be revealed in Revelation 13 to come, Paul provides the detail which matters most when understanding the character and working of this final figure:

> *⁹That is, the one whose coming is **in accord with the activity of Satan**, with all power and signs and false wonders, ¹⁰and with all the deception of wickedness for those who perish, because they did not receive the love of the truth so as to be saved. (2 Thessalonians 2:9–10)*

One might ask, "Isn't Satan already at work? Isn't he the current ruler of this world? Doesn't Peter tell us Satan *'prowls around like a roaring lion, seeking someone to devour*?" (1 Pe. 5:8) We might juxtapose these questions against what Paul is saying because we do not generally think of Satan as someone who is currently "restrained", but already operating on his own in open opposition to the Godhead. We forget the very valuable lesson from the book of Job that at present, Satan is not free to do whatever he wants, whenever he wants.

> *⁶Now there was a day when the sons of God came to present themselves before the LORD, **and Satan also came among them**. ⁷the LORD said to Satan, "From where do you come?" Then Satan answered the LORD and said, "From roaming about on the earth and walking around on it." (Job 1:6–7)*

The truth is that while he may hold some higher rank or position, he is still among all the angels and demons standing before and reporting to God, not occupying some equal position to God Himself. He has none of the qualities of the Godhead, such as omnipresence—being present everywhere; he has to walk about the earth. The point is that Satan himself has always been, to some degree, "restrained" or, if you will, operating under divine limitations. And in fact, this valuable peek into heaven provided by the book of Job shows how all of the created beings, whether still faithful to God or following Satan into rebellion, are still subject to Him and not acting independently with no constraint.

This is a very important starting point when it comes to answering the question as to exactly "who" is restraining the coming of Satan in the final person of the Antichrist. For those of us who accept there has always been nothing short of divine authority being exerted over Satan, we tend to capitalize "Restrainer" to identify Him as the Holy Spirit. Scriptural support for this identification seems to be provided by Christ when explaining to the Apostles that a change in the role of the Holy Spirit was about to be accomplished as one of our biggest benefits of the work of the cross:

> [7]*"But I tell you the truth, it is to your advantage that I go away; for if I do not go away, the Helper will not come to you; but if I go, I will send Him to you.* [8]**And He, when He comes, will convict the world concerning sin and righteousness and judgment;** [9]*concerning sin, because they do not believe in Me;* [10]*and concerning righteousness, because I go to the Father and you no longer see Me;* [11]**and concerning judgment, because the ruler of this world has been judged**. (John 16:7-11)*

A change in the working of the Holy Spirit took place in parallel to Christ's leaving—His Resurrection and Ascension, and it would appear that at some point in the eschaton a change will take place again in the shadow of Christ's returning, which initiates Satan's coming in the Antichrist. As Paul states, the *"day of the Lord"* will not come until *"the apostasy comes first, and the man of lawlessness is revealed"*. (2 Th. 2:2-3) The closest explanation provided so far for what is being described here can be best understood as a sort of "reversal of Pentecost".

In other words, prior to the outpouring of the Spirit on the Church, the Holy Spirit only worked on a personal basis through specific individuals, often kings of Israel or Old Testament prophets. Even when Jesus first appeared to His disciples immediately after His Resurrection, His impartation of the Holy Spirit to them was as individuals (Jn. 20:22) with instructions to wait in Jerusalem *"until you are clothed with power from on high"*. (Lk. 24:49) For a time the Holy Spirit continued to work in believers in the same individual manner as in the Old Testament before the seminal event of the Day of Pentecost. The reference to no longer restraining seems to indicate that as part of an anticipated spiritual darkness of historically unprecedented proportions as *"the day of the Lord"* approaches, the intensity of the situation is multiplied by the Holy Spirit reverting back to the Old Testament way of working, without which the Antichrist cannot appear.

(We must dismiss the assertion that the Holy Spirit literally and entirely departs from the earth simultaneously with the removal of the Church and "returns" to heaven as this outright violates the fact that as a member of the triune Godhead, the Holy Spirit is omnipresent. It is an aspect of His working which is withheld or "removed", not His entire, literal presence. Even though He worked differently before Pentecost, He was nonetheless always present.)

This word *"restrains"*—in the Greek, *"katecho"* (Strong's #2722), might best be understood in how it is used by Paul in Romans:

> *[18]For the wrath of God is revealed from heaven against all ungodliness and unrighteousness of men who **suppress** the truth in unrighteousness, (Romans 1:18)*

It expresses the working of spiritual suppression whether in the case of the *"unrighteousness of men who **suppress** the truth in unrighteousness"*, or the Holy Spirit who presently convicts *"the world concerning sin and righteousness and judgment"* but will no longer restrain evil to that degree and in that manner. This goes a long way in explaining how intense the apostasy, deception and persecution will become in those final days and hours as well as the unprecedented death, destruction and accompanying decent into evil characterizes those very last years.

> *[8]**Then** that lawless one will be revealed whom the Lord will slay with the breath of His mouth and bring to an end by the appearance of His coming; (2 Thessalonians. 2:8)*

This unambiguous sequence begins with the sign of apostasy, which we know to be a general condition which will increase in intensity but whose precise beginning is actually indiscernible, and then gives way to very specific milestones of a change in the working of the Holy Spirit and the public revelation of the Antichrist before the initiation of *"the day of the Lord"* by the dual work of the Resurrection and *Harpazo* in the *"Episunagoge"*—our *"gathering together to Him"*. This does not translate into the ability to select in advance the exact day or hour of the *Harpazo*, but most certainly provides all of the things which the Olivet Discourse declares will unmistakably bear witness to His impending Return.

Ultimately, in the particular New Testament church which experienced the most difficulty with the issue of eschatology, Paul actually reaffirms what is taught in the Olivet Discourse, and while the Holy Spirit supplements some of those details through him so that we have a more detailed understanding of some of the particulars, Paul does not really alter or re-state what was fundamentally taught by Christ.

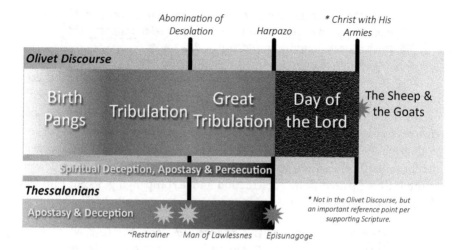

13 ❖ The Special Case of John

*I*n the Apostle John's Epistles, which were written before he had been given the vision to come which would result in the final New Testament book of Revelation, the main issues of eschatology which he briefly yet repeatedly visits is that of the Antichrist and the problem of deception.

A primary context for his writings which needs to be taken into serious consideration is they come near what John most likely realizes to be the end of his own life and ministry, but at the very end of the life as well, so to speak, of that entire first generation of the Church, and much of the second. By the time John will be imprisoned on Patmos, the Church is well into its third generation removed from those who were firsthand witnesses to the ministry of Christ. It is only natural that at such a time one communicates to their loved ones what they believe to be that which is most important.

There is a sizable gap in time between the other New Testament books and those of John's, but it is important to note that the Olivet Discourse is still the primary guide for the Second Coming, and John's works were written before the advent of Revelation. It is probably a testimony to the authority of the Olivet Discourse by the very fact that John did not see a need to replicate it yet again in his own Gospel; he allows it to stand and, as we shall see, reinforces its most fundamental points. It is difficult to believe that by this time, John was not familiar with the other Gospels, much less all of the New Testament writings prior to his own.

As noted previously, John is only one of four Apostles to whom the Olivet Discourse was originally given by Christ:

> ³*As He was sitting on the Mount of Olives opposite the temple,* **Peter and James and John and Andrew were questioning Him privately**, ⁴*"Tell us, when will these things be, and what will be the sign when all these things are going to be fulfilled?" (Mark 13:3–4)*

None of the Synoptic Gospel writers—that is, Matthew, Mark or Luke, were present and all had to obtain their accounts of that teaching from at least one of these four individuals if not some combination thereof. We have to at least consider the possibility that the reason John did not deem it necessary to publish a fourth parallel account of the Olivet Discourse in his own writings at this late date is that he was either already fully quoted in one or more of the Synoptic Gospels, or that their coverage of it was so complete that it was not necessary. (If you want to start a cult, this author suspects that Matthew, being so obviously oriented toward a Jewish audience, is the best candidate for containing John's account of the Olivet Discourse.)

It is hard to believe that as the last man standing, so to speak, and as one of the only eye witnesses of such an important event, that he would not make any necessary corrections or additions to set the record straight if such was needed. The fact that he did not may be a powerful confirmation in its own right of not just the authenticity of what was already recorded, but its foundational place in the Early Church's eschatology. But as an eyewitness of the Olivet Discourse and all that transpired in Jesus' First Coming, John would not need any New Testament source for his ministry, but was in many cases a primary source for each of them.

But a second issue which needs to be raised here is that there are many, many good Christian brethren and scholars whose view on the timing of the Rapture, in spite of the plain teaching of both Jesus in the Olivet Discourse and the Apostle Paul in 2 Thessalonians 2, is that the Church will be removed without ever having to come into contact with the Antichrist. There are many such proponents who are so dogmatic in their assertions about this that they actually accuse adherents of this position to be "looking for the coming of Antichrist instead of Christ". Then why is the Apostle John "looking" (by their standard) for the Antichrist? Why is the Apostle John stipulating that one of the ways we know for sure we are in the Last Days is the proliferation of not just many antichrists and false prophets, but the spirit of antichrist as well? If the Church is going to avoid facing the Antichrist, why does John raise the issue in the first place? And at this late date, it is absolutely impossible to make the case this is a teaching for Israel to come and not the Church, whose ethnic composition is now decidedly Gentile. The fact is that by the end of the 1st century, even before the writing of the book of Revelation, John is addressing this issue because there are already figures rising up and claiming to be Christ, and he affirms this is proof of the End Times.

We know from the conversation of the Sanhedrin in Acts 5 that there were false messiahs, two of which Gamaliel mentions by name in Theudas and Judas of Galilee. And from the historical record, others followed such as one of the most famous yet to come in Simon bar Kochba, who initiated the revolt against the Romans in 132 AD which three years later resulted in more than just Israel's conquest and total destruction; this would bring about the final end of the Jewish state and initiate the dispersement of all the Jews into the Diaspora from which it would take nearly two millennia to recover. According to what John is writing about at that time, the phenomenon of antichrists is not strictly limited to something happening within the confines of Judaism proper, but has become a problem for the Church in that sixty or so year period between the Day of Pentecost and the writing of the book of Revelation. And in keeping with what was conveyed to him firsthand in the Olivet Discourse, he knew this was a primary sign of the Last Days.

John's references to seminal sign should also be noted as being given in the context of a reminder from him that this issue was apparently so important that it was not only a part of his regular teaching to that point, but deemed so critical that it still warranted mentioning again; it is not presented as brand new material never before given. And to this body of what appears to be well-known previously transmitted information, John addresses the concept of "*the spirit of antichrist*" which establishes a satanic pattern of working in every historical period of the Church up until the very Return of Christ.

The Apostle John, whom some nickname "the apostle of love" for what he shares in his Epistles on that theme, is the Apostle who also seems to be more concerned about the Antichrist than anyone else. This issue of the importance of the Antichrist dovetails with the Olivet Discourse in that while there are many signs coming out of the milieu of the "*birth pangs*" over a longer, preliminary period which are not necessarily individually distinguishable to make a positive identification as to the arrival of the eschaton, one of the first unambiguous events specified as impossible to ignore is when the Antichrist commits the Abomination of Desolation. The Apostle John not only affirms the Olivet Discourse's contention that there will be a proliferation of false christs and false prophets in general, but in disclosing how to identify them alludes that this will lead to being able to recognize the ultimate, final one.

But we should also consider how this emphasis indicates John's adherence to the Olivet Discourse itself. Since he believes in Christ's imminent return, and he knows from that teaching it will be presaged by a proliferation of false christs, and the Church at that time is actually dealing with a rise in counterfeit messiahs, he is proving that the Olivet Discourse is, indeed, for the Church. John is providing additional warning for one of the most important "triggers" of Christ's Return.

Many Antichrists

> ¹⁸*Children,* **it is the last hour; and just as you heard that antichrist is coming, even now many antichrists have appeared; from this we know that it is the last hour.** ¹⁹*They went out from us, but they were not really of us; for if they had been of us, they would have remained with us; but they went out, so that it would be shown that they all are not of us.* ²⁰*But you have an anointing from the Holy One, and you all know.* ²¹*I have not written to you because you do not know the truth, but because you do know it, and because no lie is of the truth.* ²²*Who is the liar but the one who denies that Jesus is the Christ? This is the antichrist, the one who denies the Father and the Son.* ²³*Whoever denies the Son does not have the Father; the one who confesses the Son has the Father also.* ²⁴*As for you, let that abide in you which you heard from the beginning. If what you heard from the beginning abides in you, you also will abide in the Son and in the Father. (1 John 2:18–24)*

When John finally has the vision on the Isle of Patmos which produces the book of Revelation, it will be Revelation 13 which will be universally referred to as the definitive teaching on the Antichrist. However, what may be worth noting is that the actual term *"Antichrist"* is not specifically used anywhere in Scripture except in 1 & 2 John (not even later in Revelation), and although more details will come in Revelation, the basic teaching of the Antichrist has been around long prior to this term's publication.

In the book of Daniel, the figure John describes as *"Antichrist"* is actually assigned a variety of terms which communicate various behaviors and spiritual characteristics he will possess such as a *"beast"* (Dan. 7:8, 23), *"horn"* (Dan. 7:8, 11, 21), *"king"* (Dan. 7:24; 8:23; 11:36), *"small horn"* (Dan. 8:9), *"the people of the prince who is to come"* (Dan. 9:26-27), and *"the one who makes desolate"*. (Dan. 9:27) The terms Paul uses are *"the man of lawlessness"* and *"the son of destruction"* (2 Th. 2:3) as well as *"lawless one"* (2 Th. 2:8). When the Olivet Discourse speaks of *"false christs"*, the underlying Greek word is actually *"pseudochristoi"* (Strong's #5580). (Mt. 24:23-25; Mk. 13:21-23) It is not until John's writings when the term *"antichristos"* (Strong's #500)—that is, *"antichrist"* proper, is finally used, and it would appear that a sign of the Last Days is not merely the arrival of the final Antichrist, but the proliferation of many antichrists leading up to him. It has been expressed that the many are sent by Satan so as to disguise the final figure to come, but the clear indication by Jesus, Paul and John is that identification is not impossible, just limited to the faithful. After all, no one but the Apostles understood who and what

Judas was, and only then when Christ revealed it to them at the Last Supper, but he was, ultimately, revealed to them.

One of the most important distinctions belonging to both the many antichrist figures in general as well as the final one to come is John's specification, "*They went out from us, but they were not really of us*". Just as Judas, someone who like the Antichrist is actually called "*the son of perdition*", (Jn. 17:12; 2 Th. 2:3) was difficult to detect as having come from among the Apostles, so something like that will replay itself in the ultimate "*son of perdition*" to come. However, John's expectation is that all of these counterfeit attempts will fail because Christians will ultimately see through them due to their advantage, "*But you have an anointing from the Holy One, and you all **know***". During that time in their dealings with Judas, even the Apostles had not yet been given the Holy Spirit, which has been a staple of every born again experience going forward from Christ's Resurrection.

This is why it is recommended that everyone should read Jacob Prasch's book, *Shadows of the Beast*, which is subtitled, "How the Identity of the Coming Antichrist Will Be Revealed to the Faithful Church". (It is available in print from his website Moriel.org and as an eBook from Amazon.) This is a definitive work which exegetes Scripture on the topic of the Antichrist in concert with John's admonition that Christians should be spiritually equipped to discern between the many counterfeits intended to camouflage the final, ultimate one. A runner-up to this would be A. W. Pink's book, *The Antichrist*, published in the early 20th century. (It can be read online or downloaded for free from various places on the Internet, or purchased as an inexpensive Kindle eBook from Amazon.) Jacob's book is not about naming names or any of the many related speculations when it comes to the Antichrist, but focuses on how Scripture teaches to distinguish the singularly authentic one from the many counterfeits past and present in anticipation of the final one to come.

In the meantime, John provides a characteristic which automatically betrays the working of the Antichrist at any and every time and age, which is whenever there is a denial or attempted corruption of the relationship between God the Father and Jesus the Son. When Islam insists that God has no Son, we know without a doubt that it is an antichrist religion; when the Mormons assert that Jesus is the spirit-brother of Satan, we know without a doubt that it is antichrist; when Jehovah's Witnesses attempt to say Jesus is "a" god, we know without a doubt that it is antichrist. Whether it is an entire religion, a Christian cult, or two guys meeting on a street corner selling custom t-shirts, a denial of the Father-Son relationship reveals what is really at work.

Just as Jesus warned repeatedly in the Olivet Discourse that false christs would come and that no believers should be fooled by or drawn to them, John elaborates on this with supplemental information as to what to expect and how to identify them. It is especially important to note that in those times when we are told to expect apostasy, deception and persecution to come not just from the world, but from friends and family closest to us, the many antichrists prefiguring the final person of the Antichrist likewise "*went out from us*".

[Note: There is much debate over the Antichrist's ethnicity, but regardless of what it turns out to be, that will not prohibit him from falsely taking on Christianity for a time so that it will be ultimately fulfilled that he "*went out from us*".]

Many False Prophets

> [1]*Beloved, do not believe every spirit, but test the spirits to see whether they are from God, because **many false prophets have gone out into the world**. [2]By this you know the Spirit of God: every spirit that confesses that Jesus Christ has come in the flesh is from God; [3]and every spirit that does not confess Jesus is not from God; this is the spirit of the antichrist, of which you have heard that it is coming, and now it is already in the world. (1 John 4:1–3)*

Whereas we are first warned there are "*many antichrists*", they are inevitably accompanied by their counterparts, "*many false prophets*". And just as John expects believers to be able to be equipped in order to recognize not just the many antichrists, but the final one to come, so he sets the same expectation when it comes to false prophets. Just as an antichrist is betrayed by their denial of the Father-Son relationship, so a false prophet closely shadows this behavior in falling short where their testimony of Christ and God is concerned.

The activities of both the many antichrists and the many false prophets sheds light on the two spirits which are at work in the world today, that being God's Spirit of Truth (Jn. 14:17; 15:26; 16:13) and the spirit of error.

> [6]*We are from God; he who knows God listens to us; he who is not from God does not listen to us. **By this we know the spirit of truth and the spirit of error**. (1 John 4:6)*

The Apostle John emphasizes that those who can distinguish between these two spirits can only do so because "*he who knows God listens to us*"—that is, it is by heeding the teaching passed down to us by the New Testament writers. In other words, to successfully "*test the spirits*" as specified by John, this is accomplished by measuring their words and deeds against the standard of God's Word. This was recorded in John's Gospel as being separately affirmed by Christ Himself as well:

> ¹*"Truly, truly, I say to you, he who does not enter by the door into the fold of the sheep, but climbs up some other way, he is a thief and a robber. ²But he who enters by the door is a shepherd of the sheep. ³To him the doorkeeper opens, and* **the sheep hear his voice**, *and he calls his own sheep by name and leads them out. ⁴When he puts forth all his own, he goes ahead of them, and the sheep follow him because* **they know his voice**. *⁵A stranger they simply will not follow, but will flee from him, because* **they do not know the voice of strangers**.*"* (John 10:1–5)

John is reaffirming the teaching of Jesus captured in his Gospel, that those who listen to and make the standard the Word, whether given directly by Jesus or by Him through His Apostles, will not be deceived, whether it be a false christ, a false prophet, or a false shepherd. This might be an important parallel to the Olivet Discourse's *Parable of the Wise and Foolish Virgins*, who are differentiated by their anointing in the Word by the Holy Spirit, as well as the general antidote to deception at every level. Behind these false spiritual influences is "*the spirit of the antichrist*", which John stipulates is not merely coming, but "*now it is already in the world*".

It is interesting to note that even in secular philosophy and culture there is recognition of what has been termed the "*Zeitgeist*", a German term meaning "*the spirit of the age*". The spirit of antichrist has been at work in every historical age, exerting influence in different ways at different times, but always to ultimately achieve the same debilitating spiritual results. While secular observations often attribute the cause to something other than a purely spiritual source, Christians in possession of the truth understand this antichrist influence on the art, culture, and social and political movements of every generation which is otherwise popularly referred to in secular terms as the *Zeitgeist*.

Many Deceivers

> *⁷For many deceivers have gone out into the world, those who do not acknowledge Jesus Christ as coming in the flesh. **This is the deceiver and the antichrist**. ⁸Watch yourselves, that you do not lose what we have accomplished, but that you may receive a full reward. ⁹Anyone who goes too far and does not abide in the teaching of Christ, does not have God; the one who abides in the teaching, he has both the Father and the Son. ¹⁰If anyone comes to you and does not bring this teaching, do not receive him into your house, and do not give him a greeting; ¹¹for the one who gives him a greeting participates in his evil deeds. (2 John 1:7–11)*

Just as the many antichrists prefigure the final one to come, and the many false prophets foreshadow his ultimate counterpart, so the many deceivers provide a glimpse of the Antichrist as the ultimate deceiver of all time. It is noted by John that "*many deceivers have gone out into the world*", and this is certainly a defining characteristic of all the historical types of the Antichrist found in such examples as the Roman emperors, Napoleon, Hitler, Stalin, and a list too long to properly document here. Repeated warnings against being deceived are a hallmark of the Olivet Discourse, and nearly every New Testament writer at some point addresses the issue of deception whether it comes from false apostles, false prophets, false teachers, false shepherds, or false believers.

Countless documentaries have tried to satiate our fascination for trying to understand how the whole of the German population could be so deceived by Hitler and his associates, and yet compared to the real deal still to come, he was an amateur. This in itself should be a motivation for our taking to heart the remedy for what is coming by faithfully pursuing the Holy Spirit anointed consumption of God's Word as fervently as possible.

In verse 8, John provides a caveat of significant note, "*Watch yourselves, that you do not lose what we have accomplished, but that you may receive a full reward*". This again touches on the point made in the Olivet Discourse about Lot's wife and other supporting Scriptures that we must faithfully endure until the very end and not repeat her mistake of looking back in the final moments and thus experience an excruciating last minute loss. The right behavior is further identified by John as the difference between "*one who **abides** in the teaching*" versus the one who "***does not abide*** *in the teaching of Christ*". Take note of the qualification which "*abide*" brings to the discussion, as this carries with it the unambiguous meaning of a "lifestyle" rather than someone who merely hears the words or is familiar with the information. The repeated lesson for what to do both in preparation for, and the arrival of, deception, no matter how skilled the source of it may be, is a faith which not only puts God's Word and ways into practice, but measures all things by the same.

Some may find it ironic that the man assigned the moniker, "the apostle of love", demands separation from biblically qualified deceivers to the degree that it is specified, "*do not receive him into your house*"—that is, do not give them an opportunity to gain a foothold in our life, but to go even further and "*do not give him a greeting*". John is saying that we must not merely shut out deceivers privately, but publicly handle them so as to overtly witness to their true character, which will serve as a warning to others as well. We are not supposed to accommodate them for the sake of peace or for politeness' sake, and actually become an accessory to their crimes, so to speak, "*for the one who gives him a greeting participates in his evil deeds*". Academics may want to enter a common forum to debate each other, but that is not the biblical standard because in the eyes of those attending, it gives false teachers the credibility they crave.

This is yet another specific example in Scripture that those who deceive are never treated by the same standard of Matthew 18 which attempts to resolve personal issues of sin in private between individuals; Jesus never handled the false teachers of His day in that manner. We are commanded to publicly admonish and identify the purveyors of deception, and failure to do so on our part renders us a participant "*in his evil deeds*". Throughout the Epistles, false teachers are repeatedly and publicly identified by name.

"If Another Comes in His Own Name"

³³*"You have sent to John, and he has testified to the truth.* ³⁴*But the testimony which I receive is not from man, but I say these things so that you may be saved.* ³⁵*He was the lamp that was burning and was shining and you were willing to rejoice for a while in his light.*

³⁶*"But the testimony which I have is greater than the testimony of John; for the works which the Father has given Me to accomplish—the very works that I do—testify about Me, that the Father has sent Me.* ³⁷*And the Father who sent Me, He has testified of Me. You have neither heard His voice at any time nor seen His form.* ³⁸*You do not have His word abiding in you, for you do not believe Him whom He sent.* ³⁹*You search the Scriptures because you think that in them you have eternal*

life; it is these that testify about Me; ⁴⁰and you are unwilling to come to Me so that you may have life.

⁴¹"I do not receive glory from men; ⁴²but I know you, that you do not have the love of God in yourselves. ⁴³**I have come in My Father's name, and you do not receive Me; if another comes in his own name, you will receive him**. ⁴⁴How can you believe, when you receive glory from one another and you do not seek the glory that is from the one and only God?

⁴⁵"Do not think that I will accuse you before the Father; the one who accuses you is Moses, in whom you have set your hope. ⁴⁶For if you believed Moses, you would believe Me, for he wrote about Me. ⁴⁷But if you do not believe his writings, how will you believe My words?" (John 5:33–47)

It has been noted that not only did this literally come true in the many false messiahs who appeared within Israel not just preceding Jesus, but especially afterward as personified by Simon bar Kochba, who as an antichrist figure was endorsed by elements of the Jewish religious establishment which led to the final destruction and dispersal of Israel. This most certainly echoes what Jesus said in the Olivet Discourse, "*For many will come in My name, saying, 'I am the Christ', and will mislead many*", (Mt. 24:5) as well as in John's Epistles concerning "*many antichrists*".

Jesus notes that at His First Coming He was rejected not only in spite of the testimony of John the Baptist, and not just by their added rejection that the signs and miracles He accomplished could only come about through the authority of God Himself, but as a complete and total rejection of the very Scriptures which they laid claim to. In Western parlance, it was three strikes and they were out.

These are real-life examples of the biblical progression of events required for an antichrist figure to be embraced in favor of Jesus, that any testimony of Jesus, along with His relationship to the Father, in tandem with a rejection of God's Word, is spiritually fatal. It is important to note the relationship of how a rejection of God's Word always results in the dual rejection of any signs or wonders. What the Apostle John notes in his Epistles concerning antichrists, false prophets and deceivers was woven into his Gospel account and shown to be operating from the very beginning.

It is rejection of God's Word which is the reason for not being changed by any sign or miracle, which in turn produces a refusal to accept His messenger of truth. God's true Prophets, such as John the Baptist, have been regularly rejected as the messenger and source of God's miraculous workings because hardened hearts are produced from rejecting His Word in the first place.

This phenomenon of many antichrists has been on display for better than two millennia now, yet escalates to unprecedented levels with the nearness of the Second Coming. We live at a time when there are not only obvious antichrist figures proliferating, but counterfeits no longer simply claiming to be "Christ", but outright calling themselves the "Antichrist" himself! We have counterfeits of the ultimate counterfeit!

In his Gospel, John records repeated "I AM" statements made by Jesus, a very Hebraic way of overtly stating His divine relationship as the Son of God. (Jn. 6:51; 8:12, 23, 58; 10:9, 11, 36; 11:25; 14:6; 15:1) Just as John explained in his Epistles, that the spirit of antichrist is at work whenever the deity and/or relationship of Christ to God the Father is questioned, so it is prominently recorded in parallel in the Gospel of John throughout the entire length of Jesus' earthly ministry. The theme of Christ's rejection is visited repeatedly throughout the Gospel of John and found to be working in the character of antichrist as a prelude to the last iteration to come, steadfastly denying the Father-Son relationship.

But there is a very important warning here which explains how someone was, is, and is going to be deceived: "*You do not have His word abiding in you*". This will be replayed in the difference specified in *The Parable of the Wise and Foolish Virgins*, as well as those who are portrayed in various illustrations of the Olivet Discourse as properly ready and waiting (or not) for the Master's return. Notice that it was not enough to merely "*search the Scriptures*", that the requirement is to put them into practice and prove we believe them by living according to them. Is someone "safe" if they say they believe but continue to live contrary to His Word? So many of the teachings concerning the End Times are to avoid the consequences of replaying the character of Lot's wife, and instead setting the standard of enduring to the end, never looking back, and proving faith by consistent obedience to His Word. If we do not accept Christ through His Word, we will embrace someone and something else in His place.

"I Go To Prepare A Place For You"

> [1]*"Do not let your heart be troubled; believe in God, believe also in Me. [2]In My Father's house are many dwelling places; if it were not so, I would have told you; for I go to prepare a place for you. [3]If I go and prepare a place for you, **I will come again and receive you to Myself**, that where I am, there you may be also. (John 14:1–3)*

This direct promise of Christ fits culturally with the Hebrew marriage customs, wherein the first stage is a betrothal (roughly equivalent to what we might call an "engagement"), but was actually legally binding. The bridegroom would then depart for as long as it took to construct an addition to his father's house for him and his new wife to-be, and return at a future date to complete the marriage process when his father approved the finished work and released him. The bride had a general idea as to when he might return, but did not know the specific day or hour, and because travel in the Middle East was mostly avoided during the heat of the day, he often returned at night. Upon his surprise return, however, the invitations quickly went out and everyone was soon gathered together to the marriage feast, at which time the contract was completed and the marriage consummated. We can see many parallels in this with what Jesus states here, and as we await His Return to then participate in the Marriage Feast of the Lamb as His spotless Bride.

In spite of the danger of belaboring the point, it must still be pointed out that Jesus stated categorically He is going away for an unspecified time, a feature prominently repeated in the parables and illustrations of the Olivet Discourse.

> [27]*"Peace I leave with you; My peace I give to you; not as the world gives do I give to you. Do not let your heart be troubled, nor let it be fearful.* [28]*You heard that I said to you, '**I go away, and I will come to you**.' If you loved Me, you would have rejoiced because I go to the Father, for the Father is greater than I. (John 14:27–28)*

In the same discourse, Jesus again affirms, "*I go away*". Previously Jesus had told His disciples, "*The days will come when you will long to see one of the days of the Son of Man, and you will not see it*". (Lk. 17:22) The promise of Jesus' Return is prefaced by the reality of an interim absence of unspecified, but significant length.

> [18]*"If the world hates you, you know that it has hated Me before it hated you.* [19]*If you were of the world, the world would love its own; but because you are not of the world, but I chose you out of the world, because of this the world hates you.* [20]*Remember the word that I said to you, 'A slave is not greater than his master.' **If they persecuted Me, they will also persecute you**; if they kept My word, they will keep yours also.* [21]*But all these things they will do to you for My name's sake, because they do not know the One who sent Me. (John 15:18–21)*

In the Olivet Discourse, Jesus specifically warns that there will be persecution coming from a wide variety of sources, but here reveals that regardless of where it comes from, the root cause is "*because they do not know the One who sent Me*". This is why we must be spiritually prepared for what is to come because at its source is a greater spiritual issue than just us alone.

> ²"*They will make you outcasts from the synagogue, but an hour is coming for everyone who kills you to think that he is offering service to God. ³These things they will do because they have not known the Father or Me. (John 16:2–3)*

Jesus reveals that the same spiritual problem underlying the world's persecution of His followers is the same experienced by those who will persecute them from within the walls of religion: "*they have not known the Father or Me*". But it replays what was stated in the Olivet Discourse about persecution emanating not just from governments and the courts, but synagogues.

> ¹⁷"**Sanctify them in the truth; Your word is truth.** ¹⁸*As You sent Me into the world, I also have sent them into the world. ¹⁹For their sakes I sanctify Myself, that they themselves also may be sanctified in truth. (John 17:17–19)*

Again, the importance of God's Word in the believer's life is especially critical, both in the overall theme of the Olivet Discourse, and in Jesus' final discourse between the Last Supper and the Garden of Gethsemane. Teachings concerning the Second Coming throughout the whole of the New Testament keep coming back to the primary importance of God's Word in the believer's life.

In the Olivet Discourse, we have repeatedly noted that the main message for believers, which is restated in various ways, is a call for personal faithfulness to God's Word and ways and to prove the quality of our faith by the way we live and conduct ourselves. This is actually the primary focus of the Epistles, which in reality are a commentary on the Olivet Discourse. In John 13-17, where the very last teaching of Christ is captured on the eve of His crucifixion after the Olivet Discourse, this is the most important thing Jesus is reinforcing when it comes to how His followers are to live in the interim before His promised Return. In all of the corollary New Testament references to the End Times, there are accompanying warnings about deception and persecution, as well as admonitions regarding the importance of God's Word.

It cannot be understated that for Christians, perhaps the most valuable scriptural teaching of how we should live in the Last Days, and how we should deal with prophetic events coming into our visible fulfillment, is John 13-17. This is the End Times "road map" because it charts our actions and behavior which will properly prepare us for these things rather than documenting a series of prophetic milestones to chart. Those who put into practice what is taught here will successfully navigate what is yet to come, and may already be unfolding.

"Tend My Sheep"

> ¹⁵*So when they had finished breakfast, Jesus said to Simon Peter, "Simon, son of John, do you love Me more than these?"*
> *He said to Him, "Yes, Lord; You know that I love You."*
> *He said to him, "**Tend My lambs**."*
> ¹⁶*He said to him again a second time, "Simon, son of John, do you love Me?"*
> *He said to Him, "Yes, Lord; You know that I love You."*
> *He said to him, "**Shepherd My sheep**."*
> ¹⁷*He said to him the third time, "Simon, son of John, do you love Me?"*
> *Peter was grieved because He said to him the third time, "Do you love Me?" And he said to Him, "Lord, You know all things; You know that I love You."*
> *Jesus said to him, "**Tend My sheep**. (John 21:15–17)*

John's Gospel ends with this account of Peter being restored to ministry by Jesus, which is a powerful parallel to the parables and illustrations accompanying the Olivet Discourse, and provides a potent commentary on what is most important for His followers in the interim awaiting His Return. In both cases, the priority is placed on the same thing:

> ⁴⁵*"Who then is the faithful and sensible slave whom his master put in charge of his household to give them their food at the proper time? ⁴⁶Blessed is that slave whom his master finds so doing when he comes. (Matthew 24:45–46)*

First of all, this tells us something about the span of time for which Jesus will be away, telling Peter the most important thing to do in the meantime is to take care of the Body of Christ. But secondly, this affirms the repeated admonishment to pursue the making of disciples (not merely converts) and to see to their growth and welfare more than anything else. In what transpired between Jesus and Peter is a greater application for each of us personally of what is most important in the interim until His Return.

NT Eschatology Before Patmos

John's writings prior to being given the book of Revelation did not see it necessary to add anything to the Olivet Discourse, and even provides additional support for that being the primary teaching by which all of God's Word concerning the Second Coming—even Revelation to come—is primarily interpreted and understood.

What might be most revealing about that which the earliest generation of the Church was taught and believed where the Second Coming is concerned is not just the fact that they lived and died with the Olivet Discourse as their primary guide and with no knowledge of the book of Revelation, but by the small amount of space in which the overt points of eschatology are given within the overall writings of the New Testament authors.

Outside of Thessalonica, where there was a specific problem with eschatology demanding Paul's attention, there is relatively little offered which expands upon the Second Coming milestones provided in the Olivet Discourse compared to the topics taking up the most space by authors of the New Testament. What this means is not that these markers were unimportant, but that the Apostles took from the Olivet Discourse a different set of priorities when it comes to what is critical for Christians.

As the Synoptic Gospels were copied and began to be distributed within the Early Church, Apostolic teaching on eschatology affirmed not just a familiarity with the Olivet Discourse, but a universal acceptance of it. In fact, many of them were written and began to be distributed before the Synoptic Gospels proper, so it is particularly telling how these writings support each other. It is apparent that in the years before the Synoptic Gospels were authored, during which much of the rest of the New Testament was already written, that the primary teaching the Apostles provided was already based on the Olivet Discourse. Yes, chronologically the Olivet Discourse was given by Christ first, but many of the Apostles' teachings and writings based on it actually preceded its written publication, although it was surely a staple of Apostolic oral teaching, as were all the events and discourses of Christ's ministry.

The overwhelming message for Christians of the 1st century is that this will be a time when events taking place on the world stage are not merely an increasing frequency of wars, disturbances, pestilence, earthquakes, famines and cosmological signs, but in concert with these things, where Christians are concerned, there will be the ever more pressing rise in the parallel spiritual activities of apostasy, deception and persecution. While Jesus provides a single warning for each of the overt signs of the *"birth pangs"*, He warns of deception, apostasy and persecution multiple times. These three things are reinforced in the rest of the New Testament writings more than any other aspect of the Second Coming as well.

This is particularly powerful when combined with the parables and illustrations Jesus provides within the Olivet Discourse, which all seem to have in common a period of waiting patiently for His Return, but in the meantime continuing to carry out our duties and responsibilities of the Kingdom and to faithfully live like Christians. While *The Parable of the Fig Tree & Other Trees* speaks to recognizing the season of the nearness of His Return, all of the other parables and illustrations take it further to include a prolonged time of waiting prior to a series of identifiable events pointing to His inevitable and sudden return, faithfulness (or lack thereof) in the interim, and an arrival which has the dual effect of rewarding and welcoming the faithful, but punishing and excluding the unfaithful for their readiness or lack thereof:

➤ The illustrations of the days of Noah & Lot

➤ *The Parable of Expecting the Thief*

➤ *The Parable of the Faithful Servant*

➤ *The Parable of the Wise & Foolish Virgins*

➤ *The Parable of the Talents*

Whether consciously or by the guidance of the Holy Spirit, these are the things which the New Testament authors overwhelmingly concentrated on in the bulk of their writings so as to reinforce how Christians should consistently and faithfully live in order to fulfill these examples in order to be found spiritually prepared and ready when that time comes. This is the most important message in the Olivet Discourse for Christians, and is likewise the most important topic of discussion in the Epistles. They are actually reinforcing what should be most paramount for us: faithfulness to live a crucified, sanctified life going forward right up to the very end, rather than being obsessed with dates and times. Even when the Apostle John warns of antichrists, false prophets, false believers and the ultimate coming of the Antichrist, these topics are brought to the forefront of the discussion.

If this seems like such an obvious point to you that you wonder why it even needs to be stated, God bless you. But consider that there are many Christians who believe they have to be ready for a sign or event associated with the eschaton such as Gog and Magog or the Rapture, rather than meeting the requisite spiritual qualifications. All of the provided parables feature the consequences for believers who fail to live up to biblical standards in the interim and find themselves disqualified. Even the *Foolish Virgins* recognize the announcement of the Bridegroom's arrival, but that alone does not help them, does it? Neither is it sufficient for the *Wedding Guest* who is inappropriately clothed, a biblical metaphor for the spiritual quality of one's life and deeds, or the slave who hid the talent entrusted him.

Consider the fact that the "Church"—the Body of Christ as a whole at present, is not just comprised of people living exclusively in the Western world. Statistically speaking, there are probably a larger number of Christians living in the Third World who have little or no online access, little or no opportunity to acquire additional books and magazines, do not attend prophecy conferences, and are lucky if they even have a Bible of their own in their native language. This may be hard for some to digest, but a preoccupation with eschatology to the microscopic level it is often pursued in the Western world is a luxury only the wealthier elements of the Church enjoys at present. But do you suppose that Jesus' Second Coming will catch them unprepared? According to what is stated in the Olivet Discourse in keeping with the examples above and which are elucidated on by the New Testament writers, they are better prepared than most of their Western counterparts because of the degree to which they are putting their faith into practice. We have much more to learn from their example than they from our books, conferences and websites which are oriented more toward trying to unravel a puzzle than inspire a consistent, practicing faith.

Someone who puts into practice all that is taught in Scripture is, by definition, going to be properly prepared and ready for His Return, and such will not be caught unawares by the signs of His impending Return. Just as there were spiritually prepared and faithful examples at Christ's First Coming who recognized what was taking place even at the earliest stages of His birth, such as the shepherds, the Magi, or Simeon and Anna, and a blindness for the spiritually unprepared in the likes of Herod, the religious authorities in Jerusalem and so forth, the same is replaying once again in the shadow of His Return, particularly in the present Western world.

If a prophecy conference, website or book were doing the right job biblically where eschatology is concerned, the result would not be an increase in knowledge, but an encouragement to repent and pursue ever more persistently personal faithfulness to God's Word and ways, because this is not a test of knowledge, but a test of faith. Such would engender a fervor for preaching the Gospel while there is still time and rescuing as many backslidden and outright non-believers as possible.

But if a member of that founding generation of the Church were to draw an End Times chart before the advent of the book of Revelation, it would begin without a single, fixed starting point, but depict in some manner a gradual period of "*birth pangs*" giving way to a period of "*tribulation*" for believers, followed by a more intense shorter period called "*the great tribulation*" for the whole world kicked off by the specific milestones of Jerusalem's encirclement and the inauguration of the Abomination of Desolation by the Antichrist. This would be amputated shortly thereafter by the Rapture of the Church in concert with the onset of "*the day of the Lord*" when the wrath of God is poured out on those left behind. All of this would take place against a background of ever-increasing apostasy, deception and persecution. But not being able to point to a single, definitive starting point would speak powerfully to why the repeated definition of being "ready" or "awake" in the Last Days is consistent obedience to God's Word and ways and being found to be a biblically practicing Christian.

Their chart would not be strictly based on a seven year timeline with two rigid halves of 3-1/2 years each, but rather successive phases, a longer one called "*birth pangs*" yielding to the Church being given over to its time of "*tribulation*", and a much shorter one called "*great tribulation*" to be experienced by everyone before the *Harpazo* removes the Church from having to experience the final period assigned in Scripture as "*the day of the Lord*". The Church is first given over by the world to a period of "*tribulation*", but ultimately the whole world is given over to God's wrath in "*the day of the Lord*". Daniel's 70th Week might have become clear in hindsight, but what would be anticipated is these "phases" of activity spanning an overall period much longer than seven years, with the greater emphasis placed on the second half of that period beginning with the Abomination of Desolation.

These things are important to keep in the forefront of our thoughts as this would have shaped the way they would approach incorporating the book of Revelation into their overall understanding of eschatology. It is hard to believe that anyone from the Early Church, upon reading Revelation, would have exclaimed, "We had it all wrong! I finally get it now!" And if they were to draw an End Times chart, they would most certainly have begun with the Olivet Discourse first before attempting to incorporate Revelation.

Part Three:
Christ's Second Revelation

14 ❖ "The Revelation of Jesus Christ"

> [1]**The Revelation of Jesus Christ**, which God gave Him **to show to His bond-servants**, the things which must soon take place; and He sent and communicated it by His angel to His bond-servant John, [2]who testified to the word of God and to the testimony of Jesus Christ, even to all that he saw. [3]Blessed is he who **reads** and those who **hear** the words of the prophecy, **and heed** the things which are written in it; for the time is near. (Revelation 1:1-3)

t is of the utmost importance to always keep in mind that this is Jesus' revelation. Although revealed through an angel and written down by the Apostle John, it is often referred to by many as "John's vision" or "John's revelation", but it is specifically qualified from the outset as being, "*The Revelation of Jesus Christ*". This is again stated as a sort of second bookend confirmation at the end of Revelation:

> [6]And he said to me, "These words are faithful and true"; and the Lord, the God of the spirits of the prophets, sent His angel to show to His bond-servants the things which must soon take place. (Revelation 22:6)

For those of us who fully endorse the scriptural proposition that since Jesus is designated as the "*Word*", and therefore the whole canon of Scripture from Genesis to Revelation is actually Jesus Himself, it may seem silly to have to articulate such a thing, but such is the need to be reminded that this is not John's ideas put down in writing or as originating from him, but simply the last in a sequence coming from Christ Himself.

This is a critical point as well when it comes to our discussion of the Olivet Discourse and its relationship to Revelation; Jesus gave both teachings, and like the rest of His Word, they will not and cannot conflict with or reinterpret the other. In the same character as the recognized "progressive revelation of God" which incorporates and builds upon that which was previously disclosed and never discards the previous, Jesus first provided the Olivet Discourse and the teachings leading up to it on which it is formed, and later supplied Revelation to build upon it. Just as all His teachings on the Second Coming prior to the Olivet Discourse served as its foundation and facilitated an even more detailed overall picture, Revelation is but a continuation of the Olivet Discourse, serving to provide even greater detail.

But the most important context is that Jesus is the same Author of both, and therefore provides disclosures exclusively dedicated not just for the benefit of those who may read Scripture, but those who put it into practice and live exclusively according to it—"*His bond-servants*". As recorded in the rest of the New Testament, this is the biblical definition of those who will be found ready, accepted and rewarded upon His Return, single-mindedly dedicated servants bound exclusively to Him, especially in the character of the illustrations accompanying the Olivet Discourse.

There is a dual requirement where this Revelation of Jesus is concerned, which is actually the same requirement for the whole of His Word, that the responsibility for Scripture is not confined to "*those who **hear** the words of the prophecy*", but must be followed through "*and **heed** the things which are written in it*". This is a common New Testament theme going all the way back to the Sermon on the Mount to not merely be hearers, but doers (Mt. 7:24-27); one of the biblical definitions of an authentic faith in Christ is someone putting His Word into practice.

The underlying Greek word for "*heed*" is "*tereo*" (Strong's #5083), which Jesus used when He said, "*...if you wish to enter into life, **keep** (tereo) the commandments*" (Mt. 19:17) and, "*If you love Me, you will **keep** (tereo) My commandments*" (Jn. 14:15). There are many such examples to show exactly why this does not mean to merely be aware of Scripture, but as with the whole of God's Word, to put it into practice. There is a basic problem when Revelation is treated as if it is exempted from the exegetical axiom, "*All Scripture is inspired by God and profitable for teaching, for reproof, for correction, for training in righteousness*". (2 Tim. 3:16) And as it turns out, the biblical goal of prophecy where believers are concerned is "*edification and exhortation and consolation*", (1 Co. 14:3) and not limited to simply making a prediction or conveying information. Every verse of Revelation accomplishes at least one of these goals in that each will either edify, exhort or console the bond-servant, sometimes accomplishing the goal of two or all three simultaneously.

The context of this final but most detailed revelation concerning His Second Coming is qualified as "*the things which must soon take place*" (v.1) and "*for the time is near*". (v.3) Consistently, beginning with the Olivet Discourse, and repeatedly throughout the New Testament writings up to and including this final book of scriptural canon, the context is that we are already in the "Last Days" and, from the Godhead's point of view in eternity, the conclusion of history is close. *"God, after He spoke long ago to the fathers in the prophets in many portions and in many ways, in these last days has spoken to us in His Son..."* (Heb. 1:1-2a)

It is worth noting again that this revelation is specified as belonging to *"Jesus Christ"*, where the order of His name expresses an emphasis on what He is going to do in the earthly realm. Although the overall format of this book switches back and forth to reveal what is taking place in heaven and how it is reflected in corresponding events on earth and vice versa, the focus is nonetheless how all things on earth are going to be brought to a divine conclusion with a brief glimpse into the eternal to follow which, as it turns out, is the New Heaven and New Earth.

But from a purely eschatological point of view, there is quantitatively very little which is presented in these twenty-two chapters which is not overtly and obviously duplicated or explained in parallel elsewhere in Scripture in either of the Testaments. And the few things which are revealed for the first time serve to unveil what was present the entire time in all previous Scripture which points to them. This is why it is puzzling to find so many authors and academics on the one hand who will explain things in Revelation by visiting their parallel scriptural counterparts, especially Old Testament passages originally given centuries earlier than John's vision, but will then turn around and marginalize the Olivet Discourse provided just sixty years prior by Christ Himself. (Or even worse, completely ignore it.) It is not just the fact that they reverse the order to in some way make a case that Revelation overrides the Olivet Discourse, but all too often it is absent from their End Times charts and writings altogether.

While we will not engage in a detailed, verse-by-verse exegesis of the whole of Revelation, the effort here will concentrate on providing enough of a foundation to show the vital connection to the Olivet Discourse. Revelation deserves a dedicated study in its own right to even begin an attempt to account for all that it teaches, but the exercise here is to establish its true roots in the first revelation Christ provided to His servants prior to giving them this final Revelation. And as it turns out, without that proper foundation, whatever resulting structure is attempted will ultimately fail.

Some Essentials

No Obvious Seven Year Structure

It has been repeatedly stated, and will almost certainly be referred to again but is especially critical to consider at this juncture before we consider Revelation proper, that there is absolutely no mention of a seven year period anywhere within Jesus' revelation. The only units of prophetic time measurement revealed to John are...

> ..."*a time and times and half a time*" (Rev. 12:14) or 3-1/2 years in reference to Israel's flight into the wilderness to escape from the Antichrist;

> "*forty-two months*" (the number of months in an ideal 3-1/2 lunar year period) in reference to the timespan corresponding to when the Gentile nations will "*tread under foot the holy city*" (Rev. 11:2) and for which the Antichrist is granted "*authority to act*" (Rev. 13:5); and

> "*twelve hundred and sixty days*" (the theoretical number of days in an ideal span of 3-1/2 lunar years) assigned to the length of the ministry of the Two Witnesses (Rev. 11:3) and again to Israel's flight into the wilderness. (Rev. 12:6)

There are additional references to "*five months*" (Rev. 9:5) as the length of the 5th Trumpet judgment and six instances of "*a thousand years*" in Rev. 20:2-7 relating to the Millennial Reign.

While the three main terms in the list at first blush appear to be mathematical equivalents of 3-1/2 lunar year timespans, they have to be handled individually because of the unique people, things and/or events which are assigned to them in the text, and in any case they may not actually be perfectly equal to each other when one understands how a lunar calendar specifically works. (Another whole study in its own right.) However, that which is absolutely never to be found in Revelation, much less the whole of the New Testament, is any eschatological reference to a seven year End Times structure. Neither is it found in any of these references that one half is called "Tribulation" or the other "Great Tribulation". It is this author's opinion that by assigning those assumptions in this manner, it has distracted from focusing on what each individual reference is actually addressing, depriving us of what is not just more important, but most important. We tend to miss the point as to which things have parallels in both Daniel and Revelation, and those which are uniquely given in each.

End Times Mathematics

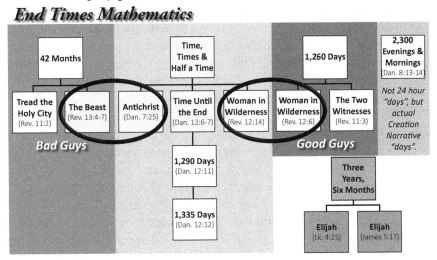

As explained in much previous detail, Jesus and the New Testament writers provide the milestones of the exact middle of that week of years (Daniel's 70th Week) by co-identifying the Abomination of Desolation, and that week's ending with Christ's assumption of His throne initiating the Millennial Kingdom. The beginning seems to be purposely cloaked, most likely disguised by the *"birth pangs"* which come with ever-increasing frequency in the character of the defining events of the eschaton. In Revelation, however, neither the beginning (the treaty) nor middle of Daniel's 70th Week is mentioned (the Abomination of Desolation), so careful examination of the text is required if parallels to such are actually present.

What seems to be a textual connection between Revelation and the Olivet Discourse is the command to flee the land of Israel when the Abomination takes place. The parallel is presented in Revelation 12 with Israel's escape from Satan into the wilderness. Revelation's provision of the forty-two month reign of the Beasts in Revelation 13 likewise appears to correspond to the reign of the Antichrist beginning with the Abomination in Daniel. The time remaining after the flight takes place is one of the forms of "3-1/2" and it is therefore difficult not to draw a parallel between them as it is the Abomination of Desolation identified in the Olivet Discourse to which is attached the command for everyone in Judea to flee. Since this is the revelation not just as to the true satanic identity of the Antichrist, but the epiphany Israel experiences that they have been deceived by this figure's treaty, the timing of their corresponding flight makes exegetical sense. While Daniel and Revelation provide timespans for these activities, the Olivet Discourse speaks in terms of the major milestones initiating these periods of allotted time without reference to their duration.

It is somewhat understandable, with the repeated feature of so many iterations of "seven" in Revelation, that many succumb to the temptation to superimpose on top of or in amongst them the seven year structure which Daniel inarguably speaks of, but this is something we must resist in our quest to understand Scripture as it was viewed in the 1st century; this will actually turn out to be quite helpful in our own century as well.

While it is clear that the Church in the centuries and millennia after the passing of the first generations became very focused on the teaching of the 70th Week, it was obviously not the centerpiece of 1st century eschatology, especially during the time the Temple was still standing, and even while Israel was still largely intact; it takes quite some time to pass before the permanency of what took place is fully appreciated. And although the events of 70 AD were devastating, it is the future and much more severe consequence of the Bar-Kochba Revolt of 132-135 AD which is going to see the dispersal of the Jewish people and occupation of their land which takes place for almost two thousand years, something still another forty years distant even from what John received on Patmos. If the 70th Week of Daniel was on their minds at this point, it most certainly did not conform to how it would be viewed and treated over the course of the twenty centuries to come. Again, this is not denying the existence of a final seven year period, but rather that it was not the primary focus of the Early Church in the same way for later generations. For believers to fully appreciate all its implications and effects, it requires some time and distance from the 1st century Church.

This revisits a point previously expounded in these pages that the "earliest" sources for Church discussions of the 70th Week are often found to be too far removed from the original generation to affirm that it was a teaching featured in their eschatology. Without a doubt it is a staple of subsequent generations and modern interpretation because of acquiring an historical perspective which can only come with time and hindsight, but exegetically speaking in strict accordance with the New Testament text, it does not appear its position can be precisely fixed in advance. The structure which is affirmed by the New Testament is that of 3-1/2 for both the First and Second Comings alike, and as it turns out, this is actually the greater emphasis presented in both Daniel and Revelation as well, and affirmed by Paul to the Thessalonians.

It is this author's opinion that this is a very serious error which can muddy one's understanding so that even though otherwise well-intentioned believers are avoiding the pitfall of predicting the date of the Rapture, they are engaging in an attempt to set into stone the date of Daniel's 70th Week, whose position in the calendar is not only never specified in Scripture, but purposely shrouded and pointing to events downstream from it. And this causes the brow to furrow skeptically even further when nearly every "Tribulation Chart" published since the invention of writing seems to choose the 1st Seal judgment of Revelation 6:1 as the corresponding first day of Daniel's 70th Week, very often not even making mention of the treaty.

This is at most a wishful guess, and at the least undermines actual Scripture since it is specified that the only thing textually associated with day one is the Antichrist's treaty with Israel. (Dan. 9:27) (It is rare to find someone who even allows the remotest possibility that there could be some gap of time, even a very short one, between the signing of that treaty and the breaking of the 1st Seal.) It is even more baffling when presented with the purported "fact" that Daniel's 70th Week and *the day of the Lord* are asserted to be the exact, same thing, when there is not a syllable of supporting Scripture for that notion in either Testament. By committing all of our efforts into a debate over the "seven", we are effectively neutralized because of the void of any discussion concerning that which Scripture deems most important, the "three and a half".

When we interpret Revelation with the Olivet Discourse as our baseline, we almost immediately see the incredible harmony of both and realize a more proper place within the whole of the eschaton for Daniel's 70th Week.

The Issue of Hindsight

It is a healthy reminder that as recorded many times in the Gospels, there were things which Jesus said and did in the course of His First Coming, which although were obvious fulfillments of Scripture in hindsight, were not recognized even by the Apostles at the time they took place. Simply stated, without a doubt absolutely everything which is stated in both Revelation specifically and the whole of the Bible at large will all come true exactly as God has specified, but it would be unwise to believe that everything can and will be discerned in advance of it actually taking place.

In spite of their extensive education in the Scriptures, no one present at Jesus' crucifixion realized at the time it was taking place how verse by verse of Psalm 22 was being fulfilled before their very eyes, much less all the other scriptural parallels to that event. The men on the road to Emmaus were dismayed at Christ's death until He showed them this took place precisely as Scripture had foretold. (Lk. 24:19-27)

Yes, most things in God's prophetic Word may be recognized in advance or when it is taking place, but some quantity will be understood only when we are finally able to look back and affirm, "Yes! That was fulfilled exactly the way Scripture said it would!" in the same way this occurred in the First Coming. Just as at least some prophetic fulfillments for the First Coming were purposely planned by God to only be understood in retrospect, it would be foolish to believe nothing like that will occur in the course of His Second Coming.

Part of the problem with this exercise we call eschatology is that we assume we have the whole puzzle in the first place, when in reality all we have is what God deemed is enough to act upon by faith. We easily feed our inflated ego by assuming we can solve the entire enigma in advance. It will only be from the vantage point of hindsight when we will be afforded the luxury of seeing how all the pieces provided actually fit together and what all the pieces really were, but in the meantime we have more than enough to affirm our trust and faith in Christ.

A Basic Outline

The Same Sequence

The most basic outline of Revelation actually conforms to the same structure Jesus' teachings relating to the eschatology of His Second Coming as were discussed in detail in *Chapter 1 • The Second Coming in the Gospels* under *A Basic Outline*. Because it is providing another level of detail, it is the corresponding yet parallel terms which are different:

➤ Ch. 1-3, "*The Things Which Are*" (This Present Age)

➤ Ch. 4-19, "*The Things Which Take Place After This*" (The End of the Age)

➤ Ch. 20, The Millennium (The Age to Come)

➤ Ch. 21-22, Eternity

Revelation & the New Testament

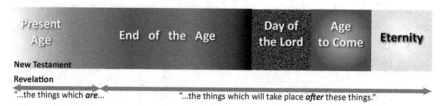

It is true that for the reader who has lived their whole life with detailed End Times charts which make scientists at NASA and the Large Hadron

Collider jealous, this can come across as a bit of a letdown, but the truth is that the basic structure of Revelation very much mirrors the categories of eschatology into which all the teachings of the New Testament can be assigned, albeit with a wealth of more detail to supplement the basic structure provided by Christ and affirmed by the New Testament writers. The labels may have changed in Revelation to explain and expound this deeper exposé, but they still correspond to the New Testament foundation established in Christ's teachings.

Again, Revelation is not a replacement for the Olivet Discourse and the New Testament teachings which all support and dovetail with it, but after more than sixty years and at least three generations of believers having formed their eschatology based first and foremost on the Olivet Discourse, for the Early Church its structure clearly duplicates New Testament teaching in this manner and would have been received as one of the many affirmations that this work is a Holy Spirit sanctified member of the canon of Scripture. This foundation serves as the basis for the Olivet Discourse, in which more detail is provided for the transition to, and the main features of, *"the end of the age"*.

New Testament & Olivet Discourse

Birth Pangs	Tribulation	Great Tribulation	Day of the Lord	The Sheep & the Goats
Olivet Discourse				
Present Age	End of the Age		Day of the Lord	Age to Come	Eternity
New Testament Revelation				

"...the things which *are*..." "...the things which will take place *after* these things."

The Olivet Discourse reveals that a transition from the *"present age"* to the *"end of the age"* comes in the character of *"birth pangs"*, increasing in both intensity and frequency until the Church experiences a period of *"tribulation"* when it undergoes the most intense time of deception, apostasy and persecution in history. This will not simply be a time of refining the Church, but provide the divinely given opportunity to complete its mission to preach the Gospel to the whole world. With the specific milestone of the Abomination of Desolation, *"tribulation"* for the Church will give way to an even more devastating period of *"great tribulation"* for the entire world which, at least for believers, will be supernaturally cut short by the harvest of the faithful—that is, the *Harpazo*, at which time the final wrath of God commences to be experienced by those left behind in what Scripture prolifically assigns to be *"the day of the Lord"*. The Olivet Discourse briefly mentions the transition to the Millennial Kingdom in the separation of the nations in the character of sheep and goats.

Scripture is providing different labels for the same things as it reveals successively deeper levels of detail for each:

> ➤ The *"present age"* in the New Testament equates to *"the things which are"* in Revelation, from which the *"birth pangs"* of the Olivet Discourse serve as its transition. This is the focus of Revelation 2-3 and that which takes place in the seven churches, illustrating the key issues for believers of deception, apostasy, persecution and personal faithfulness while we await the Parousia of Christ.

> ➤ The *"end of the age"* in the overall teachings of the New Testament are the focus of the Olivet Discourse, showing how the transition takes place in the form of *"birth pangs"*, giving way to the back-to-back periods or phases identified as *"tribulation"*, *"great tribulation"*, *"the day of the Lord"*, and finally, the Millennial Kingdom. Revelation 4-7 covers *"the end of the age"* up to the Church's removal, and Revelation 8-19 *"the day of the Lord"*, followed in the closing chapters addressing the Millennial Kingdom and eternity.

> ➤ The general parallel provided in the opening chapter of Revelation broadly describes the *"present age"* as *"the things which are"* and all which comes after beginning with *"the end of the age"* as *"the things which will take place after these things"*. Revelation concludes not only with *"the age to come"*, but a glimpse into eternity to follow.

The body of Revelation provides even more details of each aspect of the eschaton, which can be clearly seen when we include the major milestones commonly referenced delineating each phase. Each layer builds on the previous, providing more detail. This is why they employ a different set of labels:

Overall Comparison

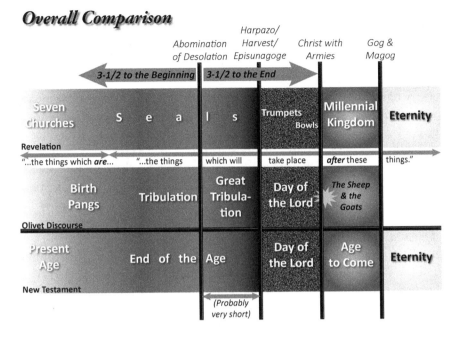

We find that the text devoted to the seven churches is a more detailed, parallel revelation of the "*present age*" and what is broadly designated to John as "*the things which are*". The subsequent "*things which will take place after these things*" which the Olivet Discourse assigns to "*birth pangs*", "*tribulation*", "*great tribulation*" and so forth are afforded an even deeper level of detail in Revelation as the Seals, Trumpets and Bowls along with accompanying parallel features such as Israel's flight, the Antichrist as the Beasts, the rise and fall of Babylon, and the Two Witnesses, among other things. Very broad terms are used because the details are themselves generally broad; but with each successively revealed level, the terms become more specific and granular to correspond to the greater parallel detail. All of these depictions show transitions because a seven year timeline is not overtly stated for any of these stages, and especially in the case of the "*birth pangs*", there may be an overlapping transition.

What Jesus and the New Testament writers refer to as "*the present age*" is described and represented in greater detail in Revelation as "*the things which are*". These are the issues and promises provided to the seven churches as representative of the whole Church which also have an application to every historical period.

This extended timeframe of "*the end of the age*" unfolds in the character of "*birth pangs*", mimicking the same kinds of activities which will have a final,

227

ultimate fulfillment in the eschaton proper in the Seals. It is no coincidence that each thing associated with a "birth pang" in the Olivet Discourse is also the substance and character of each Seal in Revelation. The *"birth pangs"* appear to mask the beginning of Daniel's 70th Week and their ultimate fulfillment in the Seals.

Activities become more concentrated and powerful in the same sequence as provided in the Olivet Discourse. The *"birth pangs"*, which parallel the Seals, give way to the world heaping *"tribulation"* upon believers, corresponding to the persecution specified by the 5th Seal. This gives way to *"great tribulation"* to be experienced by the whole world, initiated by the Abomination of Desolation. The ultimate fulfillment of this more intense period is found in the specific workings of the Seal judgments preceding the removal of the Church between the 6th and 7th Seals which corresponds to the harvest of the saved in the Olivet Discourse.

With the final Seal, which in reality comprises the full set of Trumpet and Bowl judgments, *"the day of the Lord"* is all that is left to be experienced by those left behind as God's wrath is poured out upon the kingdom of the Antichrist. It is kicked off by the same set of signs not only identified in both the Olivet Discourse and the 6th Seal, but in many parallel Scriptures referring to *"the day of the Lord"*.

The end of *"the day of the Lord"* as it gives way to *"the age to come"* is marked by Christ's return with His armies to establish His Millennial Kingdom. The beginning of *"the age to come"* is co-identified in the Olivet Discourse with the milestone judgment of the nations expressed as the separation of the sheep from the goats and in Revelation when thrones for judgment are set up. Revelation provides additional details as to what takes place during this final millennium.

Finally, the last chapters of Revelation specify the transition from the Millennial Kingdom to eternity, highlighted by the seminal "Gog and Magog" battle with the temporary release of Satan and the final judgment of the *"great white throne"* giving way to the physical changes associated with the *"new heaven"* and *"new earth"*, as well as the New Jerusalem.

New Testament eschatology is utilizing different, overlapping terms to describe the same, underlying events and activities, but in increasingly more detail with each round. Just as different terms are employed in Scripture to teach about spiritual aspects of the same thing, such as sometimes calling the nation *"Jacob"* and alternatively *"Israel"* to highlight different spiritual characteristics of the same thing, Christ's initial teachings, the Olivet Discourse and New Testament commentary on it, and Revelation are each referencing identical events and phases but each with customized labels to teach something greater in progressively more detail. Nothing is "replacing" what came before it, and not just merely steadfastly building upon them, but are completely dependent on what came before in order to be properly understood.

As a rough analogy, it is like studying the layout of Washington, D. C. from a tour guide's overview, to then looking at the founding fathers' intentions, to ultimately studying the architectural plans. Each successive level not only provides a different perspective and viewpoint, but employs a different corresponding vocabulary. Just because they each describe the Capitol Building with the differing verbiage of their particular point of view does not mean there must be three different or unique facilities. It is just that the terms and nomenclatures conform to their respective vistas. The tour guide provides a very general description, a study of the founders' intentions takes the discussion to a different level of detail in order to incorporate the philopshical viewpoint, but the descriptions from an architectural point of view become much more technical and detailed in ways not intrinsic to the previous perspectives. They can still be taken together as describing the same thing.

There is a significant difference in the overall structure of Revelation in that while the illustrations, parables and teachings concentrated at the end of the Olivet Discourse speak repeatedly to how Christians are expected to live in this present age leading up to and into the shadow of the eschaton at the end of the age, most of that parallel emphasis in Revelation is concentrated at the beginning within the seven individual letters to the churches.

The Textual Structure

In addition to the need to understand how the timeline of Revelation actually mirrors that of the Olivet Discourse and all of God's given prophetic Word leading up to it, equally critical is the ability to firmly grasp the unique textual structure of Revelation itself. Essentially it is always showing a direct relationship between what takes place in heaven and how that is played out, or at the least affects, what is taking place on earth:

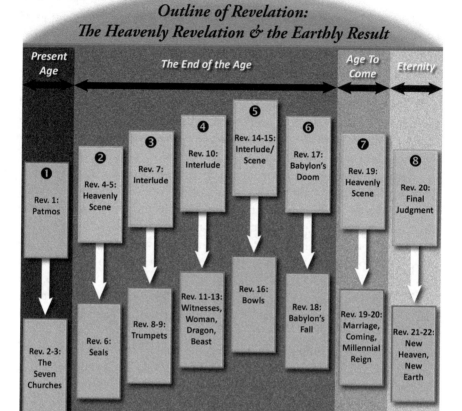

Outline of Revelation:
The Heavenly Revelation & the Earthly Result

Present Age | **The End of the Age** | **Age To Come** | **Eternity**

❶ Rev. 1: Patmos

❷ Rev. 4-5: Heavenly Scene

❸ Rev. 7: Interlude

❹ Rev. 10: Interlude

❺ Rev. 14-15: Interlude/Scene

❻ Rev. 17: Babylon's Doom

❼ Rev. 19: Heavenly Scene

❽ Rev. 20: Final Judgment

Rev. 2-3: The Seven Churches

Rev. 6: Seals

Rev. 8-9: Trumpets

Rev. 11-13: Witnesses, Woman, Dragon, Beast

Rev. 16: Bowls

Rev. 18: Babylon's Fall

Rev. 19-20: Marriage, Coming, Millennial Reign

Rev. 21-22: New Heaven, New Earth

It follows the same general timeline as already discussed, but is textually structured with a corresponding heavenly vision and earthly reaction for the *"present age"*, five such heavenly and earthly correspondences during the *"end of the age"*, and one pair each for both *"the age to come"* and *"eternity"*. It is probably no coincidence that there are a total of eight such parallels as the final one is exclusive to the new creation, and the biblical use of "eight" consistently refers to new beginnings. But more importantly, we need to recognize the special order of the text in this book as it is consistently drawing heaven and earth closer and closer until they become one and the same.

It is most definitely true that even at present, our true source of spiritual conflict originates *"in the heavenly places"*:

> *[12]For our struggle is not against flesh and blood, but against the rulers, against the powers, against the world forces of this darkness, against the spiritual forces of wickedness in the heavenly places. (Ephesians 6:12)*

But we also need to bear in mind that the end of all this can be summed up in God's intention to return things to how they were originally intended all along, where man and God lived and interacted together. This is why we see Genesis purposely reflected in the conclusion of Revelation with the presence in each of the Tree of Life, and man in direct fellowship and worship of the Godhead. In the end, what is spiritually taking place at present literally enters the physical realm so they are no longer separated.

One of the key transactions taking place in the course of the pages of Revelation are the way the barriers between heaven and earth are giving way to bring both together. We see Satan and the demons literally expelled from heaven and cast down to earth, Satan literally possess a human in the Antichrist, we have visible angelic activity taking place in pronouncements to mankind and God-directed assignments, as well as at times corresponding demonic actions such as the horde temporarily loosed from the pit upon the earth for a five month reign of torture and terror upon those not sealed by God. As we move back and forth between that which Revelation shows is taking place in heaven and how it is then reflected in earth's physical realm, the two come closer and closer together until, in the end, they are one. The Millennial Reign is actually a time when Christ and His saints reign together on earth in parallel to the nations living together under His dominion. It is the final stage of all things in the physical realm co-existing as originally intended in the Garden of Eden before giving way to their ultimate consolidation in eternity to subsequently come. The Millennial Reign parallels the Garden of Eden, but then it goes a step further when eternity future parallels eternity past.

The mistake to be avoided when it comes to our handling of the text of Revelation is to recognize how this overall pattern of alternating between the heavenly and the earthly provides our baseline guide, and to likewise understand that it is not always strictly adhering to a linear, chronological timeline. Although it is organized overall according to a recognizable chronology, at times it pauses to visit details which are taking place in parallel to each other. This is most notable in chapters 10-15. The chronology of the Seals, Trumpets and Bowls hold things together overall, but this particular passage located between the Trumpets and Bowls largely addresses activities and personalities in parallel to the grand scheme of things.

A Preparatory Checklist

It can seem like a bit of a juggling act, but there are critical issues which need to be handled throughout our embrace of the text of Revelation in order to ultimately adhere to the axiom Peter provides when it comes to the prophetic portions of God's Word…

> *²⁰But know this first of all, that **no prophecy of Scripture is a matter of one's own interpretation**, ²¹for no prophecy was ever made by an act of human will, but men moved by the Holy Spirit spoke from God. (2 Peter 1:20–21)*

When it comes to Revelation:

> ➤ There is no obvious seven year structure specified; it is rather the midway point suggested in concert with the Abomination of Desolation and the corresponding flight by Israel which is emphasized in parallel with activities mostly associated with the latter half of Daniel's 70th Week. The Seals are the final fulfillment of the *"birth pangs"* which serve to disguise the beginning.

> ➤ By God's design, at least some of these things are given for the purpose of their recognition only in hindsight, in the same manner as many fulfillments of prophecy in the course of the First Coming. We are given only as much as we need to operate by faith, but that which has been disclosed is quite comprehensive and sufficient for the task.

> ➤ The overall sequence parallels that which was originally given in all teachings leading up to the Olivet Discourse, the parallel New Testament texts, and especially the Olivet Discourse itself. They are foundational layers building on each other and providing successively greater detail. Nothing previously stated is overwritten, and that which comes later is actually dependent upon its predecessors.

> ➤ With the additional detail, Revelation provides a distinct structure in being formed around eight heavenly visions corresponding to how they are played out in the earthly realm. God's original plan and intentions are being restored as the barriers between heaven and earth are removed to bring all things back together under Him.

Such are critical in order to achieve a divinely guided interpretation of the text where the priority is given to allowing Scripture to be the chief and primary interpreter of Scripture.

A Qualifying Note

Unfortunately, in order to keep on topic, we are not able to fully exegete the whole of Revelation, but need to retain the main focus on its parallel to the Olivet Discourse. This means that we will forgo discussing the seven churches and their parallel to *"this present age"* in Revelation 2-3, and the greater details of *"the day of the Lord"* beginning in Revelation 8 going forward. We will instead concentrate on Revelation 4-8 and especially the corresponding relationship between the Olivet Discourse and the Seals, with a few additional visitations as appropriate. This is the section of Revelation which most parallels that which is revealed for *"the end of the age"* in the Olivet Discourse.

15 ❖ "...After This"

*[1]After these things I looked, and behold, a door standing open in heaven, and the first voice which I had heard, like the sound of a trumpet speaking with me, said, **"Come up here**, and I will show you what must take place after these things." [2]Immediately I was in the Spirit; and behold, a throne was standing in heaven, and One sitting on the throne. (Revelation 4:1–2)*

Is This a Corporate Solidarity?

Whether or not this *"Come up here"* command to the Apostle John is a corporate solidarity representing the Rapture of the entire Church is one of the most intense debates among Bible expositors regardless of eschatology. If it is, and what happens here to John individually represents the entire Body of believers collectively, then it is passionately asserted that this is the Rapture event when the whole Church is supernaturally removed, and the Church therefore does not participate in what comes after in Revelation 4-19 until returning for the Millennial Reign in Revelation 20; if not, an equally dogmatic case is asserted that this is just describing how the lone figure of the Apostle John is taken up to receive a heavenly vision, this is not the place where the removal of the Church takes place, and therefore the Church must endure some or all of what follows.

When it comes to how 1st century readership would have interpreted this event, however, it is difficult to make the case that such discussions ever formed or entered their minds to begin with, and therefore this whole debate is one of the strongest proofs confirming the assertion in these pages that eschatology today, regardless of the chosen "ism", often reverses the priority of the Scriptures. It is an over-realization of Revelation to the exclusion of what Jesus and the New Testament writers taught and first established long before it was published.

For at least sixty years, believers' eschatology had been exclusively formed around the Olivet Discourse, so when Revelation was finally available, they did the most natural and common sense thing of all by verifying its authenticity according to its conformity and compliance with those prior teachings. When Revelation was distributed, it was not a replacement for all previous teachings, but rather provided a more detailed explanation of what had already been provided.

Just as the Bereans tested Paul's New Testament teachings against the standard of the Old Testament, the Scriptures which they already had in their possession, in like manner the first readers of Revelation did the same thing, but with the addition of the emerging New Testament canon as well. They did not think of Revelation as a big Etch-a-Sketch® to be shaken, erased, and eschatology started all over again; this Scripture had to comply with all other Scripture previous to it. Christ Himself directly gave the Olivet Discourse, so it could not conflict with something else He provided, even sixty years after the fact, just as neither could books and Prophets hundreds of years apart in the Old Testament be found to contradict one another or any other portion of Scripture coming before or after it.

Recognizing that Revelation 4:1 is a milestone transitioning from what had been previously established by the rest of the New Testament as going from *"this present age"* to *"the end of the age"*, they never gave consideration to the interpretation that what happened to John represented the Rapture of the whole Church. This would be impossible because they already knew that it did not conform to the timing of the Rapture already given in the Olivet Discourse and confirmed by the Apostle Paul in 2 Thessalonians 2, together with other supporting Scripture. They did not read this book in a vacuum, but in the context of the teachings already established by the other twenty-six books of the emerging New Testament canon.

1st century readers already knew that the Church's *Harpazo* comes after the Abomination of Desolation and Israel's flight out of the land and as the specific milestone when the sequence transitions from *"great tribulation"* to *"the day of the Lord"*. If they thought someone was presenting something which outright conflicted with what Jesus had already established and further confirmed by the New Testament writers, the Early Church would have rejected Revelation outright from the moment they read it for the first time. That did not happen because they interpreted Revelation in the context of the rest of the New Testament which came before it, and in doing so, like the Bereans examining Paul by the standard of existing Scripture, not only found no contradictions, but that in actuality it was completely harmonious.

(Apologies for making it sound so obnoxious, but the problem is not with them, but with us.)

What they would absolutely recognize about this experience of John's is that this was not something unprecedented, but taking place for him in the same way similar episodes were experienced by others in Scripture who had individual "rapture" experiences. Some of these went through the same kind of process in the course of being shown heavenly visions, but in particular Early Church readers would have associated this activity as being in the character of Ezekiel, who was likewise "transported" or physically raptured from one location to another in the course of being given a series of visions, or in the character of what happened to the Apostle Paul. For them, Revelation 4:1 was not about "the" Rapture, but rather "a" rapture as already documented and previously experienced by other figures in Scripture past. It was a familiar phenomenon documented in Scripture for the likes of Isaiah, Ezekiel, Zechariah and Paul.

To begin with, it is important to note that John specifies "*I was in the Spirit*" both here when he is taken to heaven and at the very opening of Revelation, where in both locations he was being given a vision. While still on the Isle of Patmos, this fact was established from the outset: "*I was in the Spirit on the Lord's day when...*" (Rev. 1:10) He has a vision in each location both on earth and in heaven and for each instance independently notes, "*I was in the Spirit*". For the Apostle John, his "rapture" or command to "*come up*" in Revelation 4:1 is followed up in verse 2 with the explanation, "*Immediately I was in the Spirit*", so he could witness what was taking place in Heaven. In Revelation 9:17, John will later stipulate, "*And this is how I saw in the vision...*" to remind readers how this revelation is taking place, and John's most used affirmation of the overall context throughout the book is to repeatedly remind us that he was "*in the Spirit*". (Rev. 1:10; 4:2; 17:3; 21:10)

Anyone with even the most minimal familiarity with Isaiah, Ezekiel or Zechariah, for instance, would recognize that this was the way God has communicated through Prophets in the past, so rather than confusing it with the Church's removal, it would have actually been received by 1st century readers as confirmation of the authenticity of John's personal experience in his role as a prophet—in other words, proof of the authenticity of this message, not a symbol of an event to be unilaterally extracted out of context and applied independently to the Church. There are many rapture experiences in both Testaments which strictly involve individuals: Enoch, Elijah and Ezekiel in the Old Testament, and Philip, Paul and Christ in the New Testament. For such a thing to happen to John is not unprecedented and adheres to the character of similar examples in God's Word.

Furthermore, if we take a forward peek at Revelation 11, we will find that this exact command is given when God likewise raptures the resurrected Two Witnesses:

> [11]*But after the three and a half days, the breath of life from God came into them, and they stood on their feet; and great fear fell upon those who were watching them.* [12]*And they heard a loud voice from heaven saying to them, "*__Come up here.__*" Then they went up into heaven in the cloud, and their enemies watched them.* (Revelation 11:11-12)

The unique and personally directed command of God which in both cases initiates these individual rapture experiences is not only completely independent textually from the Greek or Hebrew associated with all other types of rapture events, but is much more in the character of what took place when Jesus called Lazarus by name out of the tomb (Jn. 11:43) or resurrecting Jairus' daughter by calling her personally (Mk. 5:41-42); it is God working on a literal, individual level. In fact, one of the key differences about the Rapture of the Church, which is the only group rapture in the whole of Scripture (there may be similarities in "rescue narratives" such as Noah, Lot, Israel, etc. but they are not specifically "raptures" but rather types teaching about it), is that the Church's removal is often specified as being accomplished by angelic agency (Mt. 13:39; 24:31; Mk. 13:27; Rev. 14:14-16); all the individual raptures (Enoch, Elijah, Ezekiel, Christ, Philip, Paul, John and the Two Witnesses) never make any such reference and appear to be the working of a member of the Godhead on a singular case basis. But in any event, no one attempts to make the case that the same command to the Two Witnesses which was given to John represents anything more than the rapture of those two individuals; neither is this a corporate solidarity representing the whole of the Church.

As established by all the individual raptures in Scripture, John here experiences something personal at the command of God and, in the character of Ezekiel or one of the Old Testament Prophets, the purpose is for the giving of a divine vision. Throughout the whole documented experience, John repeatedly reminds readers He is "*in the Spirit*".

The Heavenly Scene

> [2]*Immediately I was in the Spirit; and behold, a throne was standing in heaven, and One sitting on the throne.* [3]*And He who was sitting was like a jasper stone and a sardius in appearance;*

and there was a rainbow around the throne, like an emerald in
appearance. (Revelation 4:2–3)

The use of these kinds of descriptions by John for God would be expected by anyone even moderately familiar with the Old Testament because they are in character with the way such descriptions were given for similar special encounters. This can be seen in the experiences of Moses (Ex. 33:18-23; 34:5-8), Ezekiel (Eze. 1:25-28) and Daniel (Dan. 7:9, 10), as well as Isaiah (Is. 6:1-5). It is interesting that John first sees a circle around God Almighty in the form of a rainbow and then the circle of elders around the throne before ultimately observing the larger concentric encirclement of the huge number of worshiping angels and special beings.

There is no modern-day consensus on whether all the gem stones as translated by the NASB (or other English versions) precisely match what is considered their ancient equivalents, but the basic idea John attempts to communicate is something sparkling and transparent and glowing in a manner not experienced on earth. The presence of a rainbow around God's throne, however, is a powerful and permanent reminder of God's mercy and promise in Noah's time, a shadow of the final judgment to come. Some point out that while Noah could only observe an arc in the sky while on earth, in heaven the complete rainbow is observed so as to witness the entire circular pattern, which conveys the completeness of God's promises.

⁴Around the throne were twenty-four thrones; and upon the
thrones I saw twenty-four elders sitting, clothed in white
garments, and golden crowns on their heads. (Revelation 4:4)

It seems that this detail of "*twenty four elders*" is a sort of eschatological "litmus test", if you will. For some reason, whatever "ism" one subscribes to when it comes to their eschatology of the End Times and the way they handle God's prophetic Word, such very often forms a nexus with their dogmatic stance on the identity of these elders. Probably the most popular proposal put forward is that they are composed of the twelve heads of the twelve tribes of Israel and the twelve Apostles. Many who insist that this latter half of the group must be the founding Apostles attempt to leverage it into some sort of "proof" that the Church has thus been raptured at this point, otherwise, they continue to assert, there could not be any representatives of the Church present at this juncture.

Most often, what many are really trying to do by establishing the identity of the twenty-four elders in this manner is to make some kind of a case for their particular eschatology's timing of the Rapture by inserting something into Scripture which really is not there to begin with. The fact is that not every figure in the whole of Scripture is identified by name, but rather by their chief spiritual characteristics revealed in the course of their behavior, assigned roles and activities. For instance, many angels appear at different times throughout Scripture, but we only know the names of two of them, and not even every recorded prophet is named. And there was the case of Elijah's return in the First Coming being fulfilled by someone in his character with a completely different name! (a.k.a., "John the Baptist", not "Elijah") The biblical principle is that everyone is ultimately known by their deeds and character, not their reputation. (Just ask the church at Sardis.)

That being said, however, if half of these elders are the twelve founding Apostles, why doesn't the Apostle John recognize himself as one of them? Having spent many years with all of the other Apostles, first as disciples of John the Baptist, then of Jesus, and then from Pentecost forward to this point some sixty years later, why doesn't he recognize any of the other Apostles? He doesn't even recognize his own brother, James, or his former business partners Peter and Andrew. In fact, since in the shared vision on the Mt. of Transfiguration (Mt. 17) Peter, James and John himself all recognized both Moses and Elijah, whom they had obviously never met before and at a time with no photographs or pictures of these two historic figures to go by, why doesn't John recognize any of the elders present if they are the Old Testament heads of the twelve tribes and the New Testament heads of the Church?

Throughout Revelation, if there is a question as to identity, the issue is raised and answered, otherwise the vision, like the one on the Mt. of Transfiguration, is plainly understood as to the personalities or entities involved. But not every figure in Revelation, much less the whole of Scripture, is always specifically named, and the furthest we can stretch within the limits of what is stated in the text is they are "*elders*".

Additionally, it is not like the Apostle John, although the recipient of this vision, does not ever see anything of himself in this revelation. In describing the construction of the New Jerusalem, John will later relay:

> [12]It had a great and high wall, with twelve gates, and at the gates twelve angels; and names were written on them, which are the names of the twelve tribes of the sons of Israel. [13]There were three gates on the east and three gates on the north and three gates on the south and three gates on the west. [14]And the wall of the city had twelve foundation stones, and on them were **the twelve names of the twelve apostles** of the Lamb. (Revelation 21:12–14)

While it is the names of each of Israel's "*tribes*" which are ascribed to each of the twelve gates, it is the individual "*names of the twelve apostles*" assigned to each of the foundation stones. As one of those Apostles, John had no problem recognizing his own representation in that part of the vision.

There are two aspects of the twenty-four which undoubtedly identify them as former earth-dwelling human beings who as God's saints have been eternally transformed by the fact that they are *"clothed in white garments"* (Rev. 4:4)—a common biblical representation of spiritually good deeds and accomplishments, and possessing *"golden crowns on their heads"* (Rev. 4:4)—a feature also specifically associated as something awarded to believers. Such would unmistakably assign these individuals as former earthly citizens promoted to an elevated position in heaven—not to mention their seeming greater place of importance over the angels and everyone else. (1 Co. 6:3) And the very fact that they are called *"elders"* is itself a unique title applied exclusively throughout Scripture to humans and therefore a tripartite proof of their identity; it is just that, like many other figures encountered in Scripture, their specific former earthly identities are not revealed to us. (One possibility to consider is that, as Jesus promises, they have each received a *"new name"* as mentioned in Revelation 2:17 so that it could be these figures remain unnamed because we are not allowed to know yet.)

But as to the question of whether anyone in this group, without the aid of the Church's Rapture, could be present in heaven with these attributes provided through Christ, what is rarely addressed is the fact that the Resurrection of believers has already begun in tandem with Christ's own Resurrection. There are already resurrected believers in heaven even before the Rapture of the Church:

> *⁵⁰And Jesus cried out again with a loud voice, and yielded up His spirit. ⁵¹And behold, the veil of the temple was torn in two from top to bottom; and the earth shook and the rocks were split. ⁵²**The tombs were opened, and many bodies of the saints who had fallen asleep were raised**; ⁵³and coming out of the tombs after His resurrection they entered the holy city and appeared to many. (Matthew 27:50–53)*

A Pattern of Worship

It may be important to note that there seems to be a progression within the overall book of Revelation as to the worship of God which takes place in its various doxologies:

> ➤ In Revelation 4:9 the heavenly beings initiate praising the holiness and eternal character of God and in 4:10-11 are joined by the twenty-four elders who additionally tack on praise for His will and actions as Creator.

➤ In Revelation 5:9-10 the heavenly beings and twenty-four elders render praise for redemption through the blood of Christ. This is followed in 5:11-12 with the praise of Christ by the elders and heavenly beings joined by the angels, and in 5:13-14 by *"every created thing which is in heaven and on earth and under the earth and on the sea, and all things in them"* joining in the worship.

➤ In Revelation 11:16-19, the twenty-four elders praise God for final judgment upon the world.

This is a parallel chronological approximation of God's working incorporating His previously stated traits of *"...the Alpha and the Omega... who is and was and who is to come..."* (Rev. 1:8) The various emphases of the worship in heaven taking place correspond to the overall plan and character of God according to first rendering praise for *"who was"* (Creator), then *"who is"* (Savior), and finally for *"who is to come"* (Judge). It goes from creation past, to history present, to the final judgment to come.

A critical doctrinal point which the New Testament writers established, especially in the book of Hebrews, is that the original earthly Tabernacle and its successor Temples were a copy of their perfect, heavenly counterpart:

> *4Now if He were on earth, He would not be a priest at all, since there are those who offer the gifts according to the Law; 5who serve **a copy and shadow of the heavenly things**, just as Moses was warned by God when he was about to erect the tabernacle; for, "SEE," He says, "THAT YOU **MAKE ALL THINGS ACCORDING TO THE PATTERN WHICH WAS SHOWN YOU ON THE MOUNTAIN**." (Hebrews 8:4–5)*

It is far more likely that 1st century Christians reading Revelation would connect these twenty-four elders, who are repeatedly seen throughout Revelation in various acts of worship, as the heavenly equivalent of the twenty-four courses of Temple worship established by David in 1 Chronicles 25:2-6. The four sons of Asaph, the six sons of Jeduthun, and the fourteen sons of Heman are ultimately all assigned to minister *"under the direction of the king"* (1 Ch. 25:6) in an earthly reflection of this corresponding number of worshipers before God's throne. In other words, this heavenly scene of worship is the pattern of that which David set up on earth, the *"copy and shadow of heavenly things"*.

In fact, as time went on, and as seen in the case of Zacharias' selection to take care of the incense in the holy place which led to his encounter with

Gabriel, (Lk. 1:8-9) qualified priests and Levites were swapped in and out of these twenty-four courses when there became far more of them available than necessary for carrying out all the duties assigned to this level of service and worship. A possible heavenly parallel of this structure would mean that it is only twenty-four elders at a time who are seated as many more are rotated in and out. But at this juncture, the fact is that we do not need to know the identity and should be satisfied with the inspiration of seeing a fulfillment of what God promised for believers in heaven as illustrated for us in this group's presence and role. Scripturally, the activities they engage in are more important than their individual identity, that particular focus often diluting or outright silencing what is most important in God's Word.

The More Important Pattern

What is probably far more important about this opening scene is the pattern of the book of Revelation as previously visited. If we were to make an outline of the contents as previously noted, we would find that the vision is divided into eight major sections, each beginning with an action or scene from the heavenly realm and followed by corresponding activities in the earthly realm. Again, there is a direct association between activities and pronouncements taking place above which are replayed in parallel to corresponding events on earth below as depicted in the previous chart.

In between these "glimpses" into something taking place in heaven are related activities being directly played out on earth. Whereas the letters to the seven churches in Revelation 1-3 describe *"the things which are"* (Rev. 1:19) and have a sole and exclusive focus on what takes place on earth in *"this present age"*, Revelation 4-19 covers *"the things which will take place after"*—or what Christ and the New Testament writers refer to as *"the end of the age"*, when the final activities transpiring in the heavenly realm are concluded in their earthly counterparts.

This format of Revelation should not actually come as a surprise to us since, as born again, Holy Spirit-filled believers, we already know this to be the reality even at present. The fact is that what began in the heavenly realm before the creation of the earth is finally brought to an ultimate conclusion on the cusp of the New Creation. Whereas from time to time the Old Testament Scriptures provided a peek back in time to explain the origins of the spiritual events which resulted in what is taking place in the present course of history, Revelation is especially focused on how that interplay brings history to a unified conclusion in accordance with God's will.

Worship Around the Throne

> *⁵Out from the throne come flashes of lightning and sounds and peals of thunder. And there were seven lamps of fire burning before the throne, which are the seven Spirits of God; ⁶and before the throne there was something like a sea of glass, like crystal; and in the center and around the throne, four living creatures full of eyes in front and behind. ⁷The first creature was like a lion, and the second creature like a calf, and the third creature had a face like that of a man, and the fourth creature was like a flying eagle. ⁸And the four living creatures, each one of them having six wings, are full of eyes around and within; and day and night they do not cease to say,*
>
> *"Holy, holy, holy is the Lord God, the Almighty, who was and who is and who is to come."*
>
> *⁹And when the living creatures give glory and honor and thanks to Him who sits on the throne, to Him who lives forever and ever, ¹⁰The twenty-four elders will fall down before Him who sits on the throne, and will worship Him who lives forever and ever, and will cast their crowns before the throne, saying, ¹¹"Worthy are You, our Lord and our God, to receive glory and honor and power; for You created all things, and because of Your will they existed, and were created." (Revelation 4:5–11)*

Theologically it is important to note that all three members of the Godhead are once again specifically mentioned in these opening chapters, first God the Father in Revelation 4:2, God the Spirit in Revelation 4:5, and God the Son in Revelation 5:4. Remember, in the original manuscript, there were no verse or chapter numbers, so Revelation 4-5 is one continuous description of the heavenly scene taking place around the throne initializing the launch for *"the things which will take place after"*.

The keyword in Revelation 4-5 is *"throne"*, which is used sixteen times in these chapters alone, and forty-two times in the whole of Revelation. This is a primary theme of Revelation not to be casually overlooked, that it is God's throne which rules supreme and not that of either men nor Antichrist. Within John's vision are repeated reminders that this is the reality which is going to ultimately be implemented in every realm, bringing together heaven and earth into a consolidated kingdom or under a single throne. In the Olivet Discourse in Matthew 24-25, the final event of the judgment of the nations is described, *"But when the Son of Man comes in His glory, and all the angels with Him, then He will sit on His glorious throne"*. (Mt. 25:31)

There is the reminder given here, *"You created all things, and because of Your will they existed, and were created"*. The biblical symbolism of the thunder and lightning emitted from the God's throne would describe the judgment of God, which would be a contrast to the rainbow speaking of His parallel quality of mercy. Furthermore, it is a very powerful aspect of God's character which is initially highlighted, that He is both holy and eternal. It speaks to the fact that God has always had a plan which is about to experience completion, and it requires that the final result sanctify everything to the minimum requirements of holiness in order to abide together in His presence.

This establishment of God's throne and the completion of His plan to consolidate all things into a single kingdom is key to all that John reports after this initial heavenly vision. What is taking place going forward is the bringing to an end all earthly and satanic attempts to replace or counterfeit a kingdom of one's own making, and to purify everything and everyone remaining to the standards of God's holiness, even to the point that it will eventually end in not just a New Jerusalem, but a New Heaven and New Earth. And this would go a long way for 1st century believers who were well versed in the Old Testament so as to explain the misinterpretation of the expectancy that the Messiah would establish this throne at His First Coming. What follows from this point on in Revelation is actually a very detailed account of what will take place in order for the Messiah to fulfill those Scriptures and establish His throne on earth.

Very Familiar Parallels

In recognizing that the earthly is a pattern of the heavenly, 1st century readers still very familiar with the recently destroyed Second Temple and its precursors would have recognized the significance of *"something like a sea of glass, like crystal"*. (Rev. 4:6) In Solomon's Temple there was a large metal repository also called *"the sea"* standing before the bronze altar holding an enormous amount of water:

> [23]Now **he made the sea of cast metal ten cubits from brim to brim**, *circular in form, and its height was five cubits, and thirty cubits in circumference.* [24]*Under its brim gourds went around encircling it ten to a cubit, completely surrounding the sea; the gourds were in two rows, cast with the rest.* [25]*It stood on twelve oxen, three facing north, three facing west, three facing south, and three facing east; and the sea was set on top of them, and*

> all their rear parts turned inward. ²⁶It was a handbreadth thick,
> and its brim was made like the brim of a cup, as a lily blossom;
> it could hold two thousand baths. (1 Kings 7:23-26)

This was derived from one of the features of the original Tabernacle established through Moses which had to do with the requirement for washing between the sacrifices carried out by the priesthood:

> ¹⁸**"You shall also make a laver of bronze**, with its base of bronze,
> for washing; and you shall put it between the tent of meeting
> and the altar, and you shall put water in it. ¹⁹Aaron and his
> sons shall wash their hands and their feet from it; ²⁰when they
> enter the tent of meeting, they shall wash with water, so that
> they will not die; or when they approach the altar to minister,
> by offering up in smoke a fire sacrifice to the Lord. ²¹So they
> shall wash their hands and their feet, so that they will not die;
> and it shall be a perpetual statute for them, for Aaron and his
> descendants throughout their generations." (Exodus 30:18-21)

However, that the sea appears as solid crystal (in Revelation 15:2 believers are described as actually standing on it) and no longer required for cleansing between sacrifices, this would be a powerful illustration that the work of salvation is completed and there is no longer any need for the continuing sacrifices for sin. The fact that the perfect heavenly pattern is also absent being born on the back of oxen as in Solomon's earthly copy would be further evidence of the ultimate heavenly design in which everything is now organized around worship of the Godhead, and the earthly function to first address sin before approaching God further has become obsolete and unnecessary.

But overall, Revelation provides a description of the heavenly Temple where the Holy Spirit as seven lamps represent the seven-branched lampstand, the sea of glass the laver, there is a corresponding altar of sacrifice (Rev. 6:9-11) and altar of incense (Rev. 8:3-5), and the throne of God in heaven in parallel to the mercy seat on the Ark of the Covenant in the earthly Holy of Holies is at the center. For some, this reinforces the notion that the twenty-four elders were mimicked by the serving priesthood while the living beings are the embodiment of the cherubim embroidered on the earthly Temple's veil and embedded into the walls. As we shall see, however, the *"four living creatures"* are actually something quite different and set apart in their own right from the Cherubim.

The Four Living Creatures

Within the whole body of Scripture we are made aware of creations other than man. The list at the very least comprises angels (the only named one being Gabriel), the archangel Michael, the Cherubim (whose name many assert is derived from "guard"), and the Seraphim (whom it is also offered comes from "burning ones"). Perhaps the eagle of Revelation 8:13 belongs to this list as well. Commentators most often assign the four living creatures of Revelation to the category of Cherubim, while a lesser percentage to the Seraphim and the smallest to membership in their own separate class.

The first time we are introduced to the Cherubim in Scripture is when they are stationed "*at the east gate of the garden of Eden*" with a flaming sword to "*guard the way to the tree of life*", (Gen. 3:24) but the Cherubim is the category for which we have the most overall information and scriptural examples. In the NASB, the singular use of "*cherub*" and the plural "*cherubim*" appear 94 times in 70 verses, and examining them all reveals that there is at least three different physical varieties of Cherubim. Not every instance of a Cherub recorded in Scripture is necessarily identical to one another in appearance.

While the most sensational variety may be those who each have four faces and four wings with human hands underneath in Ezekiel 1 and 10, the Cherubim described in Ezekiel 41:18 have but two faces while the many descriptions of them embroidered into the curtain walls of the Tabernacle (Ex. 26:1, 8; 26:31, 35) or painted on the walls of Solomon's Temple (1 Ki. 6:29; 2 Chr. 3:7), and carved in the doors of Solomon's Temple (1 Ki. 6:31-35) all appear to be single-faced. The Cherubs appearing on the lid of the Ark of the Covenant (Ex. 25:18-20), as well as two very large Cherubs placed in the Holy of Holies in Solomon's Temple (1 Ki. 6:23-28; 2 Chr. 3:10-13; 5:7-8) and later replicated for Herod's Temple according to extra-biblical sources likewise appear to have been one-faced figures. (At some point the one's in Herod's Temple were modified into male and female figures which, according to the Talmudic rabbis, represented the love of God and Israel; not exactly biblically based.) These are again featured in what is popularly called Ezekiel's "Millennial Temple" as carved in the walls and doors.

There is a single instance in Solomon's Temple where Cherubim are included with lions and oxen on the ten stands of bronze between their frames, and as part of each stand's top border when they are interspersed with lions and palm trees (1 Ki. 7:27-37), but these still appear to be single-faced Cherubs. In none of these cases, however, are the Cherubs said to have faces of anything other than that of a Cherub, whereas the four-faced Cherubim in Ezekiel 1 states:

> ¹⁰*As for the form of their faces, each had the face of a **man**; all four had the face of a **lion** on the right and the face of a **bull** on the left, and all four had the face of an **eagle**. (Ezekiel 1:10)*

But later in Ezekiel 10, three of the four faces remain the same, but the face of the bull is replaced with the face of a cherub:

> ¹⁴*And each one had four faces. The first face was the face of a **cherub**, the second face was the face of a **man**, the third the face of a **lion**, and the fourth the face of an **eagle**. (Ezekiel 10:14)*

Although both the four-faced and two-faced versions are specifically identified as belonging to the classification of Cherub, as can be seen from examples in the Tabernacle and both Solomon's and Ezekiel's Temples, as well as this example of one of the faces in Ezekiel 10:14, there is some kind of a physical face unique to a Cherub which is just as different and distinguishable as a man's face is from that of a lion's or eagle's.

> ⁷*The first creature was like a **lion**, and the second creature like a **calf**, and the third creature had a face like that of a **man**, and the fourth creature was like a flying **eagle**. (Revelation 4:7)*

However, the living beings in Revelation are not multi-faced creatures, and although they are said to have many eyes like the Cherubim in Ezekiel (Rev. 4:6), there is also the significant difference of their having six wings (Rev. 4:8) rather than four. (Eze. 1:6; 10:21) The single description of Isaiah's Seraphim have far more in common with Revelation's living beings:

> ¹*In the year of King Uzziah's death I saw the Lord sitting on a throne, lofty and exalted, with the train of His robe filling the temple.* ²*Seraphim stood above Him, **each having six wings: with two he covered his face, and with two he covered his feet, and with two he flew**.* ³*And one called out to another and said,*
>
> > *"Holy, Holy, Holy, is the LORD of hosts,*
> > *The whole earth is full of His glory."*
>
> ⁴*And the foundations of the thresholds trembled at the voice of him who called out, while the temple was filling with smoke.* ⁵*Then I said,*

"Woe is me, for I am ruined!
Because I am a man of unclean lips,
And I live among a people of unclean lips;
For my eyes have seen the King, the LORD of hosts."

⁶Then one of the seraphim flew to me with a burning coal in
his hand, which he had taken from the altar with tongs. (Isaiah
6:1–6)

There is no mention of the form of the Seraphim's faces, but it cannot be overlooked that they not only have the same number of wings as Revelation's living beings, but that they are both found at the throne of God performing the same function of worship.

⁸And the four living creatures, each one of them having six
wings, are full of eyes around and within; and day and night
they do not cease to say,

"Holy, holy, holy is the Lord God, the Almighty, who was
and who is and who is to come."

⁹And when the living creatures give glory and honor and
thanks to Him who sits on the throne, to Him who lives forever
and ever, (Revelation 4:8–9)

What stands out as a key difference between what Isaiah witnessed in his time and the Apostle John for his is that the Seraphim are now joined in their activities by the twenty-four elders:

¹⁰The twenty-four elders will fall down before Him who sits on
the throne, and will worship Him who lives forever and ever,
and will cast their crowns before the throne, saying, ¹¹"Worthy
are You, our Lord and our God, to receive glory and honor and
power; for You created all things, and because of Your will they
existed, and were created." (Revelation 4:10–11)

This will be a repeated feature of John's vision when its focus alternates from what is taking place on earth to that of heaven, where the worship activities of the Seraphim and the twenty-four elders parallel one another. (Rev. 4:9-10; 5:8-10, 14; 7:11-12; 14:3; 19:4)

There is yet another unique parallel between the Seraphim and the twenty-four elders which coincides with Christ the Lamb taking the scroll from the Father:

> *⁷And He came and took the book out of the right hand of Him who sat on the throne. ⁸When He had taken the book, the four living creatures and the twenty-four elders fell down before the Lamb, **each one holding a harp and golden bowls0full of incense, which are the prayers of the saints**. ⁹And they sang a new song, saying,*
>
> > *"Worthy are You to take the book and to break its seals; for You were slain, and purchased for God with Your blood men from every tribe and tongue and people and nation.*
>
> > *¹⁰"You have made them to be a kingdom and priests to our God; and they will reign upon the earth." (Revelation 5:7–10)*

Notice that both groups are not only "*holding a harp*", but "*golden bowls full of incense, which are the prayers of the saints*". It is a Seraphim in Isaiah's case who obtains a coal from the heavenly altar in order to address Isaiah's spiritual condition, and there seems to be a parallel activity here. Notably, the new song introduced due to the Lamb's taking of the scroll extols the work of salvation for "*men from every tribe and tongue and people and nation*" whereas salvific cleansing was accomplished for Isaiah on an individual basis.

This accelerates to the point that exaltation of the Lamb involves everyone:

> *¹¹Then I looked, and I heard the voice of many **angels** around the throne and **the living creatures** and the **elders**; and the number of them was myriads of myriads, and thousands of thousands, ¹²saying with a loud voice,*
>
> > *"Worthy is the Lamb that was slain to receive power and riches and wisdom and might and honor and glory and blessing."*
>
> *¹³And **every created thing** which is in heaven and on the earth and under the earth and on the sea, and all things in them, I heard saying,*
>
> > *"To Him who sits on the throne, and to the Lamb, be blessing and honor and glory and dominion forever and ever."*
>
> *¹⁴And **the four living creatures** kept saying, "Amen." And the **elders** fell down and worshiped. (Revelation 5:11–14)*

Whereas Cherubim seem to have a specific role concerning the guarding and service of God's throne, the Seraphim as described by both Isaiah and John appear to function in the capacity of facilitating mankind's access to God's throne and have a kindred connection with man where worship and service of God is concerned.

"Zoon" vs. "Therion"

The underlying Greek term for the English rendering of "living creatures" in Revelation is "*zoon*" (Strong's #2226), the singular being "*zoa*". One of the reasons so many expositors determine that the living beings in Revelation must be the Cherubim in Ezekiel is that when they are there referred to as "*living creatures*", the Septuagint likewise employs the Greek term "*zoon*". So in fairness to this interpretation, even though the physical descriptions display obvious differences, there is a strong underlying textual connection which deserves our full attention and might actually make a reasonable case that the living beings are indeed Cherubim. Since there are at least three different types recorded in the Old Testament, it is not beyond all reason to view those in Revelation as a fourth.

But one of the things which lexicons and scholars of the original languages point out is that "*zoon*" is also used in both Testaments in general for "*animals*", mostly in the context of clean animals, but that the term "*therion*"—most often translated "*beasts*" (Strong's #2342) is employed to differentiate the unclean. By extension, it is thought that "*zoon*" is therefore used of all "*living beings*" which are approved of God and working within His reasoned character, but "*therion*" as unclean offerings are found to represent agents working against God such as when Paul uses this description for the Cretans (Titus 1:12), or more importantly, the definitive term associated with the Antichrist, the Beasts of Revelation 13.

It would appear that whereas God has angels, Satan has demons, and that corresponding to God's "*zoon*"—His living beings, Satan's parallel counterfeit is the "*therion*"—the Beast from the sea and the Beast from the land. God's agents work to effect mankind's spiritually restored access to God's throne while Satan's doppelgängers seek to permanently redirect it to the worship and service of their master. Whereas the "*zoon*" are repeatedly seen initiating and facilitating worship of the One True God, the "*therion*" are making every effort to redirect it otherwise.

This role of the living beings is going to become even more apparent as we progress through the reading of the whole of Revelation as they are going to be directly involved not only in the breaking of each of the first four Seals in Revelation 6, but generate corporate praise and worship of God at the *Harpazo* of the Church in Revelation 7, are witnesses to the worship of the 144,000 in Revelation 14, will hand out the seven golden Bowls of God's final wrath to the seven angels in Revelation 15, and together with the twenty-four elders will execute the third of four final "Hallelujahs" in Revelation 19 as the ultimate prelude to the marriage supper of the Lamb and His earthly return. This is quite a contrast to the activities of the *"therion"* of Satan who actively work against the Church, Israel and the Godhead in an effort to set up Satan's throne and deceive, persecute and destroy anyone refusing to worship Satan through the possessed *"therion"*. One is consistently seen leading to the restoration of access to the throne of God, the other to the entrance of the Lake of Fire.

Ultimately, however, the Seraphim, both in Isaiah and here in Revelation, have an interaction with mankind which is not mirrored by either angels or Cherubim. But we can see that Revelation 4-5 has something significant to contribute to our overall understanding beyond just providing an inspirational picture of heavenly praise and worship.

The Scroll

> [1] *I saw in the right hand of Him who sat on the throne a book written inside and on the back, sealed up with seven seals.* [2] *And I saw a strong angel proclaiming with a loud voice, "Who is worthy to open the book and to break its seals?"* [3] *And no one in heaven or on the earth or under the earth was able to open the book or to look into it.*
>
> [4] *Then I began to weep greatly because no one was found worthy to open the book or to look into it;* [5] *and one of the elders said to me, "Stop weeping; behold, the Lion that is from the tribe of Judah, the Root of David, has overcome so as to open the book and its seven seals." (Revelation 5:1–5)*

At the risk of inserting into Scripture something which is not actually present, the curious question which might be asked based on what is taking place here, is why this search is being initiated now? Why is it that at this particular time they are not just searching for someone *"in heaven or on the earth"* to open the scroll, but even looking *"under the earth"* for a qualified candidate? What has triggered this action? It is obvious that God the Father does not relinquish the scroll except at His appointed time, and equally obvious this is a one-time event. After all that Christ did in the First Coming, why is this ritual/event even necessary? Everything else documented in

Revelation as taking place in heaven has a corresponding parallel event on earth, so it begs the question of whether such is the case here. Is this coming about in parallel to something taking place on earth?

An obvious aspect to this situation is that this scroll, which up to this point God the Father has retained in His personal possession, is now to be unsealed according to His divine will and timing; it may simply be the answer to Jesus' own statement, "*But of the day and hour no one knows, not even the angels of heaven, nor the Son, but the Father alone*". (Mt. 24:36) But because of the overall format of Revelation touched upon earlier, that what takes place in heaven is played out on earth and vice versa, there seems to be implied that some milestone or condition is taking place on earth at this particular time which invokes, and may even correspond to, this heavenly parallel.

In the parlance of New Testament eschatology given prior to Revelation, things have finally progressed to "*the end of the age*" when, according to the Olivet Discourse, "*birth pangs*" of ever-increasing frequency and intensity are fast approaching the milestone appearance and working of the Antichrist and the anticipated parallel rise in his earthly kingdom, the final work of Satan to come. This is not something to be dogmatic about nor a candidate for forming a cult or publishing a website, but in keeping with the pattern of John's vision overall, what is taking place here in heaven might infer that some corresponding earthly milestone has also been achieved, whether it is the Antichrist's treaty initiating Daniel's 70th Week, the initiation of the "*birth pangs*" giving way to the Seal judgments, perhaps something as yet unfulfilled from Old Testament prophecy such as Ezekiel's Gog and Magog which is not specified in the New Testament, (Eze. 38-39) or anything on that order of importance. Perhaps it is the attainment of the eschatological milestone Paul identifies as "*the fullness of the Gentiles*". (Rom. 11:25)

Regardless of these questions, however, what is unmistakable is that a milestone in God's plan has been achieved which will in turn initiate the final sequence of events on earth finally bringing all things to completion. Everything to this point in the whole of history has been waiting for this seminal heavenly defining moment to take place from which there is no turning back.

Many commentators will point out that it was not uncommon for a Roman will to be sealed with seven seals, and therefore describe this scroll as a sort of will or title deed giving Christ the right, because of His sacrifice, to claim creation, something only the Heir can open:

> ¹*God, after He spoke long ago to the fathers in the prophets in many portions and in many ways, ²in these last days has spoken to us in **His Son, whom He appointed heir of all things**, through whom also He made the world. (Hebrews 1:1–2)*

There is also general consensus that the greater meaning of a scroll with writing on both sides indicates completeness and finality in that nothing more can be added to it—that is, it signifies God's complete and total judgment. In other words, its symbolism and meaning in the historical and cultural context for 1st century believers would have been well understood and not as mysterious from our more removed culture and perspective.

The titles of Christ employed in Revelation 5:5 are unmistakably assigned to the Messiah and biblically express His qualifications, but another question which does not ever seem to be sufficiently resolved is the nature of John's reaction: Why does he "*weep greatly*" because no one was "*able to open the book or to look into it*"? Since he does not know at this point what it contains, why is he so moved? It is very interesting that throughout the overall experience of the vision that from time to time John is not merely curious, but emotionally in tune with what is taking place; he is not intellectually standing apart from what he is being shown but understands what it means to everyone as a whole and to him personally as well. John picks up on the deep emotion associated not just with the need for someone qualified to handle the scroll, but the consequences if no one so qualified can be located.

But even with all the literal and physical events which will result from the unsealing of this document, there is the far greater spiritual qualification that Christ is worthy by the fact that He has "*overcome*". Christ Himself meets the standard for which all are held accountable in how He overcame the world. Just as His achievement in overcoming Satan and his world system opened the door to all that has come to Christ in eternity, likewise is our assurance of obtaining the same in the course of our own overcoming the world in His strength and power and character. This was the repeated theme proffered to the Seven Churches.

The Lamb

> ⁴*Then I began to weep greatly because no one was found worthy to open the book or to look into it; ⁵and one of the elders said to me, "Stop weeping; behold, the Lion that is from the tribe of Judah, the Root of David, has overcome so as to open the book and its seven seals."*

> ⁶*And I saw between the throne (with the four living creatures) and the elders a Lamb standing, as if slain, having seven horns and seven eyes, which are the seven Spirits of God, sent out into all the earth. ⁷And He came and took the book out of the right hand of Him who sat on the throne. ⁸When He had taken the book, the four living creatures and the twenty-four elders fell down before the Lamb, each one holding a harp and golden bowls full of incense, which are the prayers of the saints. ⁹And they sang a new song, saying,*
>
> *"Worthy are You to take the book and to break its seals; for You were slain, and purchased for God with Your blood men from every tribe and tongue and people and nation.*
>
> ¹⁰*"You have made them to be a kingdom and priests to our God; and they will reign upon the earth." (Revelation 5:4–10)*

In the whole of all the New Testament writings prior to Revelation, the word "*lamb*" is only used six times, and only four of them directly connected to Christ (Mk. 14:12; Lk. 22:7; Jn. 1:29, 36; Acts 8:32; 1 Pe. 1:19); in Revelation alone it is used thirty-one times and is the preferred title of Christ throughout the book. (Rev. 5:6, 8, 12, 13; 6:1, 7, 9, 16; 7:9, 10, 14, 17; 8:1; 12:11; 13:8, 11; 14:1, 4, 10; 15:3; 17:14; 18:7, 9; 21:9, 14, 22, 23; 22:1, 3)

But at this juncture it is important to note that what John initially hears is the announcement, "*behold, the Lion that is from the tribe of Judah, the Root of David, has overcome so as to open the book and its seven seals*" (Rev. 5:5), but when he looks up, what he sees is "*a **Lamb** standing, as if slain*". Two of the most important titles assigned to the Messiah are used to introduce Him, yet His appearance is that which symbolizes His seminal work in the First Coming on the cross. This is a critical detail which should not be glossed over. Instead of appearing in the form of either the Lion or the King ("*the Root of David*"), Jesus appears as the Lamb! Why is He announced as something different from His actual appearance?

The title "*the Lion that is from the tribe of Judah*" is derived from Genesis 49:8-10 when through Jacob it was prophesied that the scepter would pass to Judah in the character of a lion specifying the lineage of the Messiah. The title "*Son of David*" was used repeatedly in reference to Jesus in the course of His First Coming to denote His specific lineage from David, but what is specifically designated here is being called "*the **Root** of David*". This identifies Christ as having first brought David and His seed line into existence rather than just being physically descended from him as the "*Son of David*". This was a specific topic of discussion in His First Coming, how the Messiah in terms of His humanity could be descended from David (Is. 11:1, 10), but because of His divinity have also been David's Creator, here expressed as the "*Root*" or source. This was something on which Christ directly challenged the religious authorities specifically. (Mt. 22:41-46)

But having heard this introduction using what would be two especially powerful titles of the Messiah to which a Jewish Apostle would have been very sensitive in terms of their meaning and background, when he looks up, what he instead sees fulfilling those terms is "*a **Lamb** standing, as if slain*". And this embodiment of the work of the cross is what is going to be prolifically used throughout the vision going forward to the very end to communicate on every level that this is the only way which God's plan can be finally completed—through the Lamb. Revelation 4-5 is the actual nexus where all the theology of the whole of Scripture intersects with the execution of God's plan to bring everything to its ultimate fulfillment. The Lamb was the plan before the foundation of the world, the Lamb is the plan for "*this present age*", and the Lamb is the plan for "*the age to come*". The Lamb will be shown to be the fulfillment of "*the end of the age*" as well. Whether from eternity past to eternity future, it has always been about the Lamb.

"Seven" being the biblical number of perfection, Christ the Lamb is the perfection of power ("*seven horns*"), the perfection of wisdom and knowledge seeing all things ("*seven eyes*") and the perfect presence ("*seven Spirits of God, sent out into all the earth*"). These are the shared characteristics with the Godhead of being omnipotent (all-powerful), omniscient (all-knowing) and omnipresent (all-present).

Take particular note that the specific items of praise subsequently rendered by the twenty-four elders specify that it is the work of Christ the Lamb which qualifies His taking the scroll "*to break its seals*" and initiate the final execution of God's plan as revealed in the rest of Revelation:

> ➤ "*...for You were slain...*"

> ➤ "*...and purchased for God with Your blood men from every tribe and tongue and people and nation.*"

These actions of the cross are what make possible the ultimate results of what is to come from unsealing the scroll at this final juncture:

> ➤ "*You have made them to be a kingdom...*"

> ➤ "*...and priests to our God;*"

> ➤ "*...and they will reign upon the earth*".

It is only through the working of the Suffering Servant in His First Coming that anyone is qualified to participate in the working of the Conquering King in His Second Coming, but it is not two different images of the Messiah for each case, but the exact, same one of the Lamb!

The Lamb & Nothing But the Lamb

This acknowledgment of the work of the Messiah as the Lamb invokes a reaction in which not just the living beings and hosts of angels join in with the twenty-four elders, but "*every created things which is in heaven and on the on the earth and under the earth and on the sea, and all things in them*":

> ¹¹*Then I looked, and I heard the voice of **many angels** around the throne and **the living creatures** and **the elders**; and the number of them was myriads of myriads, and thousands of thousands,* ¹²*saying with a loud voice,*
>
>> *"Worthy is the Lamb that was slain to receive power and riches and wisdom and might and honor and glory and blessing."*
>
> ¹³*And **every created thing** which is in heaven and on the earth and under the earth and on the sea, and all things in them, I heard saying,*
>
>> *"To Him who sits on the throne, and to the Lamb, be blessing and honor and glory and dominion forever and ever."*
>
> ¹⁴*And the four living creatures kept saying, "Amen." And the elders fell down and worshiped. (Revelation 5:11–14)*

Far too often, in our zeal to create an End Times chart, sometimes including the seven churches but nearly always beginning with the Seven Seals, this introductory scene in Revelation 4-5 is casually skimmed without being given the due consideration it deserves for being the actual greater reason each and every thing in the whole of Revelation is taking place. In fact, this is the actual intersection of all biblical doctrine in the whole of Scripture from the very outset coming together for fulfillment in one place. The arguments related to the identity of the twenty-four elders and whether or not John's removal is also the Rapture of the Church do a disservice in the way they distract from what may be the most important theological intersection not just in the whole New Testament, but the entirety of God's Word!

Every reader is encouraged to at least temporarily suspend these alternate discussions and re-study Revelation 4-5 with a strict focus on the actual main topic, Christ the Lamb. This is the actual place where the work of the Suffering Servant in the First Coming concludes to give way to the work of the Conquering King as the Second Coming now goes into effect. A huge problem with Judaism in Jesus' day which has plagued every iteration to this present hour is to skip past the work of the cross in an attempt to go directly to the Millennial Reign, but what the born again have learned is that there is no attaining to the Second Coming without first submitting to the work of the First Coming.

Now, in these defining chapters of Revelation, this is made more vivid than ever by Christ's fulfillment of the Second Coming in His representation as the Lamb. It is going to keep being used throughout Revelation as a reminder that this is the defining difference between those who are going to be saved for all eternity at the end of these events, and those who alternatively are going to be judged and sentenced. The Conquering King is not possible without *"the Lamb of God who takes away the sin of the world"* (Jn. 1:29), who is given as a reminder at every point along the Revelation timeline going forward:

> ➤ It is the Lamb who opens each and every Seal, which in turn produces all that follows.

> ➤ Those who *"come out of the great tribulation"* (Rev. 7:14) are able to do so because of *"the blood of **the Lamb**"*.

> ➤ In Satan's final working, it is stated that he will be overcome *"because of the blood of **the Lamb**"*. (Rev. 12:11)

> ➤ It is identified as *"the book of life of **the Lamb**"* in which the names of the redeemed are written. (Rev. 13:8)

> ➤ It is the Lamb whom the 144,000 sealed follow and are referred to in the character of the work of the cross as, *"purchased from among men as first fruits to God and to **the Lamb**"*. (Rev. 14:1, 4)

➤   When the Beasts experiences their own ultimate consequences of God's wrath, it is *"in the presence of the holy angels and in the presence of **the Lamb**"*. (Rev. 14:10)

➤   When the rulers of the earth are defeated, it is stated, *"**the Lamb** will overcome them"*. (Rev. 17:14)

➤   It is *"the marriage of **the Lamb**"* (Rev. 19:7) taking place to produce *"the marriage supper of **the Lamb**"* (Rev. 19:9) so that those embracing the work of Christ the Lamb are identified as *"the bride, the wife of **the Lamb**"*. (Rev. 21:9)

➤   In eternity after the Millennial Reign, the foundations of the New Jerusalem are annotated with *"the twelve names of the twelve apostles of **the Lamb**"*. (Rev. 21:14)

➤   In eternity, *"I saw no temple in it, for the Lord God Almighty and the Lamb are its temple"*, and as for the city, *"its lamp is **the Lamb**"*. (Rev. 21:22-23)

➤   Ultimately, it is *"the throne of God and of **the Lamb**"* (Rev. 22:1, 3) which is established forever in eternity.

The plan which *"was"* from even before Creation until the first birth pang of the end of this age has always been Christ the Lamb of God; the plan which *"is"* ongoing at this present hour has always been and never strays from Christ the Lamb of God; the plan which *"is to come"* and brings to conclusion not just this age and the age to come, but the fulfillment of the whole of eternity always has been and always will be Christ the Lamb of God!

One of the very first and most powerful allusions in Scripture to Christ the Lamb is provided in Abraham's offering of Isaac, who asks the question, *"...but where is the lamb for the burnt offering?"* (Gen. 22:7) Upon this is built not just the imagery but the actual implementation of the Passover lamb whose blood at the same time saved and judged, depending on whether or not one chose to employ it. From the outset of the First Coming, John the Baptist declared Christ, *"the Lamb of God who takes away the sin of the world!"* (Jn. 1:29), and Peter will affirm, *"...you were not redeemed with perishable things...but with the precious blood, as of a lamb unblemished and spotless, the blood of Christ"*. (1 Pe. 1:18-19) And the final conclusion of all things past, present and future is brought together in Revelation with the introduction of

Christ the Lamb and His perpetual appearance throughout the End Times continuous through the Millennial Reign and into eternity itself as *"the Lamb standing, as if slain"*. (Rev. 5:6)

Textually speaking, one of the themes from this point on in Revelation will be Christ the Lamb, a clean animal classified as a *"zoa"*, contrasted by Satan's Beasts, belonging to the class of unclean animals labeld *"therion"*. This aids in explaining Satan's use of *therion* as a counterfeit of the authentic *zoa*.

For the saved, meeting the Lamb is the ultimate fulfillment of the *"blessed hope"* when we experience *"the appearing of the glory of our great God and Savior, Christ Jesus"* (Titus 2:13), but for the unsaved the ultimate, disturbing last image before going into eternal judgment is their having to behold the Lamb by which they were offered, and rejected, the only way to avoid the consequences they are about to experience.

There are those who look at the closing chapters of Revelation as the fulfillment of all the promises we are looking forward to, and those who see the 1st Seal as initializing the End Times, but everything for the past, present and future from God's point of view is revealed in a complete nexus of all these conditions in Revelation 4-5 and continually reinforced by Christ the Lamb, established in eternity before Creation, at work during the whole of history, and continuing forward into eternity beyond.

Regardless of whether we share the same eschatology and interpretation of the milestones to come, it is only those who have embraced the work of the cross through Christ the Lamb who are ultimately exempt from the consequences of what will inevitably come upon those who have not. The repeated insistence on Jesus' vision to John invoking this title and image over all others reinforces what was most important in the Olivet Discourse, most important in all biblical eschatological teaching regardless of the Testament, and what is actually most important at this very hour: accept Jesus the Lamb of God as your personal Savior!

For the saved it is the hope which empowers our faith to endure and overcome regardless of what takes place, but for the unsaved it will be the worst final image in judgment as they are ultimately held accountable to the Lamb, the very symbol of salvation so freely offered, yet ultimately rejected by them. At each point along the way, those rejecting Christ, including Satan, the Antichrist and the False Prophet personally, will in those final moments of self-realization of the price they are about to pay, be faced with Christ the Lamb, the hope of salvation.

Unfortunately, the image which is most associated with the Second Coming is that of Christ on the white horse, returning with His armies. While this is a literal, one-time event closing out the eschaton, the fact is that the biblical image for both the Suffering Servant and the Conquering King for each of the First and Second Comings is one and the same—the Lamb. There is a danger associated with substituting the Commander on the white horse with the Lamb, in that it repeats the same mistake made at His First Coming, when they wanted to skip directly to the Conquering King and bypass the Lamb.

16 ❖ The Seals and the "Birth Pangs"

Recognize The Pattern

A "seven" unfolding into another "seven" is not actually a completely unique occurrence which is only found in Revelation's interlocking cascade of Seven Seals into Seven Trumpets into Seven Bowls; the most obvious one is Joshua's conquest of Jericho where Israel marches around the city once for six consecutive days and then seven times on the seventh day. The 20th century theologian Harry A. Ironside specifically saw a parallel with Jericho as foreshadowing Revelation in this regard:

> Careful readers of the Bible will connect the seven trumpets with the fall of Jericho: that great city just across the Jordan that barred the progress of the people of Israel into the promised land—the city that fell with the blast of God alone. The priests of Israel were given the trumpets of judgment, and for seven days they marched about the city blowing the trumpets; seven times on the seventh day they did so and at the seventh blast the walls fell down flat. Jericho is a type of this present world in its estrangement from God, with enmity to the people of God. Jericho fell at the sound of seven trumpets, and the world, as you and I know it, is going to fall at the sound of the seven trumpets of doom, blown by these angels of judgment.

> Ironside, H. A. (1920). Lectures on the Book of Revelation (p. 145). Neptune, N. J.: Loizeaux Brothers.

In many of his teachings on the topic over the years, Jacob Prasch of Moriel Ministries has pointed out many parallels beyond just a "seven unfolding into a seven" in that like Revelation, Jericho has two witnesses (the spies), a silence preceding the shout and the trumpets, a type of Rapture in the rescue of Rahab and her family, both being led by Joshua ("*Jesus*" being the Greek equivalent), and so on. The greater point is that similar events in Scripture replay the same pattern in order to teach us something about the final one to come, and rather than being something entirely new, it is difficult not to find a parallel to other Scripture for nearly every aspect of Revelation, this pattern being no exception.

What took place at Jericho initiating Joshua's conquest and occupation of the Promised Land is not just a lone, historical event or a story just about supernaturally falling walls, but an additional eschatological pattern of the Last Joshua conquering and bringing us into the Millennial Kingdom in the character of the historical Joshua leading Israel into the Promised Land. 1st century Christians may have had a far greater advantage over subsequent generations in that they were first and foremost schooled in the Old Testament in the shadow of the emerging New Testament canon and readily understood how Scripture was interpreting Scripture.

Another interesting parallel is a detail which is often overlooked when it comes to the days of Noah as they mirror the Last Days, something which Christ Himself specified as a model of what is to come:

[37]"For the coming of the Son of Man will be just like the days of Noah. [38]For as in those days before the flood they were eating and drinking, marrying and giving in marriage, until the day that Noah entered the ark,	[26]"And just as it happened in the days of Noah, so it will be also in the days of the Son of Man: [27]They were eating, they were drinking, they were marrying, they were being given in marriage, until the day that Noah entered the ark,
[39]and they did not understand until the flood came and took them all away;	and the flood came and destroyed them all. (Lk. 17:26-27)
so will the coming of the Son of Man be. (Mt. 24:37-39)	

This foundation was affirmed by Peter as well in both of his Epistles. (1 Pe. 3:18-20; 2 Pe. 2:4-10)

If we examine the original Genesis account, everyone actually boards the ark and waits for seven days before the final judgment in the form of the harbinger of rain begins:

> ¹Then the LORD said to Noah, **"Enter the ark, you and all your household**, for you alone I have seen to be righteous before Me in this time. ²You shall take with you of every clean animal by sevens, a male and his female; and of the animals that are not clean two, a male and his female; ³also of the birds of the sky, by sevens, male and female, to keep offspring alive on the face of all the earth. ⁴For **after seven more days, I will send rain on the earth forty days and forty nights**; and I will blot out from the face of the land every living thing that I have made." ⁵Noah did according to all that the LORD had commanded him. (Genesis 7:1–5)

Just as there is a "seven" experienced by everyone before the final wrath of God's judgment is brought upon Jericho, there was a "seven" experienced by everyone in Noah's day before the wrath of God's judgment expressed in the Flood.

There is another reference in this regard which is also often overlooked concerning Enoch, the very first figure to be literally raptured in Scripture:

> ¹⁴It was also about these men that Enoch, **in the seventh generation** from Adam, prophesied, saying, "Behold, the Lord came with many thousands of His holy ones, (Jude 14)

Here we find a "seven" connected to his rapture as expressed in generations.

There is also a very interesting supporting parallel provided in the book of Job:

> ¹⁹"From six troubles He will deliver you,
> Even in seven evil will not touch you. (Job 5:19)

This excerpt from Job is even more compelling when examining the verses immediately following which provide a list of those six troubles. Contained therein are earthly activities which parallel those found listed both as members of the *"birth pangs"* in the Olivet Discourse and the Seal judgments of Revelation 6:

*20"In **famine** He will redeem you from death,
And in **war** from the power of **the sword**.
21You will be hidden from **the scourge of the tongue**,
And you will not be afraid of **violence** when it comes.
22You will laugh at violence and famine,
And you will not be afraid of **wild beasts**.
23For you will be in league with the stones of the field,
And the beasts of the field will be at peace with you.
24You will know that your tent is secure,
For you will visit your abode and fear no loss. (Job 5:20-
24)*

In Revelation itself, the seven letters to the churches provide this same pattern by the position of Philadelphia as the sixth church when the rapture is featured, and Laodicea as the follow-on seventh in the series as representative of those left behind. Where believers are concerned, the most important potential obstacles of the eschaton are featured in the those first six churches in regard to the issues of deception, persecution and remaining faithful to God's Word and ways; in the seventh and final one is the ultimate example of apostasy where Jesus is found on the outside knocking. For believers, it is most important to avoid the example of Lot's wife at every point along the way, even up to the very end, a vivid parallel of apostasy with the character of Laodicea as last in the overall sequence.

The Pattern of the Eschaton in the Seven Churches

Ephesus	Smyrna	Pergamum	Thyatira	Sardis	Philadelphia	Laodicea
Deals with deception & persecution while needing to regurn to its first love	Enduring the worst possible circumstances of persecution	Combating the worst extremes of deception	Battling spiritual seduction & corruption of true service & worship	Struggling to remain faithful in times of relative peace	Persevering by keeping the Word	Apostatizing because of people's opinions & spiritual blindness
"...repent & do the deeds you did at first..."	"...be faithful until death."	"...repent, or else I am coming to you quickly..."	"...whatever you have, hold fast until I come."	"Wake up, and strengthen the things that remain."	"...hold fast what you have, so that no one will take your crown."	"...buy from Me gold refined by fire...& while garments...and eye salve..."

A "six" symbolic of faithfulness through deception & persecution so as to be exempted from what is to come.

Jesus on the Outside

In each of these cases we find that events begin involving everyone, followed by a rescue or rapture occurring by the end involving a form of "seven".

Yet another parallel pattern which is often overlooked is the sequence of the Exodus judgments by which two witnesses (figuratively Moses and Aaron) battle an antichrist figure in Pharaoh in the course of executing three sets of God's judgments (consisting of three plagues each) culminating in the tenth as a type of final judgment. In other words, the three sets in Exodus roughly equate to the three sets of Seals, Trumpets and Bowls in Revelation, with something special taking place between the first and second sets of the sequence. In the Exodus affair, after the third plague, God makes a distinction going forward between His people and everyone else:

> ²⁰Now the LORD said to Moses, "Rise early in the morning and present yourself before Pharaoh, as he comes out to the water, and say to him, 'Thus says the LORD, "Let My people go, that they may serve Me. ²¹For if you do not let My people go, behold, I will send swarms of flies on you and on your servants and on your people and into your houses; and the houses of the Egyptians will be full of swarms of flies, and also the ground on which they dwell. ²²**But on that day I will set apart the land of Goshen, where My people are living, so that no swarms of flies will be there**, in order that you may know that I, the LORD, am in the midst of the land. ²³**I will put a division between My people and your people**. Tomorrow this sign will occur."'" (Exodus 8:20–23)

Everyone experienced the first set of plagues, but God's people were exempted from the next two sets. As we shall shortly see, it is precisely at this point in Revelation, between the 6th and 7th Seals, when God's people are removed and, in a replay of the Exodus pattern, do not experience the final two sets of ordered events expressed as the Trumpets and Bowls.

The activities connected to the Seals are "judgments" which God has employed in the past to be experienced by everyone at some point in history, both Israel and the Gentile nations alike. Like their counterparts in the *"birth pangs"* of the Olivet Discourse, they come in the character of forces stemming from a source of earthly agency such as war, famine, pestilence, earthquakes, and so forth. Even the cosmological signs are things which take place in the heavenly part of the realm assigned to the earth's venue. They repeatedly crop up in the Old Testament and are prolific in extra-biblical history, and God has purposely used them to judge people for their sin and unrepentance. The Seals as "judgments" are something which everyone must face, but the

Trumpets and Bowls are effected exclusively by angelic agency, and it is at that point it escalates to the level of the wrath of God being executed, not the lesser working of "judgment". And as we know, believers are exempt from the wrath of God:

> [36]"He who believes in the Son has eternal life; but he who does not obey the Son will not see life, but the wrath of God abides on him." (John 3:36)

> [9]Much more then, having now been justified by His blood, we shall be saved from the wrath of God through Him. (Romans 5:9)

> [6]Let no one deceive you with empty words, for because of these things the wrath of God comes upon the sons of disobedience. (Ephesians 5:6)

One of the primary reasons for great academic disagreement over the timing of the Rapture and the many conflicting charts depicting a Last Days sequence is rooted in not making the distinction between the first "seven" as "judgments", which everyone must endure, from the second and third "sevens" which are God's wrath to only be experienced by those remaining on the earth. Many hold to the belief that the Seals as well are the expression of the wrath of God and therefore conclude the Church is exempt from all of Revelation 4-19.

However, whether it is in the examples of what took place in the days of Noah, the days of Lot, the Exodus, the conquest of Jericho, Enoch, or the last days of Israel and Judah leading into the Captivity, consistently throughout Scripture there is a time of judgment experienced by everyone before giving way to God's wrath poured out exclusively on the non-exempt. In fact, the repeated pattern demonstrated throughout history is that judgment always first begins with God's house before escalating to an even greater degree within the ranks of the unsaved:

> [16]but if anyone suffers as a Christian, he is not to be ashamed, but is to glorify God in this name. **[17]For it is time for judgment to begin with the household of God**; and if it begins with us first, what will be the outcome for those who do not obey the gospel of God? [18]AND IF IT IS WITH DIFFICULTY THAT THE RIGHTEOUS IS SAVED, WHAT WILL BECOME OF THE GODLESS MAN AND THE SINNER? [19]Therefore, those also who suffer according to the will of God shall entrust their souls to a faithful Creator in doing what is right. (1 Peter 4:16–19)

When Aaron and Moses first arrived to initiate the Exodus sequence, the very first thing which actually happened was a persecution of Israel (Ex. 4-5) which was necessary to prepare them for what was to come, and provided the opportunity to first allow Pharaoh and the Egyptians to respond to God's message delivered to them before the "fireworks" commenced. Likewise, from the Olivet Discourse, we know that this first stage affords the opportunity for the whole world to hear the Gospel before the door on the ark is shut, so to speak, with the onset of God's wrath initiated by the 7th Seal which is actually inclusive of all the Trumpets and Bowls.

We might also consider that there is often an example of a kind of prelude revealing in some way that God is about to imminently work:

> ➤ God revealed his plan to Noah who became a visible testimony to everyone as he prepared for the Flood (Gen. 6), and Peter reveals that during this time Noah was "*a preacher of righteousness*" (2 Pe. 2:5), providing an example of preaching the Gospel in the Last Days, so to speak.

> ➤ Just before executing judgment on Sodom and Gomorrah, the Lord made his intentions known to Abraham, who became aware of what was about to take place. Abraham even made a plea on behalf of the remnant of possible remaining righteous, and Lot even had time to attempt an outreach to his sons-in-law before the fire fell. (Gen. 18-19)

> ➤ Moses and Aaron first revealed God's plan to Israel before their first appearance before Pharaoh, which resulted in a time of hardship for Israel before the formal initiation of the plagues. (Ex. 4-5)

> ➤ At Jericho, Rahab and her family were not only aware of what was about to take place because of the preparatory work of the spies, but relayed that all the people of the land of Canaan were aware of and disturbed by all that God had been doing through Israel since leaving Egypt nearly forty years earlier. (Josh. 2)

> ➤ In the days just prior to Elijah's rapture, two different groups of prophets as well as his protégé Elisha were keenly aware of the imminence of that event. (2 Ki. 2)

➤ While God had been warning Israel and Judah for nearly two hundred years through various Prophets beginning with Joel what was specifically to come, the ministry of Jeremiah leading up to and through that example of final judgment presaged all that took place.

➤ The prelude to Christ's First Coming to Israel was the ministry of John the Baptist whose function was the proper preparation for His arrival.

The takeaway here is that the assertion that the *"birth pangs"* of the Olivet Discourse provide a period of increasing spiritual activity which serves to disguise their final fulfillment in the Seal judgments is provided in these parallel examples of the End Times. Some are obviously longer than others, and there is certainly no claim being made here that they are identical, but there is a time when God's people become acutely aware of what is about to happen, and even non-believers are on edge because of what is taking place in a prelude to the actual initiation of activities.

Seals 1-4

There is a textual mechanism present which connects at least the first four Seals with the prelude in Revelation 4-5 in that each unsealing is accompanied by one of the respective living beings issuing the command, *"Come"*. (Rev. 6:1, 3, 5, 7) Taken in order, the first like a lion announces the rider on a white horse (*"he went out conquering and to conquer"*), the second like a calf announces the rider on the red horse (*"to take peace from the earth, and that men would slay one another"*), the third like a man announces the rider on the black horse (*"a quart of wheat for a denarius, and three quarts of barley for a denarius"*), and the fourth like an eagle announces the rider on the ashen horse (*"to kill with the sword and with famine and with pestilence by the wild beasts of the earth"*). As Christ breaks each of the first four Seals, each of the respective living beings just introduced ushers in something which is the final, ultimate fulfillment of what the *"birth pangs"* have been prefiguring with greater and greater intensity. In other words, this is the final and last in the series; the obstetric or seismic warnings are at last over—this is the metaphorical "birth". The significance of the accompaniment of the participation by the Seraphim is that it distinguishes these ultimate final events from their less potent *"birth pangs"* counterparts repeating and leading up to them.

> ¹Then I saw when the Lamb broke one of the seven seals,
> and I heard one of the four living creatures saying as with a
> voice of thunder, "Come." ²I looked, and behold, a white horse,
> and he who sat on it had a bow; and a crown was given to him,
> and he went out conquering and to conquer. (Revelation 6:1–2)

As stated previously, because of Satan's obsession to replace God and be God and especially to be worshiped like God, one of his favorite tactics is not just to act as a counterfeit of the authentic, but wherever possible to institute a pre-counterfeit. Notice how closely this resembles Christ coming at the conclusion of events belonging to *"the end of the age"* in Revelation 19. That is when Jesus arrives on *"a white horse...and in righteousness He judges and wages war"* (Rev. 19:11) which is feigned here. In contrast to Christ's final return in which is found *"on His head are many diadems"* (Rev. 19:12), this imitation sports a much simpler crown. And whereas the pretender is armed with a bow, Christ comes with *"a sharp sword, so that with it He may strike down the nations, and He will rule them with a rod of iron"*. (Rev. 19:15) The Antichrist, of whom we know from other Scripture initiates a false peace, initially pre-counterfeits Christ by looking just similar enough to His final appearance so he can successfully subdue as many as possible through other than the most bloody military means. The Antichrist is also known in advance to use intrigue and deception. (Dan. 8:23-25)

This all seems to speak in more detail to the Antichrist's initial use of deception and a false peace in a conquest of as many as possible before using force as a last resort. Think of this in the character of how the original Roman Empire functioned. They "conquered" far more countries and city-states by negotiating them into the Empire than having to actually wage full-on war. One of their chief negotiating tactics was to allow anyone's god(s) to be brought into their Pantheon provided the emperor was worshiped first, a precursor to Satan fulfilling his dream through the Antichrist to be worshiped in place of the One True God. Force was certainly employed if necessary, but usually only after diplomacy and negotiation failed. Many gave in so as to enjoy "Pax Romana", the peace enjoyed by the constituents of the Roman Empire.

But again, there have been *"many false christs"*, and the command of the first of the Seraphim accompanying the Lamb's initial unsealing of the scroll separates this from all the previous pretenders to signify the final arrival of the authentic final incarnation. The previous *"birth pangs"* of *"wars and rumors of wars"* are but shadows teaching something about the ultimate and most powerful fulfillment by the Antichrist in his ultimate bid to pre-counterfeit the Messiah.

> ³*When He broke the second seal, I heard the second living creature saying, "Come." ⁴And another, a red horse, went out; and to him who sat on it, it was granted to take peace from the earth, and that men would slay one another; and a great sword was given to him. (Revelation 6:3–4)*

What cannot be taken by deception in an atmosphere of false peace gives way to overt military conquest, showing that what is at work is still within the character of human agency by the designation, *"that men would slay one another"*.

These two opening "phases", so to speak, fit precisely with what we know to be Satan's preferred method of working. His preference is to first come in the character of the serpent to deceive as many as possible before resorting to the character and working of the dragon who openly persecutes and attacks. What he cannot conquer through intrigue and deception, he attempts to subjugate through open conflict; that which cannot be overcome spiritually he attempts to overcome physically.

If we peek ahead in Revelation, we are told that a reorganization of earthly kingdoms is going to take place for the sole purpose of uniting all power and authority under the Antichrist. It would therefore not be surprising to find this specific activity of war between men taking place, as it may be crucial for the rise of what is described as *"Babylon the great"*, the one-world kingdom of the Antichrist. (Rev. 14:8; 16:19; 18:2, 21) This kingdom is actually comprised of ten anticipated kingdoms to come in the Last Days for the sole purpose of consolidating power under Antichrist:

> ¹²*"The ten horns which you saw are ten kings who have not yet received a kingdom, but they receive authority as kings with the beast for one hour. ¹³*__These have one purpose, and they give their power and authority to the beast__*. (Revelation 17:12–13)*

Again, the participation of the 2nd living being in this release of the red horse and its rider distinguishes this final event from all the similar, weaker forerunners. As devastating as any previous historical military campaign, event, or full-scale war has seemed to us, they all pale in comparison to the depth and power of those which take place at this point in history signaled by the 2nd living being.

> ⁵*When He broke the third seal, I heard the third living creature saying, "Come." I looked, and behold, a black horse; and he who sat on it had a pair of scales in his hand. ⁶And I heard something like a voice in the center of the four living*

creatures saying, "A quart of wheat for a denarius, and three quarts of barley for a denarius; and do not damage the oil and the wine." (Revelation 6:5–6)

The 3rd Seal specifies in greater detail that which was generally described in the Olivet Discourse as *"disturbances"*. (Lk. 21:9) The previous dual phases of conquest are followed by tremendous economic calamity. The greater significance of this will be appreciated by the forthcoming details of the Antichrist's specific working in Revelation 13 that no one will be able to *"buy or sell"* without taking the mark of the beast. (Rev. 13:16-17) There is groundwork being laid through the 3rd Seal which not only compliments the overall conquest and control of nations sought through the dual working of the 1st and 2nd Seals, but the personal subjugation of every individual. The satanically possessed Antichrist is not strictly interested in limiting his control to just the nations, but because of his intense desire to be worshiped as God, in the end seeks to subjugate every individual heart and soul. But in the initial stages he mostly works through political and economic venues.

The inauguration of this event at the behest of the 3rd Seraphim distinguishes it as the final, most powerful event of its kind to ever be experienced, all other past historically similar economic catastrophes and corresponding disturbances being vague reflections when compared to its final fulfillment.

⁷When the Lamb broke the fourth seal, I heard the voice of the fourth living creature saying, "Come." ⁸I looked, and behold, an ashen horse; and he who sat on it had the name Death; and Hades was following with him. Authority was given to them over a fourth of the earth, to kill with sword and with famine and with pestilence and by the wild beasts of the earth. (Revelation 6:7–8)

The activities of the 4th Seal as articulated in parallel in the Olivet Discourse, when unleashed, compound exponentially the unprecedented devastation and working of the previous Seals. This is powerfully demonstrated in that at this point *"a fourth of the earth"* dies as a result, and things are still only at the very beginning of much more to come. But again, this final participation of the 4th Seraphim to usher in this Seal unleashing the ultimate fulfillment of many similar, past *"birth pangs"* leading up to these final, efficacious events is speaking to the difference in the potency of what is taking place compared to all the minor reflections which preceded it.

To understand just how big this is compared to past human history, if it took place today, the result would be just shy of 2 billion casualties, as compared to the whole of World War II in which it is estimated a total of 80-100 million lost their lives not just to the conflict directly, but the ancillary effects of the disease and famine it wrought. It is difficult to conceive of something 20+ times more destructive than the largest human conflict to date, but provides some perspective for how dramatically different these final events are from their respective historical counterparts. Mankind has never seen anything like them because the final "birth" is many times multiplied the pain of *"birth pangs"*.

The 5th Seal

> *⁹When the Lamb broke the fifth seal, I saw underneath the altar the souls of those who had been slain because of the word of God, and because of the testimony which they had maintained; ¹⁰and they cried out with a loud voice, saying, "How long, O Lord, holy and true, will You refrain from judging and avenging our blood on those who dwell on the earth?" ¹¹And there was given to each of them a white robe; and they were told that they should rest for a little while longer, until the number of their fellow servants and their brethren who were to be killed even as they had been, would be completed also. (Revelation 6:9–11)*

With the advent of the 5th Seal, a significant change of audience takes place in terms of who is the direct object of this unprecedented level of activity. By definition, persecution and martyrdom is something which can only be experienced exclusively by believers, and as horrific as past efforts against Christ's followers have been, this final instance will surpass them all.

The root cause of their martyrdom is specifically attributed to come about *"because of the word of God, and because of the testimony they had maintained"*, so again, there can be no mistaking that this is narrowly assigned to something which is not experienced by everyone, but singularly by the born again. Not just the Olivet Discourse, but as seen within the whole of the New Testament writings, deception, apostasy and persecution are spoken of where Christians are concerned far more than any other feature of the eschaton. As many martyrs for the faith have already assumed their place underneath this heavenly altar, at this juncture their number is still not complete.

Because 1st century readers rooted in the Olivet Discourse and the New Testament commentaries on it were familiar with not only the repeated warnings of the spiritual darkness to come, but were acutely aware of the timing of the Rapture stipulated to take place at a time when things are so horrific that those days have to be supernaturally "amputated"—that is, "*cut short*", (Mt. 24:22) they would correctly interpret this as speaking of the Church rather than applying only to Israel or perhaps some "new" class of Christian arising after the Church's removal as so many today teach. And they would draw the obvious conclusion that this corresponds to the "*tribulation*" spoken of in the Olivet Discourse, when the entire world turns against the Church as specified by Christ, "*Then they will deliver **you** to tribulation*". (Mt. 24:9) Not coincidentally, the "*tribulation*" in the Olivet Discourse and the 5th Seal are presented in the exact, identical sequence; they both occur in precisely the same order in both places.

The 5th Seal in and of itself is proof that the Seal judgments cannot be the expression of the wrath of God as so many assign them to be in order to stipulate that "*the day of the Lord*" and Daniel's 70th Week are the exact, same thing. God certainly brings believers through persecution and even turns what Satan intended into an opportunity to testify and work against him, but God is never the author of it. This can be easily seen in what transpired in the account of Job, where it comes at the request and working of Satan, and additionally understood in the previous discussion of the scriptural exemption of the saved from experiencing the wrath of God.

But even more puzzling is how difficult it is to understand why, on the one hand, such teachers dogmatically teach believers' exemption from God's wrath, and then turn around and say the Seals are included in that wrath. The biblical definition of God's wrath is never expressed in the form of making martyrs, which only comes about by Satan through unbelievers transacting it against believers, serving as a testimony for God in the unfortunate process. This is actually a very powerful proof that God's wrath is still to come and is not fulfilled in these opening Seal judgments.

This may also help to explain why at this juncture there is no participation by the living beings who assisted in the initiation of the previous four Seals. Since the Seraphim are seen in Isaiah 6 and throughout Revelation as connected directly with the Church in the worship of the Godhead and facilitating access to His presence, it would be an equally mountainous contradiction for them to be involved in facilitating persecution of their fellow worshipers. Just as a time came in the Exodus when the Antichrist figure of Pharaoh persecutes God's people, or the attempted assault of Lot and his household in spite of his efforts to warn them, when Satan's attempts at deception have run their course he engages in open warfare against God's followers. It must be born in mind, however, that just as each Seal is magnified in scope and effect beyond any similar "birth pang" in history past resulting in destruction on a completely unprecedented scale, this final persecution will make all previous instances look like the mere shadows they truly are.

So a time comes when the working of the Antichrist is not just aimed at the whole world in general, but singles out the Church in particular. Adherents of the Olivet Discourse would likewise understand this as a confirmation not just of what Jesus predicted in terms of prolific persecution of Christians in the End Times, but that this will actually be turned into an opportunity to witness and preach the Gospel. And it would further conform to Daniel's original disclosure concerning *"shattering the power of the holy people"*. (Dan. 12:7) This is that time of *"**your** tribulation"* identified in the Olivet Discourse.

It is a sad testimony to poor if not outright false teaching in the Church by those who insist a major End Times revival is going to come about because of the Rapture itself—that is, when the main preachers of the Gospel are removed. In actuality, it will come under the same conditions as most revivals have historically taken place, by the testimony and endurance of the Church under literal and open persecution. Instead of preparing believers for their role in what is to inevitably come while still earthbound, this false teaching not only provides the pretensive hope of escapism, but renders the preaching of the Gospel ineffective at a time when it can still rescue both those sharing and receiving it. We must resist over-emphasizing the church at Philadelphia, *"I also will keep you from the hour of testing"* (Rev. 3:10)—into some kind of promise of escape from End Times events without balancing the admonition to the church at Smyrna, *"Be faithful until death, and I will give you the crown of life"*. (Rev. 2:10) There are varied situations which the Church will encounter with varied results.

The 6th Seal

> ¹²I looked when He broke the sixth seal, and there was a great earthquake; and the sun became black as sackcloth made of hair, and the whole moon became like blood; ¹³and the stars of the sky fell to the earth, as a fig tree casts its unripe figs when shaken by a great wind. ¹⁴The sky was split apart like a scroll when it is rolled up, and every mountain and island were moved out of their places. ¹⁵Then the kings of the earth and the great men and the commanders and the rich and the strong and every slave and free man hid themselves in the caves and among the rocks of the mountains; ¹⁶and they said to the mountains and to the rocks, "Fall on us and hide us from the presence of Him who sits on the throne, and from the wrath

of the Lamb; ¹⁷for the great day of their wrath has come, and
who is able to stand?" (Revelation 6:12–17)

These signs are exactly what is so prolifically identified throughout Scripture as announcing *"the day of the Lord".* They further parallel actions stipulated in the Olivet Discourse and take place at the same time in the overall sequence, but here take hold in a final fulfillment, such as *"earthquakes in various places"* (Mk. 13:8) versus this *"great earthquake".* In particular, the features of the blackening of the sun, the moon turning red, and the accompanying cosmological signs are all documented in Scripture over and over again as specifically assigned to the onset of *"the day of the Lord"*— that time when all that is left to be experienced is God's wrath. (Examples: Is. 13:10; 24:23; 34:4; Eze. 32:7; Joel 2:10, 31; 3:15; Amos 5:20; 8:9; Zeph. 1:15) The corresponding order provided in the Olivet Discourse is maintained, however, with the *"birth pangs"* in parallel with the first four Seals giving way to *"tribulation"*—the unprecedented persecution of the Church corresponding to the 5th Seal, and then with *"the day of the Lord"* events announced in the 6th Seal to follow.

The "Birth Pangs" as Fulfilled in the Seals

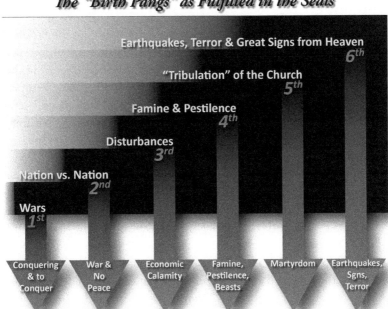

1st century readers in particular would additionally and clearly understand the connection to *"the day of the Lord"* because of the Apostle Peter's public explanation on the Day of Pentecost as to not only what was happening at that time, but additionally provided a specific timeline for the Church on earth; he not only explained its auspicious beginning, but its dramatic conclusion:

> ¹⁶*but this is what was spoken of through the prophet Joel:*
>
> ¹⁷*'AND IT SHALL BE IN THE LAST DAYS,' GOD SAYS,*
> *'THAT I WILL POUR FORTH OF MY SPIRIT ON ALL MANKIND;*
> *AND YOUR SONS AND YOUR DAUGHTERS SHALL PROPHESY,*
> *AND YOUR YOUNG MEN SHALL SEE VISIONS,*
> *AND YOUR OLD MEN SHALL DREAM DREAMS;*
> ¹⁸*EVEN ON MY BONDSLAVES, BOTH MEN AND WOMEN,*
> *I WILL IN THOSE DAYS POUR FORTH OF MY SPIRIT*
> *AND THEY SHALL PROPHESY.*
> ¹⁹*AND I WILL GRANT WONDERS IN THE SKY ABOVE*
> *AND SIGNS ON THE EARTH BELOW,*
> *BLOOD, AND FIRE, AND VAPOR OF SMOKE.*
> ²⁰*THE SUN WILL BE TURNED INTO DARKNESS*
> *AND THE MOON INTO BLOOD,*
> *BEFORE THE GREAT AND GLORIOUS DAY OF THE LORD SHALL*
>   *COME.*
> ²¹*AND IT SHALL BE THAT EVERYONE WHO CALLS ON THE NAME*
>   *OF THE LORD WILL BE SAVED.' (Acts 2:16–21)*

There is much academic debate over Peter's quotation of the Prophet Joel because all parties can agree that not every single item in Peter's list took place either on the Day of Pentecost when he delivered this message, nor in the two millennia since, but he speaks of them as if they have already taken place in their entirety. While it can be sufficiently argued that the opening activities have occurred at one time or another in terms of prophesying, visions, and dreams belonging to the agency of the outpouring of the Holy Spirit, there have never been literal fulfillments of the *"wonders"* and *"signs"* of *"blood, and fire, and vapor of smoke"*, nor *"the sun…turned into darkness and the moon into blood"*—the accompanying earthly signs. Why is Peter employing a Hebraic method of interpreting Scripture called *"Pesher"* which says that "this" is "that"—in this case, "this" being the Day of Pentecost, and "that" being the fulfillment of Joel's prophecy concerning *"the day of the Lord"*?

While most expositors will nigh unto unanimously subscribe to the notion that the Day of Pentecost initiates what is commonly referred to as "The Church Age", a time which transitions from God working through Old Testament Israel to the New Testament Church, the Bride of Christ, what they often fail to recognize in Peter's message are the parameters he is giving to define not just its specific beginning, but its precise conclusion.

Doctrinally speaking, the same adherents of the concept of the Church Age almost unanimously uphold as axiomatic that with the end of that age—that is, with the removal of the Church at whatever point they espouse it to take place, God will return to working exclusively through Israel to complete all the as yet unfulfilled promises where they are concerned. (Romans 9-11 in particular details this and warrants every believer's attention along with all the corollary, supporting Scripture.)

From God's point of view it is already seen as fulfilled because there is no possibility whatsoever of His not keeping and carrying out His Word. With the initiation of Pentecost comes the inevitable conclusion of all things in *"the day of the Lord"*; the Spirit through Peter is testifying this is such a sure thing that God already views it as fulfilled. This is a familiar device present in the divine utterances of nearly all of the Prophets in Scripture.

So Peter provides the evidence that this "age" or body of work in God's plan began on the Day of Pentecost by first citing those signs characterizing the working of the Holy Spirit which have come true to mark its beginning, but alternatively reveals what is going to happen when it expires and comes to an end with these particular worldwide events; the Church Age ends with *"the day of the Lord"* whose onset is announced with the 6th Seal, not with the 1st Seal. In God's economy, this particular time period is viewed in its whole as a step in the overall plan, something which will conclude as it gives way to the final phase of the eschaton, *"the day of the Lord"*, corresponding to the 7th Seal in Revelation. There is an irony beyond sadness that no one disputes the Day of Pentecost inaugurated the Church Age as Peter declared, but are completely divided on the issue of when he says it will end with the advent of *"the day of the Lord"*.

The earliest generations of believers whose eschatology was first and foremost shaped by the Olivet Discourse understood the direct connection not just to this passage in Revelation, but as a fulfillment of Peter's explanation of the lifespan of the Church Age. Jesus specifically assigned these events as prefacing the end of the Church Age being announced by these signs and followed by way of its removal at this juncture:

29"But immediately after the tribulation of those days	*24"But in those days, after that tribulation,*	
THE SUN WILL BE DARKENED, AND THE MOON WILL NOT GIVE ITS LIGHT, AND THE STARS WILL FALL *from the sky,*	THE SUN WILL BE DARKENED AND THE MOON WILL NOT GIVE ITS LIGHT, *25*AND THE STARS WILL BE FALLING *from heaven,*	*25"There will be signs in sun and moon and stars,*
and on the earth dismay among nations, in perplexity at the roaring of the sea and the waves, 26men fainting from fear and the expectation of the things which are coming upon the world;		
and the powers of the heavens will be shaken.	*and the powers that are in the heavens will be shaken.*	*for the powers of the heavens will be shaken.*
30And then the sign of the Son of Man will appear in the sky,		
and then all the tribes of the earth will mourn,		
and they will see the SON OF MAN COMING ON THE CLOUDS OF THE SKY *with power and great glory.*	*26Then they will see* THE SON OF MAN COMING IN CLOUDS *with great power and glory.*	*27Then they will see* THE SON OF MAN COMING IN A CLOUD *with power and great glory.*
28But when these things begin to take place, straighten up and lift up your heads, because your redemption is drawing near." (Lk. 21:25-28)		
31And He will send forth His angels	*27And then He will send forth the angels,*	
with A GREAT TRUMPET		
and THEY WILL GATHER TOGETHER *His elect from the four winds, from one end of the sky to the other. (Mt. 24:29-31)*	*and will gather together His elect from the four winds, from the farthest end of the earth to the farthest end of heaven. (Mk. 13:24-27)*	

A sidebar comment worth briefly visiting at this point is that this not only clearly mitigates against the position of Pre-Tribulationism which steadfastly refuses the direct and overt connection of the 6th Seal with the onset of *"the day of the Lord"*, but undermines Post-Tribulationism in its assertion that Christ does not come back for the Church until the very end of Daniel's 70th Week. The fulfillment of the signs specified by both Christ and Peter are nowhere to be found in the closing of Daniel's 70th Week with Revelation's working of the Bowls of God's wrath. Both positions fail to recognize that in a parallel to the character of the Exodus sequence, God's people, to a point, share the same experience as everyone else, but then a time comes when He makes a distinction by exempting them going forward; but that neither comes before everything takes place nor after it is basically all over as these two positions basically assert. In both Exodus and Revelation, it is after the first third of the judgments, and in the previously cited examples of Jericho, Noah and Enoch, the exemption only comes after everyone experiences an initial "seven".

But perhaps an equally important parallel which we should not undervalue is the simultaneous reaction of the unsaved to that of the saved. In the Olivet Discourse, Christ specified:

> [25]"There will be signs in sun and moon and stars, and on the earth **dismay among nations**, in **perplexity** at the roaring of the sea and the waves, [26]**men fainting from fear and the expectation of the things which are coming upon the world**; for the powers of the heavens will be shaken. (Luke 21:25–26)

What will be their reaction? "...*and then all the tribes of earth will mourn*" (Mt. 24:30) in contrast to the saved who "*straighten up and lift up your heads*". This is repeated as a key, opening detail of John's vision, "*Behold, He is coming with the clouds, and every eye will see Him, even those who pierced Him; and all the tribes of the earth will mourn over Him*". (Rev. 1:7) Revelation here supplies added detail to the reaction of the unsaved:

> [15]Then the kings of the earth and the great men and the commanders and the rich and the strong and every slave and free man hid themselves in the caves and among the rocks of the mountains; [16]and they said to the mountains and to the rocks, "Fall on us and hide us from the presence of Him who sits on the throne, and from **the wrath of the Lamb**; [17]for **the great day of their wrath has come**, and who is able to stand?" (Revelation 6:15–17)

In spite of their explicit acknowledgment of all these things taking place at the hand of Christ, there is not only no "revival" or reconciliation with the Lamb, but a continuation of the exact, same behavior and rebellion which led to this very dilemma in the first place: steadfast rejection of Him. Rather than ever even hinting at a worldwide revival in Revelation, this is the first of four specific descriptions of mankind's steadfast rejection and rebellion, each increasingly more potent than the last, ultimately culminating with their overt and outspoken blasphemy of God personally. (Rev. 6:15-17; 9:20-21; 16:9, 21) In other words, it only gets progressively worse from here.

It is also worth noting that the textual proof that this is the demarcation when "judgment" turns to "wrath" as the launch of *'the day of the Lord'* takes place is found in the admission not only that the source of these activities is attributed as *"from the wrath of the Lamb"*, (Rev. 6:16-17) but that it is very narrowly defined as *"the great day of **their** wrath"*, *"their"* being solely confined to *"the kings of the earth and the great men and the commanders and the rich and the strong and every slave and free man"*. In other words, every unbeliever regardless of their demographic membership or standing; as we shall see shortly, believers are on the cusp of being removed and exempted.

The Interlude & the 144,000

> [1]*After this I saw four angels standing at the four corners of the earth, holding back the four winds of the earth, so that no wind would blow on the earth or on the sea or on any tree. [2]And I saw another angel ascending from the rising of the sun, having the seal of the living God; and he cried out with a loud voice to the four angels to whom it was granted to harm the earth and the sea, [3]saying, "Do not harm the earth or the sea or the trees until we have sealed the bond-servants of our God on their foreheads." (Revelation 7:1–3)*

There is an interesting, repeated eschatological phenomenon in the insertion, at times, of a supernatural "quiet time", or what we might think of as "the lull before the storm", or perhaps being in "the eye of the hurricane". It is a specific feature in the sequence of Jericho which takes place on their seventh "seven" around the city:

> [10]*But Joshua commanded the people, saying, "You shall not shout nor let your voice be heard nor let a word proceed out of your mouth, until the day I tell you, 'Shout!' Then you shall shout!" (Joshua 6:10)*

This can also be seen when the 7th Seal initiates the Trumpet sequence to come as it is first launched with *"silence in heaven for about half an hour"* (Rev. 8:1) This supernatural withholding of the winds seems to be a dramatic pause which can be discerned by everyone in the earthly realm. It is the Hollywood cowboy and Indian movie equivalent of the cinematic hero's observation just before the big attack, "It's awful quiet out there—a little too quiet". This particular pause is quite dramatic as it comes after the tumult of the first six Seals which results in wars, economic chaos, and physical calamities all taking out at least a fourth of the planet's population. However, the worst is not over but actually yet to come.

It may be important to recognize a possible parallel between the four horsemen initiating the overall final sequence, and four angels *"to whom it was granted to harm the earth and the sea*". Again, it provides a distinction between an opening phase of activity coming about by earthly agency prefigured by earthbound horsemen, versus what now escalates to the wrath of God induced by heavenly angelic agency, and the distinctly different kinds of works each performs. There is an obvious forewarning here that judgments to come are going to inflict damage in ways those experienced thus far have not; it is dark and getting darker, bad progressing to worse.

Biblical Sealing

But in what is about to take place during this interlude between the 6th and 7th Seals, 1st century readers were most likely to draw a clear parallel to Ezekiel 9 where there was a marking of the faithful in the shadow of the final judgment of Jerusalem and Judah about to take place. It could also be argued that there was a dramatic pause in what took place just prior to Sodom and Gomorrah when the Lord and the angels first visited Abraham and engaged in a discussion of the number of faithful remaining which might at least delay God's wrath, or the week Noah and company spent in the ark prior to the actual commencement of the Flood.

In the example of the last days of Judah leading up to the Babylonian Captivity, yet another pattern of teaching about the Last Days, the end did not come about all at once as a single event, but there were actually three separate deportations. Each took place with dramatic pauses between them against a backdrop of ever-increasing apostasy and deception and, for the faithful remnant characterized by Jeremiah, persecution.

Since there probably is no more controversial or discussed detail in Revelation than the "mark of the beast", it is at least worth mentioning that while that particular activity is not revealed until Revelation 13, the first marking mentioned is being performed by God, which is actually the same pattern as what took place in Ezekiel. God "marks" His people first, and it would be a refreshing change all around if people became more concerned to first obtain God's mark so as to put to rest the hysteria so often accompanying speculation about the Antichrist's subsequent counterfeit. Yes, even the mark of the beast is a spiritual counterfeit of a corresponding authentic working of God, just as the *therion* are counterfeits of God's *Zoa*--Christ the Lamb.

We need to recognize, however, that Revelation 13 is part of a larger section which recaps what is taking place within the timeline of Revelation overall, and not presented in a strict chronological sequence. In other words, we cannot be dogmatic as to precisely when the requirement for the mark of the beast becomes public, so it may very well be underway at this point to some degree. But the first marking conveyed in Scripture is that of the faithful. Such a sequence also parallels Christ's followers in that they are "marked" in advance by the Holy Spirit:

> [21]Now He who establishes us with you in Christ and anointed us is God, [22]who also **sealed us and gave us the Spirit in our hearts as a pledge**. (2 Corinthians 1:21–22)

> [13]In Him, you also, after listening to the message of truth, the gospel of your salvation—having also believed, you were **sealed in Him with the Holy Spirit of promise,** [14]**who is given as a pledge of our inheritance**, with a view to the redemption of God's own possession, to the praise of His glory. (Ephesians 1:13–14)

> [30]Do not grieve the Holy Spirit of God, by whom you were **sealed for the day of redemption**. (Ephesians 4:30)

It is very important to carry over at least one specific detail from Revelation 7:1-3 to the following list of ethnic Israel being marked, that they are identified by the angel to John as "*the bond-servants of our God*", a New Testament designation of someone in a right and committed, born again relationship with Christ. (Acts 4:29; 16:17; 2 Co. 4:5; Gal. 1:10; Php. 1:1; Col. 1:7; 4:7; 2 Ti. 2:2; Titus 1:1; Ja. 1:1; 2 Pe. 1:1; Jude 1) This designation of "*duolos*" (Strong's #1401) is how the Apostle John describes himself in the very opening verse of Revelation and is how Jesus describes His followers in the letter to Thyatira. (Rev. 2:20) This assignation will be used in the closing verses of Revelation as well:

> [6]And he said to me, "These words are faithful and true"; and the Lord, the God of the spirits of the prophets, sent His angel to show to **His bond-servants** the things which must soon take place. (Revelation 22:6)

This is an important detail revealing that although their individual identification with each of the tribes specifies their earthly ethnicity and lineage, they are additionally singled out by their spiritual lineage as born again followers of Christ.

Additionally, this sealing cannot be separated from Christ's teaching that it is a condition which is only possible for those who have accepted Christ:

> [33]**"He who has received His testimony has set his seal to this,** that God is true. [34]For He whom God has sent speaks the words of God; for He gives the Spirit without measure. (John 3:33–34)

There are many arguments as to how these 144,000 come to Christ, mostly because of the disagreement over the timing of the Church's removal, but the text makes it clear that this group comes to faith and serves Christ the Lamb going forward by their being "*bond-servants*" who have "*received His testimony*".

The following verses are purposely formatted differently than will be found in a printed NASB to make the list easier to read:

> *⁴And I heard the number of those who were sealed, one hundred and forty-four thousand sealed from every tribe of the sons of Israel:*
>
> > *⁵From the tribe of Judah, twelve thousand were sealed,*
> > *from the tribe of Reuben twelve thousand,*
> > *from the tribe of Gad twelve thousand,*
> > *⁶from the tribe of Asher twelve thousand,*
> > *from the tribe of Naphtali twelve thousand,*
> > *from the tribe of Manasseh twelve thousand,*
> > *⁷from the tribe of Simeon twelve thousand,*
> > *from the tribe of Levi twelve thousand,*
> > *from the tribe of Issachar twelve thousand*
> > *⁸from the tribe of Zebulun twelve thousand,*
> > *from the tribe of Joseph twelve thousand,*
> > *from the tribe of Benjamin, twelve thousand were sealed.*
> >   *(Revelation 7:4–8)*

There are at least twenty listings of the tribes of Israel in the whole of Scripture, no two of which are identical, not only often including or excluding different names, but especially never displaying the tribes in the same order. (Num. 1; 7; 10; 13; 26; 34; Dt. 27; 33; Josh. 13-19; 1 Chr. 2; 2-8; 12; Eze. 48 (twice); Rev. 7) [Note: A "*Comparison of the Biblical Listings of the Tribes of Israel*" can be downloaded from the Walk with the Word website.]

Although Judah heads more lists than any other tribe, they do not lead off every list. Because some lists are focused more on the division of the land, Levi is omitted in such cases as they were not given land in the same way as the rest of the tribes because of their burden for the priesthood and specifically designated as belonging to the Lord. One of the most common variations has to do with Joseph and his sons, Benjamin and Ephraim, the three of which are shown in various combinations. This genealogical adjunct is provided to make the point that each listing needs to be studied in its own context as each is teaching a slightly different lesson from all the others, this one in Revelation being no exception.

One of the annotations which sticks out in this list as compared to all others is that "*Joseph*" is used to identify what we would normally identify as "*Ephraim*", while his other son "*Benjamin*" is presented as is. But what may be most interesting is the absence of Dan. In Judges 18, Dan is shown to be the tribe who rebels against the Lord's plan and leaves their assigned area in the far south to take away lands in the far north neither assigned to them as a tribe individually nor Israel collectively. Along the way they introduce false religion and idolatry throughout Israel as they travel its length, ultimately taking over a city in the north which becomes one of the two main seats of false worship in what will eventually become the Northern Kingdom of Israel. (Jg. 18:27-31)

It would appear that Dan has permanently lost its position and has been replaced, this being possible by the introduction of Joseph's sons Ephraim and Benjamin. In other words, just as Judas as one of the original Twelve was "removed" and replaced to keep their original number intact, so the same takes place with Israel in its removal and replacement of Dan.

One of the reasons this may matter is that there is a popular teaching, because of an interpretation of Jacob's prophecies in Genesis 49 concerning each of his sons and Dan in particular, (Gen. 49:16-17) that the Antichrist "must" be biologically descended from that tribe. This is a difficult proposition for this author to accept given that Dan is now absent or removed, but it would not be surprising because of the Antichrist's propensity to work as a counterfeit if one of his claims is an ethnic Jewish lineage to the tribe of Dan, something at this juncture which is actually extinct and replaced.

But for readers of the day, and especially the large percentage of ethnic Jewish believers still active in the Church, this feature of Revelation would actually be a very positive comfort as it confirms not only that God is not through with Israel yet—or what Paul calls a "*partial hardening*" describing a temporary condition (Rom. 11:25), but provides more detail of Israel's role in the eschaton, reconciled to, working with and worshipping Christ the Lamb of God.

Two Views of the Same Group

The 144,000 will be mentioned again in Revelation 14:1-5, and there is a parallel detail in that passage which needs to be mentioned at this time because it greatly assists in confirming not just the identity of this group, but their greater spiritual working in the overall scheme of the eschaton:

> *³And they sang a new song before the throne and before the four living creatures and the elders; and no one could learn the song except the one hundred and forty-four thousand who had been **purchased from the earth**. ⁴These are the ones who have not been defiled with women, for they have kept themselves chaste. These are the ones who follow the Lamb wherever He goes. These have been **purchased from among men as first fruits to God and to the Lamb**. ⁵And no lie was found in their mouth; they are blameless. (Revelation 14:3–5)*

When the average English reader comes to these verses, they might quite naturally interpret "*the earth*" as designating all the people and nations on the planet. However, the underlying Greek word "*ges*" (Strong's #1093) is used in Scripture in the sense of "*earth*" as "dirt" or "land". It would be the English equivalent of saying, "The farmer works the earth to produce his crop" to refer to the soil rather than the whole planet. Just as a scriptural distinction is often made by using the metaphor of the sea to represent all the Gentile nations (from which arises one of the Beasts in Rev. 13:1-10), "*ges*" or "*land*" often refers to Israel (from which arises the other in Rev. 13:11-18).

When taken together with the 144,000's description of "*first fruits*", 1st century readers would have clearly understood this very Hebraic designation to mean that these are but the first of many more to come in the character of the Old Covenant's laws concerning first fruits. Just as when Israel was coming out of Egypt, the firstborn were designated as God's as a representation of the redemption of all, the Old Testament concept of "*first fruits*" always describes the very best and first to be dedicated to the Lord, but only a sampling of what is to follow. It reinforces both the fact that this group is ethnically Hebrew, but is also born again.

This is also a specific designation assigned to Christ and directly associated with new life in Him, including both the Rapture and Resurrection.

> *²⁰But now Christ has been raised from the dead, **the first fruits** of those who are asleep. ²¹For since by a man came death, by a man also came the resurrection of the dead. ²²For as in Adam all die, so also in Christ all will be made alive. ²³But each in his own order: **Christ the first fruits**, after that those who are Christ's at His coming, ²⁴Then comes the end, when He hands over the kingdom to the God and Father, when He has abolished all rule and all authority and power. (1 Corinthians 15:20–24)*

However, what is probably the most popular assertion about the 144,000, which is something not found in Scripture and is at best an outside supposition being superimposed on God's Word, is that they are "super evangelists" who complete the work of preaching the Gospel to the entire world before the end of the eschaton is reached. While a revival of ethnic Israel can be reasonably supported by Scripture, there are a number of textual problems with this assertion where the 144,000 are concerned:

> A specific, focused persecution of Israel takes place (Rev. 12) where the people collectively flee the land of Israel into the wilderness, and according to parallel Scriptures, are later led back into the land by Christ Himself.

> Rather than scattered about the globe as persecution often does, Israel in the eschaton is described consistently as returned and altogether intact throughout the whole experience.

> It is possible that like all Christians of all ages they carry out the role of preaching the Gospel, but the designation "super evangelists" is always accompanied with the notion that they are more successful than all previous generations of Christians, and yet from this point on Revelation shows no positive response to the Gospel; in fact, it gets increasingly worse to the point that God is openly blasphemed.

While, individuals' acceptance of the Gospel cannot be automatically ruled out, this "super" role and work is never mentioned. In fact, the only mention in Revelation of the preaching of the Gospel will be in a single instance by supernatural angelic agency:

> *6And I saw another angel flying in midheaven, having an eternal gospel to preach to those who live on the earth, and to every nation and tribe and tongue and people; (Revelation 14:6)*

And because in actuality Revelation 14 appears to be part of a larger "recap" of events in the eschaton, we have to hold to the very real possibility that this first of three angelic messages (Rev. 14:6-13) might take place before the removal of the Church. The first messenger preaching *"the eternal gospel"* and warning *"the hour of His judgment has come"* and making an appeal to *"worship Him"* is followed by the second angel declaring the fall of Babylon the great, and the third warning of what will happen to those who instead worship the beast.

The only things which we can be dogmatic about in regards to the 144,000 is how this literal event shows the End Times fulfillment of God's final working to complete all of His as yet unfulfilled promises to Israel, who have something personal to bear in the eschaton as exemplified by the alternative designation of the Last Days as "*the time of Jacob's distress*". (Jer. 30:7)

The Great Multitude

> *⁹After these things I looked, and behold, a great multitude which no one could count, from every nation and all tribes and peoples and tongues, standing before the throne and before the Lamb, clothed in white robes, and palm branches were in their hands; ¹⁰and they cry out with a loud voice, saying,*
>
> > *"Salvation to our God who sits on the throne, and to the Lamb."*
>
> *¹¹And all the angels were standing around the throne and around the elders and the four living creatures; and they fell on their faces before the throne and worshiped God, ¹²saying,*
>
> > *"Amen, blessing and glory and wisdom and thanksgiving and honor and power and might, be to our God forever and ever. Amen."*
>
> *¹³Then one of the elders answered, saying to me, "These who are clothed in the white robes, who are they, and where have they come from?" ¹⁴I said to him, "My lord, you know." And he said to me, "These are the ones who come out of the great tribulation, and they have washed their robes and made them white in the blood of the Lamb. ¹⁵For this reason, they are before the throne of God; and they serve Him day and night in His temple; and He who sits on the throne will spread His tabernacle over them. ¹⁶They will hunger no longer, nor thirst anymore; nor will the sun beat down on them, nor any heat; ¹⁷for the Lamb in the center of the throne will be their shepherd, and will guide them to springs of the water of life; and God will wipe every tear from their eyes." (Revelation 7:9–17)*

One of the things we have to be understandably nit-picky about is the opening qualifier, "*After these things*". In Revelation alone it is found nine times in eight verses. (Rev. 1:19; 4:1; 7:9; 9:12; 15:5; 18:1; 19:1; 20:3) It is not uncommon to find expositors insisting that in every other instance other than this one that it "must" be a chronological device specifying the order of things, especially as it is used in the opening chapters of Revelation to make a distinction between the three major sections of the prophecy, but somehow not in this case. This exception is most often invoked by those whose position on the timing of the Rapture cannot co-exist with this being the description and assignment of its occurrence, so they must assign an alternative interpretation.

It must be affirmed that although this provides a specific window of time for the overall sequence of the eschaton in which the Rapture will take place, it is still not in violation of the axiom that no one can know the day or the hour, and in keeping with Jesus' and all the New Testament writers' assurances and warnings that we are to recognize the season and the nearness of its imminent arrival.

> [28] "But **when these things begin to take place**, straighten up and lift up your heads, because your redemption is drawing near." (Luke 21:28)

There are two very important distinctions to pay attention to, the first being that they are "*clothed in white robes*", a feature associated with those who have been redeemed as further indicated, "*they have washed their robes and made them white in the blood of the Lamb*". The other is often overlooked, that "*palm branches were in their hands*". This is exactly how God's people were to celebrate the Messiah the Conquering King in His Second Coming as part of the Feast of Tabernacles celebration symbolizing the Millennial Kingdom to come. Adherents of Judaism at that time literally waved palm branches as part of their worship during this particular feast. We know from 1 Thessalonians 4:17 that the raptured Church will at this time "*be caught up together with them*"—those who had fallen asleep in the Lord and are now resurrected, which explains such "*a great multitude which no one could count, from every nation and all tribes and people and tongues*". This is the "*Episunagoge*", the anticipated gathering of both the raptured and resurrected with the Lord.

This is further affirmed by the fact that their initial outburst of praise first assigns "**Salvation** *to our God...and to the Lamb*". This cannot possibly be assigned by anyone but the Church and anything but the "*blessed hope*" (Titus 2:13) of the two-sided coin which is the simultaneous Resurrection and Rapture. Another important detail which confirms yet again that Revelation not only conforms to the basic outline first provided by the Olivet Discourse, but itself affirms the overall eschatology of all the New Testament writings, is the specification in verse 14, "*These are the ones who come out of the great tribulation*".

The drum we keep banging because it mitigates against incorrect assumptions which have been incessantly sounded, is that neither the Olivet Discourse, the New Testament writings, nor Revelation itself organizes and confines activities to the "*end of the age*" as restricted to just a seven year period. Daniel's 70th Week is present, but found within the overall structure of three phases described as "*tribulation*", "*great tribulation*", and "*the day of the Lord*", each of which are contained within that final seven years. The Olivet Discourse makes clear that "*the great tribulation*" from which the great multitude is removed is initiated by the Abomination of Desolation. The much more intense period which follows experiences such a multiplied concentration of both physical and spiritual activity, that "*Unless the Lord has **shortened** ("koloboo" or "amputated") those days, no life would have been saved; but for the sake of the elect, whom He chose, He shortened ("koloboo" or "amputated") the days*". (Mk. 13:20)

This is further textual evidence that "*the great tribulation*" cannot possibly be assigned to the whole of the second 3-1/2 year half of a seven year period, because that phase comes to an end by being divinely and abruptly shortened with the removal of the Church; all that is left for those remaining is "*the day of the Lord*". But this parallel reference to coming out of the "*great tribulation*" precisely mirrors the timing of the harvest in the Olivet Discourse and allows yet another anchor point to show how Revelation is describing the same things, albeit with even more detail.

The Progressive Picture of the Rapture

It is not unusual to come across someone who claims that "The Rapture" does not actually appear in the biblical text who attempt to leverage this into their case opposing the Rapture in some way, sometimes even to deny it entirely. The truth is that prior to the printing press and the many English translations which would come later, the mainstream version of the Bible most often given priority was the Latin translation known as The Vulgate. Although Jerome provided this is 382 AD, it would not be adopted officially by the Catholic Church until nearly 1,200 years later in the late 16th century during the Council of Trent (1545-63).

While there were others, such as the Waldenseans (founded ca. 1173), who produced other translations of the Bible, for a very long time the Vulgate continued to be regarded (especially among scholars) as the standard until the end of the 17th century. (The Catholic Church adopted various Latin versions in its place until settling on the current one officially sanctioned.) But it was the study of the Scriptures from their original Greek and Hebrew manuscripts by a number of historic figures which ignited what we now refer to as "The Reformation". This was because of serious discrepancies in Jerome's choice of Latin words which incorrectly represented the original languages, at times seriously misrepresenting the Greek and Hebrew autographs. But when it came to this biblical event in his translation, Jerome chose to use the Latin word "*rapturo*", which was anglicized as "rapture" and adopted into common usage by nearly everyone on all levels.

While it is true we cannot find the literal equivalent in the original Greek or Hebrew for the English word "rapture", it is a word which was adopted from one of the earliest translations in the history of the Church and incorporated into the English language the same way many words originating in other languages have entered into mainstream acceptance. (How about "beautiful" from French or "gesundheit" from German?) However, this is a main source of confusion as "Rapture" has become a kind of "catch-all" for the concept of the Church's removal without always fully taking into account all the various terms which Scripture employs, and absent the full understanding as to why more than one is used. Often this has been misappropriated to make the false case that they are not referring to the same thing at all.

As touched on previously, the best example of this scriptural mechanism is found in the alternating references to the nation as "Israel" at times and then at others as "Jacob". It is a reflection of the collective whole's spiritual character referring to their literal forebearer, who before he met the Lord was called "Jacob", and afterward "Israel". It is often used to identify them in the character of the backslidden, unsaved Jacob as opposed to the born again, new creation Israel after coming face to face with the Lord. The different terms are used to illuminate alternate spiritual aspects of the same thing. We see this often in Scripture, such as when "Zion" is used for the heavenly perfect equivalent of "Jerusalem" the fallen earthly institution. The Holy Spirit is doing this to teach about more than one aspect of the same thing.

There are several terms used in Scipture which all refer to the Rapture, but each carrying a distinction so as to communicate an important yet different aspect of the same thing. And it turns out that to understand their usage sheds significant light on "the progressive revelation of God" where eschatology is concerned. By not just examining each individual term, but how and when they are used, something is being revealed by the Holy Spirit first in the Olivet Discourse, then by Paul in Thessalonians, and finally in Revelation. They not only combine to provide the best overall picture of what we commonly call the Rapture, but show how each of these texts is building upon and connecting to each other and that just one, single term is insufficient to fully describe all of this milestone's important characteristics.

The Rapture in the Olivet Discourse

The main terms Jesus employs in the Olivet Discourse are "*paralambano*"— that is, "*taken*", and "*episunagoge*"—that is, "*gathered*". As previously discussed, "*paralambano*" is used in the New Testament when describing one person taking another person to or with himself. In contrast to unbelievers who are taken into judgment by being left behind to be destroyed, believers are personally taken by Christ unto Christ Himself, each believer saved by the Savior.

This is why, in the parallel passage in Luke 17:20-37, when answering the question put to Him by the Pharisees "*as to when the kingdom of God was coming*", Jesus used the same illustrations of being "*taken*" ("*paralambano*") to emphasize a kingdom of people being removed by and to Christ personally rather than their view of a kingdom in an earthly sense. It was a response emphasizing the difference between those who will be with the Messiah and those who will not as the ultimate result of the choice whether to follow Him. Spiritual salvation is the prerequisite for this special act of literal salvation.

This is reinforced by the additional usage in both Matthew 24:31 and Mark 13:27 where this same event is described by "*episunagoge*" to depict being "*gathered*" to Christ. It is important to note the additional facet of how this takes place by angelic agency. While Paul will provide additional details for this particular aspect of the Rapture, it perfectly compliments the full meaning of being "*taken*", but refers to the Church as a whole rather than simply individual believers.

The Olivet Discourse, which is given to the Church so she will fully understand her role in the eschaton leading up to her removal emphasizes the personal aspect of the Rapture between Christ and the Church. The Bride will be personally "*taken*" by and to her Groom, and also "*gathered*" as individual members from all over the world into a consolidated whole by angelic agency to immediately be with Him. That which is being emphasized by the use of these terms is the dual nature of this event, both individually and collectively being personally brought to Him at the same time as both individual believers, and as the Bride of Christ as a whole. We are simultansoulsy singularly saved and collectively saved.

The Rapture in Thessalonians

In the next major mention of the Rapture to come some years after the Olivet Discourse through the Apostle Paul, the focus is on the timing. This is because Paul is having to address the errors and deception introduced in

Thessalonica by false teachers who misrepresented that somehow *"the day of the Lord"* had already come contrary to Paul's already given teaching. (2 Th. 2:1-12)

Paul's original explanation of the timing of this event provided in 1 Thessalonians 4:13-18 was necessary to address not just what will happen to Christians alive at the time the Church's removal takes place, but to also explain the state of Christians who had died in Christ in previous generations. While those alive experience a *"harpazo"*—that is, a sudden "snatching away", it is actually just one side of the proverbial coin. The inseparable other half is the resurrection of the dead in Christ so that ***both*** groups will be *"gathered"*— *"episunagoge"*, together with Christ. The emphasis is on the timing of not just the Rapture of the living, but the immediate onset of the Resurrection of the dead. But for those awaiting the Rapture, Paul affirms the anticipated sequence again.

Both Christ and Paul use the shared description *"episunagoge"* to help us connect each teaching to a different aspect of the same thing. Jesus compliments His emphasis on the personal nature of who is *"taken"* with the supplemental *"paralambano"*, while Paul accentuates the timing and action as being "snatched away"—that is, by employing *"harpazo"*. In both instances a common picture is provided of all believers, past or present, *"gathered"* to our Lord and Messiah. It is simultaneously an individual experience and as part of the whole Body of Christ, both past and present, both living and dead.

The Rapture in Revelation

In Revelation, the overlapping and connecting term *"harpazo"* is used and supplemented by *"erchomai"* (Strong's #2064)—"to come out" and additionally by *"therismos"* (Strong's #2326)—to harvest by the act of reaping.

A major theme throughout the whole of Revelation is the contrast between the inevitable end of the kingdom of Antichrist versus Christ's, remembering that the correct context of "kingdom" is the people, not the physical dominion. Revelation is a much more detailed account of the inescapable conclusion for those who choose to worship and serve Satan through the Antichrist juxtaposed against the servants and worshipers of Christ. The former are left behind to experience the ultimate judgment of God's wrath, the latter removed before general judgment on the whole earth gives way to that special outpouring of His wrath. In each instance, there is a sense of "escape" present in this rescue, but in this case it is focused on the collective whole.

We have just seen in Revelation 7:14 between the 6th and 7th Seals where the Church has *"come out"* of the *"great tribulation"*—that is *"erchomai"*. This action is given an additional descriptor in Revelation 12:5 when the Church escapes the dragon to be *"caught up [harpazo] to God and to His throne"*. Take note how the multitude who *"come out"* in Revelation 7:9 are immediately found *"standing before the throne and before the Lamb"*. The "snatching away" by *"harpazo"* in Revelation 12 not only connects back to Paul's reaching to the Thessalonians, but is substantiated by a direct comparison of texts within Revelation itself. Both immediately appear before the heavenly throne.

There is an additional descriptor in Revelation 14:14-16 of the Rapture as a *"therismos"* (Strong's #2326)—a *"harvest"*. The contents of Revelation 10-15 take a break from the chronological sequence of the Seals, Trumpets and Bowls to visit issues and events taking place in parallel to them. The text begins to bring us back to that sequence and does so in this particular passage by revisiting the Rapture. Whereas in Revelation 7 the emphasis is on what takes place from earth in the direction of heaven, Revelation 14 provides the alternate view of the same event as initiated from heaven and directed downward to earth.

> *14Then I looked, and behold, a white cloud, and sitting on the cloud was one like a son of man, having a golden crown on His head and a sharp sickle in His hand. 15And another angel came out of the temple, crying out with a loud voice to Him who sat on the cloud, "Put in your sickle and reap, for the hour to reap has come, because the harvest of the earth is ripe." 16Then He who sat on the cloud swung His sickle over the earth, and the earth was reaped. (Revelation 14:14–16)*

This is a powerful tie-in to the Olivet Discourse. Whereas in that instance everyone was looking up from earth upon the shout and trumpet preceding the visible return of Christ in the clouds, here was have the heavenly vantage point beginning with Christ initiating the gathering by angelic agency from a cloud. They are both pictures of the same thing, albeit from reverse perspectives.

In Revelation, Christ connects to and combines with both the teachings of the Olivet Discourse and Thessalonians textually to not only broaden our understanding of the whole working of the Rapture, but to additionally confirm its importance in separating and removing His kingdom from the ultimate satanic counterfeit. The timing is further narrowed to a window between the 6th and 7th Seals, and the act itself is confirmed as a sudden and violent "snatching away", further affirmed as the first harvest exclusively dedicated to the faithful. In Revelation 14:17-20, the subsequent second harvest takes place where the unfaithful are left behind to experience *"the great wine press of the wrath of God"*. (Rev. 14:20)

An Overlapping, Bigger Picture

We can see how the Holy Spirit is using both the literal text as well as each provided context to progressively build an overall picture to provide a greater depth of a combined and much deeper understanding of the Rapture. Christ builds upon a foundation which provides much more than just a single event whisking away the Church. It is to our collective shame that this is so often the singular fixation of our arguments not just because it so divides us, but actually exposes how little we understand all it truly involves and produces. Textually, we can see an overlapping connection to each ascending level of a greater and more detailed explanation for the greater spiritual work taking place:

"paralam-bano"	"episuna-goge"	"harpazo"	"erchomai"	"therismos"
"taken personally"	"gathered collectively"	"snatched"	"come out"	"harvest" as in a reaping
	Revelation	Rev. 12:5	Rev. 7:14	Rev. 14:15
	2 Th. 2:1	1 Th. 4:17	Thessalonians	
Mt. 24:40; Lk. 17:34	Mt.24:31; Mk. 13:27	The Olivet Discourse		

While there is certainly inherent value in studying each term individually as used throughout the whole of Scripture, they are multiplied in value when taken into consideration together in each respective context as they produce an invaluable overall teaching not just of the mechanics of this particular event, but the greater spiritual working of God through both the individually faithful and the overall collective Bride of Christ. There is far more for us to comprehend than it being a one-time miracle; it is actually the greater miraculous working of something much more profound for not only each individual faithful member of the Church and the whole Church itself, but for every believer past and present—all synchronized into a single event.

The 7th Seal

¹When the Lamb broke the seventh seal, there was silence in heaven for about half an hour. ²And I saw the seven angels who stand before God, and seven trumpets were given to them. ³Another angel came and stood at the altar, holding a golden censer; and much incense was given to him, so that he might add it to the prayers of all the saints on the golden altar which was before the throne. ⁴And the smoke of the incense, with the prayers of the saints, went up before God out of the angel's hand. ⁵Then the angel took the censer and filled it with the fire of the altar, and threw it to the earth; and there followed peals of thunder and sounds and flashes of lightning and an earthquake. (Revelation 8:1–5)

Just as we are provided a look into what first takes place in heaven in Revelation 4-5 as a prelude to what will come next on earth in the unsealing of the scroll, the opening of the next round characterized by the Trumpets first reverts to a similar heavenly scene as a prelude of what is to come. In many ways, this prelude connects to the previous one to form a sequence, taking many of the same elements to a new level, just as the Trumpets themselves escalate beyond the activities of the Seals. We need to recognize that there is a very important, direct contrast and comparison to be undertaken of similar activities taking place in both the heavenly prelude presented just prior to the breaking of the Seven Seals, and in this heavenly scene setting the stage for the Seven Trumpets, and that has to do with the censors and prayers of the saints.

In Revelation 5, it is the twenty-four elders and the four living creatures who are shown, "*each one holding a harp and golden bowls full of incense, which are the prayers of the saints*", (Rev. 5:8) but here it is a single, specific angel of whom it is said, "*much incense was given to him, so that he might add to it the prayers of all the saints on the golden alter which was before the throne*". There are shared objects between the two scenes which undergo vastly different use or treatment as well:

➤ What was first assigned to the twenty-four elders and the four living beings is now transferred to this angel.

➤ In the first occurrence these things led to praise of God for His work of salvation for the saved, (Rev. 5:8-10) but the second prefaces judgment upon the unsaved. (There was still time for repentance previously, but that opportunity has given way so that only judgment now remains.)

➤ The first time invokes the praise of "*myriads of myriads and thousands of thousands*" (Rev. 5:11) of heavenly residents, but the second time comes after the onset of "*a great multitude which no one could count*", previous earthly residents removed to heaven.

➤ Whereas in the first scene the prayers of the saints appear to be confined to having an effect in heaven after *"the smoke of the incense, with the prayers of the saints, went up before God"*, alternatively the angel *"filled it with the fire of the altar, and threw it on the earth"*. The basic direction is reversed.

➤ The prelude to the Seals was absent the visible, earthly warning signs which in this case presage the Trumpets, those signs signaling the onset of a change in what is to come from what has already been experienced. It is another confirmation of a spiritual change wherein warnings in the first round have given away to the wrath of judgment in the second.

It is no coincidence that while there are many similarities, the differences are extremely important as they serve to provide a greater explanation that although the first set of events were generalized "judgments" to be experienced by everyone, the next round has escalated to the expression of God's wrath to be dealt with exclusively by those left behind after the Church's removal.

The Timing of the Seals, Trumpets & Bowls

Yes, we are repeating ourselves a lot, but one of the previously discussed points which warrants re-inclusion at this point is that most expositors who insist on assigning all these things to having to take place in a seven year period, and further restrict each element to one of two 3-1/2 year halves of that period, most often also evenly space out each of the Seals, Trumpets and Bowls on their chart. They are most often found to assign each Seal as an equidistant milestone uniformly dividing the first 3-1/2 years, and then doing the same for the Trumpets and Bowls together in the second half. This is done to conform to their notion that the first half is "**Tribulation**" and the second half "**Great Tribulation**", that latter part incurring twice as much judgment, in their opinion, as the first. On such charts, the 1st Seal is often the very first item of the first 3-1/2 year half and the 1st Trumpet the very first milestone of the second half, or midway point.

So it is worth re-publishing the previous depiction of how prophecy was fulfilled in Christ's First Coming as a pattern or teaching of how it will take place in His Second Coming:

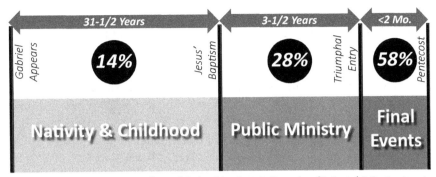

This concept, originally published by Jacob Prasch of Moriel Ministries, is derived by charting each of the more than 325 fulfilled prophecies of Christ's First Coming. This revealed a pattern in the character of a three-stage rocket, where each successive stage doubles the velocity of the previous booster to accomplish even more in a much reduced period of time.

In the 31-1/2 years from Gabriel's appearance to Zacharias to the public ministry of John the Baptist (stage 1), 14% of the all the prophecies concerning the First Coming were fulfilled; it doubled to 28% in the much shortened 3-1/2 year period for His public ministry from His baptism to the Triumphal Entry (stage 2); the far shorter final 57 day period from the Triumphal Entry to Pentecost slightly more than doubled to 58% (stage 3).

This can first and foremost be applied to the phases of the End Times articulated by Jesus in the Olivet Discourse as the *"birth pangs"*, *"tribulation"*, *"great tribulation"*, and *"the day of the Lord"*. They may not be equal in length nor arrive spaced evenly apart and progressively accelerate so as to fulfill far more in far less time as things progress toward the end. The same can be applied to the Seals, Trumpets and Bowls so that even though they are most likely confined to taking place within Daniel's 70th Week, they are not evenly distributed. This is further indicated in the very nature of the text of Revelation which seems to invoke a greater and greater urgency as we progress further into the sequence of events it describes.

At this point in most discussions of Revelation, expositors desiring to more evenly space apart the Seals, Trumpets and Bowls will state that we have reached the halfway point of their seven year chart and the 7th Seal or perhaps the 1st Trumpet is the first day of the second 3-1/2 year period—this author dogmatically asserts that we are actually on the other side of the midway point. Again, the eschaton is never described in Scripture as being confined to a seven year period, but repeatedly uses complimentary terms to describe phases which are not limited to seven years overall, but definitely contains Daniel's 70th Week within it.

The Olivet Discourse and Daniel's original prophecy identifies the middle of the 70th Week as the Abomination of Desolation, and Paul confirms that the Church must be present in order to identify the Antichrist undertaking that action in an attempt to be worshiped and recognized as a god. Revelation makes no reference to the Abomination to enable us to calculate the middle based on that milestone, and neither does it hint at the treaty which Daniel specifies is its starting point. But the Olivet Discourse also discloses that when this happens, it will be accompanied by a flight out of Israel into the wilderness, something which is spoken of later in Revelation 12.

That is part of a sizable section of Revelation which is not presented as strictly chronological, but sharing additional activities and important details going on in parallel to all the events leading up to the final sequence of the Bowl judgments. In other words, the events of the *"great tribulation"* as specified by the Olivet Discourse must all take place before the Rapture of the Church, which include the revealing of the Antichrist by way of the Abomination of Desolation, the escape of Israel into the wilderness, the pursuit by Satan and unprecedented persecution through the Antichrist in the character of the dragon (Rev. 12), and that period having to be supernaturally "amputated" for the sake of the Elect, ending with visible cosmological signs of the Son of Man and the dual reaction at seeing Him of joy for the saved, mourning for all others. (This is an incredibly succinct, bare bones synopsis which is obviously not entirely complete, but this is the heart of it.)

Since this time is cut short, it may not be very long overall. And it is important to keep in mind that the second half of Daniel's 70th Week is assigned by God through Daniel as not being precisely equal in length to the first half but actually longer. Whereas an ideal 3-1/2 lunar years consists of 1,260 days, the second half of Daniel's 70th Week is assigned quantities of both *"1,290 days"* (Dan. 12:11) and *"1,335 days"*. (Dan. 12:12) The second half is up to 75 days longer than the first. We cannot outright dismiss the possibility that this is an extra amount of time which can be used just on the other side of the midway point which would still allow the other things assigned to some form of "3-1/2" to be literally fulfilled, none of which would contradict or conflict with each other. (End Times "math" makes the SAT's a sad and pathetic wannabe.)

It may be important to note that in Revelation 12, when it is overtly stated that Satan has been personally *"thrown down to the earth and his angels were thrown down with him"*, that the Church has not yet been removed as evidenced that those he accuses and persecutes *"overcame him because of the blood of the Lamb and because of the word of their testimony, and they did not love their life even when faced with death"*. (Rev. 12:10-11) This is unambiguously describing the Church in direct conflict with Satan through the Antichrist.

This is confirmed further on in the same chapter when after unsuccessfully going after Israel, described as "*the woman*", Satan targets the Church:

> [17]So the dragon was enraged with the woman, and went off to make war with **the rest of her children**, who keep the commandments of God and hold to the testimony of Jesus. (Revelation 12:17)

Just as most persecution throughout history when targeted against Christians also takes aim at Jews and vice versa, this is textual evidence that, at this point at least, both Israel and the Church are earthbound.

Overall Comparison

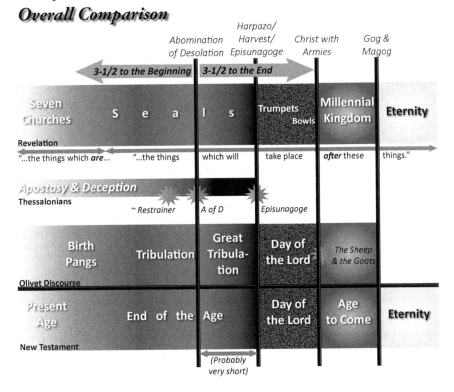

Summary of the Seal Judgments

It is worth re-visiting in a little more detail the parallel pattern of Ezekiel mentioned previously to give a bit of relief to repeating our mantra as to the Olivet Discourse and 1st century eschatology.

In Ezekiel 8, Ezekiel was taken inside the Temple and shown what was really going on, that such abominations were being increasingly committed against the Lord so that not only was the glory of the Lord going to leave both the Temple and Jerusalem, but the long opportunity for repentance and reconciliation to God had come to an end. All that was left was the wrath of His judgment to not just destroy Jerusalem and the Temple, but the entire nation and to send them into what we now call the Babylonian Captivity. Ezekiel is first given a vision of those to whom the Lord empowered to carry out these final judgments:

> ¹*It came about in the sixth year, on the fifth day of the sixth month, as I was sitting in my house with the elders of Judah sitting before me, that the hand of the Lord GOD fell on me there. ²Then I looked, and behold, a likeness as the appearance of a man; from His loins and downward there was the appearance of fire, and from His loins and upward the appearance of brightness, like the appearance of glowing metal. (Ezekiel 8:1–2)*

Just prior to giving the command to commence with the judgment, God first instructs them to mark the faithful remnant:

> ³*Then the glory of the God of Israel went up from the cherub on which it had been, to the threshold of the temple. And He called to the man clothed in linen at whose loins was the writing case. ⁴The LORD said to him, "Go through the midst of the city, even through the midst of Jerusalem, and **put a mark on the foreheads** of the men who sigh and groan over all the abominations which are being committed in its midst." (Ezekiel 9:3–4)*

We can first of all see from this where Satan got the idea for the mark of the beast. It is actually just another counterfeit in a long line of counterfeits of spiritually authentic workings of God. But it also speaks to many other levels of meaning since in the original ancient Hebrew alphabet in use at the time, this "*mark*" is specified as the letter "*tav*" which very closely resembled a cross:

In both the God-directed markings which took place in Ezekiel and those to come for the 144,000 in Revelation, it is interesting to note that they are restricted to just the forehead (Eze. 9:4; Rev. 7:3), whereas the satanic counterfeit is optionally applied to the "*right hand*". (Rev. 13:16) But whereas God's mark of the cross is an outward testimony of the greater inward spiritual marking of the giving of the Holy Spirit and a commitment to Christ, the counterfeit alternatively testifies to what inwardly possesses those who worship the beast.

But the marking of the faithful remnant immediately gives way to the onset of God's wrath upon the rest; there is no longer anything left except the consequences of judgment:

> *⁵But to the others He said in my hearing, "Go through the city after him and strike; do not let your eye have pity and do not spare. ⁶Utterly slay old men, young men, maidens, little children, and women, but **do not touch any man on whom is the mark**; and you shall start from My sanctuary." So they started with the elders who were before the temple.*
>
> *⁷And He said to them, "Defile the temple and fill the courts with the slain. Go out!" Thus they went out and struck down the people in the city.*
>
> *⁸As they were striking the people and I alone was left, I fell on my face and cried out saying, "Alas, Lord GOD! Are You destroying the whole remnant of Israel by pouring out Your wrath on Jerusalem?"*
>
> *⁹Then He said to me, "The iniquity of the house of Israel and Judah is very, very great, and the land is filled with blood and the city is full of perversion; for they say, 'The LORD has forsaken the land, and the LORD does not see!' ¹⁰But as for Me, My eye will have no pity nor will I spare, but I will bring their conduct upon their heads."*
>
> *¹¹Then behold, the man clothed in linen at whose loins was the writing case reported, saying, "I have done just as You have commanded me." (Ezekiel 9:5–11)*

The many models of the eschaton featured in Scripture never include a revival once God's wrath is finally initiated because, as stated here, "*I will bring their conduct upon their heads*", but neither is there ever found the often accompanying popular notion that when the Rapture takes place, all the babies and children will be automatically taken as well. Not only did such an occurrence not take place in Ezekiel's time, but are equally absent from the Flood, Sodom and Gomorrah, the Exodus, and Jericho and the conquest of Canaan.

This does not mean the innocent are automatically assigned to the Lake of Fire with unbelievers, because what happens afterward in eternity where God is concerned is a separate issue. But earthly death and associated horrific circumstances have never in either biblical nor secular history exempted the innocent; it is actually quite the opposite, and here in Scripture specifically stated as such. But this notion is espoused by those who have been deceived into portraying the Rapture not as an end, but twist it into an unscriptural inauguration of a false hope of obtaining afterward what everyone rejected while there was still time beforehand. (It is the mother of all ironies that almost to a man, those dogmatically propounding these things most commonly call their position the fulfillment of the "*blessed hope*", when in actuality they are the ultimate merchants of false hope.)

It is very telling that the current version of the most popular eschatology being espoused within the walls of the Church commonly embraces the notion that not only does Revelation 4-19 not apply to the Church, but neither does the Olivet Discourse. In order to support their presupposition, they must induce listeners to discard the greatest portions of God's prophetic Word specially given to the Church. And then they have to provide like exemptions from all the rest of God's Word, especially when so many things in the character of Ezekiel, which literally and historically took place, are employed by the Holy Spirit to teach about the final fulfillment of God's Word to come in contradiction to their position.

1st century believers would have recognized that everything provided to this point parallels the bulk of what was given in the Olivet Discourse, and that with the completion of "*tribulation*" and "*great tribulation*" to this point in Revelation, that the only thing which remains is "*the day of the Lord*", which they will credit Revelation for providing a wealth of more detail concerning as it ultimately leads into "*the age to come*".

Epilogue

While so many search the pages of Scripture to know more about the individual events of the eschaton, and even to construct a timeline, this can be a distraction from what the text is trying to specifically convey to believers. It is probably a higher priority to first consider the role of the Gospel in the Last Days in that it is not only the most important instruction of Christ as to what believers should do when they recognize the signs of the nearness of His Return, but the extraordinary efforts God will direct in this regard as the end draws near. It is the purpose of Christ's First Coming, and that by which everything is measured in the course of His Second Coming.

While the transition from *"birth pangs"* to *"tribulation"* to *"great tribulation"* on the one hand is a time of unprecedented spiritual darkness of apostasy, deception and persecution on a historic scale never before experienced, on the other hand we cannot ignore unprecedented last minute divine efforts to provide an opportunity to repent and escape the eternal consequences of the onset of what these earthly events precede. Consider that as the *"birth pangs"* give way to their ultimate fulfillment in each of the Seal judgments, and even though the rise of the Antichrist and False Prophet will be taking place in tandem with their world kingdom identified as *"Babylon the Great"*, there are multiple final efforts by God to reach the unsaved on several fronts:

> ➤ There is going to be visible, global angelic pronouncements of the *"eternal gospel"* (Rev. 14:6-7) and warnings against Babylon the Great (Rev. 14:8) and the beast. (Rev. 14:9-11)

> ➤ The Two Witnesses will be publicly testifying to the whole world both by word and supporting signs and wonders even if not specifically evangelizing in the traditional sense.

> ➤ The unprecedented persecution of the Church will produce unprecedented testimony and witness to the Gospel as persecution historically always has, but with a reach never before realized.

And in this study we have only given a surface-level treatment to what is going to take place among ethnic Israel when, by Christ's own unambiguous statements, Elijah will return a final time to lead Israel to their Messiah in the character of what John the Baptist initiated in the First Coming.

The false assertions propounded that there will be some kind of great, unprecedented revival after the removal of the Church, combined with the insistence that many End Times events are kept "secret" until unveiled without prior notice, obscures all of the efforts which will actually take place in the preceding shadow of the *Harpazo* initiating *"the day of the Lord"* when all that is actually left is the wrath of God for those remaining. It is the ultimate use of misdirection to deceive the Church while it is still day, knowing that *"night is coming when no one can work"*. (Jn. 9:4) It's not night yet, but such false teaching has prematurely deceived too much of the Church into operating that way.

In the closing days, in the character of when God Himself shut the door on Noah's ark and the opportunity for those left behind was lost forever, those who are going to choose the beast over Christ are going to have experienced not only the witness of Christian martyrs and the working of the two most powerful prophets of God ever sent, but visible angelic pronouncements not just warning about what is to come, but offering the *"eternal gospel"* itself. The subsequent unmitigated effects of the wrath of God to come by angelic agency in the Trumpet and Bowl sequences is first contrasted by the unprecedented final efforts to offer an opportunity to avoid experiencing them. But before the door is shut, no one will have been excluded without ample opportunity coming in multiple, overlapping efforts. Or as *"the Preacher"* phrased it:

> ⁶*A time to search and a time to give up as lost;*
> *A time to keep and a time to throw away. (Ecclesiastes 3:6)*

While there is still time to *"search"* and *"keep"*, God uses every resource—man, prophet, and even angel—to provide the opportunity to avoid being given up "*as lost*" and, in the parlance of *The Parable of the Dragnet* (Mt. 13:47-50), literally thrown away.

> [47]*"Again, the kingdom of heaven is like a dragnet cast into the sea, and gathering fish of every kind;* [48]*and when it was filled, they drew it up on the beach; and they sat down and* **gathered the good** *fish into containers, but* **the bad they threw away**. [49]*So it will be at the end of the age; the angels will come forth and take out the wicked from among the righteous,* [50]*and will throw them into the furnace of fire; in that place there will be weeping and gnashing of teeth. (Matthew 13:47–50)*

All of this, however, is going to take place before the removal of the Church.

The Final Takeaway

Probably the interpretation presented here which is most likely to go against the grain of every eschatology is that the basic timeline is not a seven year tribulation divided into two halves called "Tribulation" and "Great Tribulation" followed by the Millennial Reign, but rather a rough parallel based on the pattern of the First Coming.

> ➤ First is a much longer period of "*birth pangs*" likened to the 31-1/2 year of prophetic fulfillment at the First Coming from Gabriel's appearance to Zacharias through Jesus' childhood into adulthood.

> ➤ This is followed by His 3-1/2 year ministry from His baptism to Pentecost, replayed in the eschaton by the second half of Daniel's 70th Week initiated by the Abomination of Desolation. The starting point of the first half is purposely obscured, and it is important to note that neither Christ nor any New Testament writer stress or even mention "*seven years*" as a whole, but place all their emphasis on the last 3-1/2. Although Daniel divulges the "*seven*", he, too, stresses the last 3-1/2 as being the most important.

➤　This intense period Jesus calls *"great tribulation"* will be cut short for the sake of the Elect by the *Harpazo* of the Church, and what remains is *"the day of the Lord"* when those who are left behind will experience the full and final wrath of God.

What is involved is not just the *Parousia* of Christ (2 Th. 2:8), but the *parousia* of the Antichrist. (2 Th. 2:9) The issues of greatest concern to Christians are apostasy, deception, persecution, and maintaining faithfulness to God's Word and ways throughout. It is a time for us to be looking upward in positive, faithful anticipation of the nearness of these things working for our salvation, while for the unsaved the very same activities work to produce ever-hardening hearts and will instead invoke Final Judgment leading to the Lake of Fire; all the servants of Christ will instead be brought back for the Millennial Reign before the final transition to eternity.

For those who are not quite convinced but still make the sincere attempt to handle Scriptural literally and rely first and foremost on allowing Scripture to interpret Scripture, such are encouraged to consider the complete eschatological absence in the New Testament of a seven year period and why both Christ and Daniel actually place the emphasis on the second half of Daniel's 70th Week. And all are encouraged to engage in the exercise of examining Scripture chronologically, first establishing that which is axiomatic in Scripture which came before Revelation, and therefore must be given its rightful place in the handling of the last book of the canon of Scripture.

Each Generation's Light

If one studies the history of the Church, and in particular what they had to say for their time concerning eschatology—the Return of Christ, it is somewhat understandable to find present-day observers who will assert that since every generation seems to think it was living in the Last Days—and was wrong because He did not actually return, then at present we must be likewise deceived or, at the least, in extreme error.

> *3Know this first of all, that in the last days mockers will come with their mocking, following after their own lusts, 4and saying, "Where is the promise of His coming? For ever since the fathers fell asleep, all continues just as it was from the beginning of creation." (2 Peter 3:3–4)*

Part of the answer to this is that God has repeated many of the patterns of the End Times for each generation, albeit not necessarily all of them in the same way, but enough to test their faith and provide foreshadowing examples of the ultimate fulfillments to come. Every historical age has had to deal with apostasy, deception, persecution, false prophets, false christs, and the relentless pursuit of the spirit of antichrist. But a greater part of the answer is found in the definition of "*apokalupsis*" itself in its portrayal of an unveiling where things become clearer the closer one gets as the veil is being lifted. Previous generations have been generally right for the light provided to them, but perhaps constrained by their distance from the veil and the details they could discern behind it from their particular vantage point.

The Earliest View

Broadly speaking, over the ensuing 1,700 years following the giving of Revelation, the mainstream interpretation of God's Word transitioned from the 1st century practice to take it quite literally, to mostly treating it allegorically. While we can trace a remnant who have always maintained the right, literal handling of God's Word, the majority—both within and without the Catholic Church proper, routinely treated not just the prophetic portions of God's Word allegorically, but often His Word in its entirety. To a degree this is understandable in that there were so few literal events or parallels, and as time went on, it was believed that prophecy, at least, must be speaking largely in symbolic terms. Adhering to a literal interpretation of God's Word, in the absence of prophetic fulfillments, was in itself an act of faith.

Even when the Reformation provided a palpable reaction to this way of handling Scripture and set the Church back on the road to the standards of using literal hermeneutics, when it came to the prophetic portions there was still a common tendency to continue to handle them allegorically, or at least with a different set of rules from the rest of Scripture. When perusing the past historical writings of the Church during this time, particularly from the Reformation onward, some of the most noted scholars and expositors are commonly found assigning an allegorical meaning to God's prophetic Word, often naming this pope or that as the Antichrist, or this country or that as Babylon the Great and so forth.

A significant factor contributing to this which we often do not take into consideration is that over those many centuries, the literal proof of the historical facts of much of the Bible had disappeared, become lost, and could not be verified. For instance, the location of Nineveh was completely forgotten and buried under centuries of topsoil so that its location was no longer known. A mainstream viewpoint emerged wherein Nineveh was considered by many to be a biblical allegory (just a "story") rather than a literal place, contributing to the false notion that the whole of the book of Jonah could not therefore be taken literally and was at most just an allegory or Hebrew legend. Without a literal, physical Nineveh, many asserted there could be no literal, physical swallowing by a giant fish, so it was spiritualized as a parable or allegory.

Most Old Testament biblical sites outside of the Holy Land were lost to antiquity (as well as many within it) along with evidence of the various people groups associated with them. It is not uncommon to read in writings during this period a standard assertion, for instance, that the Hittites were just another of many allegorical inventions to merely illustrate a teaching in the Bible, but that they never actually existed. We forget that for more than eighteen centuries from the birth of Christ onward that there was no such thing as archaeology, anthropology, and very little in the way of ancient linguistics in the manner existing at present.

In other words, they were so far away from that veiled door we now refer to as the eschaton—all things relating to "*the end of the age*" and "*the age to come*", that all they could make out was a blurry little light. It was a time when the remnant who maintained the right interpretation and understanding of these things could only really do so by faith. If we pause long enough to consider, those few were spiritual giants who maintained, even in the face of the majority opposing them, their belief in the literalness and plain text of Scripture by faith alone.

The First Big Adjustment

But this all dramatically changed in the early 1800's when something happened that the Church had heretofore never experienced: many prophecies—not all, of course—but many prophecies began to be literally fulfilled. A European ruler rises to form a confederation in the person of Napoleon Bonaparte, who famously snatches the crown and anoints himself king in what seems to be an act of self-deification. He not only re-establishes a Jewish Sanhedrin, but begins to repatriate Jews back to Israel. He takes his troops to the Middle East and not only engages the Mamelukes in battle, but is famously found at the literal site of Har-Magedon and is quoted as admiring this place as being perfect for the final conflict mentioned in the Bible. His European campaign appears to many to duplicate many of Daniel's characteristics of the last kingdom to come.

Obviously Napoleon was not **THE** Antichrist and this was not **THE** Second Coming, but the literal, parallel fulfillment of so many scriptural details had an awakening effect on the Church where God's prophetic Word is concerned, and just like it was in the 1st century, it began to be treated literally again. What we might now call in hindsight one of the "*birth pangs*" had the effect of showing how God's prophetic Word could, indeed, be literally fulfilled.

In parallel to this, by the mid-19th century, the first results from a new science being developed called archaeology were starting to take hold where not only actual artifacts and manuscripts could be physically examined and displayed, but began to uncover all those places and people groups which for so long had been thought to just be allegorical. With such a treasure trove of documents in ancient languages retrieved, the literalness of not only history was being restored to the Church, but the very Scriptures themselves.

Many in the Church were shocked when Nineveh was not only rediscovered, but it turned out to be the size of present-day London. Likewise like a series of dominoes, the names and places and peoples of the Bible were corroborated as literal and real, and we probably do not fully appreciate the blessing of living at a time when all such details in Scripture have been verified and accepted as not just authentic, but historically accurate. The revival of the Bible's historicity has fueled a revival in how we handle it.

It Was All About "Millennialism"

All of these, as well as other contributing factors beginning with Napoleon, shifted the central focus of eschatology. For approximately the next 150 years, although again we will find a remnant who resisted its wholesale adoption, the mainstream focus was the Millennial Reign. The Church had moved closer to the veiled window, and at that distance what they could make out, naturally, was the outline of the largest object behind the veil—the Millennial Kingdom.

Roughly from 1800 to 1948, give or take, when we examine the writings devoted to eschatology, they are overwhelmingly fixated on the Millennial Reign. People and even entire denominations would label their beliefs by claiming to be Pre-Millennial, Post-Millennial, A-Millennial, and sometimes even Pan-Millennial. In other words, most of the charts and timelines created at this time were ordering the sequence of events and the Return of Christ in relationship to one's belief about the Millennial Kingdom.

All of this was greatly amplified in and around World War I, which so many Christians believed was fulfilling Scripture so as to itself be the End Times and impending Return of Christ, and along with even more efficient methods of printing books, magazines and newspapers, produced a nearly incalculable amount of material regarding Millennialism. There are those who can be found that did not waver from their faith in the literalness of Scripture and did not assign anything and everything as a prophetic fulfillment, and as a parallel benefit there arose various movements dedicated to seeing Israel literally restored and the Jewish people returned to their homeland. This might also have been yet another "birth pang" of prophetic activity, which some appraised correctly, but many misinterpreted.

And Then Came "Tribulationism"

However, things took an order of magnitude leap forward when, in the wake of World War II, the nation of Israel was reconstituted and Jews began to return to the land. The Church now found itself even closer to the veiled door and could make out things in the foreground in front of the Millennial Reign which must be navigated first, the most notable being what has been most commonly referred to as the seven year Tribulation.

The issues of eschatology regarding one's position on the Millennial Kingdom were given less importance and gave way to the common practice of instead defining one's self as Pre-Tribulational, Mid-Tribulational, Post-Tribulational, and yes, a few here and there who posited being Pan-Tribulational. (Pre-Wrath is not going to begin to enter the mainstream until the mid- to late-80s.) Now all events associated with the eschaton, particularly the *Harpazo* of the Church, were defined in relation to what is commonly referred to as the Tribulation, but obviously readers of this work will understand by now the preference for the term "Daniel's 70th Week" instead.

Even among many subscribing to opposing eschatologies, events such as Israel once again gaining statehood, the reoccupation of Jerusalem in 1967, the many wars which Israel obviously won with divine intervention, and other things such as the way being paved for a common currency, the ecumenical movement bringing all religions under one umbrella, the one-world movement, and so forth, are considered to at least be components of the *"birth pangs"* Jesus spoke about.

This tiresome discourse is attempting to make the case that when it comes to what each generation has offered as their interpretation of eschatology, to a large degree they have been right for the light provided at the time at the respective distance they found themselves in relation to that veiled window. The fact is that more and more becomes clearer and clearer the closer we get and, as the veil is being removed, to finally and plainly reveal the entire picture.

It Is Time For The "Half"

But in respect to what has been presented in these pages, whereas the historical emphasis transitioned from Millennialism to Tribulationism, what is being proposed here is that we have entered a time where the focus has narrowed even further to "the half"—the second half, that is, of Daniel's 70th Week which is initiated by the Abomination of Desolation.

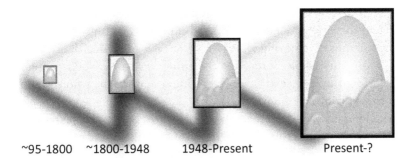

~95-1800 ~1800-1948 1948-Present Present-?

As noted repeatedly, we can very well already be in that first phase of the eschaton experiencing the *"birth pangs"* as we approach the formal execution of that final week of years, but the defining event for believers is the Abomination of Desolation revealing the Antichrist and kicking off that most intense of final periods for the Church, *"the great tribulation"*, culminating in being cut short by the *Harpazo* and initiating the final phase which remains, *"the day of the Lord"*. The beginning of the first half of Daniel's 70th Week seems to be purposely shrouded in order to place the focus on the chief defining characteristic emphasized by Christ Himself, the Abomination of Desolation.

To be sure, there are other prophetic events recorded in Scripture which are neither mentioned in the New Testament nor provided with a specific date for their fulfillment which very possibly could be members of the *"birth pangs"* foreshadowing the onset of Daniel's 70th Week, but we have certainly entered a time when we now need to narrow our focus even further from the thousand, to the seven, to the three-and-a-half. Admittedly, this may not yet be the end of that process.

And Finally...

> *⁷Clean out the old leaven so that you may be a new lump, just as you are in fact unleavened. For Christ our Passover also has been sacrificed. (1 Corinthians 5:7)*

In both Testaments, *"leaven"*—the biblical equivalent which in modern times is better known as "yeast", is used as an illustration of sin. Especially when combined with *"bread"*, a repeated biblical metaphor for God's Word, there is a very powerful and repeated scriptural caveat of the direct cause-and-effect relationship when it comes to our spiritual condition and its effect on our understanding of God's Word. This is the greater meaning of the Old Testament requirement not just to present unleavened offerings (Lev. 2:11; 6:17) and the Feast of Unleavened Bread connected with the Passover which not only required removing all leaven from each individual household, but from within the whole borders of the entire nation of God's people. (Ex. 12:15; 13:7) Intolerance of sin is just as important for the whole group as it is for the individual.

But Jesus expanded this metaphor to show that sin has a direct relationship with something else invoking the same characteristics as leaven: the handling of God's Word. The false teachings of the Pharisees, Sadducees and Herodians were all identified by Christ as *"leaven"* (Mt. 16:6, 11-12; Mk. 8:15) and even went so far as to define the counterfeit spiritual condition of *"hypocrisy"*. (Lk. 12:1) In other words, sin and false teaching—the ultimate mishandling of God's Word, are two sides of the same coin. Where one is present, so is the other. No individual or group can justify sin in any form or on any level without twisting God's Word into something never intended in order to allow it to remain. A lifestyle which includes unaddressed sin leads to the complete opposite of faithfulness—that is, the very definition of hypocrisy.

This is an additionally important detail to fully grasp because we live in an age where common wisdom maintains, especially when it comes to eschatology, that what is required is a certain level of formal education, or at the least, some kind of scholarly qualification. This is not a biblically-based belief. Regardless of one's scholastic, technical or otherwise qualified resume, the biblical requirement is always faithfulness to God's Word and ways. And especially when it comes to eschatology, God has made it clear that those to whom such things are revealed are pre-qualified by the degree to which they put His Word into practice, not the number of degrees they've earned from earthly institutions.

> [29]*"The secret things belong to the LORD our God, but the things revealed belong to us and to our sons forever, **that we may observe all the words of this law**. (Deuteronomy 29:29)*

> [14]*The secret of the LORD is for those who fear Him,*
> *And **He will make them know His covenant**. (Psalm 25:14)*

Knowing such deep things of God cannot be achieved without exclusive devotion and obedience to putting God's Word into practice. The prophetic portions of God's Word carry the same qualification as the rest of God's Word, that it cannot simply be read or studied, but must be part of a Scripture-practicing lifestyle, the meaning in the above when it comes to those who "**_observe_** *all the words*" who by doing so are proven to have an authentic covenant relationship with God through Christ.

One of the biblically wisest of the wise specifically articulated the qualification of spiritual faithfulness as being the chief requirement for the understanding of all things eschatological in the Last Days:

> [3]"**Those who have insight** *will shine brightly like the brightness of the expanse of heaven, and those who* **lead the many to righteousness**, *like the stars forever and ever. (Daniel 12:3)*

And he even passed along the fact that the tribulation which believers would experience in the shadow of Christ's Return would purposely serve to distinguish between the wicked and the righteous, a distinction between those who have insight because of their adherence to God's Word and ways and those whose wickedness is evident when they forego putting it into practice:

> [10]"*Many will be purged, purified and refined, but the wicked will act wickedly; and none of the wicked will understand, but those who have insight will understand. (Daniel 12:10)*

When this is fully grasped, it is not difficult to understand why the accompanying instructions co-located with God's prophetic Word consistently address the need for personal faithfulness. A life dedicated to God's Word by definition cannot abide sin, which turns out to be the only avenue made available for the understanding not just of eschatology as a general topic, but for recognizing its ultimate fulfillment as it occurs in real time. Sound doctrine is the result of a biblically-based crucified and sanctified life; false and mistaken beliefs the inevitable casualties of the tolerance of sin.

However, if this foundation is achieved, every believer must still be so thoroughly versed in God's Word, that when End Times events finally unfold, they are not captive to an "ism" or someone's book, but will allow the Holy Spirit unfettered reign to align Scripture with what is taking place. This was a common problem at Christ's First Coming frequently documented by the Gospels, that both the teachers of the day and their students—the general population of Israel schooled in the synagogue, could not properly process what was taking place before their very eyes because they were so invested in their preconceived notions of how the Messiah would fulfill Scripture. Those similarly "schooled" in the Church need to avoid repeating this error. Much of what is taught comes out of an academic environment focused on mimicking secular institutions and methodologies rather than preserving first and foremost the overriding authority of God's Word.

But at the risk of sounding completely and maniacally ego-centrical, one of the main sources of confusion within the ranks of the Church may be our willing, albeit unbiblical, acceptance of all positions on eschatology, claiming that it is not a doctrinal issue over which we should divide. Even when particular points completely and unambiguously contradict each other, "for the sake of love" we are supposed to tolerate these differences because we have assigned them to a category which we say is largely just opinion and open to interpretation. This is completely incongruous with the plain standard of Scripture:

> [19]So **we have the prophetic word made more sure**, to which you do well to pay attention as to **a lamp shining in a dark place,** until the day dawns and the morning star arises in your hearts. [20]**But know this first of all, that no prophecy of Scripture is a matter of one's own interpretation,** [21]for no prophecy was ever made by an act of human will, but men moved by the Holy Spirit spoke from God. (2 Peter 1:19–21)

Because of our conditioning this may be hard to digest, but eschatology is not open to opinion and is actually supposed to enjoy the same degree of rigid agreement as the rest of biblical doctrine. We are supposed to be as dogmatic about the meaning of the prophetic portions of God's Word as we are about those teaching the fundamentals of salvation, justification, etc. There is no exemption from the right handling of God's Word when it comes to prophecy, and the hard truth is because the mainstream members of the Church have bought into the notion that we can "agree to disagree", much deception has taken root at present which will eventually produce an unwanted harvest of results at the worst time possible. The cure for this is not to reconcile earthly learning institutions, but the individual pursuit of being a "Wise Virgin" where God's Word and ways are concerned. The practice of absolute truth in the course of our daily walk with Christ is actually the same standard for His whole Word, the prophetic portions included; it is the same standard for the academic elite and laity alike.

Side-by-side with the discussions of the milestones and personalities specifically assigned a role in the eschaton, this commentary has repeatedly attempted to highlight the even more important accompanying texts devoted to explaining to Christians what they are supposed to do about such things. Such almost always relate to remaining faithful and grounded in God's Word, rejecting the various seductions of deception and false teaching, and fervently carrying out the work of the Kingdom, particularly in the preaching of the Gospel. Another problem at present is the deference to Christian academics who have never actually engaged in ministry, are not actually seeking to disciple others, and are carrying out the work of academia rather than the Kingdom—all of which, of course, are compounded by the unprecedented reach and impact afforded by modern technology. It is difficult at present to see how Christ's commandment to *"make disciples"* (Mt. 28:19) is being achieved by the means of social media and the Internet, which too often seems to disintegrate into just making noise.

For believers, these accompanying instructions are far more important than any chart they might construct or glossary of milestones they may maintain. In fact, it is this author's contention that the associated parables provided by Christ both before and in the course of the Olivet Discourse are far more important where they are concerned, because such reinforce how we should actually live in and navigate through the eschaton.

We must never forget that eschatology properly aligned with the whole counsel of God's Word, in the same character as the whole counsel of God's Word, is ultimately not an issue of knowledge, but faith.

> *"However, when the Son of Man comes, will He find faith on the earth?" (Luke 18:8b)*

Grace and blessings in Christ. † † †

Appendix "A":
The Olivet Discourse in Parallel

[20]Now having been questioned by the Pharisees as to when the kingdom of God was coming, He answered them and said, "The kingdom of God is not coming with signs to be observed; [21]nor will they say, 'Look, here it is!' or, 'There it is!' For behold, the kingdom of God is in your midst."

[22]And He said to the disciples, "The days will come when you will long to see one of the days of the Son of Man, and you will not see it.

[23]They will say to you, 'Look there! Look here!' Do not go away, and do not run after them.

[24]For just like the lightning, when it flashes out of one part of the sky, shines to the other part of the sky, so will the Son of Man be in His day.

[25]But first He must suffer many things and be rejected by this generation.

[26]"And just as it happened in the days of Noah, so it will be also in the days of the Son of Man: [27]They were eating, they were drinking, they were marrying, they were being given in marriage, until the day that Noah entered the ark, and the flood came and destroyed them all.

[28]It was the same as happened in the days of Lot: they were eating, they were drinking, they were buying, they were selling, they were planting, they were building; [29]but on the day that Lot went out from Sodom it rained fire and brimstone from heaven and destroyed them all. [30]It will be just the same on the day that the Son of Man is revealed.

> ³¹*On that day, the one who is on the housetop and whose goods are in the house must not go down to take them out; and likewise the one who is in the field must not turn back.*
>
> ³²*Remember Lot's wife.* ³³*Whoever seeks to keep his life will lose it, and whoever loses his life will preserve it.*
>
> ³⁴*I tell you, on that night there will be two in one bed; one will be taken and the other will be left.*
>
> ³⁵*There will be two women grinding at the same place; one will be taken and the other will be left.*
>
> ³⁶*Two men will be in the field; one will be taken and the other will be left."*
>
> ³⁷*And answering they said to Him, "Where, Lord?" And He said to them, "Where the body is, there also the vultures will be gathered." (Lk. 17:20-37)*

[Note: Strictly speaking, Luke 17:20-37 is not recorded by Luke in his parallel record of the Olivet Discourse and provides a message and teaching in and of itself. However, so as to avoid making this into something independent in meaning from the whole of what Jesus taught on the End Times, it is necessary to properly show how it fits in with the Olivet Discourse. Therefore, in this chart, it appears twice, above as a self-contained teaching, and then again below as it mirrors the appropriate points within the Olivet Discourse overall.]

¹*Jesus came out from the temple and was going away when His disciples came up to point out the temple buildings to Him.*	¹*As He was going out of the temple, one of His disciples said to Him, "Teacher, behold what wonderful stones and what wonderful buildings!"*	⁵*And while some were talking about the temple, that it was adorned with beautiful stones and votive gifts,*
²*And He said to them, "Do you not see all these things?*	²*And Jesus said to him, "Do you see these great buildings?*	*He said,* ⁶*"As for these things which you are looking at,*
Truly I say to you, not one stone here will be left upon another, which will not be torn down." (Mt. 24:1-2)	*Not one stone will be left upon another which will not be torn down." (Mk. 13:1-2)*	*the days will come in which there will not be left one stone upon another which will not be torn down." (Lk. 21:5-6)*
³*As He was sitting on the Mount of Olives,*		³*As He was sitting on the Mount of Olives opposite the temple,*

the disciples came to Him privately, saying,	Peter and James and John and Andrew were questioning Him privately,	[7]They questioned Him, saying,

and what will be the sign when all these things are going to be fulfilled?" (Mk. 13:3-4)	And what will be the sign when these things are about to take place?" (Lk. 21:7)

and what will be the sign of Your coming, and of the end of the age?" (Mt. 24:3)

[4]And Jesus answered and said to them, "See to it that no one misleads you. [5]For many will come in My name, saying, 'I am the Christ,'	[5]And Jesus began to say to them, "See to it that no one misleads you. [6]Many will come in My name, saying, 'I am He!'	[8]And He said, "See to it that you are not misled; for many will come in My name, saying, 'I am He,'

and, 'The time is near.'

and will mislead many.	and will mislead many.

Do not go after them.

[6]"You will be hearing of wars	[7]"When you hear of wars	[9]When you hear of wars

and rumors of wars.	and rumors of wars,

and disturbances,

See that you are not frightened, for those things must take place, but that is not yet the end.	do not be frightened; those things must take place; but that is not yet the end.	do not be terrified; for these things must take place first, but the end does not follow immediately."

[7]For nation will rise against nation, and kingdom against kingdom,	[8]For nation will rise up against nation, and kingdom against kingdom;	[10]Then He continued by saying to them, "Nation will rise against nation and kingdom against kingdom,

...and earthquakes.	there will be earthquakes in various places;	[11]and there will be great earthquakes,

and in various places plagues

and in various places there will be famines...	there will also be famines.	and famines;

and there will be terrors and great signs from heaven. (Lk. 21:8-11)

[8]But all these things are merely the beginning of birth pangs. (Mt. 24:4-8)	These things are merely the beginning of birth pangs. (Mk. 13:5-8)

⁹"Then they will deliver you to tribulation, and will kill you, and you will be hated by all nations because of My name.

⁹"But be on your guard; for they will deliver you to the courts, and you will be flogged in the synagogues, and you will stand before governors and kings for My sake, as a testimony to them.	¹²"But before all these things, they will lay their hands on you and will persecute you, delivering you to the synagogues and prisons, bringing you before kings and governors for My name's sake.
¹¹When they arrest you and hand you over, do not worry beforehand about what you are to say,	¹³It will lead to an opportunity for your testimony. ¹⁴So make up your minds not to prepare beforehand to defend yourselves;

but say whatever is given you in that hour; for it is not you who speak, but it is the Holy Spirit.

¹⁵for I will give you utterance and wisdom which none of your opponents will be able to resist or refute.

¹⁰At that time many will fall away and will betray one another and hate one another.

¹²Brother will betray brother to death, and a father his child; and children will rise up against parents and have them put to death. ¹³You will be hated by all because of My name,	¹⁶But you will be betrayed even by parents and brothers and relatives and friends, and they will put some of you to death, ¹⁷and you will be hated by all because of My name.

¹⁸Yet not a hair of your head will perish.

¹¹Many false prophets will arise and will mislead many.

¹²Because lawlessness is increased, most people's love will grow cold.

¹³But the one who endures to the end, he will be saved.	but the one who endures to the end, he will be saved.	¹⁹By your endurance you will gain your lives. (Lk. 21:12-19)

¹⁴This gospel of the kingdom shall be preached in the whole world as a testimony to all the nations,	¹⁰The gospel must first be preached to all the nations. (Mk. 13:9-13)

and then the end will come. (Mt. 24:9-14)

²⁰"But when you see Jerusalem surrounded by armies, then recognize that her desolation is near.

¹⁵"Therefore when you see the ABOMINATION OF DESOLATION which was spoken of through Daniel the prophet, standing in the holy place (let the reader understand),	¹⁴"But when you see the ABOMINATION OF DESOLATION standing where it should not be (let the reader understand),

¹⁶*Then those who are in Judea must flee to the mountains.*	*then those who are in Judea must flee to the mountains.*	²¹*"Then those who are in Judea must flee to the mountains,*
¹⁷*Whoever is on the housetop must not go down to get the things out that are in his house.*		¹⁵*The one who is on the housetop must not go down, or go in to get anything out of his house;*
¹⁸*Whoever is in the field must not turn back to get his cloak.*		¹⁶*and the one who is in the field must not turn back to get his coat.*

and those who are in the midst of the city must leave, and those who are in the country must not enter the city;

²²*because these are days of vengeance, so that all things which are written will be fulfilled.*

¹⁹*But woe to those who are pregnant and to those who are nursing babies in those days!*	¹⁷*But woe to those who are pregnant and to those who are nursing babies in those days!*	²³*Woe to those who are pregnant and to those who are nursing babies in those days;*
²⁰*But pray that your flight will not be in the winter,*	¹⁸*But pray that it may not happen in the winter.*	

or on a Sabbath.

²¹*For then there will be a great tribulation, such as has not occurred since the beginning of the world until now, nor ever will.*	¹⁹*For those days will be a time of tribulation such as has not occurred since the beginning of the creation which God created until now, and never will.*	*for there will be great distress*

upon the land

and wrath to this people;

²⁴*and they will fall by the edge of the sword, and will be led captive into all the nations; and Jerusalem will be trampled under foot by the Gentiles until the times of the Gentiles are fulfilled. (Lk. 21:20-24)*

²²*Unless those days had been cut short, no life would have been saved; but for the sake of the elect those days will be cut short. (Mt. 24:15-22)*	²⁰*Unless the Lord had shortened those days, no life would have been saved; but for the sake of the elect, whom He chose, He shortened the days. (Mk. 13:14-20)*

²²*And He said to the disciples, "The days will come when you will long to see one of the days of the Son of Man, and you will not see it.*

23Then if anyone says to you, 'Behold, here is the Christ,' or 'There He is,' do not believe him. 24For false Christs and false prophets will arise and will show great signs and wonders, so as to mislead, if possible, even the elect. 25Behold, I have told you in advance.	21And then if anyone says to you, 'Behold, here is the Christ'; or, 'Behold, He is there'; do not believe him; 22for false Christs and false prophets will arise, and will show signs and wonders, in order to lead astray, if possible, the elect. 23But take heed; behold, I have told you everything in advance. (Mk. 13:21-23)
26So if they say to you, 'Behold, He is in the wilderness,' do not go out, or, 'Behold, He is in the inner rooms,' do not believe them.	23They will say to you, 'Look there! Look here!' Do not go away, and do not run after them.
27For just as the lightning comes from the east and flashes even to the west, so will the coming of the Son of Man be.	24For just like the lightning, when it flashes out of one part of the sky, shines to the other part of the sky, so will the Son of Man be in His day

25But first He must suffer many things and be rejected by this generation.

28Wherever the corpse is, there the vultures will gather. (Mt. 24:23-27)	[See v.37] (Lk. 17:22-25)
29"But immediately after the tribulation of those days	24"But in those days, after that tribulation,

THE SUN WILL BE DARKENED, AND THE MOON WILL NOT GIVE ITS LIGHT, AND THE STARS WILL FALL from the sky,	THE SUN WILL BE DARKENED, AND THE MOON WILL NOT GIVE ITS LIGHT, 25AND THE STARS WILL BE FALLING from heaven,	25"There will be signs in sun and moon and stars,

and on the earth dismay among nations, in perplexity at the roaring of the sea and the waves, 26men fainting from fear and the expectation of the things which are coming upon the world;

and the powers of the heavens will be shaken.	and the powers that are in the heavens will be shaken.	for the powers of the heavens will be shaken.

30And then the sign of the Son of Man will appear in the sky,

and then all the tribes of the earth will mourn,

and they will see the SON OF MAN COMING ON THE CLOUDS OF THE SKY with power and great glory.	26Then they will see THE SON OF MAN COMING IN CLOUDS with great power and glory.	27Then they will see THE SON OF MAN COMING IN A CLOUD with power and great glory.

²⁸*But when these things begin to take place, straighten up and lift up your heads, because your redemption is drawing near." (Lk. 21:25-28)*

³¹*And He will send forth His angels*	²⁷*And then He will send forth the angels,*

with A GREAT TRUMPET

and THEY WILL GATHER TOGETHER His elect from the four winds, from one end of the sky to the other. (Mt. 24:28-31)	*and will gather together His elect from the four winds, from the farthest end of the earth to the farthest end of heaven. (Mk. 13:24-27)*

³²*"Now learn the parable from the fig tree: when its branch has already become tender and puts forth its leaves, you know that summer is near;* ³³*so, you too, when you see all these things, recognize that He is near, right at the door.*	²⁸*"Now learn the parable from the fig tree: when its branch has already become tender and puts forth its leaves, you know that summer is near.* ²⁹*Even so, you too, when you see these things happening, recognize that He is near, right at the door.*	²⁹*Then He told them a parable: "Behold the fig tree and all the trees;* ³⁰*as soon as they put forth leaves, you see it and know for yourselves that summer is now near.* ³¹*So you also, when you see these things happening, recognize that the kingdom of God is near.*
³⁴*Truly I say to you, this generation will not pass away until all these things take place.*	³⁰*Truly I say to you, this generation will not pass away until all these things take place.*	³²*Truly I say to you, this generation will not pass away until all things take place.*
³⁵*Heaven and earth will pass away, but My words will not pass away. (Mt. 24:32-35)*	³¹*Heaven and earth will pass away, but My words will not pass away. (Mk. 13:28-31)*	³³*Heaven and earth will pass away, but My words will not pass away. (Lk. 21:29-33)*

³⁴*"Be on guard, so that your hearts will not be weighted down with dissipation and drunkenness and the worries of life, and that day will not come on you suddenly like a trap;* ³⁵*for it will come upon all those who dwell on the face of all the earth.* ³⁶*But keep on the alert at all times, praying that you may have strength to escape all these things that are about to take place, and to stand before the Son of Man." (Lk. 21:34-36)*

³⁶*"But of that day and hour no one knows, not even the angels of heaven, nor the Son, but the Father alone.*	³²*But of that day or hour no one knows, not even the angels in heaven, nor the Son, but the Father alone.*

³³*"Take heed, keep on the alert; for you do not know when the appointed time will come.*

³⁴It is like a man away on a journey, who upon leaving his house and putting his slaves in charge, assigning to each one his task, also commanded the doorkeeper to stay on the alert.

³⁵Therefore, be on the alert—for you do not know when the master of the house is coming, whether in the evening, at midnight, or when the rooster crows, or in the morning— ³⁶in case he should come suddenly and find you asleep. (Mk. 13:32-37)

³⁷What I say to you I say to all, 'Be on the alert!' "

³⁷For the coming of the Son of Man will be just like the days of Noah. ³⁸For as in those days before the flood they were eating and drinking, marrying and giving in marriage, until the day that Noah entered the ark,	²⁶"And just as it happened in the days of Noah, so it will be also in the days of the Son of Man: ²⁷They were eating, they were drinking, they were marrying, they were being given in marriage, until the day that Noah entered the ark,

³⁹and they did not understand

until the flood came and took them all away;	and the flood came and destroyed them all.

so will the coming of the Son of Man be.

²⁸It was the same as happened in the days of Lot: they were eating, they were drinking, they were buying, they were selling, they were planting, they were building; ²⁹but on the day that Lot went out from Sodom it rained fire and brimstone from heaven and destroyed them all. ³⁰It will be just the same on the day that the Son of Man is revealed.

³¹On that day, the one who is on the housetop and whose goods are in the house must not go down to take them out; and likewise the one who is in the field must not turn back.

³²Remember Lot's wife. ³³Whoever seeks to keep his life will lose it, and whoever loses his life will preserve it.

³⁴I tell you, on that night there will be two in one bed; one will be taken and the other will be left.

⁴⁰Then there will be two men in the field; one will be taken and one will be left.	³⁵There will be two women grinding at the same place; one will be taken and the other will be left.
⁴¹Two women will be grinding at the mill; one will be taken and one will be left.	³⁶Two men will be in the field; one will be taken and the other will be left."

[See v.28]

> [37]*And answering they said to Him, "Where, Lord?" And He said to them, "Where the body is, there also the vultures will be gathered." (Lk. 17:26-37)*

[42]*"Therefore be on the alert, for you do not know which day your Lord is coming.*

[43]*But be sure of this, that if the head of the house had known at what time of the night the thief was coming, he would have been on the alert and would not have allowed his house to be broken into.* [44]*For this reason you also must be ready; for the Son of Man is coming at an hour when you do not think He will.*

[45]*"Who then is the faithful and sensible slave whom his master put in charge of his household to give them their food at the proper time?* [46]*Blessed is that slave whom his master finds so doing when he comes.* [47]*Truly I say to you that he will put him in charge of all his possessions.* [48]*But if that evil slave says in his heart, 'My master is not coming for a long time,'* [49]*and begins to beat his fellow slaves and eat and drink with drunkards;* [50]*the master of that slave will come on a day when he does not expect him and at an hour which he does not know,* [51]*and will cut him in pieces and assign him a place with the hypocrites; in that place there will be weeping and gnashing of teeth. (Mt. 24:36-51)*

[25:1]*"Then the kingdom of heaven will be comparable to ten virgins, who took their lamps and went out to meet the bridegroom.* [2]*Five of them were foolish, and five were prudent.* [3]*For when the foolish took their lamps, they took no oil with them,* [4]*but the prudent took oil in flasks along with their lamps.* [5]*Now while the bridegroom was delaying, they all got drowsy and began to sleep.* [6]*But at midnight there was a shout, 'Behold, the bridegroom! Come out to meet him.'* [7]*Then all those virgins rose and trimmed their lamps.*

[8]*"The foolish said to the prudent, 'Give us some of your oil, for our lamps are going out.'*

[9]*"But the prudent answered, 'No, there will not be enough for us and you too; go instead to the dealers and buy some for yourselves.'* [10]*And while they were going away to make the purchase, the bridegroom came, and those who were ready went in with him to the wedding feast; and the door was shut.*

[11]*"Later the other virgins also came, saying, 'Lord, lord, open up for us.'*

[12]*"But he answered, 'Truly I say to you, I do not know you.'*

[13]*"Be on the alert then, for you do not know the day nor the hour. (Mt. 25:1-13)*

¹⁴"For it is just like a man to go on a journey, who called his own slaves and entrusted his possessions tothem. ¹⁵To one he gave five talents, to another, two, and to another, one, each according to his own ability, and he went on his journey.

¹⁶"Immediately the one who had received the five talents went and traded with them, and gained five more talents. ¹⁷In the same manner the one who had received the two talents gained two more. ¹⁸But he who received the one talent went away, and dug a hole in the ground and hid his master's money.

¹⁹"Now after a long time the master of those slaves came and settled accounts with them. ²⁰The one who had received the five talents came up and brought five more talents, saying, 'Master, you entrused five talents to me. See, I have gained five more talents.'

²¹"His master said to him, 'Well done, good and faithful slave. You were faithful with a few things, I will put you in charge of many things; enter into the joy of your master.'

²²"Also the one who had received two talents came up and said, 'Master, you entrused two talents to me. See, I have gained two more talents.'

²³"His master said to him, 'Well done, good and faithful slave. You were faithful with a few things, I will put you in charge of many things; enter into the joy of your master.'

²⁴"And the one also who had received the one talent came up and said, 'Master, I knew you to be a hard man, reaping where you did not sow and gathering where you scattered no seed. ²⁵And I was afraid, and went away and hid your talent in the ground. See, you have what is yours.'

²⁶"But his master answered and said to him, 'You wicked, lazy slave, you knew that I reap where I did not sow and gather where I scattered no seed. ²⁷Then you ought to have put my money in the bank, and on my arrival I would have received my money back with interest. ²⁸Therefore take away the talent from him, and give it to the one who has the ten talents. ²⁹For to everyone who has, more shall be given, and he will have an abundance, but from the one who does not have, even what he does have shall be taken away. ³⁰Throw out the worthless slave into the outer darkness; in that place there will be weeping and gnashing of teeth. (Mt. 25:14-30)

[31]"But when the Son of Man comes in His glory, and all the angels with Him, then He will sit on His glorious throne. [32]All the nations will be gathered before Him; and He will separate them from one another, as the shepherd separates the sheep from the goats; [33]and He will put the sheep on His right, and the goats on the left.

[34]"Then the King will say to those on His right, 'Come, you who are blessed of My Father, inherit the kingdom prepared for you from the foundation of the world. [35]For I was hungry, and you gave Me something to eat; I was thirsty, and you gave Me something to drink; I was a stranger, and you invited Me in; [36]naked, and you clothed Me; I was sick, and you visited Me; I was in prison, and you came to Me.'

[37]"Then the righteous will answer Him, 'Lord, when did we see You hungry, and feed You, or thirsty, and give You something to drink? [38]And when did we see You a stranger, and invite You in, or naked, and clothe You? [39]When did we see You sick, or in prison, and come to You?'

[40]"The King will answer and say to them, 'Truly I say to you, to the extent that you did it to one of these brothers of Mine, even the least of them, you did it to Me.'

[41]"Then He will also say to those on His left, 'Depart from Me, accursed ones, into the eternal fire which has been prepared for the devil and his angels; [42]for I was hungry, and you gave Me nothing to eat; I was thirsty, and you gave Me nothing to drink; [43]I was a stranger, and you did not invite Me in; naked, and you did not clothe Me; sick, and in prison, and you did not visit Me.'

[44]"Then they themselves also will answer, 'Lord, when did we see You hungry, or thirsty, or a stranger, or naked, or sick, or in prison, and did not take care of You?'

[45]"Then He will answer them, 'Truly I say to you, to the extent that you did not do it to one of the least of these, you did not do it to Me.'

[46]"These will go away into eternal punishment, but the righteous into eternal life." (Mt. 25:31-46)

Appendix "B": The Didache

The Didache (pronounced dih-deh-kay) is one of the few extant Christian writings for which there is a high degree of confidence it originated from believers of the actual 1st century Church. Also known as *The Teaching of the Twelve Apostles*, it was given serious consideration for inclusion as part of the New Testament canon. Although modern scholars have divided it into some sixteen chapters and assigned associated verses, it is actually about the size of one of the Epistles such as Galatians or Colossians, and very little of its contents is not mirrored in the text of the New Testament. Those elements which do not have direct equivalents almost always appear to be summing up or elaborating further what is already given in the New Testament rather than presenting something new or completely without precedent. The majority of its text seems to parallel Christ's teachings in the Gospels, but there are obvious restatements of teachings found in the Apostolic Epistles appropriately interspersed as well. If it had been included as part of the New Testament canon of Scripture, it would not have provided anything which would conflict with the rest of the text of those books. It appears that its author(s) took important New Testament teachings and ordered them into groups of related topics in what is essentially an organized consolidation of essential doctrine.

Although this work was known for a long time because it was referenced by early Christian figures, it was not until 1873 when a copy of an actual Greek manuscript was discovered in a monastery in Constantinople when we first came into actual possession of this writing. But because the recovered volume also included the 1st & 2nd Epistles of Clement of Rome along with the Epistle of Barnabas—additional important writings of note which were also highly sought, it would be another seven years before *The Didache* was formally studied and translated over a subsequent three year period and finally made generally available.

There appear to be repeated references to this work in Christian writings during the first five or six centuries of Church history, often referred to simply as the "Teaching" or "Teachings" of the Apostles. The recovered manuscript is dated 6564 according to the Greek calendar, the equivalent to 1056 AD by modern reckoning. Ancient language experts recognize that this document, in contrast to other extra-biblical writings discovered to date, more closely parallels the Greek syntax and style of the New Testament, providing additional strong and affirming evidence of its 1st century heritage. Because Greek, like every language, changes over time, this in itself can be used to date a book's authorship in much the same way Shakespeare's use of English can be leveraged. Like the New Testament itself, its usage of Greek is markedly different from that of even the earliest of the so-called "Church Fathers"—prominent Church figures in the centuries following the death of the original Apostles, substantiating the experts' belief in its 1st century authenticity.

It is documented concerning the first generation of the Church in the wake of Pentecost, "*They were continually devoting themselves to the apostles' **teaching***". (Acts 2:42a) There is more than a single Greek word which is rendered "*teaching*" in the New Testament, this instance being "*didache*" (Strong's #1322), which is strongly associated with doctrine. It is used prolifically in the Gospels to describe Christ's teaching and additionally for the Apostles' in the rest of the New Testament. Occasionally (as in Gal. 6:27) the underlying Greek word is "*katecheo*" (Strong's #2727) which is describing oral instruction.

The contents of *The Didache* consistently reflects the theme of New Testament doctrine and are absent any parables, allegories or what we might call "homiletic" teaching, that which is more in the character of a sermon expounding on a point or two of doctrine. Basically this is an organized summary of the Christological doctrines presented in the whole of the New Testament with no obvious exclusive references to John's writings—that is, the Gospel of John, 1-2-3 John, and Revelation. Those few which may echo something similar to Johannine texts have stronger parallels elsewhere in the New Testament canon. This also contributes to evidence of its early origin in Church history, and particular during that sixty year stretch when the Early Church had not yet received the book of Revelation.

However, when it comes to the area of eschatology and what the Early Church believed, if this is accepted as a legitimate 1st century writing in the same way many later works are accepted and quoted, or at the least that it still comes from an earlier date of publication and is therefore "closer", it gives overwhelming credence to the proposal that their primary guide for Jesus' Return was the Olivet Discourse and the Apostolic commentary on it. In the last chapter of *The Didache* provided below, readers will clearly see that the entire work concludes with that which can only be objectively described as a summary statement of the Olivet Discourse, accompanied by the fact that neither in that chapter nor the whole of this writing is present an overt reference to Revelation, which was not yet available.

It is not difficult to understand why so many scholars who insist on quoting early Church writings to justify their positions often ignore this very earliest of them all, instead opting to cite figures who will come much later, sometimes two to three hundred years distant, when it does not support their particular position. But if they gave full approval to the authority of this work by their own stated standard of "the closest must be the truest", such would have to retract their stance that the Olivet Discourse has no application or meaning to the Church, but only to Israel once she has been left behind to experience what they call "*The* Tribulation". The actual full title of this work is *The Teaching of the Lord through the Twelve Apostles to the Gentiles*. They would have to explain how an obvious summary of the Olivet Discourse was given "to the Gentiles" as an Apostolic doctrinal staple of Christian faith when many modern commentators are saying it only applies to future Israel alone.

Furthermore, the fact that it concentrates on the Olivet Discourse and is absent any details or references to Revelation or John's other writings attests to its coming from "the Apostles", since all save John passed away with no knowledge of those works. Even if someone organized this work after the Apostles had gone to the Lord, it would still make sense that they never passed along Revelation in the course of their ministries. And it must be kept in mind that although John would author his writings at a much later date, anything earlier including "the Apostles" as a whole would still include at least his sanctified blessing of what was published, much in the same way he was obviously in attendance at the crucial council meeting in Acts 15 which resulted in the Apostles as a whole communicating their findings to the Church at large. In other words, as one of only four original witnesses to the Olivet Discourse, this must have been John's own primary teaching on the eschaton as well.

So for those who are dogmatic in their insistence of quoting early sources in order to sanctify a particular eschatology, take note of how this earliest of them all so closely parallels a basic outline of the Olivet Discourse:

CHAPTER XVI

WATCH for your life. Let not your lamps be quenched, and let not your loins be ungirded; but be ye ready, for ye know not the hour in which our Lord cometh. 2 And be frequently gathered together seeking the things which concern your souls; for the whole time of your faith shall not profit you except ye be made perfect in the last season. 3 For in the last days the false prophets and the corrupters shall be multiplied; and the sheep shall be turned into wolves and love shall be turned into hatred; 4 for when lawlessness waxeth great, they shall hate and persecute and betray one another; and then shall appear the deceiver of the world as the Son of God; and he shall work signs and wonders, and the earth shall be delivered into his hands, and he shall work iniquities such as have never been from everlasting. 5 Then shall the work of men come into the fire of trial, and many shall be offended, and shall perish; but they that endure in their faith shall be saved by the curse itself. 6 And then shall appear the signs of the truth; first the sign of a spreading out in heaven; next the sign of the sound of a trumpet; 7 and the third a resurrection of the dead; howbeit not of all, but as it was said, the Lord shall come and all His Saints with him; 8 then shall the world see the Lord coming upon the clouds of heaven.

Allen, G. C. (Trans.). (1903). The Didache or The Teaching of the Twelve Apostles Translated with Notes (pp. 9–10). London: The Astolat Press.

Appendix "C": "Intra-Seal"

*[**Author's Note**: Here is as brief a summary as possible of the various eschatological positions, the one endorsed by this author being "Intra-Seal". Keep in mind that this is the broadest encapsulation and variations within each overall camp will inevitably be encountered.]*

As previously noted, Church literature throughout its entire history has not employed the exact, same terms to describe and define various eschatological positions. Although we can trace a remnant who by faith adhered to the literalness of Scripture, resisting alternate interpretations for events in their times which either fell short of a complete fulfillment of God's prophetic Word or were entirely absent, there are themes and topics which dominated the respective landscape of particular periods. Such shaped the overall discussion as to those period's view of the Second Coming.

The most obvious example is from circa 1800 to World War II when the overwhelming emphasis was on "Millennialism" and the fundamental change since Israel's attainment of statehood to present, when it shifted to "Tribulationism". Whereas the timing of the Rapture and the overall sequence of the eschaton at one time was defined as Pre-Millennial, Post-Millennial, Pan-Millennial and even A-Millennial, the favored terms at present have narrowed to Pre-Tribulational, Mid-Tribulational, Post-Tribulational and even a few self-identifying as Pan-Tribulational. Since the mid- to late-80s, a newer term emerged from this category which is not only the fastest growing in terms of number of adherents, but has essentially incorporated those who previously called themselves "Mid-Tribulational", which is the category of Pre-Wrath. But prior to that, during much of Church history, these terms are not usually found and an examination of their writings is needed to determine if they were actually teaching a particular "ism", albeit without the nomenclature we presently employ.

Whereas for about 150 or so years the Church seemed to fixate on the timing and structure of the eschaton in relation to the Millennial Kingdom, for the past 70 or so years that dialog has narrowed down to the final seven years of history which was originally revealed in Scripture as the 70th Week of Daniel, but which became popularly called *The* Tribulation.

All of the current Tribulational positions are using their names to identify up front a preference for the timing of the *Harpazo* in relation to this seven year period:

> ➤ Pre-Tribulationism places the timing of the Rapture entirely before the 70th Week, positing that the Church is completely exempt from it. Proponents support this position by co-defining "*The* Tribulation" as being the exact, same things as *"the day of the Lord"*. Because *"the day of the Lord"* is that time devoted to the exclusive pouring out of God's wrath, and believers are exempt from His wrath, it is asserted, therefore, believers escape the entire final seven years. There are those within this camp who further assert that the Church's removal could take place quite a long time prior to *The* Tribulation, some published estimates being up to 70 years. This usually goes in tandem with their adherence to "The Doctrine of Imminency", narrowly defined to mean that Jesus comes for the Church in a "secret" Rapture with no prior warning whatsoever, and with no events required to precede or even "trigger" the *Harpazo*. In the West, at least, this is probably still the majority view, but not as popular as it once was.

> ➤ Mid-Tribulationism places the timing of the Rapture at the exact middle of *The* Tribulation, which is accomplished by assigning the Seals to the first half and the Trumpets and Bowls to the second half. This sequence allows for the Rapture to take place at the midway point of the final seven years in concert with the great multitude who come out in Revelation 7 between the 6th and 7th Seals. Over the past 30-40 years, holders of this view have mostly folded themselves into Pre-Wrath and it is rare to still find outspoken proponents of a pure Mid-Tribulational position.

➤   Post-Tribulationism places the timing of the Rapture at the end of *The* Tribulation, usually in concert with Christ's return on the white horse with his armies in Revelation 19. This not only requires a parallel explanation for the multitude who comes out in Revelation 7, but alternate interpretations for why the Church must then endure the entire seven years, the last major parts of which are obviously the outpouring of God's wrath.

➤   Pan-Tribulationism, as encountered when it is actually offered, is usually a cover for someone who is either disinterested in the overall discussion of eschatology, or might be understandably weary of the pitched battles in which opposing factions often engage. It is usually accompanied by a shrug of the shoulders with the qualifier, "Whenever He comes is fine by me". It is not a position so much based on Scripture as it is a reaction to all the various interpretations of God's prophetic Word or a total disregard of same.

➤   Pre-Wrath is the newest eschatological term to arise, which assigns the timing of the Rapture to Revelation 7 between the 6th and 7th Seals. Its name is largely a reaction to Pre-Tribulationism which asserts that the entire seven years is all God's wrath from which the Church is exempt. Pre-Wrath posits that the first six Seals are "judgments" which everyone must endure, believer and non-believer alike, and that it is the 7th Seal (comprised of the entirety of the Trumpets and Bowls) which escalates to God's wrath from which they are exempt. Unlike the original proponents of Mid-Tribulationism, however, the removal is not synchronized with the exact middle of *The* Tribulation. In this case, the 7th Seal does not occur until a point shortly after the midway milestone of the Abomination of Desolation, which is where "judgment" gives way to "wrath". They assert the Church therefore goes into *The* Tribulation and is removed at some point early in its second half.

The modern discussion of eschatology begins primarily with establishing one's interpretation of the timing of the Rapture takes place in relation to

The Tribulation, but the differences between them do not end there. It is this author's burden to be in agreement on certain particular points within each of these camps, and stark disagreement with others. This is why I prefer the "Intra-Seal" position, a term coined by Jacob Prasch of Moriel Ministries.

While this position mirrors the timing of the *Harpazo* with that of Pre-Wrath between the 6th and 7th Seals, a major secondary issue is absolute disagreement with that position's most oft-stated definition of the Archangel Michael as the restrainer of 2 Thessalonians 2. The Intra-Seal position in this case embraces the common Pre-Tribulational interpretation that the Restrainer is the Holy Spirit. But it is not just the timing of the Rapture which differentiates this position from Pre-Tribulationism, but its parallel assertions of a "secret" Rapture, their Doctrine of Imminency which asserts no prefiguring events leading up to the Rapture even though Jesus repeatedly warned us to be aware of the signs of His Return, and especially the growing movements in that camp to discredit both the Olivet Discourse and 2 Thessalonians 2. The difficulty with Post-Tribulationism is not just the lack of acknowledgement of the multitude coming out in Revelation 7, but the absence of distinction when it comes to the Church and God's wrath. A Pan-Tribulationist is usually found to be someone who needs to be made accountable to the Word...

> ¹⁹*So we have the prophetic word made more sure, to which **you do well to pay attention** as to a lamp shining in a dark place, until the day dawns and the morning star arises in your hearts. (2 Peter 1:19)*

But it is not enough to merely stop there.

It is this author's assertion that the classic positions published in the arena of eschatology have all fallen victim to allowing a redefinition of critical, scriptural terminology which have a tangible, ultimate effect on the flock we are charged with feeding. The best interpreter of God's Word is always God's Word, and yet we have not just allowed a redefinition of key terms and phrases to take place, but have embraced them ourselves as sanctified synonyms:

> ➤ There is not a single, overt reference, much less inference in Scripture that Daniel's 70th Week and *"the day of the Lord"* are the exact, same thing.

> ➤ There is not a single, overt reference, much less inference in Scripture that the whole of Daniel's 70th Week in its entirety is called "*The* Tribulation".

➤ There is nowhere specified in Scripture, as so popularly taught by adherents of even opposing eschatologies, that the entire first half of the 70th Week is called "**T**ribulation" and the entire second half "**G**reat **T**ribulation".

➤ There is nowhere in Scripture stating that the final seven years is synchronized and coincides with the 1st Seal of Revelation 6. The only thing Scripture specifies in this regard is the signing of the Antichrist treaty.

➤ Jesus did not qualify the Olivet Discourse by proclaiming, "This doesn't apply to the Church, but only to Israel in *The* Tribulation after the Church is gone." This is an error generated in Christian academia known as "Dispensationalism", which many have taken to an extreme to actually slice-and-dice the New Testament into portions they claim are only for Gentile believers and portions only for ethnically Jewish believers. Such proponents have no rational explanation for why nearly the entire first generation of the Church, including all but one original Apostle, were allowed to pass away with only the Olivet Discourse to sustain their belief in the Second Coming. They never ponder why the Church existed for 60 or so years without Revelation and with only the Olivet Discourse as its guide.

➤ There is no eschatological mention of a final seven year period anywhere in the New Testament. Daniel's 70th Week can only be inferred from Christ's and Paul's reference to its defining mid-point in the Abomination of Desolation. The emphasis is actually on the second half.

➤ And most certainly it has only been in our immediate history when Christian academics have attempted to slice-and-dice 2 Thessalonians 2:3 so as to reverse the order to make the contra-scriptural case that the Church will be removed and never actually encounter the Antichrist.

These may be the most prominent, but certainly not all-encompassing, of the errors which have resulted from our accepting the use of terms as being "biblical" when they are not. They may be found within Scripture, but they have been lifted out and assigned alternate meanings.

If we accept just the plain provision of the text, it is clear that the pattern of the First Coming is replayed in the Second Coming. Prophetic fulfillment took place over a nearly 35 year period from the appearance of Gabriel to Zacharias (Lk. 1:5-25) to the Day of Pentecost. The most important emphasis was on Christ's 3-1/2 year public ministry initiated by His baptism by John. But nearly half of all fulfillment of God's prophetic Word concerning the Messiah's First Coming transpired in the final 57 day span between the Triumphal Entry and the Day of Pentecost. It began gradually, gaining the same kind of momentum as a boulder rolling down a hill, covering more and more ground in less and less time.

Likewise, in His Second Coming, many obstetric waves or "*birth pangs*" come (which this author asserts we are already experiencing) until they achieve an ultimate, final fulfillment in the Seals of Revelation 6-7, the whole of these things not strictly confined to a seven year period. The most important emphasis, however, is the 3-1/2 year reign of the Antichrist initiated by the Abomination of Desolation, a spiritual yet public counterfeit of Christ's baptism and subsequent ministry. Prophetic fulfillment again escalates in the time remaining just like that boulder hurtling down the slope.

But the first half is not "Tribulation", because Jesus specifies that is something which happens exclusively to the Church. (Mt. 24:9-14) In fact, "*tribulation*", or "*thlipsis*" in the Greek, is overwhelmingly used in the New Testament to describe something which does not happen to the world, but exclusively to believers. It is only when it is used in conjunction with "*great*" — "*megale*", as in "*great tribulation*" when it becomes something assigned to the whole world. Jesus specifies that the a period of "*tribulation*" near the end of the first half of Daniel's 70th Week will take place as a precursor to the "*great tribulation*" the whole world will experience initiated by the Abomination of Desolation. It is this period which will be cut short for the sake of the Elect when the Church is removed, partway into the second half, and all that remains for those left behind is to experience God's wrath in what Scripture prolifically ascribes to "*the day of the Lord*".

The misuse of these terms by the major eschatologies have not just led to general error, but to additional conflicts with God's Word for many other details.

It has been this author's experience that the rank-and-file member of the flock who in faith accepts Scripture for Scripture's sake sees the plain truth of the matter quicker and easier than the academic who has had to endure the years long process of what is essentially studying more what other men have said than God. Much has been introduced from the outside and injected into a mixture which does not exist when the plain text is accepted for the deeper things of God's Word just as they are for the basic fundamentals.

But for the benefit of those who might still wonder why different timelines and approaches matter, aside from the very serious issue of rightly handling God's Word, consider the fact that Jesus spent far more time in His teachings, the Olivet Discourse included, warning believers to be ready, to not be deceived, to be awake and found living and working as a biblical Christian should when He returns. We are supposed to be preparing for His coming for us whether it is by the most common means of death leading to Resurrection, or the one-time Rapture. In either case, whether we are *"taken"* by Him today should our individual life conclude, or collectively with the Church when it experiences the *Harpazo*, we are supposed to be preparing ourselves to meet Him. The fundamental problem with an incorrect eschatology is that it leads to being ill-prepared, or in one prominent case, to the deception that no preparation is really necessary at all. The danger is not purely or even mainly intellectual, but wholly and completely spiritual.

> *"However, when the Son of Man comes, will He find **faith** on the earth?" (Luke 18:8b)*

Index

CPSIA information can be obtained
at www.ICGtesting.com
Printed in the USA
LVHW080736150721
692757LV00010B/690